At War with King Alcohol

CIVIL WAR AMERICA

Peter S. Carmichael, Caroline E. Janney, and Aaron Sheehan-Dean, *editors*

This landmark series interprets broadly the history and culture of the Civil War era through the long nineteenth century and beyond. Drawing on diverse approaches and methods, the series publishes historical works that explore all aspects of the war, biographies of leading commanders, and tactical and campaign studies, along with select editions of primary sources. Together, these books shed new light on an era that remains central to our understanding of American and world history.

MEGAN L. BEVER

At War with King Alcohol
Debating Drinking and Masculinity
in the Civil War

The University of North Carolina Press *Chapel Hill*

This book was published with the assistance of the Authors Fund of the University of North Carolina Press.

© 2022 The University of North Carolina Press
All rights reserved
Set in Arno Pro by Westchester Publishing Services
Manufactured in the United States of America

The University of North Carolina Press has been a member of the Green Press Initiative since 2003.

Library of Congress Cataloging-in-Publication Data
Names: Bever, Megan L. (Megan Leigh), 1984– author.
Title: At war with king alcohol : debating drinking and masculinity in the Civil War / Megan L. Bever.
Other titles: Civil War America (Series)
Description: Chapel Hill : University of North Carolina Press, [2022] | Series: Civil War America | Includes bibliographical references and index.
Identifiers: LCCN 2022008947 | ISBN 9781469669533 (cloth ; alk. paper) | ISBN 9781469669540 (paperback ; alk. paper) | ISBN 9781469669557 (ebook)
Subjects: LCSH: United States. Army—Military life—History—19th century. | Soldiers—Alcohol use—United States—History—19th century. | Masculinity—United States—History—19th century. | Drinking behavior—United States—History—19th century. | Drinking of alcoholic beverages—United States—History—19th century. | United States—History—Civil War, 1861–1865—Social aspects.
Classification: LCC E607 .B485 2022 | DDC 973.7/1—dc23/eng/20220408
LC record available at https://lccn.loc.gov/2022008947

Cover illustration: Detail of After Winslow Homer, "Thanksgiving in Camp," *Harper's Weekly*, November 29, 1862 (courtesy of Harris Brisbane Dick Fund, 1929, Metropolitan Museum of Art).

Portions of chapters 5 and 6 were previously published in a different form as "Prohibition, Sacrifice, and Morality in the Confederate States, 1861–1865," *Journal of Southern History* 85, no. 2 (2019): 251–84.

For my parents

Contents

Introduction: A Revival of the Temperance Cause? 1

CHAPTER ONE
Supplying the Spirit Ration in the Union and Confederate Armies 13

CHAPTER TWO
The Drinking Practices of Officers and Enlisted Men 35

CHAPTER THREE
Mishaps, Morality, Masculinity, and Military Discipline 60

CHAPTER FOUR
Military Regulations and Civilian Sellers 85

CHAPTER FIVE
Controlling the Traffic in the Union and Confederate States 112

CHAPTER SIX
Drinking, Duty, and Disloyalty 138

Epilogue 167

Acknowledgments 173

Notes 175

Bibliography 213

Index 235

At War with King Alcohol

Introduction
A Revival of the Temperance Cause?

When Abraham Lincoln and Hannibal Hamlin won the 1860 presidential election, members of the American Temperance Union rejoiced: "Two thorough temperance men" had been elected to the presidency and vice presidency.[1] For decades, reformers had been fighting a moral crusade against the demon rum, and now, with Lincoln and Hannibal Hamlin at the helm, abstainers believed that their time had come. Campaign season had been distracting, but the "political excitement" of the election had passed, explained the *Templars Magazine,* and temperance reformers seemed to be under the impression that there was "nothing of general interest to engross the public" in December 1860.[2] Something had to fill the void, and temperance reformers thought that time was perfect for "a revival of the Temperance Cause."[3] A few decades earlier, the temperance movement had counted more than a million followers among its ranks, but in the 1850s, membership in the American Temperance Union (and similar organizations) declined (in part because Americans consumed less liquor).[4] Reformers, though, blamed slavery for distracting Americans from the more dangerous problem of drunkenness.[5] Now that Lincoln's election had settled the slavery controversy (in their minds), temperance reformers could regain the public's attention.

When the slavery controversy continued after the election of 1860, temperance reformers panicked that their cause might again be sidelined. Secession and war brought significant complications for the temperance movement. Liquor, when available, flowed pretty freely during the war years because the massive Union and Confederate armies (and their navies) integrated spirit rations into their health regimens. Soldiers, immersed in military culture, used liquor with a frequency that horrified temperance reformers. It seemed like soldiers everywhere drank, and Northern and Southern communities had to grapple with the liquor problem in a new context of war. In the North, most civilians opted to continue to regulate liquor, much to the chagrin of temperance reformers who still hoped for prohibition. But in the Confederate South, support for prohibition gained ground at the state level. In both regions, reformers worked diligently to link sobriety to national survival, and they expressed dismay when not all Americans reached the conclusion that prohibition was in their respective nation's best interest. Even as they disagreed about the best solutions to controlling liquor, however, many Americans—Union and Confederate, soldier and civilian—believed that excess drinking was unpatriotic because it threatened their nation's survival. In short, while 1860 certainly did not usher in the grand revival of the temperance movement for which reformers hoped, the war years linked mainstream conversations about drinking and the liquor traffic with national well-being in a literal sense. Americans in both sections used the manufacturing and consumption of liquor to assess who was loyal or not, linking liquor control with national health. Northerners and Southerners accepted expansions of state authority to curb liquor consumption (and were thus poised to pivot toward prohibition in the postwar decades).[6] Yet Americans did more than discuss prohibition and the expansion of state authority. Through conversations about drinking, soldiers and civilians debated appropriate definitions of masculinity. Men, especially veterans, emerged from the war convinced that democratic expressions of masculinity that included moderate liquor consumption were more appropriate for channeling wartime trauma than the teetotaling masculinity championed by middle-class temperance reformers.

Thus, the 1860s caught the temperance movement in a state of transition because national conversations about the loyalty, masculinity, and the role of the state were also in states of flux. Although support for temperance had existed since the founding of the republic, the movement gained steam in the antebellum decades. Increasing commercialization, urbanization, and democratization in the 1820s seemed to many Americans to be incompatible with heavy drinking. As factory jobs brought more people to cities and hardened divisions between middle and working classes, middle-class managers and factory owners preached that workers needed to be sober while on the clock. Drunken men lost their jobs, went into debt, and left their families to suffer, so the temperance story went. More than being poor workers, though, drunkards would likely vote unqualified men into important offices. In a land of universal manhood suffrage, alcohol threatened social stability. Middle-class, native-born white men worried that immigrant working men were even more susceptible to drunkenness than their native-born counterparts, contributing disproportionately to crime and poverty in their neighborhoods with their immoral habits. To address rampant liquor consumption, concerned white men and women of the middle classes established the American Temperance Society in 1826, and similar societies cropped up in cities throughout the urbanizing North. These temperance societies preached the value of self-control—of which sobriety was a key component—which dovetailed nicely with many of the members' evangelical faith. Caught up in the Second Great

Awakening, middle-class evangelicals adhered to a new form of Christianity that stressed perfectionism—the need to purify one's self and one's community (local and national) in order to usher in the second coming of Christ. Temperance reformers, then, believed more was at stake than creating sober workers who clocked in on time, earned a steady paycheck, and voted responsibly. These men's sobriety facilitated the millennium.[7]

Middle-class evangelicals dominated the ranks of the American Temperance Society (which would become the American Temperance Union [ATU] in the 1830s), but support for temperance was so widespread by the 1840s that working-class organizations formed as well. The Washingtonians and the Sons of Temperance emerged as two popular organizations for working-class men, many of whom were reformed drunkards. Unlike the evangelical-dominated ATU, the Washingtonians and Sons focused on providing a fraternal culture that could replace the camaraderie and recreation that men had previously found in concert halls and bawdy houses. To an extent, both organizations embraced the language of perfectionism in a secular context, but the Sons of Temperance put more emphasis on forming local societies based on pledges of sobriety and secrecy, offering men a social outlet similar to the Masons or Odd Fellows. In the 1850s, the Independent Order of Good Templars formed, following a similar model. Membership in the societies grew quickly, and while the Washingtonians declined, the Sons of Temperance and the Templars maintained active chapters in Northern and Southern states throughout the 1850s.[8] While these organizations largely comprised native-born white men (who often had close ties with nativist organizations), African American temperance organizations sprang up in Northern cities as well. The African Methodist Episcopal church, specifically, tried to reach out to Black communities with the promise that temperance principles would bring racial uplift.[9]

Temperance was possibly the most popular social movement during the antebellum decades, counting about 12 percent of the American adult population among its members at its height, but reformers approached the problem of drunkenness with different and evolving strategies.[10] In its early years, the movement focused on excessive drinking, arguing that moderate consumption fell within the bounds of a temperate lifestyle. By 1836, however, the American Temperance Union had changed its tune and crusaded for total abstinence, hoping to spread its influence by targeting moderate drinkers along with habitual drunks. Reformers relied at first on a strategy of moral suasion: convincing drinkers that it was in their best moral (and financial) interest to sign a pledge of a lifetime of sobriety. Pledge-signing worked to an extent, and the actual influence of the temperance movement stretched well beyond the roles of the ATU,

Washingtonians, or Sons. By 1850, many Northern communities had passed license laws to regulate alcohol sales, and consumption plummeted. These license laws disappointed reformers. They curbed, rather than eliminated, drinking. Worse, regulatory measures undercut the total abstinence crusade by permitting moderate drinking. In response to license laws and the limited effects of moral suasion, the ATU turned by the 1850s to a new strategy: legal suasion. Temperance reformers in Northern states mounted crusades to convince state legislatures to pass legal prohibition. Maine enacted such a measure in 1851. Other Northern states followed suit, referring to their laws as "Maine Laws."[11]

Southern states hesitated to jump on the prohibition bandwagon in the 1850s, but that does not mean that temperance reform was solely a Northern phenomenon. Some historians have argued that white Southerners felt wary of radical movements that sought to upset the status quo, and they recognized a close relationship between temperance reformers and abolitionists.[12] Other historians disagree, arguing persuasively that the limited support for temperance in the South probably had more to do with the fact that the great majority of white Southerners lived on farms. Distilling, after all, effectively preserved fruits and grains, a necessary part of Southern agricultural life. By the middle of the nineteenth century, however, sizable towns popped up in various regions of the South, and the middle-class citizens of these communities tended to regard alcohol as a nuisance and to promote abstinence. In other words, support for temperance existed in the South before the war, and if the movement counted fewer members in the slaveholding states, these historians contend that it was because much of the South was rural, and temperance was largely an urban phenomenon.[13] When historians weigh Southern support for liquor control, they also must consider the ways that slave codes masked prohibitory measures. Southern states prohibited enslaved people (and free people of color) from consuming liquor. So while rural white Southerners, especially planters, may not have admitted to being temperance reformers, they favored controlling access to liquor among Black workers whom they deemed of too low status to drink responsibly.[14] They just did not need Maine Laws to solve their problems (as they perceived them).

In fact, by the middle of the 1850s, most Northerners had decided that Maine Laws were not solving any problems either. Unenforceable and increasingly unpopular, by 1860, many states repealed their prohibition measures. License laws remained, which curbed the worst excesses and suited most Americans fine. Plenty of respectable—white, financially stable, middle-class, professional—Americans supped wine with their communion wafers and at their dinner tables. In the South as well, wealthy families considered consuming alcohol a marker of social status. Moderate drinking and state regulations kept liquor businesses turning steady profits. Nevertheless, hardline supporters of prohibition remained committed to ridding the United States of liquor completely. They believed drinking was a sin, and only by eliminating it entirely could American society progress toward the millennium. Yet as the second party system collapsed over slavery's expansion, temperance reformers could not find for themselves a party firmly devoted to their prohibition crusade. When the Republican Party refused to incorporate support for prohibition into its state and national platforms in the 1850s, prohibitionists were angry. Their zeal left them unable to process that prohibition had become unpopular. By the election in 1860, their frustration boiled over. "What is Southern slavery to the slavery of rum?" asked Boston reformers. "What are all the agonies and tortures and racks of Alabama and Georgia and Mississippi compared with what may be witnessed, and is plead, and apologized for in all the cities and towns of this rum-ridden community.... If we go to our Legislature and ask for help, how are we treated? Disturb us not; wait till we have knocked off the shackles in Southern climes." Temperance reformers blamed the slavery controversy for distracting their supporters from a more pressing crisis.[15]

Although the temperance community—especially in the North—expressed disappointment when Lincoln's election did not immediately turn the public's attention back to the sins of the liquor traffic, reformers quickly used the war to reframe the fight against drinking in terms of (literal) national salvation. "The very patriotism which has led our population to rise as one man to save our national life, they cannot but feel will equally lead it, as it ought, to become a sober, self-governed, and manly people," insisted Vermont reformers.[16] Suddenly, drinking behavior mattered because the fate of the nation literally seemed to hang in the balance. Northerners needed to preserve the Union. Confederates wanted national independence. In both cases, sobriety was imperative.[17] Northern reformers targeted soldiers, spirit rations, and sutlers (private merchants who peddled goods ranging from boots to lemonade, pie, and whiskey), arguing that soldiers with access to liquor would be defeated on the battlefield and would compromise the morality of their cause. Confederates targeted not only drunken soldiers but also distillers, whom they believed put profits ahead of preserving food for soldiers, women, and children. For reformers, Union and Confederate, the complete elimination of liquor offered the best chance to win the war. Yet they continued to face a problem: not all Americans agreed that complete sobriety was essential to national salvation.

This became especially evident when reformers confronted the mobilization of massive armies of volunteer soldiers. Questions of drinking and national survival became intertwined with wartime definitions of masculinity. Temperance reformers continued to promote an evangelical and middle-class version of masculinity that privileged self-control and complete sobriety. They assumed that soldiers who adhered to this definition of restrained manhood would be successful on the battlefield. To an extent, reformers' ideals paired neatly with notions of republican citizenship, an ideal that a fair number of volunteer officers attempted to emulate (especially when they first set off for war). Public service, selflessness, and virtue would best suit men charged with leading their fellow citizens into battle. But these ideals, to an extent, were out of step with the regular army's definitions of masculinity. Certainly the military emphasized discipline, but it was a more authoritarian and coercive model. It did not champion an individualistic pursuit of personal morality. For officers, standards of masculinity were more aristocratic—specifically, rank included a privilege to drink and keep private stores of liquor.[18]

Complicating matters even further, many volunteers, enlisted men and officers, had neither a military nor an evangelical middle-class background on which they based their masculinity or their beliefs about the morality of drinking. For one thing, middle-class ideals were more common in the North, where there were more sizable communities with professional and perfectionist enclaves, than they were in the South. That is not to say that there were not middle-class Southern men. But far more Southerners lived on plantations and farms and regarded liquor as a part of the daily rhythms of life. Planters adhered to older, more aristocratic forms of masculinity and luxury, which included social drinking. Farmers distilled seasonally to preserve their crops. Rural families used liquor medicinally and as a beverage. And Southern men, outside of evangelical circles, had few reservations about incorporating liquor into their recreation. Of course, plenty of Northerners also lacked such reservations. Although the temperance movement, particularly the Washingtonians and Sons, had tried to instill the values of sobriety among the urban working classes, reformers had by no means succeeded in making their sober ideal the dominant form of masculinity. Especially among immigrant communities of Irish and German Americans, drinking remained a vital component of recreation and community bonding.[19]

When men from these various backgrounds joined the Union and Confederate armies, these ideals of masculinity collided. Scholars have often pointed out that Union and Confederate soldiers brought with them to war conceptions of masculinity so different that it shaped their responses to the crisis.[20] When it came to the relationship between drinking and masculinity, however, there were no noticeable regional differences. Instead, Union and Confederate soldiers and officers alike selected components from the various definitions of masculinity to suit their wartime drinking needs. Some soldiers were teetotalers. Others were chronic drunks. But by and large, soldiers and officers adopted attitudes toward drinking that fell somewhere between those two extremes. Most men took their cues from official military policies, which generally allowed officers to drink and keep private stores and allowed enlisted men to have rations in cases of medical necessity, exposure, and fatigue. Over the course of the war, soldiers adapted these official uses to fit their individual health and recreational regimens. Liquor, they believed, fortified their bodies and minds and kept them able to serve in and survive the war. Yet while teetotalism was never popular among most men in the ranks, soldiers stopped well short of subscribing to definitions of masculinity that allowed them to drink with senseless abandon. Repeatedly, soldiers loudly condemned fellow enlistees and officers who drank so heavily that it disrupted their duties or caused a misuse and the abuse of manpower and resources. Officers, as well, lambasted their comrades who took their drinking privileges to an extreme. When drinking interfered with duty or the well-being of other men, soldiers had little tolerance for it. Reckless drunkenness violated their sense of responsibility to each other and to their respective countries.

This tolerant attitude toward drinking may have well-suited many uniformed men's needs during a war in which they constantly struggled to maintain their health in the midst of disease and trauma, but it left civilian reformers and military officials struggling to keep troops well-disciplined. Reformers worried about the physical and moral health of the men, and they returned to their antebellum strategy of moral suasion to convince soldiers that it was in their best interest (practically and eternally) to stop drinking. They sent tracts and hosted temperance societies within the ranks. Plenty of soldiers found comfort and solidarity within the wartime temperance community. But moral suasion only went so far (as reformers well knew). For soldiers who were unpersuaded by the temperance community, military officials stepped in to deal with the myriad mishaps resulting from drunkenness. But soldiers—even those not guilty of infractions—chafed under the military's authoritarian and corporal discipline. The difficulty for Union and Confederate military authorities, however, was that drunken mishaps could not simply be curtailed by punishing individual soldiers after the fact. Instead, armies had to develop mechanisms for controlling soldiers' widespread access to liquor.

In other words, Union and Confederate militaries had to find ways to cut off soldiers from sellers—a process that necessitated an expansion of military authority over civilian populations. Confederates closed liquor shops entirely as part of declarations of martial law that swept throughout the upper South in the war's first year. Union officers, while they had little compunction about arresting civilians or declaring martial law, usually stopped short of closing shops entirely. Instead, they limited their authority to targeting civilians who sold liquor directly to soldiers. Because Union officials attempted to keep order in contested and occupied spaces while also restoring the Union, the regulation of sales suited Union officials better than the Confederate decision to close shops entirely while white Southerners worked to eliminate internal dissent in their bid for independence.[21]

The actions of the Union and Confederate militaries in many ways mirrored their respective societies' responses to the wartime liquor problem. Most Northerners entered the war years still skeptical of the efficacy of statewide prohibition laws. The temperance community, naturally, believed the war made sobriety more important than ever, and they pleaded with Congress to cut off soldiers' rations and prohibit sutlers from selling liquor within the camps. Outside of the ranks of the teetotalers, Northerners expressed little concern about drunken soldiers. In fact, after troops mobilized, most mishaps created by drunken armies occurred in Confederate and border communities, far away from the minds of most Northerners. Instead, Northern communities continued their discussions of license and Sunday laws, which had begun before the war. The federal government, for its part, dabbled with regulating liquor rations and sutlers' stores, but for the most part contented itself to tax the liquor trade, raising revenue for its war effort. Temperance reformers felt as though their state and federal authorities gambled with the soul of the nation, legitimizing sin through the taxation and regulation of liquor.

Just as Northern temperance reformers had their hopes for launching a popular push for prohibition dashed, Confederate states took sweeping actions to end the manufacturing and trafficking of liquor. This regional shift in support for prohibition seems ironic, at first glance, because antebellum Southerners had had comparatively less use for banning liquor than their Northern counterparts. Nevertheless, the war brought drunken soldiers to Southern towns, where they clashed with civilians. Food shortages were rampant throughout the Confederate South. Confederate state legislatures felt they had little choice but to prohibit distilling in order to preserve grain and to protect women and children from starvation and drunken soldiers. These wartime experiments with prohibition were messy. The Confederate national government had little interest in prohibition, preferring instead to harness as much of the Southern distilling capacity as possible to supply its medical departments, which were chronically short of whiskey and brandy. This led to showdowns between Richmond and various Confederate governors. Ultimately, the Confederacy's national distilling needs triumphed over state-level bans on production.[22] Confederate prohibition, like the Maine Laws of the 1850s, proved unenforceable. That being said, the shift in white Southerners' attitudes toward prohibition is essential for understanding the state of the temperance movement during the 1860s. Whereas the movement in the North seemingly stalled during the war, it gained momentum in the South. When conversations about state and national prohibition gained steam again in the years following the war, white Northerners and Southerners were both on board.

Equally significant, the war broadened the conversation—in the Union and the Confederacy—about the relationship between drinking, patriotism, and national duty. Not all Americans jumped on the total abstinence train by any means, but they discussed the ramifications that excessive drinking had on the war effort. Rumors of drunken generals circulated in the wake of defeat. Northerners and Southerners alike assumed that whiskey fueled and corrupted enemy soldiers. When liquor dealers sold alcohol to troops, distilled scarce grain into whiskey, and took advantage of wartime shortages to speculate, Americans regarded them as not only unpatriotic but sometimes even disloyal. By war's end, so widespread was the notion that liquor was a national enemy that Americans applied the twin labels of "drunkenness" and "disloyalty" to any group of people that appeared to threaten national goals: secessionists, guerrilla bands, Copperheads, or draft dodgers.[23]

This had profound implications for recent immigrants and African Americans. As historians have shown, both Black and immigrant communities spent the war years fighting for full inclusion in American society. Often, they had to defend their wartime service against nativist and racist claims that they did not belong. Irish and German Americans had spent the antebellum decades defending their cultural heritage from nativist attacks. For both communities (broadly speaking), drinking was integral, which nativist Americans assumed facilitated crime and immorality. During the war, when immigrant regiments faltered in battle, native-born citizens blamed liquor. That some recent immigrants opposed the draft did not help. German American brewers found themselves lumped in with the demonized liquor-traffickers. If patriotism meant sobriety, many immigrants failed to live up to the mark in the eyes of nativist Americans. African American men, likewise, had to overcome rumors rooted in slavery and racism that they had a predilection for drunkenness. Black evangelical and middle-class reformers had worked for decades to counter this notion, championing temperance for their own communities. During the war, examples of Black sobriety were used to contrast Black patriotism and service to the war effort with the drunken antics of white soldiers and secessionists. Black men deserved citizenship because they exemplified ideals of self-restrained masculinity better than their white counterparts.[24]

Weaving together conversations of drunkenness, war, masculinity, and the power of the state requires examining a diverse group of sources. To untangle military policies regarding supply and liquor regulation, records at the National Archives and Records Administration and the *Official Records of the War of the Rebellion* proved invaluable. Likewise, legislative journals of state and national governments reveal a great deal about taxation, licensing, and prohibition. Temperance periodicals, such as the *Spirit of the Age* and the *Journal of the American Temperance Union*, as well as tracts and minutes from temperance and church meetings shed light on the wartime opinions of the reform community. But this study also relies heavily on the personal observations of soldiers and officers caught in the midst of war. Those observations reveal how soldiers consumed liquor in camps and during battles, as well as how soldiers understood their drinking. The combination of soldiers' accounts, when blended with newspaper reports and government records, illuminates the debates over the meaning of liquor for different groups of Americans.

This study examines the relationship between wartime uses of liquor and its effects on the trajectory of temperance sentiment in the 1860s, and it is organized topically rather than chronologically. Early chapters focus on the military's uses for liquor and the consequences of soldiers' drinking. The conversation over the problem of liquor slowly broadens to include civilians in subsequent chapters and culminates in a broad examination of the relationship between drinking, duty, and loyalty. Despite my attempts to look broadly at questions of temperance and drinking, this study has limits to its scope. Most of the actors are men. Almost all of them are white and native-born. While enslaved and free people of color and immigrants appear in the study, they sometimes appear as targets of white and nativist rage or of temperance reformers' crusades. What emerges is a debate between middle-class temperance reformers, Northern and Southern politicians, literate citizens, and military authorities on whether or not alcohol was acceptable, in any capacity, in a modern society at war. When the voices of immigrants, women, and African Americans appear, they are responding to a debate whose parameters were set largely by affluent white men. I also focus on questions about alcohol and temperance as they related specifically to the war effort. Temperance organizations, especially in the Northern communities, engaged in license and Sunday Law campaigns, debates about family drinking, and discussions about drinking on railroads, but because these discussions had little to do with the war, I chose not to analyze them in depth.

I also do not attempt answer the question of whether certain generals were drunk on certain days or whether intoxication can be blamed for catastrophes on the battlefield.[25] I do not offer an answer to the question of whether or not General Ulysses S. Grant was an alcoholic, although I show that Americans have been curious about it since the war began. Biographers of Grant have devoted years of research trying to determine the extent to which he drank and whether it affected his career.[26] The same holds true for other generals who have been infamous for their supposed drinking or abstinence: Jubal Early, Irvin McDowell, Joseph Hooker, Robert E. Lee, and Stonewall Jackson. Instead of attempting to figure out when they were drunk and if it mattered, I have examined public debates over their character and drinking habits as it related to their performance on the battlefield. What I have found overwhelmingly is that the American public assumed that unsuccessful generals (such as McDowell) were drunkards while successful ones (such as Grant) were sober. Primary evidence about each general's behavior shows that what Americans thought was not always true: McDowell was a teetotaler; Grant was not. That did not matter. So entrenched was sobriety in American conceptions of masculinity and success that many civilians could not fathom a victorious drunken general. Likewise, they had trouble believing that a sober man could fail. This study, then, is one of perception. It looks at how ideas about drunkenness shaped Americans' understanding of the war and how, in turn, ideas about war and national duty shaped definitions of masculinity and drunkenness.

Temperance reformers worried that the war would lead to the failure of their movement. And, in one sense, this is true. There was no energetic push for prohibition in 1861, and the Union and Confederate armies' reliance on liquor contributed to drunken men roaming Northern and Southern cities. But perhaps because of the liquor-related problems that ran rampant through the armies, the war unleashed a complicated conversation about the dangers of drunkenness to national success. Civilians worried that the fate of their nation might rest in the hands of drunken soldiers and officers. Union attempts to secure the border and occupy Southern cities depended on controlling men's access to liquor. And white Southerners, surprisingly, were willing for Confederate states to prohibit distilling. Even though most Confederate measures passed under the guise of pragmatic necessity, beneath the surface (barely, in some cases), there existed a moral impetus: the state acted to protect women and children from dangers caused by alcohol. Like the Maine

Laws of the 1850s, Confederate prohibition faltered. Yet moral reformers reemerged during Reconstruction, using the newly powerful federal government to enforce morality. After the war, temperance reform ceased to be a largely Northern phenomenon. White Southerners joined the crusade for prohibition as well, although they preferred local and state measures to federal laws.[27] Despite legislative success, however, the prohibition crusade that emerged after the war never successfully curtailed drinking as a component of masculine culture. A close examination of the war years illuminates why: many men used liquor in different ways to cope with the war's brutality, and they emerged from the war unconvinced that drinking compromised their masculine duty as citizens.

CHAPTER ONE

Supplying the Spirit Ration in the Union and Confederate Armies

In November 1861, the *Journal of the American Temperance Union and New York Prohibitionist* reported on an ugly rumor: the spirit ration might be returning to the army. As temperance reformers understood it, the army had been sober since 1832, when Congress abolished the regular distribution of whiskey to soldiers, and they shuddered at the notion that Congress might consider reinstituting spirit rations. Surely soldiers would be better off if they were kept completely sober. They hoped that even if Congress made allowances for liquor, "a large portion of our patriotic army would spurn the offer."[1] By the next summer, when both Union and Confederate soldiers received medical rations to support their health, reformers wasted no time expressing their concerns about the risks these rations posed to the soldiers. "Will not the prevention be worse than the disease," asked worried Northern teetotalers. Malaria, typhoid, and typhus were harmful, but reformers concluded that many a father would "infinitely prefer that his son should be brought home a victim to typhoid" than for the boy to return from war a "miserable slavering drunkard." They offered a solution: cold water.[2] Confederates agreed. Although their rhetoric was less hyperbolic, Southerners encouraged soldiers to "take more pains to get water" because "drinking spirits" was "injurious" to good health.[3] Unfortunately for these reformers, their opinions were at odds with those of military officials and medical officers who believed (like many of their civilian counterparts) that liquor had important qualities that promoted health.

When the war began, both Union and Confederate armies rooted their policies on alcohol use in this quasi-temperate tradition, regulating the distribution of spirit rations. In many ways, mainstream cultural opinions about drinking shaped the armies' policies on alcohol during the Civil War. Drunkards made poor soldiers. Surgeon Charles S. Tripler explained this clearly in his 1858 manual on recruiting men for service. The soldier who drank was "first in a mutiny and last in a battle, he is, at once, an example of insubordination, and a nuisance to his comrades." Tripler believed that men who looked and acted like drunks should not be allowed to enlist.[4] Many in the U.S. Army, including General Winfield Scott, shared Tripler's views. Yet the army distinguished between consumption and drunkenness, and it supplied spirit rations to men, in certain conditions, because medical officials also believed that limited amounts of alcohol were useful in keeping the army healthy. Beginning with the Revolution, the daily spirit ration had been provided to the rank and file—in line with British military tradition. By the 1820s, the army began taking steps to eliminate the daily ration. The widely popular temperance movement clearly had some effect, and by 1832, the daily spirit ration had been eliminated, and whiskey was only used in hospitals and on fatigue duty (performing manual labor other than fighting).[5] This regulated distribution became the basis for policies on liquor at the war's beginning.

Complete abstinence from liquor was impractical, from the armies' points of view, because liquor not only contained stimulating medicinal properties but also could be used as a substitute for food and water shortages. Traditionally, many Americans consumed liquor for its supposed nutrients and its ability to steel the body against illness. Regulating alcohol's distribution most commonly fell to licensed distributors and tavern keepers—men of good character who sold responsibly.[6] Union and Confederate policies regarding alcohol reflected these common practices. Both Union and Confederate medical officials believed that liquor acted medicinally to stimulate men against illness and battle wounds, and their ideas about liquor's usefulness expanded beyond the medical departments and encouraged officers to issue rations to stave off the effects of exposure and fatigue. Yet while most military officials believed that the regulated consumption of liquor kept soldiers healthy, supply, rather than medical manuals and general orders, dictated how much liquor soldiers consumed. Chronic shortages especially plagued Confederates. Yet despite the regulations—and, ironically, the shortages—Union and Confederate officials had difficulty preventing officers and soldiers from overusing medicinal spirits. And the problem of alcohol abuse ultimately created tensions in an environment where medicinal liquor was essential. This left temperance reformers wringing their hands and making desperate attempts to combat mainstream military medical practice. Reformers fought a losing battle, and ultimately, the military's reliance on medicinal rations laid the foundation for a martial masculine culture in which drinking was commonplace.

THE USE OF ALCOHOL FOR MEDICINAL PURPOSES was still prevalent in the 1850s and 1860s in both Northern and Southern states, much to the chagrin of temperance reformers. Many Americans kept private stores of liquor on hand to use to treat minor ailments, and physicians also believed alcohol to be an important component to many courses of treatment. Thus, when war broke out, both Union and Confederate medical departments included alcohol among their stores. Furthermore, liquor's medicinal properties ensured that subsistence departments stocked it to enable commanding officers to distribute it at their discretion (as the supply permitted).

Alcohol's importance stemmed from physicians' belief that it acted as a stimulant—that is, a medication that increased "vital activity" in the body. Although alcohol, like narcotics, has a dulling effect on the senses, in the nineteenth century, many physicians understood that to be only a side effect of imbibing. In short, while it would seem like common sense that alcohol would have been used for its valuable pain-relieving properties, physicians did not focus on those characteristics in their manuals (although liquor's numbing properties undoubtedly increased its popularity among soldiers, whether they consciously realized its effects or not). Most physicians hoped for quite the opposite result: that alcohol would energize the body to enable it to combat wounds and disease.[7] Stimulating the body with alcohol, however, could be risky. William A. Hammond, surgeon-general of the U.S. Army, believed that alcohol, in its pure forms, could be "a violent poison." He noted that when people became intoxicated, "the nervous and circulatory systems become excited, the mental faculties are more active, the heart beats fuller and more rapidly, the face becomes flushed, and the senses are rendered more acute in their perceptions." These sensations, of course, were what physicians were hoping to induce. The problem, Hammond pointed out, was that if one became too intoxicated, "temporary insanity" and the "complete abolition of the power of sensation and motion" quickly replaced the stimulating effects.[8]

Military surgeons believed the benefits of alcohol as a stimulant outweighed the dangers associated with too much alcohol consumption. In fact, even Hammond believed that the moderate consumption of alcohol kept soldiers healthy. Brandy, whiskey, and sherry were all essential components to the hospital stores of the Union army.[9] When it came to stocking Confederate hospitals, surgeon Edward Warren had similarly specific opinions about which alcohols made the best stimulants. "Pure" whiskey was best in most cases because it was "less irritating to the stomach."[10] Pure whiskey may have been ideal, but medical ledgers from hospitals and medical purveyors in Alabama, Georgia, and Virginia reveal that the lack of centralization within Confederate supply networks contributed to haphazard access to this preferred spirit. The war's carnage created grain shortages, and Virginia (where crops were trampled throughout the conflict) had more severe liquor shortages in its hospitals than its Deep South counterparts in Georgia and Alabama.[11] Due to these shortages, Confederate physicians tried to rely on apple brandy, which was more available in "the present condition of the County," as its distillation was not being widely prevented early in the war. The drink was "the purest, most palatable" stimulant available.[12] In short, when it came to prescribing alcohol, Warren's manual indicates that all alcohol stimulated; the goal was simply to find an alcohol that tasted the best and settled most easily in patients' stomachs.[13]

By the war's midpoint, Confederates fell well short of their goal of providing adequate medicinal whiskey or brandy. Instructions from the surgeon-general provided physicians and their stewards information about how to acquire alcohol from the natural resources of the Southern states. When it came to alcohol, the rich indigenous plants held potential, and *Resources of the Southern Fields*, a medical botany guide published by the Confederate surgeon-general, instructed Southern physicians on how to extract alcohol from grapes, birch sap, agave, apples, barley, blackberry, cherry, and spruce. The guide included instructions for distilling, brewing, and wine-making as well.[14] That the Confederacy searched desperately to find substitutes for liquor speaks to its invaluable medical properties as a stimulant.

That Union and Confederate physicians understood alcohol to fortify the body served as a basis for distributing spirit rations. In 1861, Union and Confederate armies developed policies for distributing spirit rations through their medical and subsistence departments that, on paper, seemed quite clear. Union military regulations of 1861 provided that all soldiers received not only medicinal rations but also a daily ration of one gill of whiskey (about four fluid ounces or half a cup) in cases "of excessive fatigue and exposure." Confederates adopted similar policies.[15] In reality, these whiskey rations came intermittently in Union and Confederate armies, and they ranged from a tablespoonful to a gill.[16]

For surgeons working in the field hospitals, the availability of alcohol through the medical departments ensured that they would be able to provide relief to wounded men. In these cases, alcohol's stimulating effects worked two ways: alcohol could reinvigorate a body that had lost a lot of blood, and it could "restore nervous energy" when men suffered from shock.[17] When it came to field amputations, liquor seems to have worked in concert with anesthesia.[18] Surgeons believed that a small dose of whiskey or brandy stimulated the heart after they administered an anesthetic, and they repeated the dose (an ounce) when the patient's pulse became weak.[19] Liquor mitigated the effects of the "shock attending amputation," Warren explained.[20] So essential was brandy to field surgery that Confederate surgeon John Julian Chisolm advised that regimental surgeons and their assistants should carry it in their knapsacks any time soldiers were on the move or engaged. For wounded men, brandy could "revive those exhausted from hemorrhage."[21] As useful as brandy was, however, Chisolm emphasized that caution was imperative when using it to strengthen a weakening pulse after a head injury. He believed too much stimuli could worsen a head wound.[22]

Union physicians agreed that keeping liquor stocked in field hospitals was paramount. As with most issues involving supply, the Union army had more resources than its Confederate counterpart, especially in Virginia, and supply seemed to follow its armies. In general, the longer Union forces had a foothold in a territory, the more likely soldiers were to have access to liquor through the Commissary of Subsistence.[23] Like Confederates, Federals believed that wounded men required alcohol. In the Army of the Potomac, the commissary often sent wagons of whiskey to the front or to the field hospitals.[24] Surgeon and medical director Charles S. Tripler also suggested that medical officers for the Army of the Potomac carry on their person "a small canteen of whisky or brandy."[25] In the western theater, even the medical director of temperance-minded General Oliver O. Howard's 11th Corps recognized the necessity of providing whiskey to wounded men. During an attempt to reopen the Tennessee River near Brown's Ferry, surgeon D. G. Brinton noted that the acting medical director sent for a barrel of whiskey—when he learned that there were wounded soldiers.[26] Whiskey's importance remained steady throughout the war, from the perspective of Federal officers. During the Appomattox Campaign, the surgeons-in-chief of the 2nd and 3rd Divisions of the Army of the Potomac tossed the food stores out of two ambulances that were headed to the front and restocked them with supplies to treat wounded men, including whiskey.[27]

When it came to treating camp diseases ranging from skin infections to fevers, the armies similarly relied on alcohol's stimulating qualities. Confederate surgeons believed that brandy was "constantly required" to counteract the "debility" and "depressing effects" of erysipelas, gangrene, and typhoid and typhus fevers.[28] Union medical professionals used liquor not only to treat camp diseases but also to prevent them from ever taking hold. When it came to preventing malaria, medical director and surgeon Charles S. Tripler admitted in September 1861 that the Army of the Potomac was still feeling its way in combating the disease. Americans had learned long before the war to associate low-lying and swampy areas with sickness, but no one knew in the 1860s that mosquitoes carried the disease.[29] That being said, the British military had perceived for decades that the bark from the cinchona tree would guard against malaria.[30] This knowledge prompted the U.S. Sanitary Commission to recommend in July 1861 that the military use quinine (derived from the bark) as a preventative. Yet quinine was nearly unbearably bitter to swallow without being diluted with liquor. Early in the war, Tripler only recommended prophylactic quinine (with or without liquor) to prevent malaria, although he had it kept in medical purveyors' stores. Tripler believed "prejudice and aversion" among the soldiers made them hesitant to take a daily quinine and whiskey ration. Because of this, he thought it would not "have been practicable to have forced it upon the whole army" (despite the recommendation of the Sanitary Commission).[31]

Having thousands of soldiers take a daily whiskey ration might have been impractical so early in the war, but word spread quickly that whiskey and quinine seemed quite effective in preventing disease. From Gauley Mountain in November 1861 to Pittsburg Landing in April 1862, generals perceived that prescribing quinine and whiskey rations diminished their sick lists.[32] By late spring of 1862, Surgeon Jonathan Letterman had made the distribution of medicinal rations the official policy of the Army of the Potomac. During the Peninsula Campaign, worried commanding officers took Tripler's recommendations seriously in malarial regions—some even doubled whiskey rations. After the Battle of Fair Oaks in June, so prevalent was malaria that "the surgeon-general ordered each soldier to be furnished with a small quantity of whisky and quinine, mixed, every morning before going on daily duty." Although some men declined their whiskey, everyone took the quinine. One chaplain who "neglected" to take either found himself incredibly ill.[33] By June 1862, General Robert E. Lee likewise authorized Confederate division commanders throughout the Department of Northern Virginia to issue spirit rations whenever their men camped near swamps.[34]

This continued use of medicinal liquor by the armies despite the risks of abuse sent temperance reformers into a tizzy. Reformers had long feared that the prescriptions for alcoholic tonics undercut their movement by increasing drunkenness in the respectable (middle) classes (especially among women). By the 1860s, reformers used the language of science to convince these respectable Americans that their drinking harmed their health. Citing scientific research, temperance activists argued that alcohol had debilitating effects and only cold water could prevent disease. They were not alone. Advocates of everything from vegetarianism to water-cure also increasingly cited supposed scientific experts to prove the health benefits of certain diets. These interrelated movements promoted the consumption of bland foods and drinks that would reportedly increase longevity (and righteous living), and all favored, in some way, the abstinence from certain foods, such as meat or alcohol, that they believed would overstimulate the body and lead to ill health.[35] Because temperance reformers believed that alcohol overexcited the body, they argued that the prescribing of alcohol as a medicinal stimulant constituted, perhaps, the greatest threat to the success of the temperance movement. Medicinal alcohol physically debilitated its users, who were otherwise sober.[36]

Reformers went to great lengths to cite expert, scientific, opinions about the uselessness of alcohol as a medicine. Often quoting the testimony of temperance-minded British physicians and scientists, reformers spent the early 1860s arguing that physicians who relied on the supposed healing powers of liquor were superstitious quacks.[37] At a temperance convention in Maine in April 1861, the "best authorities" went on record "in favor of limiting" the use of ardent spirits to "a few extreme cases, where the question of life or death warrants the expedient" use and where the liquor was dispensed only at "the hands of the skilful [sic] and conscientious physician." When more careless doctors prescribed whiskey "as a common remedy," on the other hand, they contributed to the ruin of society by leading many well-intentioned and trusting patients down the road "to miserable and fatal habits of intemperance." "Increase[d] drunkenness" followed the careless prescribing of alcohol, as many people took to swigging medical whiskey in an attempt to cure "every even slight ailment." This "superstition," reformers argued, was a greater obstacle facing "the temperance reformation than any other cause."[38] When abstainers decided "that alcohol is good as medicine," they, "like Samson," lost their "strength and power."[39] Reformers went further, citing an unnamed "eminent" American "whom the bottle has destroyed" after he "fell into intemperance under medical prescription," and the wine he used "as a daily tonic . . . became his conqueror."[40]

Temperance reformers did more than simply advise Americans to suffer stoically through their illnesses without the aid of medicinal spirits. Instead, reformers (and the growing alternative health community) recommended that Americans adopt regimens filled with exercise and cold water as preventatives and curatives. "There is much difference between strong drink and strengthening drink," cautioned members of the ATU, and people who wanted to adopt healthy routines should know the difference: water was key.[41] A professor of chemistry noted further that consuming only water had freed him from headaches, "nervous irritation," and thirst; it also led to increased "clearness of mind."[42] The promotion of cold water led reformers to redirect their efforts. As the ATU explained, the war against alcohol had evolved from a struggle to save the lower classes from the abuse of liquor; instead, reformers needed to redouble their efforts to convince the "respectable" classes to put down their bottles entirely. Amassing evidence that the moderate consumption of alcohol increased an individual's mortality by "one-third and sickness one-half," reformers urged middle-class Americans (who had assured their insurers that they fell into the category of "moderate" consumers) that they risked damaging their organs if they continued to consume liquor, wine, and beer.[43]

The preference for water over alcohol spread among a subset of educated Northerners throughout the war years. Even beyond the American Temperance Union, adherents to the water-cure method espoused the benefits of total abstinence. In 1863, when a new series of the *Herald of Health and Water-Cure Journal* began circulating, it exposed its readers to the idea that the medical profession posed the greatest threat to national (and international) temperance reform. In its first issue, doctor and editor R. T. Trall implored renowned American reformer Edward C. Delevan to redirect the entire focus of the temperance movement. "Whatever importance may be attached to the moral, the religious, the social, and the economical arguments in favor of total abstinence from alcoholic beverages, there is yet one thing needful," argued Trall: "this is the recognition of the *physiological* or *scientific basis*" for temperance.[44] As long as medicinal alcohol existed, Americans would continue to become intoxicated. Trall's plan was straightforward; he would debunk the science behind prescribing alcohol medicinally while converting the forty thousand members of the American medical profession to his theories. Trall did not believe alcohol worked as a stimulant, in the medical sense. The excitement caused by alcohol did not restore vitality. People needed rest instead of whiskey. Trall saw no reason to support the temperance movement on moral grounds, but he saw Delevan and his followers as pragmatic allies. As long as physicians prescribed whiskey, dram shops would remain open and prohibitory laws would be largely ineffective.

Trall and Delevan's alliance took on extra meaning during the war. The mistaken notion that alcohol could restore vitality explained "why 'whisky rations,' and sometimes double rations, are forced on our soldiers now in the field; why the officers of our army are dying of grog-doctored typhoid fever faster than they are falling by rebel bullets and bayonets; and this is why all the power of our government can not or does not prevent the mercenary sutlers from robbing and murdering our country's defenders with the alcoholic poison."[45] For temperance reformers, the war created a new sense of urgency, as many newly minted soldiers would be subjected to illness while also consuming more alcohol. Reformers were particularly concerned about Northern soldiers fighting in Southern climes for the first time. Military officials, they knew, would institute whiskey rations to stave off the effects of malaria, yellow fever, and other illnesses, but reformers argued that even in warm climates, water replenished the body while whiskey caused "mischief."[46] Reformers seemed not to take into account that there might only be swamp water to drink.

Though the Confederacy lacked a well-organized national temperance organization, white Southerners wrestled with when and how to properly use alcohol to treat their illnesses. The Raleigh-based *Spirit of the Age*, a reform-minded paper partially devoted to temperance, occasionally reminded readers during the war years that unlike wine, which was a "whirlwind of fire," water was "pure" and "ever refreshing—invigorating to the wearied body, fevered brain, and thirsty tongue." God provided water that replenished "the whole system—mental and physical."[47] Less preachy, in some ways, than the American Temperance Union but also quite clear was the Southern stance on alcohol and health: a teetotaling life was the healthiest choice, and ardent spirits not only wreaked emotional and moral turmoil but also offered no relief in times of illness. Beyond not offering any health benefits, the *Spirit* further blamed alcohol for leading young men to "self murder," a "double death" that transformed "a fair, robust frame" to "a shrinking, suffering, living corpse, with nothing of vitality but the power of suffering and with everything of death but its peace."[48] Southern reformers undoubtedly believed that alcohol left Confederate men walking around in corpse-like stupors, but the reformers devoted less effort to arguing that whiskey specifically endangered soldiers. Nevertheless, their efforts to organize volunteers to provide moral activities to pass the time for soldiers convalescing in Confederate hospitals indicate that some Southerners were concerned about boredom-induced debauchery.[49]

Union and Confederate physicians were unpersuaded by temperance reformers' concerns and continued to rely on liquor, as much as supply allowed. Later in the war, the regular issuing of quinine and whiskey to ward off malaria and similar illnesses in swampy areas became commonplace—especially in the Union ranks where supplies were available. In August 1863, regulations required that "working parties" in the 16th Army Corps headquartered near Memphis, Tennessee, take a daily half gill of bitters—which included whiskey and quinine.[50] The swampy lands of the Virginia Peninsula prompted many Union officers to issue "whiskey and quinine" rations to "obviate local malarial influences" affecting men digging drainage ditches near Petersburg.[51] By these cases later in the war, commanding officers took surgeons' guidelines and expanded them not only to cover malaria but also to combat the effects of exposure and excessive fatigue.

WHEREAS REGULATIONS ORDERING the distribution of rations to stave off malaria were straightforward enough, the rules governing the use of rations outside of the medical department varied considerably. Because of the stimulating properties of whiskey, whiskey rations had myriad uses and were available (sometimes) through subsistence departments. Both Union and Confederate armies made provisions for men to receive rations of alcohol in cases of "exposure" and "fatigue," and they left that decision in the hands of commanding officers. Because of this, rations fluctuated from regiment to regiment because commanders relied on their own judgment. Regulations allowed for high-ranking generals to stipulate policy for all the men under their command—if they chose. But often, officers generally decided to pass the authority down the chain of command. At times, regimental and company commanders found that the authority to distribute rations had been left to them.

This meant that the availability of whiskey outside of medical departments depended largely on location and the commanding officer's drinking habits. In the summer of 1862, Union generals George McClellan, Benjamin Butler, and Henry Halleck issued orders abolishing liquor rations in their respective departments.[52] As the war went on, however, such sweeping decrees proved impractical. After stopping in Stevenson, Alabama, en route to Chattanooga, General William G. Le Duc told the soldiers of the 2nd Minnesota Regiment that they could have a barrel of whiskey from his stores if they obtained permission from their commanding officer, Colonel George. When the colonel agreed—his only stipulation being that the men could not become intoxicated—the Minnesotans "at once had the head knocked out of the barrel." Commanding officers knew that distributing rations carried a risk of intoxication and disorder. But in the case of the 2nd Minnesota, the men mostly held up their end of the agreement by not becoming drunk, and after a brief respite, they continued on their way to Chattanooga.[53] Other generals, like Le Duc, followed the practice of leaving distribution to lower-ranking officers.[54]

Most officers could easily determine what constituted "exposure." In the same way that Americans knew to associate swamps with fevers, they also believed that cold and damp air could wreak havoc on their lungs.[55] In September 1861, the *Lynchburg Republican* reported that a soldier who had been "drenched with rain and chilled with cold, without fire to warm or dry him, is almost obliged to be sick unless he has some stimulant to stir his blood and make it bound freshly through his veins." Providing troops with "a gill of liquor per day" would be "a better preventive and cure of disease than all the apothecary shops and doctors in Christendom."[56] In 1863, Confederate officers in the South Carolina Lowcountry provided double rations to soldiers working in mud or water.[57] Augustus Cleveland Brown of the 4th New York believed the whiskey rations he and his comrades received as they camped near Stevensburg, Virginia, in April 1864 had "beneficial results." The weather had been so nasty and "the term 'mud' scarcely conveys an idea of the condition of the soil."[58] In cases of exposure, officers used whiskey for its own stimulating properties, which they believed would guard men against harsh weather.

Using liquor to stave off the effects of swampy regions or inclement weather was logical, but commanding officers also had to judge for themselves what constituted "extreme fatigue." Officers took it upon themselves to distribute rations not only for men who were performing fatigue duty but also for those serving picket duty (the somewhat isolating task of standing guard to protect a position), marching, or doing any other task that might be considered abnormally strenuous. Men digging trenches and mending roads commonly received rations. In May 1862 during an advance by the Army of the Tennessee, John Quincy Adams Campbell and the 5th Iowa Infantry received whiskey rations after repairing a road crossing the Tennessee-Mississippi border (the temperate Campbell dumped his whiskey ration on the road, greatly exasperating nearby comrades).[59] Confederate soldiers digging trenches in Blandford near Petersburg, Virginia, received similar perks. Knowing that his men worked "night and day without cessation" and were "constantly exposed to the weather and the dampness arising from the ground incident to mining operations," Captain Hugh T. Douglas requested that his engineering troops receive whiskey rations.[60] In these instances, officers defined fatigue duty—and its accompanying rations—straightforwardly.

In other cases, however, commanding officers accounted for not only physical fatigue but also mental exhaustion when they chose to issue rations. In May 1864, Union soldiers stationed near Huntsville, Alabama, worked one day in "a heavy rain" tearing down a machine shop and loading the bits and pieces onto a train so that they could be made into gun platforms. Jenkin Lloyd Jones of Wisconsin and his fifty comrades completed their tasks and "marched up in line to McBride's headquarters, where whiskey rations were freely issued to all that wanted." The men drank greedily, and the whiskey, along with news of Grant's success in Virginia, "brought forth thundering acclamations" and an unruly march through town as the drunken men stumbled home for dinner. Technically, the whiskey rations relieved the fatigue from working in the rain, but Jones made it clear that the liquor (and the good news) livened the men's spirits as well. The "noise and fun" turned the "disagreeable" circumstances into "humorous" ones. In this case, the risk of a bit of drunkenness was worth it to raise enlisted men's morale.[61] While it may not have been official policy to treat morale with liquor, commanding officers understood that soldiers' mental and physical well-being were connected, and they broadened definitions of "fatigue" rations to include mental exhaustion; they celebrated promotions with wine, whiskey, and cigars; the removal of poor officers with "a good drunk"; victory over the enemy with blackberry pies and a keg of beer; and the surrender of a foe with "poor whiskey."[62]

The relationship between whiskey and morale becomes even clearer when one considers how officers rewarded men completing especially arduous tasks with rations and bonus pay. Union soldiers charged with burying the dead at Antietam drank copious amounts of whiskey to enable them to dump Confederate bodies into mass graves.[63] At Petersburg in August 1864, the Union army's 10th Army Corps, situated near the city, gave division commanders the authority to issue half a gill of whiskey to their men who performed fatigue duty. Whiskey was only part of the men's compensation; they also earned overtime pay. Any man who did not want his whiskey would trade it in for in additional wages. Commanding general Benjamin Butler believed that whiskey and additional wages would convince more soldiers to volunteer for the otherwise unappealing tasks.[64] Butler's thoughts make it clear that from the soldiers' (and in fact many officers') perspective, the whiskey was not simply issued because it stimulated the body physically against harsh conditions. The spirits, along with the pay, also served as a reward and kept morale from sinking so low it endangered the men's physical fitness.

This dual significance is evident with picket duty as well. In March 1862, Tripler noted that the "severity" of exposure that men experienced while serving picket duty could be mitigated by giving the men "a whisky ration twice a day."[65] Tripler focused on the men's physical health. But when reading the soldiers' accounts, it is apparent that the rations served a psychological, comforting, purpose. Describing the general misery, David Day recalled how a picket stood "concealed behind a tree in the drenching rain, solitary and alone, absorbed only in his own reflections and looking out for the lurking foe" on stormy nights. Most men were "very anxious" about going out, but the men on detail managed to comfort "themselves with the thought that they can have all the whiskey they want when they get back the next morning."[66] Like Day, Charles Francis Adams Jr. longed for the "home comfort one attaches to the bivouac" after a night of duty. As he "walked sulkily along," soaking wet, Adams attempted to console himself by thinking "of one crumb of comfort"—"drinking hot whiskey punch and eating plum-cake."[67] For both Day and Adams, their concerns were different than Tripler's. While Day and Adams recognized that picket duty was cold, wet, and miserable, they looked to the whiskey to provide comfort—to raise their spirits—whereas Tripler was attempting to ward off disease.

Providing rations for men digging in the mud or serving picket duty in the cold made sense given instructions to limit the effects of the weather and exhaustion, but Union officers had to use a greater amount of judgment during or after marches. Marching certainly tired soldiers, and many times they marched through rain and mud. But marching also required discipline and order, as men who became intoxicated straggled and created headaches for commanding officers. Balancing the need for relief with the need to keep order proved tricky. In July 1862, Surgeon Jonathan Letterman stipulated that before undertaking a march, all soldiers in the Army of the Potomac ought to have "a cup of coffee," and "after their arrival in camp each man be given a gill of whisky in a canteen three-fourths filled with water."[68] Henry Warren Howe of the 30th Massachusetts noted that "rations of whiskey were served" to him and his fellow soldiers after they had spent the day on a foraging "tramp" along a two-mile stretch of Mississippi River bayou populated by alligators, snakes, and secessionists.[69] Long marches could leave men "tired, hungry, ragged, covered with mud, and sore," as David Day, of the 25th Massachusetts, explained. It took "a good ration of whiskey," along with bacon and hot coffee, for Day and his comrades "to limber up and feel a little more natural" on the morning after a march.[70]

Finally, in addition to using liquor to mitigate the harsh physical effects of military life, Union and Confederate armies used liquor as a substitute for other provisions. Long before the 1860s, Americans had grown accustomed to using whiskey to mitigate poor diet.[71] As early as August 1861, Northerners worried that the soldiers' diet was inadequate. Reporting on the health of the army, the *New York Times* noted that as the men moved farther away from Washington, the vegetables needed to prevent scurvy and malnutrition became scarcer. While pondering solutions to the problem, the newspaper also reported "that the regiments which had been allowed to supply themselves with lager-beer or a malt-liquor, have suffered less from the want of vegetables and fresh meat, and have had fewer cases of diarrhea than other regiments." If the goal was to make "each man the best possible instrument for fighting," then providing spirits was one way to achieve it.[72] Supply records indicate that the Union army indeed thought that whiskey provided additional subsistence, and they counted it among their supplies. In September 1864, correspondence between the Department of the Cumberland's chief quartermaster J. L. Donaldson and Major General Montgomery C. Meigs, quartermaster-general of the U.S. Army, indicated that supplies, including whiskey, were abundant.[73] When inventorying the provisions he had on hand at Chattanooga in October 1864, Captain M. H. Bright, commissary of subsistence, counted forty days' worth of whiskey along with other necessities such as meat, bread, coffee, sugar, beans, rice, and vegetables.⁷⁴ Once Union soldiers began moving through Georgia, however, supplies fluctuated. After completing the march to Savannah, Private Alonzo Miller of the 12th Wisconsin welcomed the dinner of fried pork, crackers, coffee, and whiskey that replaced his breakfast of beans.⁷⁵

Even so, soldiers complained about intermittent rations of equally unreliable quality. Men sometimes admitted to having trouble drinking what they described as rather poor government liquor. As Francis Adams Donaldson of the 118th Regiment Pennsylvania Volunteers explained, he kept "an old bottle half full of lemon peel" to mix with the commissary rations to knock "the rawness off." Donaldson could not be sure "whether it was the beverage or the lemon flavor," but he felt downright "unpleasant about the stomach."⁷⁶ David Day of the 25th Massachusetts further explained the problem. It seemed that after "a barrel of whiskey has stood out all day in the sun and got about milk warm," it became a bit harder to drink. Soldiers with "rather tender gullets" had to "make up all manner of contortions of face trying to swallow it." They eventually succeeded but often had to "run about fifteen rods to catch their breath."⁷⁷ Officers worried less about foul-tasting whiskey. Their supply wagons tended to include wine instead of whiskey.⁷⁸

While Northerners entertained the notion of using fermented beverages to fight scurvy and supplemented their rations with whiskey, sometimes poor tasting, Confederate commissaries substituted whiskey for coffee when they could. Chronic coffee shortages plagued the Southern armies and left Confederate soldiers without warm beverages in cold weather. In addition to not having winter clothing, John Henry Cowin of the 5th Alabama Regiment reported bleakly that the soldiers had "to draw regular *bust head* [strong and rough tasting] whiskey now instead of coffee," an unfortunate occurrence that could turn a man into "a fool."⁷⁹ Using whiskey to mitigate other subsistence shortages proved inadequate. Early in the war, Confederates learned to rely on domestic supply due to the blockade, and when it came to whiskey, Commissary-General Lucius Northrop chose to contract with civilian distillers to keep the military supplied.⁸⁰ But while the Union army relied on supplies sent from not only from occupied ports and Northern cities, such as Boston and New York, which were removed from the fighting, Confederates had more difficulty producing and shipping supplies—including liquor.⁸¹ By late 1862, food shortages were so widespread throughout the Confederacy that many states prohibited the distillation of grain in order to preserve food.

While Confederate soldiers could not rely on whiskey to stave off hunger, their officers worked to ensure that soldiers had medicinal whiskey. Because whiskey was so valuable in the Confederate medical department, some officers sent confiscated alcohol directly to the hospitals. When William Daniel Dixon and his comrades found "2 demi johns [a large bottle with a narrow neck] and a number of bottles of wiskey [sic] besides 2 boxes of brandy cherries" while searching the premises of the camp bake house, they sent the liquor to the hospital (and arrested the baker for selling the liquor at 20 cents a glass).[82] Colonel Thomas L. Rosser reacted similarly after confiscating some "blockade goods" from the U.S. gunboats *Satellite* and *Reliance* in August 1863. He let his men pick over most of the items, but the whiskey he "brought up and turned over to the medical department, having given a small quantity to the surgeons of the county, who certified that the community greatly needed it."[83]

Sober-minded Union officers did not always share this commitment to transferring whiskey to medical departments. Instead, they insisted on destroying it regardless of its supposed uses as medicine and subsistence. Union colonel D. H. Hughes of the 28th Iowa came across well over a hundred barrels of whiskey hidden in a swamp in rebel territory in Missouri. The soldiers found the barrels alongside quinine and morphine, but Hughes destroyed nearly all of it. Its medicinal value did not outweigh the trouble of transporting it.[84] Though this undoubtedly seemed expedient to officers, such decisions angered fellow soldiers who viewed it as waste. Writing from Union Camp Pleasant Hill in Kentucky in September 1861, Friedrich Bertsch of the 9th Ohio Infantry could not understand why General Jacob Cox "destroyed with holy indignation several barrels of whiskey found." German American Bertsch opposed temperance and prohibition in general and advocated moderate consumption instead of teetotalism. In his opinion, which he shared with the *Cincinnati Volksfreund*, the whiskey would have provided "the best medicine for many in this season," and he could not see how the fear that some soldiers might become drunk outweighed the suffering of other men deprived of medicinal whiskey. "Intelligent allocation," rather than temperance, should be (and was) the military's policy on whiskey. Officers who forced abstinence were simply "unjust."[85]

Despite these exceptions, officers generally made it a priority to ensure that their men had access to liquor whenever possible. Whiskey's health-promoting qualities made it essential and generally outweighed concerns over drunkenness. But while there was widespread agreement that liquor could stimulate sick and wounded bodies, relieve exhaustion and fatigue, and even mitigate the effects of malnutrition, the fact that some officers and soldiers recognized that drinking provided mental relief and raised morale eventually led to complications when soldiers overconsumed. Despite these risks of intoxication, whiskey and brandy remained invaluable components of both Union and Confederate medical (and subsistence) stores.

VARYING REGULATIONS AND FLUCTUATING SUPPLIES made controlling access to alcohol nearly impossible, especially in hospital settings. Even when commanding officers went to great lengths to keep medicinal spirits from thirsty soldiers, preventing the careless use of alcohol proved difficult. Both sides dealt with the chronic abuse and waste at the hands of hospital staffs, and beyond the medical department, the problems created by alcohol multiplied. Some enlisted men and officers attempted to steal or falsely requisition whiskey from the hospital stores. More troublesome were alcohol's intoxicating effects. Military records and personal accounts contain numerous tales of sickness caused by alcohol prescriptions and overindulgence. Despite liquor's many important uses, its ability to wreak havoc on the health of the army presented medical departments and commanding officers with numerous headaches.

Unfortunately, drunken physicians proved to be one of the greatest risks associated with medicinal alcohol. Ideally, medical departments sought physicians possessing sound moral character. In 1862, the Confederate secretary of war provided for the release of any man from the medical corps who lacked professional or "moral habits."[86] Members of Union and Confederate medical corps enumerated specific moral habits in their evaluation of surgeons: men should be sober themselves but should also make certain that scarce whiskey rations reached patients. De Witt C. Peters, assistant surgeon in the U.S. Army, noted that one doctor tending to prisoners of war in Richmond was "a very kind man" who "did all in his power to promote the health and comfort of the sick. His careful planning ensured that the sick prisoners had "a sufficiency of whisky" that was "not being drank up by outsiders so much."[87] Kate Cumming sang the praises of Dr. Redwood, like the good surgeon in Richmond, at Levert Hospital in Mobile, Alabama, whose penchant for "strict discipline" was so infamous that jokes circulated throughout the region that the careful doctor refused to provide any ailing surgeon with a whiskey ration "until he put his name down as a patient."[88]

These doctors were ideal for their jobs, but military authorities' determination to weed out drunken members of the medical corps proved difficult, especially as the war dragged on. Hospital workers regularly complained about drunken doctors. While on board a Union steamer, Burt Wilder remarked that "too many of the doctors use too much" whiskey. Teetotalers were few and far between.[89] Some workers blamed the long hours. Union nurse Sally Gibbons Emerson supposed that the doctors and contrabands working nonstop on the crowded steamer *Lizzie Baker* could only "be kept up with whiskey." She herself lived on crackers and punch.[90] Perhaps exhaustion played a role in the overreliance on alcohol, but more often nurses groused about physicians who simply took advantage of access to hospital stores. Surgeon Carl Uterhard, serving with the 119th New York Infantry Volunteers, knew that "unbelievable [sic] amounts of money are being spent on things to nurse the sick and wounded, but no patient ever sees any of it. Large shipments of *Whiskey*, for example, are sent to the sick soldiers every month, but the respective regimental doctors drink it all with their friends." The regimental surgeon in the 119th New York "behaved so badly" that a group of doctors brought him up on charges of "incessant drunkenness and incompetence in his operating." Uterhard hoped a subsequent court-martial would lead to the man's discharge from the army. Even so, Uterhard took no chances, pilfering what he needed to treat his patients from the incoming supply of goods and hiding it away before the regimental surgeon ever had a chance to get his hands on it.[91]

The male nurses and stewards working in the hospitals had such a knack for drunkenness that others questioned their masculinity and sense of duty. When the Army of the Potomac was near Fairfax, Virginia, in August 1862, General Herman Haupt became exasperated that many "of the nurses who came on last night were drunk and very disorderly." The War Department had issued a broad call for volunteer nurses to care for wounded Union soldiers after the Second Battle of Bull Run. These newly minted nurses came from the ranks of Northern men who had not yet bothered to enlist. Or, as Haupt put it, they were members of the "drunken rabble" who had joined as nurses to avoid the danger of soldiering.[92] Elsewhere, patients reported that hospital stewards tended to become drunk when they were supposed to be on duty or that they took whiskey intended for the patients. Both Union and Confederate prisoners of war accused their stewards of intoxication. At times, stewards intercepted liquor stores intended for their prisoners.[93] At a parole camp in Maryland, stewards ordered extra whiskey stores for themselves. In April 1863, the commissary-general of prisoners, Colonel W. Hoffman, noticed that although the hospital had but 122 patients, the staff had purchased $995 in stores that included "twelve barrels of ale and one barrel of whiskey." The report included no explanation about how the stewards used the spirits "for the benefit of the sick," and Hoffman concluded that the purchases were "extravagant."[94]

Female nurses noted repeatedly male staffers' proclivity for sneaking liquor and drinking excessively and even pondered if men, in general, lacked the moral fortitude to care for wounded soldiers. Building on Haupt's opinions that male nurses were drunken wastes of men who were not good for service, Elizabeth Blackford expressed her disgust with "the majority" of the doctors serving wounded Confederates in the Taliaferro factory in Lynchburg, Virginia, in 1864. They had "free access to the hospital stores and deem their own health demands that they drink up most of the brandy and whiskey in stock." As a result, the doctors and surgeons were "fired up most the time" and treating the "suffering" soldiers with "a cruel and brutal indifference." The abuses were, in Blackford's mind, "a disgrace to their profession and to humanity."[95] Confederate nurse Phoebe Yates Pember reported how the wounded men in her care "began to make serious complaints that the liquor issued did not reach them." She concluded that the female nurses were not guilty, as the "liquor would be no temptation to them." Pember suspected the male staff members and began employing only women to deliver whiskey to the wards. This solved her problem.[96] Pember's actions reflect the notion that she and plenty of other women believed: that women were better nurses than men because they were more moral.[97] Men—specifically those men who chose to be nurses rather than to enlist—were especially lacking in self-control.

Intoxicated male doctors eventually prompted many female nurses to invoke military protocol to restore discipline in the hospitals where they worked. Mary Phinney von Olnhausen, while serving as a nurse near Beaufort, North Carolina, in 1865, had an especially trying time with a drunken doctor, an "ignorant, bad man without a particle of principle or judgement [sic]." This doctor had a knack for sleeping until noon, leaving von Olnhausen alone in her ward for days before an additional surgeon arrived to "rescue" her. He continued to wreak havoc at the hospital, deciding late one night to go "on a lark" with local "artisans, navy officers, [and Black workers] who were impressed with a guard to be made to sing" before running through town "screaming and shouting," and then returning to the hospital to wake "all the patients." The traumatic and exasperating experiences left von Olnhausen "more down on whiskey than ever."[98] But von Olnhausen and other hospital workers she knew reached their limits when putting up with disorder and abuse. Near the war's end, von Olnhausen witnessed the infamous Mother Mary Bickerdyke go up against a "Dr. S. of Alexandria" who habitually inspected her kitchen while drunk. Bickerdyke "took him by the nape of the neck, led him out, called a guard, and told them to take this drunken man to headquarters and she would have him court-martialled [sic]."[99] Neither woman had further problems with Dr. S. But more importantly, they invoked military justice to demand that surgeons sober up enough to perform their duties.

Hospital workers used liquor excessively, at least in part, because they had incredible access. To limit soldiers' access, Confederate officials often controlled access to liquor by only dispensing spirits in limited quantities to men who had prescriptions. After visiting with wounded and "much exhausted" soldiers near Winchester, Confederate physician David Bagley requested "two bottles of whiskey" to be used as stimulants. Confederate surgeon James D. Robison refused because only soldiers treated by the surgeons directly could receive any sort of medication, including whiskey.[100] In part, requiring prescriptions helped Confederates to preserve scarce whiskey. In 1864, circulars to Confederate medical departments in Virginia, South Carolina, Georgia, and Florida stipulated that whiskey rations would not be given for "trivial complaints" and could only be given to men whose prescriptions noted their names, regiments, and specific diseases. Even with prescriptions, men could only receive six to eight ounces at a time. Surgeon General Samuel Preston Moore prohibited the prescribing of alcoholic stimulants "except in such cases as imperatively demand[ed]" it. Medical officers should instead treat soldiers with "more judicious and economical" medications.[101] Confederate nurse Kate Cumming explained how similar policies played out in the field hospitals of the Army of Tennessee. The staff measured every ounce of alcohol and daily recorded each purchase and distribution. Hospital druggists oversaw all distributions of liquor to the wards.[102] The limits made officers testy. When a captain at Castle Thunder prison in Richmond tried to pull rank to obtain spirits from the medical department to liven up a dinner party, he found himself denied access. After multiple attempts failed, he told the steward a false story about having a man with a broken leg in immediate need of liquor. When the steward still refused, the captain had him "put in the cell for refusing to prescribe for a patient."[103]

Even when physicians and nurses tried to limit access, sick and wounded soldiers could become intoxicated on medicinal rations, exacerbating issues of chronic drunkenness within the ranks. Physicians may have prescribed alcohol for its stimulating properties, but men tended to notice its numbing and intoxicating effects more acutely. Some soldiers seemed especially prone to intoxication even from relatively small amounts of alcohol. As Simon Cummins explained to his concerned parents, when he had his occasional swallows, he could "feel it in my head some."[104] Other soldiers noticed this as well. Mason Whiting Tyler not only suffered "from a severe attack of fever and ague" in August 1864 but also complained of being unable to fully perform his duties because of the additional "crazing effects of whiskey and quinine taken to counteract the fever."[105] Patients sought its numbing effects, and one of Burt Wilder's soldiers went "out of his head and threatened to attack" the medical officer after he was not given additional whiskey.[106]

Surgeons knew well that men could become dependent on alcohol, but even so, soldiers' and officers' overuse of spirits prompted less ire than that of drunken physicians and hospital stewards. Confederate field surgeons watched for the effects of "the abuse of spirituous liquors, opium, and tobacco" when they evaluated patients for pain.[107] Officers outside of the medical departments also knew of the connections between alcohol and various health problems. General William Dorsey Pender lost a comrade, Colonel R. H. Gray of the 22nd North Carolina, to drunkenness. Although Pender lauded Gray as "a fine soldier, and a nice gentleman," drinking killed him, and Pender lamented that he had not known of the troubling behavior in time to intervene.[108] Rather than doubting Gray's manhood or sense of duty, Pender clearly regarded drunkenness as a disease that killed an otherwise good man.

Hospital workers tried to redirect men's energies before their intemperance became severe.[109] The Confederacy's guide for hospital inspectors indicates that the surgeon-general's office sought to reduce problems of intoxication and other vices in the Southern hospitals. Regulations required inspectors to make certain that "noise, profanity, intemperance and waste [were] forbidden and punished" but also to check that hospitals had chaplains, religious services, current newspapers, and libraries.[110] Union hospitals similarly tried to direct ailing men's energies away from ardent spirits. Many hospital newspapers included advertisements for the Sons of Temperance and other organizations. The papers espoused the virtues of temperance. The only debate, it seems, was whether soldiers could drink liquor medicinally. The pledges of the temperance men published in the *Cartridge Box* at the hospital in York, Pennsylvania, vowed to "not drink any intoxicating drinks unless ordered by proper medical authority." Other editors of the *Army Square Hospital Gazette* in the Department of Washington took a stronger stance, promising men that "the sick and wounded cold water man always withstood diseases, wounds and operations better than those who drank liquor."[111]

Of course, soldiers abusing medicinal liquor was exactly what temperance reformers had feared all along. To reach men directly, the ATU and others embarked on a tract-distributing crusade. "The Wounded Soldier," published in October 1862, told the story of a young man who survived a bout of typhus because he relied on water rather than whiskey. It warned—while citing the "highest medical authorities"—that "intoxicating liquors produce such a state of the system, as, in active diseases and gun-shot wounds, prevents the necessary curative effect of medicines and medical treatment."[112] The following year, "The Sick Soldier" celebrated the sober-minded Tom, who, recovering from sickness and fatigue in a camp hospital, used "the invigorating morning breeze" and a plumped-up pillow to send him "into reveries of home and friends" and improve his mental state instead of relying on "such ignoble aid as strong drink." Tom and other soldiers had been sacrificed by their parents for God and country, and they had to resist "evil" even in sickness, to return themselves to good health so that they could continue to do their duty.[113] According to the ATU, the tracts had "saved our whole nation from going to destruction" by keeping "thousands" of Americans, soldier and civilian, from ending up in "the drunkard's grave."[114]

Yet temperance reformers most certainly did not speak for all respectable civilians, as the activities of middle-class volunteer efforts make clear. Rather than jumping on the cold-water bandwagon, plenty of civilians attempted to bolster the Union and Confederate medical departments' liquor supply. These citizens' efforts indicated that many middle-class Americans (unlike most temperance reformers) considered alcohol to be a necessary stimulant. The Union army had a well-established network through the U.S. Sanitary Commission (USSC) and U.S. Christian Commission (USCC). Civilians kept soldiers supplied with food and spirits, at times running afoul of Northern temperance organizations that strongly objected to whiskey in hospitals or convalescent homes. Despite some temperance reformers'—and the American Temperance Union's—official stance on abstinence, civilian volunteers' behavior in the USSC and USCC indicates that Northern Protestant reformers were anything but united on their views about medicinal whiskey.[115] Union soldier Mason Whiting Tyler told his parents in October 1864 that the Sanitary and Christian Commission volunteers in Winchester, Virginia, had supplied more than two thousand wounded Union soldiers with "hot soup, coffee, tea, and hot whiskey punch."[116] Even far from the front lines, Northern volunteers seemed comfortable providing spirits to ailing soldiers. Iowan Annie Wittenmyer would become an active member of the Women's Christian Temperance Union in the years following the war. During the conflict, however, her temperance principles did not prevent her from requesting and sending spirits to Iowa soldiers convalescing in the state's military hospitals. Her Christian Commission notes regularly included orders for wine.[117]

There are many similar examples among the Confederates. According to Emma Holmes, Charleston citizens sent more than $5,000 in donations to their wounded soldiers in Virginia hospitals in the early winter of 1863. Mayor Charles Macbeth gave the funds to Rev. R. W. Barnwell, who "spent $1,000 in purchase of good French brandy, Madeira & Sherry, for the use of those patients who needed more delicate stimulants than the whiskey furnished by [the] government." Holmes believed Barnwell to be a "soldier's friend" and hoped that "showers of blessing" would be "poured upon him from every part of the Confederacy." Holmes gave no indication that the Rev. Barnwell compromised the soldiers' physical or spiritual health by providing medicinal spirits (although, clearly, wine was seen as less problematic than whiskey).[118] Although reformers believed that the risks of chronic drunkenness far outweighed any dubious medical benefits, they were out of sync with the opinions of the medical community and most civilians when it came to medicinal alcohol.

That being said, chronic overuse presented a conundrum for military authorities in both the Union and the Confederacy because it showed that despite their best efforts to control access, soldiers drank too much. Men preferred liquor's intoxicating and numbing efforts to its supposed qualities as a medical stimulant. Despite the risks, however, liquor remained invaluable to subsistence and medical departments.

AS MUCH AS REFORMERS WANTED SOLDIERS to forgo liquor and choose cold water instead, army life led most men to conclude that that solution was completely impractical. For one thing, water was not reliably safe. But also, military officials followed medical guidelines when it came to using liquor. While they fully recognized the risks associated with liquor's abuse, their need to keep the armies healthy and malaria-free outweighed the threat of drunken soldiers (or so they thought). Liquor was so important, in fact, that both Union and Confederate medical and subsistence departments went to great lengths to supply it to their men.

Most commanding officers and the enlisted men who served under them chose to follow the military's guidelines: that liquor had medical and subsistence benefits and that men should drink whiskey (or other spirits) whenever their well-being necessitated it. As a result, both Union and Confederate armies' policies created a culture in which men throughout the ranks would use liquor freely.

CHAPTER TWO

The Drinking Practices of Officers and Enlisted Men

One night in December 1862, Union soldiers encamped beside a river in southeastern Missouri woke to find water filling their tents. Some men abandoned their possessions. Others scrambled away from the river and toward nearby hills. Still others remained trapped on a shrinking island, surrounded by rushing water. When the ordeal ended, many of the soaked soldiers decided to dry themselves out with liquor. Among the drinkers was the 8th Indiana's Captain Hiram T. Vandevender, an officer purported to be "an earnest seeker" of God. For him to imbibe was unexpected—so much so that the Baptist chaplain, William Taylor Stott, was horrified by Vandevender's fall from grace. Stott hoped that Vandevender's soul could be "reclaimed" despite the bender.[1] Whether or not Vandevender shared Stott's concern about his soul is hard to know. He died a few months later during the siege of Vicksburg, and the citizens of his home county have lauded his patriotic sacrifice ever since.[2] Nevertheless, on that December night, Stott feared that Vandevender gambled with his salvation when he chose to drink liquor with his comrades after a harrowing flood.

This event exemplifies the tensions over drinking that occurred in the Union and Confederate ranks. Soldiers and officers, like William Stott, who belonged to the sober ranks of society believed that teetotalism and salvation went hand in hand. They had grown up immersed in an evangelical and middle-class culture in which temperance required complete abstinence from ardent spirits. One sip could send an individual tumbling down the slippery slope to hell (and financial ruin, which was, perhaps, a more tangible torment). For teetotaling soldiers, the military culture that allowed men to drink to stave off illness, exposure, and fatigue was anathema to their understanding of manhood. But for many soldiers—both Union and Confederate—the military's regulations made sense, and so they interpreted the rules broadly enough to allow themselves to drink whenever it suited their purposes (provided, of course, that they could find the booze). In fact, many soldiers came from families that did not value abstinence, and quite oppositely, used liquor medicinally. Other men, who had been sober in civilian contexts, believed drinking within the context of military life—when they were sick, wet, or scared—was acceptable. Taken together, these soldiers created an environment in which they could interpret military regulations loosely enough that they could drink for self-care without threatening their masculinity. At times, self-care included recreational drinking, and, in some instances, resulted in excessive misuse of liquor.

Looking at Civil War soldiers gives us an opportunity to examine the extent to which middle-class values pervaded American culture in the mid-nineteenth century. Because the culture of reform loomed so large in the political culture of the 1840s and 1850s, scholars often have this view of the antebellum nineteenth century as an era where men practiced self-control and the values of hard work, sobriety, and thrift reigned supreme. In many ways, of course, these evangelical middle-class values dominated municipal and state politics—especially in Northeastern and Midwestern cities—and historians are correct to emphasize the pervasive culture of restrained manhood.[3] To an extent, these values played a powerful role among soldiers and officers in both the Union and the Confederacy. Soldiers' value of family, republicanism, and country were often intertwined and required masculine behavior rooted in self-control and discipline.[4] But these middle-class and evangelical values did not extend to every corner of every neighborhood and farm in the Union or in the Confederacy. In the case of temperance, specifically, native-born and immigrant workers and rural Americans, for example, had less need for complete sobriety. Middle-class values may have been a powerful force, but they were by no means entirely dominant.[5]

The parameters of drinking culture within the Union and Confederate militaries reveal the complications and limits of middle-class cultural dominance. In western contexts, the military often served as a facilitator of middle-class masculinity—instilling discipline and thrift among the rank and file from the rural and unruly working classes. But historians have shown that in the United States in the 1860s, the military operated differently (for better or worse).[6] Volunteer soldiers hesitated to conform to military culture—preferring instead to cling to the notions of democracy and individualism. A close look at soldiers' and officers' interpretations of liquor regulations confirms that within the United States (and the Confederacy), the military offered no clear avenue to middle-class manhood. Instead, military regulations created environments in both the Union and Confederate armies in which alcohol was more acceptable than it would have been in the typical 1860s middle-class or evangelical home.[7]

Officers' and soldiers' preference for drinking created an environment where alcohol use abounded. Still, it would be a mistake to conclude that because men in the armies drank, they tossed all hints of self-restrained manhood aside. Rather, soldiers debated constantly which uses of liquor were acceptable and which were not. Drinking might have been allowable, in most men's minds, but a soldier—and an officer, especially—still had to be able to do his job well. Men who misused or abused liquor caused concern and at times received ire from their comrades.

LIQUOR USE PREVAILED IN THE MILITARY despite seemingly widespread societal opposition to drinking because military tradition in the United States allowed officers to drink. In the decades before the Civil War, professional officers tended to adopt an attitude toward drinking that more closely modeled aristocratic behavior. When volunteers joined the ranks of junior officers, they complicated these notions because they carried with them republican ideals of the citizen-soldier. To serve their nations effectively, citizen-officers needed to eschew liquor.[8] In practice, men consumed spirits socially, taking advantage of the small indulgences afforded to them by their rank. Officers' predilection for drinking facilitated much of the liquor consumption among the rank and file, because they interpreted military regulations and doled out rations.

The military regulations that allowed officers to drink provided the groundwork for men to redefine for themselves when it was acceptable for them to consume liquor. Officers could keep liquor in their private stores. They could purchase liquor from camp sutlers and civilian dealers. They could have liquor sent to them by their families in care packages. Some officers even reported receiving wine in their supply wagons, while enlisted men complained of foul-tasting commissary. Although some of these young men who became officers espoused beliefs of republicanism and middle-class values that prompted them to adhere to principles of self-control and sobriety, other men rose through the ranks via company and regimental elections and had not the slightest interest in teetotalism. Plenty of officers drank, and as the war went on and became increasingly brutal, they found little reason to join the ranks of the cold water army. The availability of alcohol enticed them. Imbibing took the edge off of the war's brutality.

Soldiers tended to believe that taking an officer's oath turned temperate men into drunks overnight. Shortly after the Union capture of Vicksburg, Jenkin Lloyd Jones, a Wisconsin private, remarked the "whiskey is used by our officers more freely than water" even though these "men left home with great pretensions of temperance."[9] Even men who "were not habitual drunkards," he explained, could lose "their discretion" after a close brush with danger. "Prompted by the devil or some other demon," officers consumed barrels of whiskey, which transformed into "raving maniacs" so many "men working in sober earnestness." Wives and mothers would have been horrified to see their husbands, sons, and fathers of their children "staggering through our camp in this condition." Churches and temperance lodges felt themselves "disgraced" by the conduct. Appalled, Jones questioned his "faith in human nature."[10] As if illustrating Jones's point, in another instance, a young man "became so elated" after being sworn in as first lieutenant "that he got drunk, and has not been heard of since."[11]

The sober-minded Rufus Kinsley of Company D of the 8th Vermont explained this phenomenon more thoroughly. "Many men who never drank at home, and who had no difficulty in resisting the temptation while *in the ranks* of the army, no sooner pocket their Commission, than they become drunken" because the pressure to drink socially mounted immediately. Young officers imbibed when their superior officers offered them liquor. It would not do "to reproach other officers by refusing to drink with them."[12] Even when superior officers did not supply the booze, junior officers found that drinking was a privilege of rank, and the luxurious parties and greater access to rations and private stores removed almost all barriers between officers and liquor. The middle-class definitions of masculinity that existed on the home front simply had less influence in the military.

A few officers chose to abstain. General Robert McAllister of the Army of the Potomac epitomized self-control and other virtues. The man, with a "soft and calm" voice that never swore and a "closely shaven" face, had "the air of simplicity and modesty." The officer "never touches liquor of any kind, not even beer," but fellow Union officer Regis de Trobriand noted that he stopped short of requiring those around him to embrace abstinence. By "preach[ing] by example only," McAllister found favor with his men. Yet de Trobriand further pointed out that his troops regarded him as a mother, an indication that soldiers associated teetotalism with femininity rather than masculinity, and "when the day of battle came the mother led on her children as a lioness her cubs." Lest his feminine simile cause confusion, he clarified that as a lioness, McAllister "was a most exemplary man"; "because" of this—not despite it—he was a "most energetic soldier."[13] To be an effective leader in battle, an officer had to embody characteristics of temperance and self-control in order to mold and protect the young soldiers in his command.

Colonel William W. Jennings and Lieutenant-Colonel H. C. Alleman, commanding the 127th Pennsylvania, adhered to similar principles as McAllister. But many officers faced difficulty in deciding whether to abstain or not, regardless of the principles the man had held in peacetime. Alleman abstained entirely from liquor and often required his men to do likewise. During the Battle of Chancellorsville, however, Alleman needed a group of three hundred volunteers to build a bridge across the Rappahannock near Fredericksburg. Knowing the conditions would be dangerous, Alleman, despite being a teetotaler, vowed to provide his volunteers with "as much whiskey as you can drink—or at least as much as is good for you!" His comrades considered this "sacrifice of moral principle" an act of mercy, as the men volunteered for a job where they could not defend themselves. After Alleman broke open the barrels of whiskey, the men obeyed his orders to imbibe "with amusing alacrity."[14] This proved to be a onetime dispensation, and shortly after Chancellorsville, Alleman refused to distribute whiskey rations, violating an order that his men should be regularly supplied with liquor. Despite being threatened with the loss of his sword for disobeying orders, Alleman stood "firm as a rock." He forbade his men from being "poisoned with their abominable 'whisky rations.'" Fellow teetotaler J. Chandler Gregg observed the incident and lauded Alleman and Colonel Jennings for their "uncompromising opposition to this curse of humanity."[15] Alleman and his comrades' moral stance seemed to take into account both circumstance and rank when determining whether or not a soldier could consume alcohol. Troops volunteering for the most arduous and dangerous tasks could use whiskey to steady their nerves. But under any other circumstances, liquor compromised men's ability to do their duty and rendered officers useless and detrimental to the cause.

Men like McAllister, Jennings, and Alleman—who continued to adhere to bourgeois and evangelical definitions of masculinity—seemed to be the exception rather than the rule. That officers considered drinking a privilege became clear as soon as camp-life doldrums set in. In many cases, officers had the financial means to enjoy dinner parties and balls where ardent spirits flowed freely. As he traveled through the Confederacy in 1861, British observer William Howard Russell noticed immediately the copious hospitality of the naval officers stationed at every battery. Officers welcomed their British guest with bourbon. In New Orleans, young Zouaves "full of life and spirits" invited Russell to a "very comfortable dinner, with abundance of champagne, claret, beer, and ice," courtesy, it seemed, of the local quartermaster.[16] A few months later, when Russell visited the 6th U.S. Cavalry, encamped near Richmond, he found the dinner tables similarly spread with "whiskey, champagne, hot terrapin soup, and many luxuries."[17] To be sure, both events were held to impress Russell, but officers' accounts indicate that the Englishman's brief experience was hardly unique. New York volunteer Don Redro Quarendo Reminisco repeatedly noted Union officers' penchant for "drinking copious libations of their good old champagne wine."[18] Private Dietrich Gerstein echoed Reminisco's observations, while making clear the mockery officers made of middle-class values. The officers of the Union army, Gerstein thought, were in "a better category" of men. They had not come from the "crude masses," who rashly ran into battle after becoming drunk on beer and liquor. Instead, he noted sarcastically, the Union officers had finer tastes—they clouded their minds with champagne.[19]

As the champagne, wine, and liquor flowed freely, the frivolity spun out of control. Near the camp of the 118th Regiment Pennsylvania Volunteers in May 1863, Captain Dendy Sharwood decided to host a shindig for his fellow officers, a task for which he was well suited, having been the owner of a hotel before the war. Sharwood treated his guests to a generous supply of gin cocktail, fish house punch, claret punch, and ale, and "to satisfy the craving of the appetite the Gin Cocktail was sure to produce" the officers also found "enormous tubs" of cold beef, boiled ham, chicken salad, and ham sandwiches. The cocktails and sandwiches led to "song and ribald jest," and not surprisingly, Sharwood's tent quickly "filled with a writhing mass of drunken men." The officers exchanged pledges of love and friendship, and one young man giddily climbed a spruce hedge repeatedly, much to his comrades' amusement. The next morning, sober Captain Francis Adams Donaldson alone reported for duty while all of his friends lay "asleep on the floors, under the tables, and on the ground surrounding" Sharwood's tent.[20]

Captain Sharwood used his business connections to buy booze and sandwiches, but other officers relied on the sutlers or their wives to fortify them. Sutlers who followed the soldiers could sell alcohol to officers, although regulations usually prohibited them from selling to enlisted men, especially privates. Officers took full advantage, in some instances using sutlers' stores to remain in a perpetual stupor.[21] A keg of beer purchased from the sutler could certainly make a long evening more enjoyable.[22] Likewise, when Charles Fessenden Morse wished to relieve the "monotonous routine" of life in Cantonment Hicks near Frederick, Maryland, he worked with his wife to plan a feast for seven officer friends. Turkey, grouse, pie, and pudding arrived in packages from home, and the guests, who were "hungry as bears," washed down their "splendid" dinner with sherry and Madeira.[23] Union colonel Charles S. Wainwright was so accustomed to having his wine that he expressed great consternation when he ran out of claret and could not travel to Washington to restock. Likewise, when the camp sutler only stocked the "poorest Jersey brand" of champagne, Wainwright found it undrinkable. Luckily, he had "a bottle of common Madeira" in his private stores.[24]

Officers typically came from middle-class or affluent backgrounds, but they incorporated moderate (in their eyes) drinking into their conceptions of masculinity. That their wives provided the care packages suggests that they did not disgrace their families. Still, the propensity of drunken fun to spin out of control left fellow officers concerned that their comrades overused liquor and fell short of standards of masculinity.

OFFICERS DRANK AS A LUXURY because it was their privilege to do so. But when looking over most soldiers' accounts of their drinking habits, it becomes clear that many men (officers and enlisted alike) agreed with military officials that liquor should be an essential component of their personal health care regimens. In other words, liquor was not simply an extravagance but also a medicine, from the soldiers' perspective. In addition to the rations supplied by their surgeons, plenty of soldiers went to great lengths to keep themselves "medicated." Wounds were horrific, childhood diseases ran rampant through the camps, and, especially early in the war, field hospitals were incapable of providing adequate care. Left to their own devices, many soldiers and officers resorted to folk remedies, and liquor played a vital part in the process.[25] They tended to use spirits to revive themselves, even if they did not always articulate that they perceived alcohol to work as a stimulant in the same way that physicians did. Men simply believed that poor weather and exhaustion made them sick, and they drank brandy and whiskey to treat various physical and mental illnesses. Soldiers interpreted notions of fatigue and exposure broadly and also used liquor to treat homesickness and boredom. But the men had not abandoned all notions of morality that they had learned from their families. Ironically, troops often drank when they tried to replicate the comfort and security of their homes.

It was not simply that soldiers adopted military ideas of medicinal liquor when they joined the ranks. Instead, many men arrived in camp already believing that liquor carried important medicinal benefits. Confederates' letters home indicate that ardent spirits were common home remedies. The deeply pious Jones family of Georgia went to great trouble to ensure that family members remained well stocked with brandy and wine throughout the conflict. Whether they used it to treat wounds or chest pains, brandy, ale, and wine (blackberry or Madeira) were an integral part of their medicinal habits.[26] The family even added spirits to external compresses, mixing together brandy and mustard to treat typhoid fever, while also applying brandy-soaked cloths to a swollen throat.[27] Although the Joneses firmly supported sobriety among soldiers and lauded Confederate general Thomas "Stonewall" Jackson for keeping liquor out of reach of the troops, when it came to their health, the reverend and his family relied on brandy and porter, per their doctor's advice.[28] The Jones family was emblematic of temperance reformers' worst nightmare: the Christian family who drank for health. This indulgence, for the reform community, was the first step on the slippery slope into drunkenness.

But the Joneses were hardly an anomaly in the South. Confederate soldiers did not wait for the chronically undersupplied medical department to prescribe them liquor. Instead, they searched out their own remedies. Texan Theophilus Perry became quite concerned when he could not to find brandy or whiskey to treat a cough that had been afflicting him "for several weeks." He hoped to buy some rum to "make a little flip or egg-nog" that he could use as an expectorant.[29] His fellow Texan, Elijah P. Petty, used "about 4 fingers of brandy" and a bath in a spring to treat a fever brought on by a "severe cold," a case of piles, and a "very sore and painful" ripped fingernail. The brandy and bath readied Petty for "the full discharge of my duty and more."[30] Mississippian Robert A. Moore blamed a rainy march for landing him on the sick list with the measles. He purchased some brandy and ginger and concocted a brandy-infused ginger tea, which "made the measels [sic] go a little easier."[31] Edmund DeWitt Patterson recalled that he passed out "from excessive heat" on a march to Chancellorsville, Virginia, and a comrade's "pouring brandy down" his throat brought him back from being "almost dead."[32] So common was the use of medicinal liquor that soldiers' families provided medicinal spirits when they could. While fighting in Virginia, Mississippi private David Holt stopped to visit "the home of [his] forefathers." Holt was sick, and his Uncle Jim decided to "make one addition" to the treatment prescribed by Holt's doctor. The soldier's uncle had in his cellar "a barrel of fine old rye"— the rye had been grown on his farm and his neighbor had distilled it into whiskey for him. A daily dose, taken with sugar, would ward off sickness.[33]

While Confederates spent more time than their Union counterparts acquiring their own spirits to improve their health, Union soldiers wrote about liquor's medicinal properties similarly as they consumed their official rations. In July 1861, Friedrich Bertsch noted that "the total lack of wine and whisky" left many soldiers at Camp Middle Fork near Beverly in western Virginia stricken with diarrhea. Without liquor, the soldiers drank "all kinds of water" and slept in a leaky henhouse.[34] After a round of picket duty in Murfreesboro, Tennessee, Minnesotan James Madison Bowler caught a severe cold and "paid $1.00 for a pint of whisky to make cherry bitters," in hopes of curing his nagging cough, sore throat, and dysentery.[35] Union officer Augustus D. Ayling also found that a "day of cold and east wind and rain" made his recovery from typhoid fever and chronic diarrhea all the more difficult. Before going to bed, the lieutenant "took a good big drink of wine and got several naps before morning."[36] In other words, military life did not necessarily introduce men to new forms of medicinal liquor. It merely confirmed their preconceived notions that spirituous treatments were essential.

Plenty of soldiers, however, expanded the uses of alcohol beyond the military's policies to treat themselves for depression. Severe homesickness—known more commonly as "nostalgia"—plagued soldiers in both armies, often causing physical symptoms that accompanied mental distress.[37] Soldiers sought many remedies for homesickness, one of which was the bottle.[38] "Sometimes I am so low spirited that I am sorely tempted to indulge largely in this favorite pastime [drinking], but I can scarcely think that to be the proper remedy for my ailment," confided a Pennsylvania captain to his brother on the day after Christmas 1862. He wrestled with himself about how much whiskey an unhappy soldier should consume.[39] Confederate surgeon Junius Newport Bragg jokingly warned his wife that he had "a big jug of whiskey and the very first time you do not write me a long letter and one every week, or two or three a week, as you see proper, I shall most certainly imbibe."[40] His tone was playful, but there is little doubt that his wife understood that it was her letters that kept her husband from being overwhelmed with homesickness. These letters indicate that men—even surgeons—understood liquor to have more than stimulating properties. They clearly described alcohol's numbing effects when drinking to curb mental angst.

Soldiers' misery came not only from missing their families but also from the imminence of death, which, when coupled with the anonymity of army life, created a volatile combination that prompted some men to adjust their definitions of appropriate masculine behavior. Lieutenant Charles B. Haydon of the Kalamazoo Light Guards lamented that the men in his regiment acted "like devils" when drunk, but added that he and the other officers had "to tolerate some things which you would not at any other time" when dealing with undisciplined soldiers. Knowing that battle and its carnage lurked around the corner, Haydon believed, made everyone—officers and enlisted men alike—want to be drunk, and he perceptively acknowledged that many of his men would not "drink much after they had been out of the army a few days." Those familiar words "Eat drink & be merry for to morrow you die" resonated with these young men, who knew they might be dead in a month's time. When men arrived in a city with comrades, "money and opportunity," indulging in ardent spirits, along with other forms of amusement, could take their minds off the death and destruction that awaited them on the battlefield.[41] Soldiers found increasingly that the values with which they had marched off to war mattered less after the fighting began. Self-control, sobriety, moral courage—it all seemed less important in the midst of the horrific carnage.[42] What began as self-care to ward off the effects of sickness morphed into reckless regimens to mitigate the effects of war's emotional toll.

As a result (and because commanding officers so often doled out whiskey rations to raise morale), soldiers seemingly developed the common assumption that they were entitled to liquor when they performed any physically or mentally arduous task. When slated for sentry duty, men found ways to procure their own spirits in the absence of official rations. Some soldiers dealt with the effects of the weather by becoming intoxicated before their shifts ever began, exasperating those who spent extra time in the cold before being relieved.[43] But in the Union army, there seemed to be an understanding that sentries could demand a tribute of liquor from those wishing to pass into the camps. As Alfred Bellard recalled, a soldier presented him with "a suspicious looking bottle" in place of the countersign. After "taking a refreshing pul [sic] at the contents," Bellard let the men pass; the "countersign" had been correct.[44] This seems to have been common. Even Benjamin Butler, who was notorious for limiting his soldiers' access to alcohol, understood that it took liquor to move past the guard. When Henry Warren Howe tried to cross a bridge near Hampton Village, Virginia, the sentry turned him back for not having a pass. "Why didn't you shake a whiskey bottle at him?" asked a frustrated General Butler, whose orders had not been delivered.[45] When it came to fighting exposure and fatigue, soldiers took the military's guidelines to heart but interpreted them excessively, creating disruptions.

THE SENTRIES PROVIDE A GOOD EXAMPLE of the ways in which soldiers broadly interpreted military liquor regulations in order to expand definitions of acceptable drinking. Technically, enlisted men had no authority to procure their own spirits, but that they scrounged up their own liquor was a well-known secret. Overwhelmingly, soldiers expanded the definition of "exhaustion" to include any instances when they were bored, tired, or lonely. In other words, drinking under the umbrella of self-care became a common way for men to pass the time while in camp. Because liquor provided both physical and emotional relief, soldiers tended to view its recreational use acceptably, especially when they encountered other men who drank. As a result, the use of recreational whiskey revealed discrepancies between middle-class, working-class, and rural soldiers, who all adhered to different notions of when drinking was acceptable. Men created temporary camp homes that were decidedly not middle-class, and they rethought their previously held ideals of manliness and sobriety.

When soldiers arrived in camps, they went to great lengths to make themselves as comfortable as possible. Especially during winter months, camps dotted the Southern countryside, and the tent cities (as they appeared) often included row upon row of little semi-permanent cabins. Soldiers made their winter quarters as comfortable as they could, building furniture for themselves and even, at times, adding landscaping to make their accommodations as home-like as possible.[46] These "homes" kept the soldiers warm and busy, and for plenty of soldiers, recreational drinking was an essential component to their comfort (an irony that must have shocked temperance folk, who believed that home provided the best prevention against drinking). Plenty of men drank simply to cope with the boredom of camp life. The long winter nights became especially tedious, and soldiers went to great lengths to make life more bearable. Many times, though, their evening activities more closely resembled activities of a concert hall than a family parlor. Soldiers filled long evenings with games and snacks.[47] For better or worse, drinking typically livened things up; for officers who passed the hours playing cards and backgammon in their tents—sometimes gambling, sometimes not—nothing, it seemed, spiced up a game of whist like cakes, wine, or an occasional toddy.[48] Others engaged in livelier games like "Whiskey Poker" or spent their evenings enjoying James River oysters, which, apparently, tasted best with "a couple of bottles of good Scotch."[49] In the "dull" camps, where "mails come by chance & there is nothing to be had save meal, eggs & whiskey," ardent spirits provided a break in the loneliness and monotony.[50] Only a few men avoided such foolishness. For many, games and drinking provided more comfort than sitting soberly with memories of home and family.

Long evenings passed slowly, but winter weather also increased the desire to imbibe. Men from both the North and South came out of a tradition of rambunctious pastimes involving alcohol and the great outdoors.[51] A fresh blanket of snow beckoned enlisted men in both Union and Confederate armies, who had been cooped up in their cabins, to engage in snowball fights.[52] "Boys on a drunk" tended to enjoy the winter weather more freely than their sober comrades. One group of drunken Wisconsin soldiers stationed in Richmond, Minnesota, took to the river to skate, even though it was "not quite safe on the rapids."[53] When they were not playing in the snow, soldiers went to great lengths to keep warm in camp, keeping whiskey near their beds for the cold nights.[54] A cold day called for a drink as well, and a soggy soldier, like Edmund DeWitt Patterson of the 9th Alabama, could warm himself with some "Old Peach Brandy" if he managed to acquire it from a "jolly old farmer" on a rainy October day.[55] For these officers and soldiers, the lines between drinking for health and drinking for happiness were closely intertwined. Oyster roasts, drunken skating, card games, and the perceived warming effects of peach brandy provided welcome escape from the drudgery of camp life. While some relatives (and temperance reformers) may have expressed alarm when word reached home, most soldiers seemed to enjoy these pastimes without worrying if they would ultimately lead to their ruin.

That being said, men from teetotaling families were often shocked by the prevalence of drinking when they arrived in camp. Seymour Dexter lamented that in the 23rd New York Volunteers he had "seen more drunkedness and swearing" than ever before. A graduate of Alfred University in New York, Dexter commented that he and the other alumni of the institution remained sober, not willing to abandon their principles and tarnish their alma mater's reputation. Before the war, school had provided a domestic haven for the boys, but moving from the academy to camp at Elmira Heights proved jarring for Dexter and his comrades.[56] Reporting on the 44th Massachusetts Volunteer Regiment, comprising largely young men of the professional classes, Zenas T. Haines commented matter-of-factly to the *Boston Herald* that approximately half of the men were drinkers.[57] Conditions in Haines's regiment may have been better than in others. The *Richmond Enquirer* complained that many Confederate soldiers were "slaves to a low appetite."[58] These early reports confirmed families' and temperance reformers' worst fear—away from home and school, young men faced a host of trials and vices that caused them to reevaluate their commitment to sobriety (if they had ever valued it to begin with).

These competing notions of manliness became more noticeable during holidays. Military culture that allowed celebratory drinking spilled over into other festivities. Plenty of soldiers had not come from abstemious families, and their behavior frustrated more sober-minded men. Although men typically joined regiments with friends from their hometowns, they arrived in camps with men from all over the United States. Regiments of farmers and urban workers found themselves at times near regiments comprising largely recent immigrants (mostly from Ireland and Germany). Middle- and working-class men crossed paths, and cold-water Baptists shared tents with urban rowdies who had never darkened the doors of a church. When the conflicting values that they held collided, whiskey flowed more freely and gatherings became quite rambunctious.

Irish and German regiments celebrated religious and cultural festivals with spirits whenever they could find them. Union troops in New Orleans observed St. Patrick's Day 1863 with religious services and "a general spree" of drunkenness, horse-racing, and fighting.[59] In 1864, Confederate soldier John Edward Dooley passed his more subdued St. Patrick's Day with a church service, wine, and apple brandy.[60] The Irish Brigade, on the other hand, observed its St. Patrick's Day 1864 with the men and their guests munching on sandwiches and sipping whiskey punch while watching horse-races. These parties were by no means clandestine events. High-ranking generals in the Army of the Potomac—including George Meade—were among the guests.[61] Germans in the Army of the Cumberland were less lucky. Wilhelm Stangel and other members of the large German American 9th Ohio Infantry received orders to march right before a carefully planned Turners festival—complete with speeches and lager beer—was set to commence.[62] A sober festival— while perhaps more evangelical in nature—had less lively distraction to offer tired soldiers.

American patriotic holidays stirred debates among soldiers concerning whether they should be occasions for drunken frivolity or sober reflection, illuminating cultural tensions. For Alfred Bellard and his comrades, celebrating their patriotic holidays "in proper style" included tapping kegs of beer, getting tight, and "having a free fight, which resulted in black eyes and bloody noses."[63] Picnicking, fishing, and becoming a "little 'boozy'" were the preferred Independence Day pastimes of the 28th Wisconsin Infantry.[64] When members of the predominantly German 9th Ohio Infantry had "no 'Speech,' no money, no beer, no wine, and even no schnapps, only good fresh spring water" for their Fourth of July celebration, they concluded that the celebration was very "dry" (double meaning intended) and insinuated that America's Independence Day could be more appropriately enjoyed by incorporating more "German customs."[65] Soldiers in the Missouri State Guard likewise lamented a lack of supply to celebrate the Fourth of July. In 1862, General M. Jeff Thompson complained to Union general Ulysses S. Grant that his men had "neither whisky nor ice to have a very gay celebration today, neither have we powder to waste." The Missourians hoped, instead, to content themselves with the "news from Richmond."[66] From these soldiers' perspectives, being good republican citizens included drinking in celebration of the Republic.

Other soldiers, however, purposefully observed patriotic holidays in a drier fashion. July 4, 1862, left Union soldier Luman Tenney feeling "most disgusted" because the "officers gave the freest license to the men" and everyone "caroused." Two of Tenney's comrades fought, contributing to his displeasure.[67] Rufus Kinsley also preferred to commemorate the holiday more soberly (and reflectively), especially in 1865. Celebrating emancipation, Kinsley rejoiced that "for the first time in history . . . the old Liberty Bell in Independence Hall [spoke] the truth." The "hollow hypocrisy" that had tarnished the holiday in the past had disappeared, and Kinsley spent his day with a small circle of friends, reading Henry Ward Beecher and James Redpath's *John Brown*. The rest of the officers, he noted disapprovingly, opted for "a grand revel."[68] When the officers of the 5th Iowa Volunteer Infantry indulged in feasting and drinking on George Washington's birthday, it similarly disturbed John Quincy Adams Campbell. "Satan was more honored than Washington by it," grumbled Campbell.[69] For Kinsley, Campbell, and others, liberty and its heroes deserved loftier (and more thoughtful) recognition than a lusty swig from a keg or jug. Not coincidentally, these men came from evangelical reforming families who believed that drinking and other sins would lead to the downfall of the republic the soldiers intended to celebrate.

Perhaps no occasion revealed clashing beliefs over liquor quite like Christmas. The holiday had made pious (and middle-class) Americans nervous for generations because of its potential to devolve into bacchanalian chaos. Historically, Christmas had been a time when people turned the social order on its head and celebrated with drinking, eating, and demanding gifts from their social betters. In the nineteenth century, American evangelicals attempted to rein in Christmas and bring order through religious reflection and by giving gifts that promoted self-discipline and education.[70] Within the ranks of the Union and Confederate armies, the limits of the pious middle-class Christmas were evident. Officers—especially Union officers—approached Christmas as a time to give patronage. And soldiers' tales of Christmas reveal that frivolity, homesickness, and a mix of emotions expressed themselves—sometimes through drunkenness. To a greater extent than most other holidays, life in the army disrupted familiar domestic traditions, and soldiers went to great lengths to recreate the festivities.[71] Their makeshift celebrations often involved alcohol.

In the Union armies, many officers made it a priority to ensure that Christmas was a merry occasion for their men. Although the amount of alcohol involved varied from place to place, soldiers in various armies report receiving rations of commissary whiskey for the holiday. Members of the Irish Brigade remembered using their canteens of "wretched 'commissary'" to facilitate their reconstructions of celebrations from both New England and Ireland, and drank and danced "around the fire, jigs, reels, and doubles."[72] For soldiers in the Army of the Potomac camped near Fredericksburg in December 1862, government whiskey flowed freely. At his headquarters, General Joseph Hooker and twenty-five guests celebrated the holiday (and his promotion) with a "grand" dinner and copious toasts.[73] In 1863, officers in the 23rd Indiana Infantry gave "the soldiers beer and *Whiskey* as a Christmas present and that made them all lively."[74] Of course, drunken men could cause trouble. While Hooker and his men were "getting drunk and keeping up a terrible uproar," the privates of the 2nd New Hampshire Volunteers attempted to take a sutler's tent by "main force" after he refused to sell them whiskey to supplement their allotted government rations.[75] So engrained among Union officers was the notion that whiskey rations accompanied Christmas that prisoners of war occasionally reported receiving rations from the Union officers guarding them. Members of the Moccasin Rangers captured in rural western Virginia around Christmas 1862 received a "pitcher of whisky" from the Captain John Baggs who accompanied them.[76]

Confederate armies, on the other hand, were much less able or willing to formally incorporate drinking into their Christmas celebrations. Certainly chronic shortages of liquor within the Confederate armies contributed to the lack of whiskey rations. But at least in 1862, while Union general Hooker doled out drams, soldiers encamped nearby in the Army of Northern Virginia complained that "General [Robert E.] Lee saw to it that the opportunity [to become drunk] was wholly lacking," much to the chagrin of his soldiers.[77] Most men could find their own Christmas spirits, even if the commissary department failed them. A few friends in Walker's Texas Division pooled their resources to purchase "some whisky at $40 per gallon to have a frolick" on Christmas Day.[78] Soldiers in the 17th Mississippi paid between thirty and fifty dollars per gallon to buy liquor for a "grand camp dance" to celebrate the holiday.[79] Other soldiers received care packages from home full of spirits and other holiday treats.[80]

These affairs do not serve as evidence that young men abandoned their moral principles when left to their own devices, but rather they reveal that many soldiers came from families where Christmas was not a pious and sober occasion. The complaints about holiday drunkenness were few and far between and seem to be somewhat limited to evangelical chaplains.[81] Otherwise, that both Confederate and Union soldiers received packages from home attests to their families' approval of holiday spirits. These boxes containing turkeys, partridges, cakes, rum, and whiskey arrived through express delivery, and men combined their gifts in order to make appealing spreads for Christmas dinner.[82] Soldiers desired to re-create a homelike atmosphere on Christmas Day. For Confederate soldiers, civilians stepped in as substitutes for friends and family. Elijah Petty enjoyed "egg nog & cake in abundance" with "some nice young ladies" during Christmas 1861.[83] Edmund DeWitt Patterson spent his first Christmas of the war in a "house full of ladies with loads of delicacies of all kinds," but he and his friends kept "a suspicious looking jug stowed away ... with plenty of one thing needful in it." With eggs and sugar close by, the men hoped the women would occupy themselves long enough for them to concoct "a good 'egg-nog.'"[84] Union corporal Robert Rossi and his own friends "made punch" as well—on both Christmas Eve and New Year's Eve. On the latter holiday, they "had a lot of fun and didn't get to bed until around 3, all of us dutifully drunk."[85]

When soldiers wrote about holiday drinking, however, they typically indicated that liquor only took the edge off their doldrums. Many soldiers expressed significant homesickness and sadness around the holidays, and procuring whiskey seems to have been part of their desperate attempts to keep their misery from overwhelming them. When no one from home sent packages, two German soldiers and their friends experienced "a melancholy disposition." After all, "who can put on a jolly social gathering without song and without wine and—even more dreadfully—without beer and without hard liquor?" Far away "from the old familiar circle of friends ... and dear families," soldiers concluded that their Christmas Day would be "lonely, sad, and thirsty."[86] If spirits had been a part of Christmas traditions at home, their absence in the army could have a gut-wrenching effect. Thomas Wentworth Higginson, lauding the discipline of his regiment of U.S. Colored Troops, the 1st South Carolina Volunteers, noted that he had only heard one request for whiskey, on Christmas Day, by a man who "spoke with a hopeless ideal sighing, as one alludes to the Golden Age."[87] August Horstmann told his parents that his holidays were so uneventful that he did not "even know when they were. Nothing at all, not the slightest festivity, no joyful shooting in the air, no punch, no beer or wine, and no change in the bill of fare to remind us that these otherwise so richly celebrated days had gone by."[88] Irvin Cross Wills wanted nothing more than to enjoy "a cup of egg-nogg [sic]" but "no whiskey could be got. He had never in his life celebrated Christmas without eggnog. It was "dull."[89] These expressions of immense sadness speak to the significant role that liquor played in the soldiers' attempts to relieve themselves of the mental exhaustion associated with living in camps away from family and friends. These expressions of low spirits become most acute at Christmas.

Access to liquor in no way guaranteed a happy holiday. Charles Francis Adams Jr. complained to his family of his Christmas dinner of "tough beef" and "commissary whiskey" in 1862.[90] Eggnog, whiskey, and apple brandy could not keep Christmas from being "dull" for many soldiers. Floridian Robert Watson drank a little, but "did not feel marry [sic] as my thoughts were of home."[91] Unfortunately, whiskey proved a poor substitute for home, and recalling the festivities of past holidays left some men feeling gloomy. Christmas in the army appalled pious men. Homesick soldier John Baxter Moseley wrote of his wife on Christmas Day 1864, reporting "the drinking men are having a gay time & there are few who don't indulge." He was "sorry to see it."[92] Despite General Lee's attempts to cut off the flow of liquor in the Army of Northern Virginia, in Richard Lewis's camp near Fredericksburg in 1862 there was such a "terrible spree" during Christmas that all the men experienced "a day of reckoning and judgement [sic]" like they had never experienced before.[93] That so many Confederates became drunk on Christmas suggests that Lewis's critiques represented a minority opinion about drinking. When soldiers had access to liquor at Christmas, most imbibed and believed that their raucous frivolity was an acceptable way to re-create the festivities they missed from home.

No holiday achieved quite the level of debauchery as payday in the Union armies. Unlike Christmas tippling, which men typically enjoyed, soldiers condemned men who drank their earnings, believing that they shirked their masculine responsibilities to their country and their families. Ideally, payday occurred once a month, but in reality, the armies disbursed pay much less frequently. Because soldiers were paid so irregularly, officers worried that they would be unable to prevent the utter chaos that arrived when men had money in their pockets.[94] Officers and men documented the drunkenness that generally followed the disbursement of funds. Junior officers had their hands full trying to keep order amid payday's "evils."[95] Quarreling soldiers often had to be corralled.[96] Some commanding officers learned to let it run its course. In April 1862, Elijah Cavins of the 14th Indiana expressed to his father that "all the whiskey will be drank up in a few days."[97] General William T. Sherman likewise assured General Grant that the reports of rampant drunkenness among the soldiers in Memphis had merely been a temporary nuisance caused by payday. Most of the time, Sherman explained, his measures to close liquor shops and inspect packages for contraband liquor worked successfully.[98]

The lack of discipline vexed officers, and many soldiers were equally appalled at the amount of money squandered on booze—money that they believed should have been sent to families. Temperance reformers—especially women—had complained for decades that drinking men violated their masculine duty to support their families either because they could not hold steady jobs or because they spent their earnings on liquor.[99] The Union army exhibited similar notions of a man's responsibility to his family. A moderate drinker, Charles B. Haydon spent a dollar of his pay to enjoy a bottle of ale, but many of his comrades spent twenty to thirty-five dollars drinking and gambling.[100] Some men in Henry Warren Howe's Massachusetts regiment lost up to 250 dollars after a particularly large payday.[101] These benders could leave soldiers strapped for cash—and, problematically, unable to support their families. Officers in the 192nd Regiment Pennsylvania Volunteers cautioned their men "not to expend [their pay] foolishly, nor to invest any of it in whiskey."[102] William Wheeler expressed enormous relief when his "boys behaved much better than could have been expected" after going four months without pay. His men paid off debts and sent money to their homes.[103] This was not always the case. Georg Bauer complained that all too often men wasted money on "cards and drink, and in a short time, all the money is boozed up ... and the family gets nothing." Bauer believed that Union soldiers earned enough to support their families, and he accused drunken soldiers of being "foolhardy, shabby father[s]."[104]

Although Confederate soldiers wrote less about drinking on payday than their Union counterparts, in one case, a Confederate soldier disagreed that drinking away his pay made him a bad husband. In disagreeing, he illustrated how the war broke down traditional economic arrangements for many families. Enlisted men earned little, and although the army provided white soldiers uniforms and rations, supporting a family could be difficult. Union surgeon Daniel Holt received a candid answer from one Confederate soldier when Holt asked how a man could support a family on eleven dollars per month. "*I get eleven dollars a month and spend it the same day I draw it, for a pint of whisky!*" explained the rebel. The soldier had no reason to send home money. His wife supported their family by running his print shop in Memphis, Tennessee. Moreover, she sent him hundreds of dollars to sustain him while he fought Yankees. In short, his duty was to fight, while her duty was to provide for the family. From his perspective, he was not shirking his patriotic or manly duties by drinking up his paycheck—he was simply putting his meager earnings to the best use. His wife may not have shared his perspective; plenty of Northern and Southern women certainly faced economic hardship after their husbands enlisted and left them as the primary breadwinners.[105] Nevertheless, the rebel's explanation impressed Holt, who concluded that because Confederate scrip was so useless, the soldier, by serving, was sacrificing his life and comfort for "home and fireside." Rather than being a sign of his lack of moral fiber, his pint of whiskey became his reward for serving his country without receiving any meaningful monetary compensation.[106] The debate over payday drinking reveals that even though soldiers may have rejected teetotalism—and even believed that drunken frivolity was acceptable in certain celebratory contexts—when it came to supporting families, men critiqued drinkers who wasted their funds and left their wives and children with nothing. Nevertheless, that the Confederate soldier explicitly pointed out that he performed his duty to his home by fighting suggests that perhaps enlisted men were not behaving thoughtlessly when they drank their pay so much as it reveals that they shifted their notions of masculine duty and believed that liquor left them better able to protect their families by fighting.

By drinking on payday, holidays, and long winter evenings, soldiers and officers demonstrated that liquor was central to their mental (and not just their physical) well-being. It provided comfort and emotional fortification as men faced death and missed their families. As a result, men adopted definitions of manhood that were at odds with evangelical and middle-class values.

THE HAPHAZARD REGULATIONS coupled with soldiers' and officers' tendency to use alcohol for self-care and comfort created an environment where abuse was as rampant in camps as it was in hospitals. The abusive use of alcohol could take a variety of forms. Some men—especially officers—simply misused liquor (for other than its expressed purposes) or acquired it through theft or other nefarious means. Other men, however, were chronic drunks. These perpetually intoxicated officers and soldiers created more significant problems. The men who served under them and with them argued that they felt misused by them and left vulnerable.

Much misuse occurred when soldiers found ways to capitalize on distributed spirit rations. Basically, when an army or navy distributed rations, not every soldier wanted his. Plenty of men simply did not drink. The navy generally provided whiskey rations three times a day for all men who wanted it. Sailors who chose to abstain could earn extra pay, although most men chose liquor.[107] Outside of the navy, soldiers made similar arrangements. Alonzo Miller, for example, sometimes traded his whiskey for extra coffee.[108] Often, nondrinking soldiers passed their rations along to their buddies who drank. William Wiley of the 77th Illinois noted that after his regiment was issued rations in the wake of Lee's surrender, some of the men refused to drink and others, to compensate, "took a double portion and got gloriously drunk."[109] Virginian William Clark Corson explained that he and his buddy Billy Price had learned to take full advantage of the whiskey issued by the Confederate government. Price and Corson "contracted for the rations of all the fellows that don't drink" in order to "have a lively time."[110] The exasperated officers commanding the 5th Alabama decided to put a stop to men "getting tight" on doubled rations. They required the men to drink their rations in the presence of their company commanders. Soldiers could pass their rations along to a friend, but the company commander kept the whiskey out of reach for an hour. Spacing out the drinks prevented disorder.[111]

Officers had more opportunity than enlisted men to abuse whiskey, and their penchant for overindulging frustrated their commanders and the enlisted men who served under them. Soldiers preferred their commanding officers to exhibit at least a pinch of the self-control that middle-class evangelicals espoused. Because officers regarded access to liquor as a privilege of their rank, tensions existed within the cultures of the Union and Confederate armies between men who drank and men who drank too much. Unlike the temperance-minded, who regarded even the smallest sip of liquor as a problem, officers tended to look at job performance when evaluating whether or not their comrades drank too much. Many men within the military worried that commissions attracted drunkards. Fellow officers—and, importantly, soldiers—chastised officers who drank to the point that it prevented them from performing their duties. As a result, the debates about proper manly behavior among officers (and soldiers) ensued.

The perception that officers had a predilection to drink excessively was widespread in both Union and Confederate armies. Captain Jacob Ritner estimated that at least two-thirds of the officers in his regiment were drunks.[112] Other soldiers noted similarly high numbers and even pondered if drunkards had a special knack for rising through the ranks. Part of the problem, from the perspective of sober-minded men, was that enlisted men elected their own company officers. Too often, the men did not bother to consider their comrades' drinking habits before voting for their promotion. When Elliott H. Fletcher and other men of Mississippi County, Arkansas, were mustered at Osceola in June 1861, they "unanimously elected" a captain who showed up drunk to their mustering.[113] Hoosier soldier William Taylor Stott barely managed to win an election for captain after his liquor-drinking opponent tried to buy votes by getting "some of our men drunk."[114] Sobriety triumphed over drunkenness in his 18th Indiana, but elsewhere in the Union army and navy, officers noticed that drunkards seemed to have an advantage. Admiral David Dixon Porter asserted that "rum sucking, good for nothing" retirees were "being placed in such good commands and positions." It was bad enough when incidental drunkenness occurred among the officers on a ship, but appointing "a chronic drunk" to a position of power created a new type of problem—"not having seen them sober you cant [sic] prove whether they were drunk or not."[115] Even General Benjamin Butler, who was reputed not to "tolerate" such problems, had trouble with drunken officers throughout the war, despite taking measures to cut the flow of ardent spirits through the Department of

Virginia.[116] In December 1863, Butler implored Secretary of War Edwin Stanton to stop promoting officers to positions in the U.S. Colored Troops without first requesting information about their conduct. It seemed that an order for a promotion had just arrived for a man sitting in the guardhouse charged with desertion and drunkenness. He "desires me to let him out for the purpose of taking his commission, with the promise that he will not do so again," explained Butler in exasperation.[117]

Soldiers judged their superior officers harshly because they believed their commanders had to set an example of patriotic manliness. For an officer, proving one's leadership skills in battle was the ultimate test of his manhood, and it was under fire that officers earned or lost the respect of the men who served under them. Men overwhelmingly condemned habitual drunkards, but when it came to fighting, soldiers expressed divided opinions about whether or not liquor helped or hurt. Some soldiers thought that sobriety and bravery had little to do with each other. One Massachusetts soldier assured his mother that she need not "make a great fuss at home" over the issue of drunken officers. He reminded her that in times of peace, plenty of men spent "thier [sic] time in getting drunk and getting over it." Officers were no different. A man who might spend his evenings in a stupor could likely be "perfectly sober rushing up to the Cannons mouth amid a storm of lead and iron, and amid such sights and sounds as would alone kill the race of disabled men who have crept out of the draft on the strength of a corn on the toes or a scratch on the fingers."[118] When it came to performing one's patriotic duty, plenty of soldiers wanted a man who served willingly on the battlefield. What he kept in his canteen was immaterial, as long as he did not shirk. Some officers certainly decided that making it through the bloody ordeals required that they and their men take a few swigs of whiskey. Fighting sickness, Colonel Mason Whiting Tyler "lived on whiskey" in order to withstand a day with his regiment on a skirmish line.[119] Tyler implied that the whiskey gave him the staying power he needed to provide leadership to his men, who relied on him, by fortifying him physically (as the army intended whiskey rations to do) and by taking his mind off the misery of illness. For better or worse, whiskey transformed men and sometimes helped them endure combat. After the capture of Union City, Tennessee, a war correspondent described rebel soldiers as "valiant haters of Yankees"—"frantic" and "whiskey-brave" soldiers whose performance in battle was "superhuman." Whiskey had not compromised their performance, but instead had enhanced it.[120]

That being said, a habitually intoxicated officer could wreak havoc on the cause by wasting manpower because he deprived his men of the support they needed to prepare for battle. After a visit to Atlanta in May 1864, nurse Kate Cumming worried that drunken officers endangered the struggling Confederacy. Rumors of "drunkenness and evil of all kinds" circulated, and Cumming believed that "if one half of the tales are true," the officers did "much harm to our cause." She had heard of one intoxicated officer who had dragged a soldier behind a gun-carriage for twenty miles. Even more unacceptable, from Cumming's perspective, this officer "was never sober enough at the time of any of the battles to lead his men." The military seldom brought such men to justice, and Cumming felt certain that their behavior brought about disastrous consequences.[121]

Enlisted men expressed similar frustration when their officers behaved hypocritically, regarding drinking. Officers, for example, notoriously searched care packages that soldiers received from their families. Don Pedro Quarendo Reminisco, whose memoirs recount common happenings in Union camps, sarcastically noted that officers searched packages from home for evidence of "a liquor brand or stamp." Cheap "contraband" was "emptied on the ground," but finer liquors were sent to the hospital under "pretence of discipline in camp." Then, doctors, colonels, and other officers enjoyed "the spoils" and "indulged in them like Lucifer."[122] While assigned to the CSS *Savannah* late in the war, Floridian Robert Watson noticed a similar problem among Confederate officers near Wilmington. The Confederate army allowed enlisted men one gill of whiskey per day, but "the balance of the men get none," because officers drank the majority themselves and spent their time "fiddling, dancing, and drinking whiskey all day and nearly all night."[123] So ingrained into their minds was the notion that imbibing was a privilege of rank that plenty of officers seemingly had no remorse when it came to stealing alcohol from their own troops, rejecting all notions of responsible leadership.

Drunken officers' spectacles disillusioned enlisted men. Colonel William Weer of the 10th Kansas, for example, decided one night to defend the honor of his men (who had been charged with cowardice) with a speech at a dress parade in camp at Forsyth, Missouri. Unfortunately, the perpetually intoxicated Weer struggled, his speech morphing into nothing more than the "freaks of a drunken man" who "held on the pummil of his saddle as if there was danger of his falling off."[124] He disgraced the men who served under him. Confederates suffered similarly. When Texan Ludwig Lehmann and his comrades found their colonel, James B. Likens, "lying in a *Mudhole*" as they marched through South Carolina, they left him there—"dead drunk and out cold"—and expressed satisfaction when Colonel Likens finally strolled into Columbia and was arrested.[125]

As problematic as officers who could not stay in their saddles were those who disrupted the flow of supplies. Illinois soldier Frederick Hess became so enraged with his officers, who cared more about "their Whiskey" than whether or not their men had "anything to eat or not," that he hoped that "about a dozen of them would get a ball put through them."[126] Confederate soldier Robert Patrick found that working under a tipsy officer in the 4th Louisiana Infantry's Commissary and Quartermaster Departments was similarly unbearable. Major T. J. Woolfork, the quartermaster of Cantey's Brigade, remained in a drunken stupor day after day. His intoxication not only made him terrible at his job but also exacerbated his corrupt business dealings. Most egregious to Patrick was that Woolfork made a habit of selling shoes and blankets to Confederates officers' slaves in exchange for bottles of whiskey. While the officers engaged in their illicit trading, enlisted men went without blankets or shoes. Patrick regarded Woolfork as "a damned fool, who knew "nothing about business" and prevented Patrick from completing his tasks properly. Even if Woolfork "had the capacity his unsteady habits would render him entirely unfit for business," grumbled Patrick. He decided that describing Woolfolk as "unsteady" did not really capture the situation: "He is the most regular man in his habit that I ever saw. *He gets drunk every day regularly.* Nothing could be more systematic than his drunkenness." His habitual intoxication made him "the poorest apology for a quarter-master, or as I may say, for a man that I ever saw."[127]

Enlisted men may have been largely powerless to curb an officer's drunkenness, but junior officers risked charges of insubordination to report their drunken superiors whom they believed misused their services. After the 22nd U.S. Colored Troops (USCT) endured a "disgraceful rout" on October 27, 1864, at Boydton Plank Road near Petersburg, Virginia, the captains wished to place the blame for the defeat "where it properly belongs"—at the feet of Colonel Joseph B. Kiddoo. They thought it was "rather asking too much of thinking men to risk their lives, which are valuable, if not to themselves to the country in its present hour of need, to carry out the sublime views and plans of a whisky-crazed brain." Colonel Kiddoo wasted national resources with his reckless behavior and the other officers of the 22nd USCT implored the commander of the Army of the James to investigate the colonel to prevent "the recurrence of such a disgraceful affair."[128]

With their criticism of their drunken superiors, these enlisted men and junior officers presented clearly their definitions of what a proper officer—and a proper man—should be. It was a definition that middle-class temperance reformers would have recognized. For decades, temperance reformers had argued that drunken men not only endangered themselves but also threatened the people—namely, women and children—who depended on them for shelter and food. In many ways, enlisted men similarly depended on their officers to keep them well supplied and healthy so that they would be prepared to fight. When officers neglected these duties because of drunkenness, their men offered scathing condemnations of their manhood.[129] Patrick knew that Major Woolfork's perpetual condition of intoxication made him a poor excuse for a man because he left the Confederate soldiers who depended on him hungry and nearly naked. Likewise, when a lieutenant colonel in the Union army was found to be "beastly" drunk and "unable to attend to his command" for three days, his commanding officer, Colonel Nathan W. Daniels, threatened to court-martial him. In his view, a drunken man was no use as a commander; the soldiers would not "rely upon him in any event of emergency."[130]

THESE TENSIONS THAT EXISTED BETWEEN soldiers' drinking and soldiers' drunkenness illustrate that to a certain extent, life in the military required different codes of behavior than middle-class neighborhoods and evangelical congregations. Although plenty of volunteer soldiers and officers went to war with civilian conceptions of duty and self-control, they had to reconfigure their ideals when it came to drinking. Men from temperate backgrounds mingled with plenty of soldiers who had different cultural proclivities. But more than that, teetotalism was profoundly impractical, and men in the ranks were often left on their own to manage their physical and mental exhaustion with liquor.

In this environment, Union soldier James Kendall Hosmer indicated that most soldiers had little interest in adopting complete sobriety as a masculine trait. War, to Hosmer, necessitated a broader, different, conception of manhood and morality. Noting that prewar values of patience, honesty, and temperance were sorely lacking among many men and officers in camp, Hosmer learned to "put as much confidence in men as ever, to believe in intrinsic goodness of the human heart." For the first time, Hosmer had formed relationships with "rough men"—coarse and lacking religion. Yet, he observed that they "would help others generously; they would bear privation cheerfully"; and they faithfully attended to sick and dying comrades. Finding his preconceived notions of respectability turned upside down by the war, Hosmer concluded that unselfishness was a manly trait of the highest value.[131] Increasingly throughout the war, soldiers reevaluated masculine and patriotic values on the battlefield.[132] Men in the armies sometimes favored solidarity and camaraderie over pious self-control, and by making room for "roughness" and drunkenness, they redefined masculinity for themselves.

And yet, Hosmer's alternative definition prioritized selfless behavior. Soldiers lambasted both men whose drinking precluded them from "helping others" and "bearing privation" and officers who stole from their men or neglected their responsibilities. So while many soldiers certainly rejected notions of sober masculinity—if they ever embraced them to begin with—they stopped well short of embracing a masculinity of selfish drunkenness.

Nevertheless, the centrality of drinking for physical and emotional comfort created a chaotic environment. Union and Confederate militaries struggled to control overindulgence—not just in the medical departments, but throughout the camps. Chronically drunken officers were not the only problem. So many mishaps occurred from too much drinking that both Union and Confederate camps became targets of civilian reforming efforts, and military officials searched constantly for ways to deter soldiers from intoxication.

CHAPTER THREE

Mishaps, Morality, Masculinity, and Military Discipline

Devil's Leap, a hill near Germanna Ford along the Rapidan River in Virginia, was thickly wooded in December 1863. The 5th New York Cavalry had been instructed to build their winter quarters near the hill, but Confederates, who were encamped across the river, wanted the Devil's Leap's timber for their own quarters. The men of the 5th New York Cavalry needed to work quickly. Rain fell. They were cold, wet, and miserable. The camp's adjutant kept the construction on task, pooling the men's carpentry skills in order to get the shelters up as quickly as possible. But on December 30, the building process hit a snag, of sorts. The adjutant took a break from construction to enjoy "a jollification time with an old crony." After what must have been a pleasant evening of drinking, the adjutant decided "to make use of one of the deep-dug sinks." Unfortunately for the adjutant, he lost his balance and tumbled into the latrine trench head-first, "spoiling his entire suit of clothes."

The adjutant suffered no long-term ill effects of his tumble, although work on the camp ground to a halt for a few hours—presumably because the man was hung over and doing his laundry. Most of the cavalrymen found the incident to be hilarious. Less enthused, the camp's chaplain hypothesized that a drunken nosedive into the latrines might actually save many soldiers from the "more awful" pit of hell.[1] The adjutant's misfortune illustrates the typical progression of drunken antics in both Union and Confederate armies. Officers set the tone of drinking to excess, especially when they were cold, sick, and bored. Yet while the adjutant's antics result in hilarity, in many cases, officers' drinking spread to enlisted men and caused a whole range of mishaps. The disruptions were so severe that they exacerbated tensions between soldiers and officers, and they left chaplains, concerned civilians, and military officials wondering how to curb drinking and reinstill discipline. Civilian reformers and military chaplains worried about drinking's immoral effects on the men. But military officials resorted to corporal punishment and other forms of harsh discipline to control drunkenness. No approach was particularly successful.

While the lack of control over drunken mishaps probably did not affect the overall outcome of the war, unruly drunks certainly contributed to insubordination and a lack of discipline in camps. Scholars have argued that the

Union and Confederate armies experienced problems with discipline. In the Union army, especially, many enlisted men hesitated to adopt the disciplinary norms of the regular army, preferring instead to cling to democratic ideals to resist the military's attempts to remold them into a fighting machine.[2] Drunken soldiers' resistance to military and civilian efforts to discipline them confirms these historians' arguments. That soldiers and officers drank to relieve their physical and mental exhaustion—even if it contributed to disruptions in military routines—speaks to men's lack of interest in having their manhood shaped by either middle-class evangelicals or by military officials. Instead, soldiers combined their appropriation of military uses of liquor and their adherence to working-class and rural definitions of masculine recreation to form new definitions of manhood. When it came to military discipline, soldiers resisted martial traditions. Instead, they favored a more democratic solidarity with the drunken soldiers against demeaning military practices, even as they condemned harmful drunkenness among themselves.

A MILITARY CULTURE WITH unsuccessfully regulated drinking contributed to a lack of discipline in the armies. Intoxicated soldiers created a variety of disturbances and mishaps, ranging from fairly innocuous complaints of noise to the more serious problems of murder and mutiny. Officers, when they drank, abused men under their command. The problem of disruptive soldiers and officers led men to debate among themselves how much drinking was too much. Even as soldiers believed that spirits were medically beneficial and invaluable in staving off the effects of exposure and fatigue, they drew the line in instances where drunkenness caused officers or soldiers to harm other men.

The irony in the fact that the armies' policies that allowed drinking also enabled the wide use of liquor that undercut discipline is most evident when examining how company-grade officers' use of liquor during marches and in battle led to chaos. Perhaps the most infamous instance of whiskey-related trouble occurred during Burnside's Mud March after the battle of Fredericksburg. Charged with the task of getting demoralized troops to move during horrible weather, officers in the Army of the Potomac turned to whiskey rations. The unhappy men drank willingly, but officers lost control as drunken fights broke out.[3] Later in 1863, Confederates had similar troubles (albeit on a smaller scale) while on their way to Pennsylvania. After crossing the Potomac River in Maryland on a rainy, muddy day, Confederate soldiers stopped to eat dinner. As the men prepared their fires, they received hearty rations of whiskey to combat the nasty weather. "About one-third got pretty tight" from the "stiff drink." Unfortunately, orders came to march again, and the tipsy soldiers "dragged" themselves toward Pennsylvania—"many slipped down and literally rolled over in the mud for it rained all the time."[4] Enlisted men had only consumed what the military allowed, but their officers' decisions contributed to their misery.

Officers' intermittent decisions to provide rations during marches created an environment in which enlisted men sometimes felt entitled to obtain their own libations while journeying from place to place. During the Shenandoah Valley Campaign of 1864, officers of the Army of Northern Virginia found stragglers "who had been after whisky." Though the men had been successful in their hunt, General John B. Gordon poured out the whiskey on the turnpike.[5] On the rare occasion that soldiers arrived at a destination without "irregularity," company and brigade commanders rejoiced. Jonathan Huntington Johnson of the 15th New Hampshire Infantry proudly told his wife that his men had marched twenty miles in six hours. They had sore toes, but no one had become drunk.[6] A safe and sober arrival at a destination filled officers with pride at their men's discipline.[7] Officers may have rejoiced when their men marched soberly, but when things went poorly enlisted men tended to place the blame for drunken disorder with undisciplined officers. When marching from Bristoe to Manassas, General Dan Sickles's Excelsior Brigade became "so drunk that nothing could be done with them." They were sent back to camp, oblivious to the other brigades' taunts of "Johnny stole a Ham, and Sickles killed a Man." Such hijinks blamed Sickles's lack of character for his men's drunkenness, and even raised doubts about the drunkards' patriotism; some thought such men as immoral as thieving rebel soldiers.[8]

Moving soldiers by rail exacerbated the problems by throwing civilians into the mix. Officers had little notion of how to prevent chaos. British observer William Howard Russell spent a "hideous" night in a train carriage with soldiers singing loudly after downing copious amounts of "forty-rod" (strong) whiskey. The officers, he lamented, had lost control of their men.[9] Temperance reformers had their worst fears about the trains confirmed. One irate passenger wrote to the *Journal of the American Temperance Union* that he only encountered intoxicated soldiers—some by lager beer, others by something that "looked clearer and smelled stronger." Although he noted that women escaped the indecent scenes, respectable men who could not ride in the ladies' car had to put up with raucous shouting and singing that continued until all the drunks fell asleep.[10] Temperate soldiers found traveling with their drunken comrades "very disagreeable."[11] But there seemed to be little that commanding officers could do to prevent the raucousness. Every time the train stopped, soldiers had additional opportunities to find trouble. When moving men on the railroad from La Mine Bridge to Saint Louis, Major R. H. Brown ordered ten men to keep the soldiers from straggling, stealing farm supplies, and finding whiskey.[12] By winter of 1865, Assistant Secretary of War Charles A. Dana, Major-General Henry Halleck, and Brigadier-General John Rawlins all tried to cut off access to liquor on the Baltimore and Ohio Railroad to prevent drunken disorder.[13]

Steamer transport provided no safer alternative. In one incident in the winter of 1861, soldiers awaiting a steamer to Maryland arrived at the dock, only to wait four hours to board. This gave the men plenty of time to find whiskey to take the edge off the blustery winter weather. Soon, officers and companies engaged in a "free fight." The ruckus that continued on board only ended after two men lost their balance and tumbled into the icy water.[14] Both steamers and trains put soldiers in towns while they waited to board—increasing their access to liquor. That the men could stand still while on board seemed to remove their inhibitions about becoming drunk. The results were more disruptive—to the point of being deadlier—than straggling on marches. Officers seemingly had little ability to control their men once a handful became intoxicated and tended to exacerbate the violent disorder rather than mitigate it. What is more, even if commanding officers tried to prevent men from finding liquor in towns along the rails and rivers, soldiers' drinking during transport had its origins in company-grade officers supplying liquor to boost morale.

This same tacit approval to drink on duty occurred during battle as well, when some company officers decided that whiskey rations would fortify men for an engagement, the same way it shielded them from the elements. Officers who distributed whiskey rations before battle gambled—at times, disastrously. Union and Confederate commanders risked it. When officers in the 30th Massachusetts believed that combat was imminent and that the enemy awaited them near Winchester, they served a ration of whiskey.[15] During a break in the action at Ball's Bluff, Confederate colonel W. H. Jenifer requested a barrel of whiskey be sent for his men (knowing that other provisions were unavailable).[16] More common were commanders who supplied rations right after an engagement. After falling back to White House during the Battle of Gaines Mill, Colonel H. S. Lansing of the 17th New York Volunteers saw to it that his men received a spirit ration as they stacked their arms.[17] In July 1864, Confederate major general Bushrod R. Johnson requested that that one brigade be given a ration of whiskey after being subjected to "sharpshooting and shelling" that "was quite brisk."[18] A few days before the war's end on March 30,

1865, Major-General Nelson A. Miles made a similar request for his troops stationed near Petersburg. Assured that the enemy knew their position, Miles had the division band brought up and issued a ration of whiskey among the soldiers so that they could relax for the night.[19] These uses of the whiskey ration—whether they came before, during, or after the engagement—were all rooted in the same logic: that liquor had a fortifying effect on the (sometimes hungry) men engaged in an exhausting and traumatic experience.

Unfortunately, whiskey rations did not guarantee measured behavior from soldiers. During the siege of Petersburg, Captain Augustus Cleveland Brown of the 4th New York Heavy Artillery noticed that the captain of the company positioned next to his was in a tight spot. The officer was "as brave a man as ever lived," but he had given his men a ration of whiskey just before they became engaged. Much to their captain's (and Brown's) horror, the men began "dropping into a little ditch just outside of the line of trees." Brown recalled that the captain stood, "with tears streaming down his face," screaming at his men, prodding them, and "begging them to get out and keep in line and not disgrace themselves or him."[20] The crying officer and his fears of disgrace encapsulate the complicated relationship between liquor, soldiering, and patriotic masculinity. Fighting bravely was a key marker of masculinity during the war.[21] As a company-grade officer, this man had a duty to ensure that the soldiers under his command performed well. He tried to ensure that, using whiskey, and as a result his men appeared cowardly in front of their comrades. He appeared foolish as well.

The debacle Brown witnessed was simply one incident in a much larger internal debate reverberating throughout the Union and Confederate ranks. Officers and enlisted men disagreed over who was responsible for the mishaps that compromised military discipline. Within these debates, it becomes clear that within the military conflicting ideals of masculinity clashed. The older notion—somewhat aristocratic—that drinking was a luxury that accompanied the professional career of an officer competed with newer definitions of masculine patriotism, which infiltrated the military through the volunteer ranks. Among officers, especially, republican ideals—which favored sobriety—somewhat supplanted aristocratic ones, in rhetoric if not in practice. Enlisted men, on the other hand, absolutely expected that their officers would exhibit self-control whenever soldiers' lives were on the line.

The contradictory ways that soldiers and officers responded to drunken mishaps revealed these conflicting ideals. When high-ranking officers bemoaned the culture of excessive drinking, their tone was one of exasperation that their comrades performed their jobs unseriously. In one instance, Union general Darius N. Couch and assistant adjutant general Seth Williams complained that intelligence took more than a day to wind its way through the Army of the Potomac's 2nd Corps because many officers throughout the Union army believed their duties consisted of reading books, playing cards with politicians, "drinking whiskey, and grumbling."[22]

Lieutenant-Colonel H. C. Alleman likewise concluded that officers who drank were "unfit to command our brave patriotic men" in battle, because intemperance repeatedly "wrought disaster, and caused blunders, and mistakes on many a bloody field." Men too inebriated to "drive a decent mule team" had no business directing "an important campaign." Sobriety was as essential in commanders as was an understanding of military science.[23] These officers' frustration suggests that the idea of the officer's job as luxurious faded within the context of a brutal war, in which a lack of efficiency caused by drunken officers could affect engagements.

Enlisted men expressed concerns far more acute than lollygagging officers. They worried less about large-scale disruptions and more about the direct effects intoxicated officers had on their well-being. Building on their critiques of chronically intoxicated officers who acted foolishly or wastefully, soldiers expressed fury at the shenanigans of their drunken officers when it led to abuse and compromised the soldiers' ability to be good fighters. While squads of the 77th Illinois Infantry tried to capture rebels and sheep one night while encamped near Falmouth, Virginia, in October 1862, William Wiley reported that Captain Robert Erwin of Company I "got on a big drunk" and had his men "out in line at all hours of the night."[24] At Vicksburg in July 1863, Wiley reported that the men "marched hard all day" because the officers "rushed us through as if we were on a forced march." With no enemy in the vicinity, Wiley and others wondered why they were "being run" back to camp like "greyhounds." It turned out that a few of the "head officers had got too much Mississippi rum . . . to know what they were doing." Wiley and the other men objected to the grueling march by setting up "the most unearthly howling like a pack of hounds" any time General Thomas Kilby Smith came within earshot.[25] Other soldiers wrote of being constantly subjected to "double-quicks" and extra drilling for the pleasure of drunken officers.[26] Men believed these useless drills wasted energy and manpower and hurt the war effort. Confederate soldier Robert Watson became so "heartily sick of it" that he supposed that if the extra drilling and abuse "continue much longer" he would "certainly desert and go to some other command."[27]

With their complaints of abuse, enlisted men revealed their complicated attitudes toward liquor. To be certain, soldiers often appreciated when their commanding officers supplied some whiskey after a long march or a hard-fought battle. They could respond with "a thundering cheer" to show appreciation for liquor.[28] Yet the disorder that generally followed left soldiers such as Jenkin Jones wondering if the whiskey was indeed a perk. Jones believed that Union officers who used whiskey "more freely than water" caused additional headaches by serving whiskey to their men.[29] Men clearly had no tolerance for drunkenness that resulted in mismanagement. The matter-of-fact-ness with which Robert Watson had made up his mind is telling. The Floridian had no intention of abandoning his duty to fight, but as he saw it, drunken officers misused, even wasted, him and his fellow soldiers at a time—January 1865—when Confederates had limited manpower. The officers' behavior was so appalling that only by deserting to join another outfit could Watson escape abuse and fulfill his patriotic obligations.

Not all soldiers threatened to desert, but they echoed Watson's feelings of powerlessness, and their reflections reveal that the standards of acceptable behavior within the military were truly contested. If plenty of officers believed that consuming liquor conspicuously came with a privilege of their rank, enlisted men disagreed. Overwhelmingly comprising volunteers, the rank and file brought with them ideas of republican citizenship (even if they were not from middle-class or evangelical families)—and with it the notion that soldiers and officers had a duty to act selflessly in defense of their country.

DRUNKEN OFFICERS CAUSED AN ADDITIONAL PROBLEM: their bad behavior spread to the impressionable young men serving in the ranks. After intoxicated officers turned the Confederate army in Arkansas into a disorganized mob that ravaged the countryside, a disgusted Colonel Cyrus Franklin went so far as to inform President Jefferson Davis that he refused to subject his men to "any drunken officer." As Franklin saw it, dangerous raids put troops into harm's way because the whiskey drinking affected the soldiers.[30] Other soldiers and officers knew that drunkenness could cause an insidious culture of indiscipline. Complaining to his wife about the lack of discipline in the Army of the Potomac, Levi Bird Duff remarked that only half of the officers and enlisted men fit for duty showed up to drill. The problem, he thought, stemmed from the officers in the 105th Pennsylvania Volunteers, who disappeared on drunken sprees "for several days & when they are present they never look after the interest or the comfort of the men." Appalled by such scenes, Duff began to question General George B. McClellan's leadership. The idea that more important tasks prevented McClellan from noticing the drunkards in his army carried no weight with Duff. "They stare him in the face every day," he remarked to his wife, and "unless he is blindfolded he must see them."³¹ While officers may have blamed enlisted men from rough backgrounds for the lack of discipline in camps, when it came to drinking, enlisted men saw it differently: officers who drank excessively and provided rations foolishly created the atmosphere that enabled soldiers to drink too much.

A widespread lack of discipline trickled down through the ranks. Soldiers reported nights of disturbed sleep because of drunken men. John Daeuble of the 6th Kentucky complained one night that he "could not get a half hour's sleep the whole night because of a continuous noise" coming from intoxicated soldiers. Another night when he served picket duty, a drunken soldier awakened his entire regiment by stealing the regimental flag and running noisily through the lines. Daeuble and his exhausted comrades conked the drunk on the head to quiet him down.³² Their response to the soldier suggests that men had little patience for drunken noise in the middle of the night. But Regis de Trobriand knew of a regiment in the Army of the Potomac where "the soldiers were often disturbed in their sleep by the obscene refrains and drunken cries from the tent of the commanding officer." The behavior had a "deplorable effect."³³ Again, officers perpetuated the behavior that enlisted men mimicked.

At first blush, it might seem that noise would be a minor disturbance but reports that it had a deplorable effect suggest that soldiers considered it a prelude to more serious forms of disorder that resulted in violence. In some instances, the violence came at the expense of Black men whom Union troops plied with alcohol to provide entertainment. In September 1863, in one camp near Vicksburg a group of minstrels, "quite sprung, some of them, by whiskey," "kept on with their fun till midnight," and well past the order for lights out.³⁴ Soldiers in Chauncey Herbert Cooke's camp were more malicious. After a Black man began teaching the soldiers new war songs, the troops tipped other African American men pennies to sing Southern songs while the whites drank in saloons. Singing for pennies, however, only temporarily satisfied the white soldiers. A few rounds later, soldiers gave Black men five cents for "butting." The men were "kept about half drunk to give them grit" as they "would back off like rams and come together head to head."³⁵

Not coincidentally, every form of camp recreation that involved alcohol had the potential to devolve into violence. Jenkin Lloyd Jones and his comrades spent one evening playing music with a banjo, fiddle, clarinet, bones, and tambourine. The evening passed enjoyably until the quartermaster passed around "some bottled whiskey." The music "broke up in a drunken row."³⁶ After Alabama soldiers received a dose of "bust head, tangle foot whiskey" in

April 1865, men of the 6th Alabama challenged a company of men from the 5th Alabama to a brawl.[37] A "snowy day" in camp brought not only boozy snowball fights but "bloody heads" when men became so intoxicated they fought over whiskey stashes.[38] Elsewhere, St. Patrick's Day ended with "fistfights," and payday brought "black eyes," "noses skinned & bloody," and "hard knocks to the bowels" after men used their money to purchase more than a dozen bottles of spirits.[39] Charles Haydon witnessed a "melee" that also resulted in "everything in the old tent" being "turned bottom side up," and despite not being involved, he "laughed . . . nearly to death but got very little sleep."[40] What seemed like reckless fun to Haydon and other rabble-rousers also threatened camp discipline, and the injuries sustained in fights served as evidence that drunkenness was a disruptive—if standard—form of camp recreation.

Instances of brawling reveal soldiers' own debates about manliness and patriotism. While soldiers' widespread acceptance of medicinal liquor rations indicates that they were more comfortable with regular drinking than many civilians, men in the ranks tended to draw the line when intoxication led soldiers to hurt their comrades or disturb others in camp. After Confederate soldier John Overton "got drunk . . . and kicked up the devil" when the guards tried to subdue him, his longtime friend Robert Patrick recalled that Overton used to be "considered a respectable man and mingled in good society." Now he was a drunk and "scarcely tolerated."[41] Although Patrick seemingly blamed the war, on some level, for Overton's devolution into chronic drunkenness, a Union surgeon attempted to place the blame for all disorder on men who were never patriots in the first place. In a camp near Culpeper, Virginia, John Gardner Perry blamed the "drunken rows and disturbances" that occurred "almost every night" on the "substitutes and conscripts."[42] While both Patrick and Perry seemingly agreed that drunken brawling was unmanly and unpatriotic, they disagreed about the root cause of the behavior, illuminating the competing ideas of masculinity and warfare within the camps. While Patrick expressed clear disappointment in his friend's behavior, he signaled that the atmosphere of war caused the change. Perhaps because Perry worked as a surgeon—and had less personal interaction with the rank and file—assuming that men motivated by money or threat of force caused the constant ruckus was easier for him than contemplating that war turned respectable patriots into intolerable drunks.

That men bristled at brawling was no wonder. Liquor and weapons were a volatile combination, and intoxicated men often "got to fooling with their arms."[43] Drunken fights sometimes escalated into shootings and murders. One "semi-drunken" Texas soldier wildly fired six shots at a drayman, dropping his horse with the final bullet. Soldiers laughed at his being "a *disgraceful bad shot.*"[44] In other instances, men hit their targets. One soldier in the Excelsior Brigade "deliberately shot a member of the same company for no cause whatsoever" while "under the influence of liquor."[45] A drunken soldier shot Joseph Herring of the 7th Illinois Cavalry in the arm; Herring's "suspender buckle" knocked the ball off its course and saved him from death.[46] Even more corrosive to discipline, soldiers attacked their officers in the midst of drunken fury. Stephen Minot Weld reported almost off-handedly in his diary one day that he was "troubled" both by "bed-bugs" and a drunken corporal who "wanted to run me through."[47] Major Joseph D. Bullen of the 28th Maine was killed after being shot by a drunken fellow.[48] Other soldiers became murder victims themselves when they became too drunk to know their whereabouts—killed by comrades, thieves, and guerrillas.[49]

Plenty of intoxicated men wandered—both accidentally and purposefully—suffering isolated consequences but also contributing to more systemic patterns of disorder. When a group of Confederate soldiers decided to run the blockade near Goose Creek, South Carolina, one night in search of whiskey, pickets caught them on their way back to camp. One drunken soldier fell into the creek and ended up in the guardhouse. His comrade fell into the same stream a short time later and drowned.[50] When an intoxicated soldier became lost and caused his friends to have to run quickly to catch up to their company, they expressed anger at his "stupidity." In a different instance, Confederates captured two Kentuckians who stumbled drunkenly into their lines.[51] Whether they deserted or absent-mindedly strolled into enemy territory, these drunken men created a nuisance for officers attempting to keep soldiers disciplined in camp and prepared for battle.

Perhaps the most serious threats to camp discipline came from whiskey-induced mutinies. In August 1861, after initial three-month enlistments expired for many volunteers, members of the 79th New York Volunteers, who had enlisted for three years, misunderstood the terms of their contracts and panicked when not allowed to return home despite experiencing fierce fighting at Bull Run. They at first refused to strike their tents, but soon men began to drink and "the wildest confusion took place." William Thompson Lusk and other officers were terrified—caught between Colonel Isaac Ingalls Stevens's orders and their drunken men's cocked weapons. After the mutineers passed out from drunken exhaustion, their officers finally reasserted their authority.[52] Rebellions of much smaller scale occurred in Union and Confederate armies when men drank too much and collectively decided to disregard military discipline.[53] When Pennsylvania reserves became mutinous after the Second Battle of Bull Run, Levi Bird Duff lamented that the youths were "about to prove a great disgrace to the state" with their drunken disobedience.[54] The same military structure that enabled drinking could easily be dismantled by the lack of discipline drunkenness caused. Officers set the tone by overindulging, but when enlisted men followed suit, their commanders often could not effectively corral the drunken men.

THE DISORDER CAUSED BY DRUNKEN SOLDIERS and officers left civilian observers horrified, if not surprised. In fact, many Americans (or at least parents, wives, and temperance reformers) believed that soldiers would be susceptible to the temptation of strong drink because they had been removed from the safe havens of their homes and tossed into military life, with its ubiquitous drinking. Reformers worried that these young men would "drink to their ruin" in an effort to assert their manliness—to "appeal to sociability, to honor and bravery."[55] The *Journal of the American Temperance Union* lamented that the young men, living together "away from their homes" while being subjected to "great excitements," would be in "constant danger of being drawn into habits of drunkenness from which they will never escape." Both abstainers and drinkers alike would be ruined by whiskey after spending time in the army, where fatigue rations (issued any time they performed fatigue duty) would be thrust upon them as they tried to process the trauma of war's "excitements." Men had to take it upon themselves to "seek their own safety and welfare" by pledging themselves to total abstinence.[56] Temptation lurked everywhere, but both Union and Confederate reformers hoped that self-restraint and the "memory of home" would keep soldiers from becoming ensnared by alcohol.[57]

This notion of "home" about which temperance reformers wrote referenced a specific urban middle-class (and republican) ideal that many Americans believed promoted self-control and sobriety. Since industrialization began in the early decades of the nineteenth century, middle-class Americans—especially urban Northerners—had developed social aspirations that balanced a public masculine world of work, politics, and vice with a private domestic realm of feminine virtue. Men participated in business and political life during the day and returned to their homes at night, where their wives had established a moral atmosphere. With the outbreak of war, young men, who were most susceptible to the sinful temptations of the public world, were isolated from their families—wives and mothers—and lacked those important domestic influences. The homes that soldiers created in camp were anything but the teetotaling havens reformers idealized. Temperance reformers and families scrambled to find a solution: to re-create some sense of "home" to keep their men sober. Restoring the moral balance was imperative, because an army of drunken soldiers would not only be bound for hell but would lose the war.

The belief that these young soldiers were particularly prone to sin when left to their own devices was a logical extension of reformers' concerns about hordes of unmarried clerks and working-class men who had descended on their cities in the antebellum decades. By 1861, reformers well knew the narrative of the urban worker who spent all his free time and his earnings in houses of public amusement, watching plays, gambling, drinking, and visiting prostitutes. Applying it to soldiers required only simple shifts in the story's setting. Whereas sobriety in the prewar decades facilitated a self-disciplined manhood that fostered economic success and moral uplift, sobriety during wartime led to well-disciplined armies full of patriotic soldiers who could save the nation.[58]

Civilians had to transform the atmosphere of the camps to create armies of sober soldiers. To that end, temperance reformers and family members encouraged enlistees to take action against temptation before they ever left home. In 1861, temperance regiments formed in both Northern and Southern states, and reform organizations encouraged new volunteers to sign pledges. In the Confederacy, the "Oxford Grays," who encamped near Raleigh, North Carolina, all signed pledges to abstain from alcohol during the course of the war. Wishing "to go at it *cool*," the men determined to "give old Abe and his man Scott a *warm* salutation." Another Georgia regiment commanded by a minister believed that by signing the temperance pledge they would invoke the favor of God so that they could never be conquered.[59] Northerners were no different. The state of Maine reportedly sent a regiment comprising entirely "Maine Law men." Another regiment of abstainers brought cheers from New York's temperance community when they camped in Central Park.[60] In Wisconsin, the Madison Lodge of the Independent Order of Good Templars marked with little flags those soldiers who took the pledge before leaving for war. More than half of the lodge's new male members in 1861 and 1862 were soldiers attempting to guard their morals before heading into the fray.[61] The Grand Division of the Sons of Temperance of Virginia reported that more than two-thirds of its members had volunteered to fight.[62] Simply taking the pledge, however, would not guarantee safety and salvation, seasoned temperance reformers knew, and they encouraged abstainers to remain vigilant. Men could easily avoid liquor at home, but life in camp would make matters much more difficult. Reformers in Raleigh urged North Carolina troops to avoid all temptations so that when the war ended it could be said of them, "There goes one, who in all that terrible conflict, never violated his pledge; never brought disgrace upon his profession."[63] Social pressure and the desire to guard one's moral reputation were reformers' best hopes for keeping young soldiers away from the bottle.

For the many soldiers not belonging to temperance regiments, letters from mothers and wives reminded them of home and warned them that indulging in spirituous beverages was unacceptable manly behavior. Correspondence indicates that plenty of men paid heed to what these women had to say.[64] Shortly after joining the Union army in the summer of 1861, Charles Harvey Brewster assured his mother that the camps had not even "one tenth of the temptations . . . that there are in civil life." Liquor and gambling were both prohibited, so Brewster's mother need not worry that life in the army would ruin her son's character.[65] Brewster may have been exaggerating the orderliness of camp life to set his mother at ease, and other women certainly checked up on their husbands and sweethearts. One Minnesota soldier sobered up after his sweetheart let him know she had "heard of his being drunk in Hastings."[66] Harriet Jane Thompson pleaded with her husband not to "get in the habit" of drinking while away from home. Her requests may have fallen on deaf ears, however, as her letter indicates that she and her husband had had plenty of disagreements about his drinking before the war ever began.[67] Thompson's moral influence over her husband may have been precarious, but Palmetto sharpshooter Bobby Hubbard's wife had "laid the law down." When his friends became "corned on lively drinking," Hubbard remained sober. None of his comrades questioned it. Hubbard did not drink because his wife forbade it.[68] Iowa captain Jacob Ritner kept his wife's picture with him at all times. When pressured to drink, he showed it to his comrades. He often thought of his wife "and *our* children" when he was "tempted to do anything mean or bad," and he openly questioned how other men with families could justify their drinking and carousing.[69] For these men, the domestic and moral authority of their wives carried significant weight despite long separation. Fear of returning home a failed husband or father kept them sober.

Ritner and others stayed sober to please their wives and mothers, but soldiers also worried that their reputations might be compromised if word reached their communities that they had become drunks. Most Civil War regiments were organized by community, and men enlisted and fought alongside cousins and neighbors. If a soldier developed immoral habits, word of his downfall reached home. One soldier in a Jeffersonville, Indiana, hospital nearly went to pieces when he found out that a nurse had mistakenly reported him drunk. "There must be a mistake somewhere," he wrote to the matron. He simply could not believe anyone would make such a "cruel" accusation about a man who had a "lovely wife" whose "future happiness depend[ed] on the character of her husband." He needed his friends and family to know he was sober.[70] Soon after Alabamian William McClellan enlisted, his family heard that a number of the soldiers from their hometown "got drunk at Decatur," and they became "anxious to hear" from the young soldier.[71] Although Seth James Wells had "seen more vice and drunkenness than I ever supposed existed" while traveling over four thousand miles, he hoped that he was "morally no worse than when surrounded by kind relatives and friends."[72] Simon Cummins credited the discipline of army life with keeping him "straight as a candle." By avoiding "devilry" while in the army, Cummins hoped to earn the respect of friends and relatives when he returned home. Cummins believed that drinking would tarnish his patriotic reputation, stating that he "would be ashamed to come back a poor drunken rowdy." In April 1865, he rejoiced that he had heeded his father's advice to remain sober and had survived the war without ever adopting "degrading habits" while he had "worn the blue uniform."[73] These men conflated their self-disciplined manhood with their patriotism, and they guarded it carefully for the sake of their families and neighbors.

As much as some young men sought to guard their reputations and make their communities proud, others worried that brothers and friends prone to heavy drinking would find their habits worsened by life in the army. Hoosier soldier Elijah Cavins assured his wife that he did "not drink near as much here as he did at home," but that his brother Ben Cavins fared poorly. By September 1861, Elijah Cavins had worked successfully to get Ben discharged from the army. Ben could not "perform the duties of a private soldier in this country," and Elijah's letter to their father indicates that the cold and damp conditions had left Ben seeking solace in the bottle. Oddly, Elijah thought Ben might be able to remain sober if promoted to second lieutenant, but he pointed out that farm labor might be the best way to "recuperate his constitution."[74] Undoubtedly, Ben Cavins's poor health—and the military culture that treated exposure with liquor—contributed to his drinking problems. Nevertheless, other soldiers, like his brother Elijah, found army life to be sobering.[75] For Minnesota native William Govette, it took serious illness to free him "from the effects of liquor." His buddy Madison Bowler confided to their concerned friends at home that, for the first time ever, he had observed Govette's "naturally warm free-hearted disposition." Bowler hoped that the newly sober Govette would "not drink again," even when his health returned.[76]

Whether men took pledges before they left home or relied on family and friends to keep them sober, it becomes clear that soldiers connected morality, sobriety, and discipline. Men took seriously their familial duties, as well as their patriotic ones. Yet their families worried that the military apparatus that required their husbands' and sons' patriotic duty would also rob them of their masculine morality through its carnage and threats to their health. As such, family members at home—especially wives—worked diligently to affect soldiers' behavior from afar. Social pressure certainly kept individual soldiers disciplined while they lived in camps, but its effects were limited.

WHILE FAMILIES MAY HAVE HELD SOME SWAY over the behavior of individual soldiers in their lives, temperance reformers wanted more systematic efforts to combat drunkenness in the ranks. Yet reformers worried less about day-to-day discipline than they worried for the collective moral health of the armies. Anxious civilians flooded Union and Confederate troops with tracts and temperance papers. Northerners, often working with the U.S. Christian Commission, established temperance clubs. Chaplains and officers on both sides hosted meetings and encouraged men to take pledges. These clubs appealed to bored soldiers who were, perhaps, interested in temperance. Some men became teetotalers as a result, but the effects of these efforts were limited. Nevertheless, the work of reformers and chaplains were the only forces within the camps that sought to use moral suasion to convince men that their masculinity (and perhaps salvation) depended on sobriety. The men who joined the clubs indicated a strong desire to reclaim a moral form of masculinity that did not involve destruction.

Weeks after the war began, John Marsh, editor of the *Journal of the American Temperance Union* (*JATU*), issued a call for donations to send fifty thousand tracts to the newly recruited soldiers.[77] By July, the American Temperance Union had published eight tracts which could be sent in batches of one thousand to any quartermaster in the Union army free of charge. They desired that all regiments would receive approximately six thousand tracts to be distributed among the men.[78] Chaplains expressed their thanks in the pages of the *JATU*. "There is great need of such material in every regiment," exclaimed one chaplain, who hoped that the donated tracts would enable him and others to minister more effectively to the "peculiarly needy men." Another, noting the "considerable leisure" time the men had on their hands, believed it "an act of mercy to supply them with reading matter."[79] Over the course of the war, the American Temperance Union raised more than eighteen thousand dollars—enough money to send approximately 7.2 million tracts to the Union army. Donations came from across the North, from temperance reformers and Sunday school classrooms not only in New York and New England but also from the Midwestern states.[80] Confederate efforts were much less centralized, but various societies worked tirelessly to send tracts to Southern soldiers. Tracts published by temperance reformers in Raleigh, North Carolina, could be sent to soldiers at a rate of 1,500 per dollar.[81] A more prolific publisher, the South Carolina Tract Society, published by 1863 more than 170 tracts for soldiers, twenty-three of which discussed the dangers of intoxicating drink.[82]

Both Union and Confederate tracts covered a wide range of topics in similar fashion—all of which attempted to reform military drinking culture by espousing the virtues of the sober life. Some tracts exploited the imminence of death to implore the young soldiers to avoid the bottle. The war's carnage disrupted Victorian customs of death, leaving men and their families fearful that when young men died on the battlefield or hospital, away from their peaceful and virtuous homes, their souls might be in jeopardy. Families sought reassurance in honorable military deaths, and soldiers tried to greet death bravely and stoically.[83] Reformers knew of the importance of a "good" death, and tracts published by North Carolinians urged the men to flee from all sins, and reminded them that swearing led to gambling, which led to intemperance, which led to death followed by eternal torment. Drunkards had no place in heaven, and an intemperate soldier not only risked his own soul but also brought potential anguish to his family. Another tract reminded the young men that mothers, wives, and sisters were "pained not only at your absence, but the uncertainty of seeing you again in this life; and they long to be persuaded that whatever may befall you in this war, they will meet you in heaven."[84] Northern tracts published by the American Temperance Union focused on the same themes, although the organization emphasized a sense of duty to family and friends more than it used the threat of eternal damnation. Intemperance could scar a soldier like the bite of a lobster could scar a fisherman, creatively explained one tract presumably aimed at New Englanders. Brave men who avoided vice (not just drinking but also swearing and gambling) protected themselves from accidents—from crime and from death caused by a lack of discipline. A cowardly drunk brought "home to his friends and county, disgrace and infamy."[85]

Reformers, North and South, may have guessed that appealing to young men's sense of morality and self-disciplined masculinity might only go so far. Plenty of tracts attempted to appeal to the soldiers' more pragmatic concerns about staying alive, and in the process, they directly confronted military policies that used liquor rations to treat illness and exposure. Going against the medical community, tracts instructed soldiers to rely on cold water and temperate habits. Confederate advocates of cold water used a sketch of British captain Hedley Vicars, who had been killed during the Crimean War, to show soldiers that they need not take their "gill of rum" in order to remain healthy (whether soldiers found this ironic is unclear).[86] A Northern tract, "The Wounded Soldier," told of a young soldier with "habits of great self-denial and self-control" who was severely wounded on the battlefield just as he came down with a bout of typhoid fever. Miraculously, the young man recovered from his wounds without an amputation and returned quickly to "the battlefield ready again to do service for his country." According to his surgeon, "If he had been a drinking man, he never would have recovered; at least the limb must have been amputated, and the fever might have terminated his life."[87] If the threat of eternal damnation or familial scorn did not convince a young man to put down the bottle, surely the prospect of avoiding an amputation might. Likewise, these tracts suggested to soldiers that military policies did not always have their best, individual interests at heart. Preserving one's sense of self (and one's morality) required resisting the military's attempts to turn a man into a generic, ration-drinking soldier.

Some men truly appreciated the reading material supplied by the American Temperance Union, the South Carolina Tract Society, and other publications. Soldiers in both armies enjoyed passing the time by reading, and available material ran the gamut from smutty dime novels to literary classics to temperance and religious publications.[88] Union soldier Robert Winn, serving in the 3rd Kentucky Cavalry, spent as much of his leisure time as possible devouring any religious publication he could find. His interests included Baptist and Presbyterian theology, the Great Tribulation, abolition, and temperance. When possible, the young man forwarded selected issues of favorites such as the *Christian Banner* and the *Good News* home to his family in Hancock County.[89] Wisconsin native Guy Taylor specifically asked his wife to mail him copies of the *Wisconsin Chief*. Taylor had been active in his local temperance lodge before leaving for war, and he knew that in camp, temperance articles were scarce. "You don't hear a word in faver [sic] of temperance hear [sic]. It is all whiskey and it is a killing more men then the balls are." Once his paper arrived in the mail, Taylor set off to organize his own temperance crusade.[90]

In many regiments, temperance societies appeared, especially during winter quarters, to help soldiers cope with the temptations of camp life while providing them with leisure activities to alleviate boredom. Throughout the Union army, the U.S. Christian Commission (USCC) facilitated temperance efforts, using volunteers to distribute literature and set up weekly temperance meetings. At its first annual meeting, the USCC estimated that approximately three hundred thousand temperance documents had been distributed to Union soldiers.[91] In many places, they reserved chapels on Wednesday evenings for temperance meetings. Overall, USCC civilian volunteers reported some success at reaching men as they moved in and out of their camps.[92] Temperance meetings provided interested soldiers a place of support and alternative ways to pass the time as they navigated their vice-ridden camps. The meetings also regularly offered the pledge to bring more young men into the ranks of the cold-water army.

Christian Commission workers thought their efforts were successful, and many soldiers undoubtedly found the meetings reassuring as they worked to uphold the pledges they signed before they left home. At Camp Distribution, USCC station leader James P. Fisher estimated that more than three thousand men had pledged to avoid all intoxicating beverages. The official report of the USCC listed a higher number, 3,700 men.[93] Volunteers working at Fort Leavenworth had similar success, reporting that "many hundreds" had signed the pledge and joined the church.[94] Fifty soldiers a week joined the temperance crusade in Washington.[95] One Iowa officer's testimony at a USCC meeting in Helena, Arkansas, illustrates how temperance meetings worked to replace the customary community bonds. Before leaving for war, the Iowan, like many men, had promised his wife that he would "maintain" his "Christian character unsullied." But military life had taken its toll. Irregular church services, coupled with coarse company, led to swearing, drinking, and gambling. Thinking of his wife at home only compounded the problem. The soldier, disappointed in himself, "drowned" his "thoughts in the morning with liquor." Reading between the lines of his letters, his wife figured out that her husband no longer walked the straight and narrow path, and she reminded him that death awaited him and, unless he changed his behavior, hell might await him as well. Shaken by his own behavior and his wife's warnings, the soldier confessed his vices to the attendees of the temperance meetings and vowed publicly "to stand up for Christ as valiantly as for my country." Volunteers with the Peoria Committee noted aptly that war had disrupted family influences and that this once "strong man" had been "broken down" by isolation and war's carnage, which led to intemperance.[96] From reformers' perspective, domestic influences could only carry a soldier so far, and many men needed additional support from camp-supported temperance organizations to keep them sober after years of fighting and camp life began to take a toll on their moral masculinity.

When organizing temperance groups, chaplains and officers sometimes worked to establish chapters of already existing societies. Among Union troops, the Sons of Temperance was popular. Enlisted men (and some officers) found joining the Sons to be an enjoyable way of counteracting the rampant drunkenness of the camps. Recognizing the need to provide alcohol-free recreation in its camps, the Grand Division of Massachusetts authorized the formation of the 16th Massachusetts Regiment Division. Chaplain Richard Fuller thought the organization provided "wholesome recreation and intellectual and moral stimulus in the army, deprived as we are of those enjoyed at home." Fuller knew that "the old-fashioned, total-abstinence society" would not flourish in an army camp, and with his Division, he created a club where his soldiers had the opportunity to share literary creations and recite essays they had written. The soldiers would be sober, of course, but Fuller designed his organization "to be of great intellectual and moral value."[97] The Sons of Temperance may have provided literary entertainment in an alcohol-free environment, but some soldiers, like Seymour Dexter, doubted the organization's ability to reform with a simple pledge any man who recently had been willing "to wallow in the slough of intemperance."[98] Men undoubtedly attended merely to pass the time.

Effective or not, chaplains worked tirelessly to promote temperance societies. Chaplain Louis N. Beaudry began preaching temperance sermons in the 5th New York Cavalry within months of taking his post in the spring of 1863. He initially noted with some frustration that a drunken soldier disrupted his religious meetings with "his discordant singing and offensive breath." Some men attended temperance meetings with no intention (at least initially) of signing a pledge. By the winter of 1864, Beaudry experienced a change of heart and realized that these intoxicated soldiers deserved attention rather than disdain. After Beaudry formed the "Fifth New York Cavalry Temperance Club," the meetings drew crowds. The chapel "was completely jammed," as men sat for hours on end, listening to lectures on the risks of intemperance to their physical and moral health. Fewer than ten days after the club had been formed, more than ninety soldiers had signed the pledge, and the club's popularity had spread to an Ohio regiment encamped nearby. Planning lectures consumed most of Beaudry's energies, but hope for achieving a "complete victory over this great evil" spurred him on. "Men are now signing the pledge whom we had given up for desperate cases," he noted in early March. Harboring none of the skepticism of Seymour Dexter, Beaudry believed that soldiers reclaimed their lives "of sobriety and honesty which we possessed in our former quiet homes." The military may have chipped away at men's morality, but chaplains like Beaudry used temperance organizations to help soldiers reclaim the masculinity they were losing in the camps.[99]

Unlike Northern chaplains, who often had the support of groups such as the USCC to organize temperance clubs, Confederate chaplains acted largely on their own. The Sons of Temperance, however, had a presence in the South, and even after separating from the national organization in 1861, the Sons continued to operate in Southern cities.[100] In early 1862, the Richland Rifles, along with other companies in the First Virginia Regiment, organized a division at Camp Huger, similar to the Massachusetts Division formed in the Union army.[101] A few weeks later, the Springfield Division in Virginia initiated ten soldiers, including members of the nearby Texas Invincible.[102] As in the Union camps, temperance meetings in the Confederate army served to build community. One Roman Catholic chaplain, James Sheeran, serving with the 14th Louisiana, tackled the problem of drunkenness differently from his Protestant colleagues. He did not organize a temperance society, but after one of his visits, "two notorious drunkards" reformed themselves, began "giving an edifying example to their companions," and credited the priest with their transformation. For his part, Sheeran acknowledged that the "graces of the sacraments" had more to do with the change in habits.[103] Regardless of the method, the results were the same. Chaplains' sincere efforts had a sobering influence on the men who trusted them for guidance.

Efforts to bring about temperance reform worked when soldiers themselves invested in their own sobriety and decided that abstaining was in their best interest—morally or pragmatically. Taking matters of morality into their own hands, the enlisted men of the 14th Massachusetts at Fort Tillinghast in Virginia organized their own weekly temperance meetings. They hoped their chaplain would make an appearance to lend his support, but that hardly mattered to these highly motivated soldiers.[104] Of course, some soldiers found the pledges a bit confusing, and, becoming caught up in the moment, sometimes signed up for the cold water army without fully understanding what awaited them. Young Chauncey Herbert Cooke thought his pledge permitted him to drink cider and assumed he could drink beer as well. He assured his mother that he was deceived about the nature of his pledge but that she need not worry about him, as he had never "touched a drop of whiskey." Furthermore, he "felt as guilty as a thief" after drinking the beer.[105] Undoubtedly, Cooke's mother rested a bit easier knowing that her son had signed his pledge. Despite some confusion about the meaning of "cold water," Cooke seemed to have taken his oath to heart.

Temperance pledges distinguished between those who signed for "life" and those who signed for the duration of the war. Even if some soldiers hesitated to swear off ardent spirits for the rest of their lives, plenty of men decided that serving in the army necessitated sobriety; they considered morality and discipline in the ranks to be intertwined. Friends Robert Winn and Matthew Cook made a pragmatic decision to abstain. Winn pointed out that a drink of whiskey had "knocked down a sober man . . . because he had not become a proficient in the *noble!* art of self-defence."[106] Cook agreed that whiskey could lead to all kinds of trouble. "We are all Teetotalers here by compulsion," he assured Winn's sister, Martha. A soldier had "plenty else to think about," and drinking muddled a man's head unnecessarily.[107] Whiskey could weaken a man physically and mentally, soldiers knew, and avoiding the beverage kept them stronger and on their guard. But some men hoped their commitment to sobriety would stick even after they returned home. Wisconsin soldier Wilhelm Franchsen stopped drinking at first simply because he wanted to save his paycheck. Then, he stopped drinking his whiskey rations. Finally, he thought that by the time he returned home, he would have "conquered my old fondness of liquor."[108]

Enlisted men understood the necessity of keeping sober, but officers seemed much less inclined to join the ranks of the temperance army. Only a few teetotaling regimental commanders took the lead in organizing temperance groups in camps. Reformers on the home front praised them for it, believing that the rank and file would follow their example. When the 11th Massachusetts organized its club, the commanding officer, Lieutenant-Colonel Porter D. Tripp, joined first. Seventy soldiers followed him.[109] Colonel Samuel N. Black of the 62nd Pennsylvania and thirty-four of his officers also signed pledges, which they "kept with unswerving fidelity." When Black was shot in the chest while leading his men, that he died sober and "without a groan" earned "special mention" in his *New York Herald* obituary. Civilians admired his personal habits as much as his military and political careers.[110] When most of the officers in the 25th Iowa went on a drunken spree near Bridgeport, Alabama, Captain Jake Ritner expressed gratitude that the officers of Company B remained "all right and minding their own business."[111] Soldiers and civilians lauded officers who promoted temperance habits by example, but sources indicate that officers hesitated to take pledges and abide by them. When General Robert McAllister organized a temperance club in the First Massachusetts, he noted that only one line officer signed the pledge.[112] Even when officers attached their names, plenty of soldiers expressed cynicism about their sincerity. Connecticut noncommissioned officer Lewis Bissell noted that his colonel and most of the officers in his regiment signed a temperance pledge at Fort Worth, Virginia, around Christmas 1863 and expressed frustration that the lieutenant-colonel appeared determined not to add his name to the list. Bissell suspected their convictions lacked sincerity and decided to wait and see if the officers would abide by their pledges before adding his own name.[113] Evidence suggests that plenty of enlisted men took temperance seriously, regardless of what their superiors decided to do.

Reformers proudly reported when soldiers took the pledge, but understanding the rates of success of chaplains' methods is harder to get at. Many men who attended temperance meetings in camp were evangelicals before they enlisted. The meetings merely bolstered their convictions. But the vivid examples of drunkards who reformed at the meetings indicate that for temperance societies to work, the men had to attend the meetings (voluntarily) often enough embrace the message. Merely two months after first organizing his club, Beaudry had convinced more than two hundred soldiers to sign the pledge. General Robert McAllister reported more than seventy members in his temperance society in the winter of 1864.[114] These numbers indicate that in regiments with temperance clubs, about 10 to 20 percent of the soldiers abstained. This may seem insignificant at first blush, but for comparison, the antebellum temperance movement included about 12 percent of the United States' population in its heyday. This suggests that enthusiasm for temperance within the ranks was at least as high as it had been in the decades before the war.[115] Equally important, temperance clubs in camps allowed men to reclaim a sense of family and moral discipline that military culture did not provide.

NEVERTHELESS, AS HAD BEEN THE CASE in antebellum society, moral suasion had only limited effects on curtailing drunkenness within the ranks, and the military had to develop more coercive strategies to convince men not to drink. Whereas civilians had tried legal suasion (licensing and prohibition) in the 1850s, Union and Confederate militaries focused more on their ability to punish soldiers who thwarted regulations regarding drinking. But the punishment occurred only after the drunken mishaps, and soldiers chafed at its demeaning nature. If the goal was to deter other soldiers from making drunken mistakes or turn them into sober fighting machines, the military justice system had limited effect at instilling discipline or convincing soldiers that it was unmasculine to drink.

Rebellious soldiers compromised the authority of commanding officers so seriously that Union and Confederate militaries took severe action to punish drunkenness and disorder. Captain Raphael Semmes of the CSS *Alabama* made it clear that not only would drunkenness not be allowed as an excuse for offenses committed aboard ship but "that intoxication was a crime in itself."[116] On land, camp commanders tried to emphasize this as well. Of the more than twelve thousand Union court-martial cases that involved drunkenness, over 60 percent of the cases listed drunkenness as the primary offense, in one form or another. Courts charged soldiers, for example, with not only drunkenness and a violation of the 45th article of war (being drunk) but also with conduct prejudicial to good order, quitting and sleeping on post, neglect of duty, being absent without leave, and disobedience.[117] By late spring 1861, soldiers in the 17th Mississippi and the 25th Iowa knew well that whiskey drinkers risked serious punishment.[118] In most cases of drunkenness and these related charges, enlisted men found themselves facing fines or reductions in pay along with some form of hard labor (usually with ball and chain), with corporal and public punishments being less common.[119]

When officers opted for corporal punishment, however, it usually generated enough attention that men recorded it. In December 1861, David Day reported that his evening dress parade in his training camp usually included a list of "unlucky wight[s]" being publicly punished for being "too drunk to perform the duties of a soldier."[120] With emasculating public humiliation and threat of punishment, commanding officers hoped to halt drunken amusements before they ever had a chance to devolve into violent disorder. Augustus Cleveland Brown ordered one private tied "up by his thumbs."[121] Payday drunks in the 3rd Kentucky Cavalry were "dipped" into the "very cold" river to sober them up.[122] Officers commonly tied miscreants to wagons and trees.[123] Others became more creative. One Union captain liked to have his intoxicated soldiers alternate between being tied up and digging and filling holes in the frozen ground.[124] Officers in the 2nd Connecticut punished soldiers returning to camp from a night of drinking by making them "carry a heavy stick of timber or be tied up to the wheel" for hours at a time for multiple days. Two especially unfortunate men had to hold up a wheel to which they were both tied.[125] In 1865, officers in both the 177th Ohio and 200th Pennsylvania made intoxicated soldiers march back and forth for hours with boards painted with the words "DRUNKARD" strapped to their backs. The Ohio soldiers also carried a "large stick of wood on the shoulder" while they marched.[126] Officers intended these public and physically harsh punishments to serve as a deterrent to other men.

Plenty of soldiers found themselves performing extra duties or losing other privileges after their drunken sprees. In October 1861, the 13th Massachusetts descended into a "perfect Pandemonium" when the soldiers became drunk on a stormy march. The men fought, one soldier shot another, and still another "broke the head of a fourth with the butt of his musket." Though General Nathaniel Banks had detailed the regiment "to go to Williamsport on special duty," he sent them back to camp and decided to "send off another [regiment] with more discipline and less whiskey."[127] In other regiments, commanding officers worked to instill this sense of duty through extra guard duty.[128] When individual soldiers continued to be habitually drunk, commanding officers tried punishments such as reducing them in rank or canceling furlough applications.[129] Other men were sent home. Two Georgians were "discharged and left in Atlanta for getting drunk."[130]

The court-martial cases illustrate, though, that in many instances the drunkenness merely exacerbated other more serious crimes like desertion and various forms of violence. Desertion cases make up the largest grouping of more serious crimes to which drinking contributed. But even among drunken deserters, fines and hard labor remained the most common punishments.[131] So often, though, mishaps turned violent. Mississippian Ed Lockard became so intoxicated that he "cursed the officer of the day," earning himself some time "under guard & came very near getting some bayonets run in him" because of his unruly behavior.[132] An Irish Confederate made such noise after being arrested that he had to be gagged until he sobered up.[133] Some drunks slept it off under guard, but others faced additional punishments. For attacks on superior officers and other violent crimes like mutiny or homicide, soldiers could expect hard labor (usually with a reduction in pay). Execution was much less common but happened (especially in cases of mutiny).[134]

Fining soldiers and sending them off for hard labor certainly punished the drunken miscreants, but soldiers' accounts suggest that when officers attempted to use public punishments as a deterrent, they risked backlash from enlisted men who perceived the punishments as barbaric. After a drunken soldier in the 2nd Massachusetts was tied to a tree for several days, his comrades began yelling for him to be cut down. Extra guards had to help the officers restore order, and the man had to be punished out of his comrades' sight.[135] Unit solidarity against excessive punishment is indicative of the problems plaguing military discipline: officers who lacked the capacity to keep troops calm and disciplined also lost control when trying to restore order. Some became abusive. Others accidentally injured or killed men. A colonel in the 4th Iowa Cavalry who "hate[d] a drunken man as bad as a snake" one Christmas ordered a group of intoxicated soldiers stripped of their uniforms, tied by hand and foot, and left to lie on the ground all night. Other officers intervened to prevent the holiday drinkers from freezing to death.[136] Confederate Harry Burns and a few comrades likewise became too intoxicated one Christmas and ended up "in irons and kept on the spar deck for several days and nights [in] the bitter cold" until a doctor prevented the punishment from going further.[137] Soldiers had their cheeks and heads split open when officers used their guns and swords to subdue them.[138] One of the more severe instances occurred in the 118th Pennsylvania. In October 1863, Captain Francis Adams Donaldson had repeated problems with a Private Shields, a substitute serving in his company, who liked to get "drunk on Jamaica Ginger, drinking a whole bottle at a time." Donaldson refused to allow the often inebriated private to leave the camp, warning him that if he went on another spree, the captain "would kill him." True to form, Shields left camp, became drunk, and "secured a musket and had intimidated the guard." Donaldson reacted quickly and, after a fight ensued, slammed his "musket down upon [the private's] head and felled him to the ground." The blow fractured Shields's skull, and although Major Charles Herring assured Donaldson that he had acted in the best interest of his men, Donaldson seemed haunted by earning the reputation as a "man killer" among the regiments encamped nearby.[139] So unregulated and reckless were the armies' responses to drunkenness that enlisted men tended to resist attempts of officers to instill discipline through violence and often assumed that commanders like Donaldson were abusive.

By resisting corporal punishment for drinking, enlisted men asserted their rights to exist as men free of harsh military authority. Soldiers were somewhat persuaded to stop drinking by the appeals of voluntary camp temperance clubs, which appealed to their nonmartial identities as moral family men. But military discipline at the hands of officers (who had the right to drink and at other times even facilitated drinking in the ranks) caused enlisted men to unite against practices that they perceived forcibly reshaped their masculinity through undemocratic means.

PROBLEMS OF DRUNKENNESS persisted throughout the war. While drunken mishaps may not have affected the overall trajectory of the war, they certainly contributed to a lack of discipline and a waste of resources and manpower (especially when the mishaps became violent). That families, civilian reformers, military officials, and even the soldiers themselves tried to find ways to reform habitual drunkards speaks to the seriousness of the problem.

Even as these methods of reform came up short, they reveal the myriad connections between ideas of morality and discipline. Whereas civilians tended to focus on reforming men morally to ensure their health and salvation, military justice systems focused pragmatically on restoring discipline. But soldiers reacted to needless violence—whether it came from drunkards or draconian punishments. And they interpreted the violence as a moral problem because it demeaned and endangered human beings. In short, while no method of reform—personal, social, or judicial—was able to effectively curtail chronic drunkenness, the soldiers themselves consistently condemned any behavior—especially that of officers—that led to gratuitous violence. Ultimately, they resisted both civilian and military ideals of masculinity and discipline.

CHAPTER FOUR

Military Regulations and Civilian Sellers

As the Union army mobilized men in 1861, New York City found itself the new home of increasing numbers of recruits. Military officials knew that if recruits had unfettered access to liquor shops, trouble would ensue. Initially, New York placed its soldiers in Camp Washington on the "isolated but healthful" Staten Island. There, army officials believed they could maintain discipline among the volunteers with the help of civilian authorities because there was no access to the city save a ferryboat and the island had few "temptations" to offer. There were occasional violent confrontations around village liquor shops, and the morning sick report "often swelled" with bruised and hung-over soldiers. Yet for the most part, reasonable discipline was maintained.[1] By October 1861, however, Camp Washington was filled to the brim, and seasoned regiments were moved to the newly formed Camp Ledlie, located at the Palace Garden in Manhattan. As its name suggests, the Palace Garden "had been previously used as a place of public amusement." The building also was in a neighborhood filled with drinking houses.[2] And the Palace Garden was not the only urban "encampment" near large supplies of liquor. In January 1862, Charles Francis Adams Jr. found himself "barracked in a German amusement building and grove."[3] Nearby bars and beer gardens offered too many temptations, and officers' "absence at night" created a situation where drunken soldiers brawled. After drinking "about as much liquor as the landlord thought was for their good," soldiers refused to leave Willer's lager-beer saloon in New York City. A fight ensued, and one soldier "received a severe scalp wound." The soldiers went on a rampage and proceeded to destroy private property and terrify civilians as they roamed the neighborhood wielding their muskets and demanding justice for their injured comrade.[4] Attempts to control the soldiers' access to alcohol generally failed, and soldiers readily invented tales of sick relatives to obtain passes for short furloughs that would enable them to go out into the city to drink.[5]

The problems of New York City suggest that when it came to controlling the flow of liquor, the decentralized nature of Union and Confederate armies coupled with the myriad civilian sellers created environments where access to liquor was nearly impossible to control. When soldiers were encamped, they visited sutlers' wagons and found lone sellers who lurked nearby. More often, soldiers marched through small towns and occupied cities, causing all sorts of trouble whenever they stumbled into dram shops. In cases where men determined that sellers were taking advantage of them, the disorder escalated. Preventing drunkenness, in other words, required military officials to erect barriers—legal and literal—between the soldiers and their civilian suppliers.

The problem at hand, though, was the extent to which military officials had the authority to regulate civilians who came within close range of soldiers. Sutlers—who received their licenses to peddle from the government—clearly fell within the purview of military authority. But when it came to private civilian sellers, the military had to expand its authority. Yet the extent to which Union and Confederate officers were willing to expand their authority to regulate civilians varied. Confederate generals such as Kirby Smith were notorious for implementing martial law in the name of national security. Federal forces, likewise, curtailed civil liberties and arrested disloyal persons in contested and occupied territories.[6] When it came to liquor sales, however, the issue at hand seemed to be where controlling (soldiers') drunkenness fell among each respective army's priorities for keeping order.

Although Union soldiers seemingly had more access to civilian sellers through most of the war than their Confederate counterparts (especially in urban areas), Confederate officials were more likely than Federals to enact sweeping closures of dram shops throughout a region, often resorting to martial law. Union officers, instead, were likely to target soldiers' drinking, while allowing local shops to operate limitedly. When federal officials flexed their muscles to control the civilian traffic, they often targeted larger-scale smuggling operations, and while they prohibited individual sales to soldiers, they hesitated to close shops with such sweeping measures as Confederate officials. In addition to the obvious practical benefit of curtailing soldiers' drunkenness, concerns about disloyalty and immorality sometimes sneaked into officers' reasoning for closing shops (especially in the Confederacy), suggesting that more than mere practicality was at stake in Union and Confederate strategies for controlling the flow of liquor. For Federal officials, whose goal was to knit the Union back together, strains of conciliation and a desire to work with civil authorities ran through their efforts to regulate liquor sales in contested and occupied regions. But for Confederates, who were attempting to establish an independent nation that reclaimed the morality that the United States had forfeited, the widespread closing of shops served a moral purpose by cracking down on political dissenters and the perceived threat that drunken soldiers posed to loyal civilians.

SOLDIERS' INTERACTIONS with civilian merchants began, perhaps unsurprisingly, in the camps themselves, with a visit to the camp sutler's tent. Long a staple of American military life, sutlers were private merchants who peddled good ranging from boots to lemonade, pie, and whiskey. Ideally, sutlers operated in accordance with military regulations that required the licensed vendor to set standard prices and only peddle authorized goods. Any violation resulted in the revocation of the sutler's license and confiscation of the wares. But once civil war erupted, sutler regulations became wholly haphazard. There was confusion about who had the authority to make contracts with vendors. In the Union, the secretary of war, state governors, generals, and even regimental commanders granted privileges to sutlers.[7] This caused confusion for commanding officers attempting to ascertain whether a vendor had the right to be present in his camp. Regulations varied, and the high demand for liquor led many peddlers to raise prices, lower the quality, and sell whiskey under the table. By doing so, they gained a reputation for unscrupulousness, provoked soldiers' ire, and contributed to discipline problems.

In the war's early months, many merchants sold wares without explicit permission of the army. Sensing an opportunity to "pull off a real *coup*" as soldiers descended on Washington, D.C., Emile Dupré established a military supply shop in "a very nice iron building" in the city, with an inventory that included "the finest wines." His business boomed. His brother Alexander, likewise, sold "cigars and liquor to the soldiers," despite having little aptitude for business.[8] Other opportunists took advantage of the hordes of young men mobilizing in northern Virginia. In late July, Colonel Israel Richardson sent the 2nd Michigan's sutler packing after he caught him selling beer to the soldiers. This hardly solved the problem. A few weeks later, his guard spent an afternoon emptying the contents of three peddlers' wagons, which included at least ten barrels of beer and whiskey.[9] Richardson clearly considered both beer and whiskey to be forbidden, but the regulations varied. In Indianapolis, the sutler serving the overwhelmingly German-speaking 32nd Indiana "delight[ed] the thirsty souls with a foaming glass of beer" because only whiskey was forbidden.[10] Whether these peddlers actually had licenses, and what those licenses permitted, differed considerably from place to place, leaving Union officers unable to keep control of the liquor within their ranks.

In the Confederacy, the details surrounding sutlers were even murkier. Confederate soldiers and official reports reference sutlers much less frequently than Union sources, and even when sutlers appear in the record, it is unclear if the peddlers had licenses or if men who sold goods near camps were simply referred to generically as "sutlers."[11] Nevertheless, there were opportunities for peddlers located close to the camps. Less than a day after setting up shop near Leesburg, Virginia, one Confederate sutler had "sold about

100 bottles of whiskey."[12] Confederate enlistees made willing customers. But Confederate general William Dorsey Pender expressed exasperation regarding his sutler, a Mr. Frank. Frank had been authorized to sell goods in camp but had been expressly forbidden to sell liquor. Disregarding Pender's orders, Frank sold whiskey to officers. Pender kicked him out of the camp but seemed puzzled by the sutler's contradictory behavior. On the one hand, the man was "very gentlemanly in deportment and very accomodating [sic]," but at the same time, his "whole existence seems to be bound up in money."[13] Pender found the sutler's lack of attention to duty distasteful. Throughout the war, civilians—especially in the Confederacy—lambasted war profiteers and extortionists who put personal profit ahead of public service to the war effort. Soldiers and officers who were sacrificing comfort and safety for their countries certainly viewed sutlers in this vein, and Pender's consternation with his sutler's character fits into this framework.[14]

Sutlers (licensed or not) perceived their duty as making money, and opportunity abounded. By the end of 1861, the U.S. Sanitary Commission reported that in 169 regiments encamped near Washington, D.C., the sutler was prohibited from selling whiskey, but in thirty-one, he was allowed to sell liquor. The USSC noted further that in 177 of the regiments, "it appeared that the men did in fact, get liquor with more or less freedom and facility from the sutlers or otherwise."[15] Whatever restrictions the army had put in place were not working. One Union soldier, William Need, even went so far as to complain to Simon Cameron in 1861 that sutlers were "suck[ing] the blood ... out of loyal defenders of the American Government."[16] By early 1862, Colonel Samuel Starr, commander of the 5th New Jersey, had lost his patience. Starr was well known for his harsh discipline and "severely dealt with" two men from Washington who decided to sell illegally to soldiers "at a fabulous price." Despite being civilians, the vendors were arrested, court-martialed, and "sentenced to receive 20 lashes on their bare back and to be set adrift in the Potomac in an open boat without oars."[17] When it came to sutlers who interfered with military discipline, Starr had little hesitation about expanding the military justice system to punish them, even though they were technically civilians.

The chaos surrounding ineffective sutler regulations motivated the Union government to act. Congress passed a law in March 1862 giving a board of inspectors-general within the army the authority to stipulate lists of goods and prices for sutlers. It also authorized the army to punish merchants who violated their licenses. It is clear that Congress intended that no intoxicating liquors be included on the list of approved goods.[18] What is less clear is how effective—if at all—the regulations were. In part, the rules continued to vary, with some regiments prohibiting all sales of liquor and others allowing sutlers to sell to officers but not to enlisted men. There was no shortage of violent confusion on the ground. An August day in 1862 found a brigade commissary in the Army of the Potomac's 3rd Corps in such a "speculative" mood that he began selling "whiskey by the canteen full very indiscriminately" (which resulted in a drunken mutiny).[19] Likewise, when the sutler serving the Illinois soldiers encamped near Peoria "got to making bad whiskey," the men became so angry that they made "an assault on his works," destroying his tent and stealing his goods. The officers encouraged the shenanigans.[20] The enlisted men may have purchased and consumed the spirits willingly, but whereas veterans understood that sutlers might cut corners on quality in order to stretch their profits, fresh volunteers were shocked by the merchants' seemingly unscrupulous behavior.[21] Soldiers took military justice into their own hands

Without a doubt, sutlers were opportunists, and the war offered "a splendid chance to make money."[22] That being said, actual accounts of pricing do not generally reflect that sutlers profited more greatly than other wartime merchants (when it came to selling spirits). There were isolated reports of "extravagant prices."[23] For the most part, the cost of whiskey near the camps remained on par with prices on the Southern home front, and soldiers appeared to appreciate the peddlers. One sutler in Huntsville, Alabama, offered to sell the officers and enlisted men of Union general Horatio Van Cleve's division canteens filled with lager beer for fifty cents a quart. A "stream of soldiers" took him up on the offer.[24]

Most soldiers purchased spirits by the gallon, and prices increased throughout the war, especially with Confederate inflation.[25] Until the fall of 1863, whiskey prices typically ranged from about three to five dollars per gallon throughout the Confederacy, and it is clear that a few enterprising sutlers took advantage by selling spirits to soldiers at ten to forty dollars per gallon.[26] For example, officers in the 25th Iowa "found a sutler" near the Tennessee River who sold them whiskey "at three dollars a quart," whereby most of them got drunk and began "raising Cain ... all over the Camp."[27] Other civilian sellers sold gallons of Christmas whiskey to Confederate soldiers for thirty to fifty dollars.[28] As high as these prices seem, by 1864, however, the typical price of whiskey on the Confederate home front was ten to twenty-five dollars per gallon.[29] Soldiers may have overpaid (especially at Christmas) when they purchased from a sutler (licensed or not), but in reality liquor experienced less inflation than other scarce goods. Still, these whiskey prices were extraordinarily higher than what Union soldiers would have found in antebellum Northern markets.

Regardless of the prices, soldiers and officers continued to purchase spirits, and sutlers continued to skirt regulations to rake in the profits. The

4th New York Heavy Artillery dealt with a licensed sutler, King, while encamped in Culpepper County, Virginia. Augustus Cleveland Brown noted with some disgust that many of the officers made "large purchases of useless sutler's stores" after a hefty payday and had "a reception in the private tent of the sutler." Whiskey flowed abundantly.[30] A clever dealer near Cleveland, Tennessee, smuggled liquor to Union troops under the labels of "Canned Fruits, Canned Berries, Cordials, and Bitters" and sometimes did not even bother with those disguises but instead sold liquors "greatly beyond the list of articles authorized by law."[31] Opportunities to imbibe were seemingly endless in the Union lines. In fact, Confederate soldier James Cooper Nisbet commented on the disparity after he was captured in Atlanta in July 1864. While he was under provost guard, he observed an "enterprising sutler dispensing lemonade, beer, ice cream and other luxuries." He remarked on how "strange" the sutler seemed to him, and Nisbet "was forcibly reminded of the difference in the resources of our government and the United States."[32]

Nisbet's illustration of a sutler's tent as a peaceful shelter of refreshment did not quite capture the whole scene. Rather, the abundance of sutlers in the Union lines contributed to environments of chaos within the camps. As they had earlier in the war, soldiers continued to disparage the quality of sutlers' whiskey. Soldiers at Camp Randall, prone to drinking excessively and "rais[ing] ned," one night "tried to tear down the sutler's house."[33] When soldiers felt that sutlers were taking advantage of them—and undercutting the war with their profiteering—they felt completely justified in enacting vigilante military justice. Soldiers were willing to lash out violently against sutlers, but Union officials were much less likely to punish sutlers physically, even if they subjected them the military authority. The merchants following the 141st Pennsylvania were put on leave after they sold whiskey to men of all ranks "on the sly and upon a large scale." Other sutlers who sold to privates were fined, sometimes as much as one hundred dollars.[34] When sutlers sold to officers, however, there were few consequences. After General Grant prohibited all whiskey sales within the camps around Petersburg, officers in the 36th Wisconsin began to "bye off the sails wagons," with tacit approval from the Union military.[35] Even near the war's end, the Union army still had not figured out how to adequately regulate sutlers' sales.

ALTHOUGH SUTLERS FELL UNDER THE PURVIEW of military discipline because of their contracts, frustrated officers had their hands full keeping soldiers from acquiring whiskey with the assistance of other, unlicensed, civilians. Soldiers' access ranged from family suppliers to rural stills to towns full of patriotic or opportunistic shopkeepers. Problematically, soldiers also clashed violently with sellers whom they believed to be extorting them (as they had done with sutlers). Nevertheless, in plenty of cases, commanding officers had no clear plan of how to stem the flow of illicit spirits. The military's habit of punishing drunken soldiers after the fact did nothing to curb suppliers' actions. Instead, officials had to act (at times on the fly) to expand their authority over civilians in their attempts to limit soldiers' access to liquor and to prevent clashes between soldiers and civilians.

Early in the war, plenty of liquor found its way into camps courtesy of soldiers' families, who hoped to support their men in arms by providing them comforting libations. In the war's opening months, it was not uncommon for Confederate volunteers to receive visits from male relatives who arrived in camp bearing gifts. Robert A. Moore's father brought a bottle of whiskey with him when he traveled from Mississippi to Leesburg, Virginia, to visit his son.[36] In the 5th Alabama, John Henry Cowin and his friends counted on the whiskey supplied by his father, Samuel, who also enlisted in the same regiment.[37] Far more common were the liquors that arrived in soldiers' care packages. Virginian Marx Mitteldorfer received a jug of whiskey from his Uncle Moritz. Several months later, he renewed his request, asking his family to send more whiskey.[38] While encamped near Petersburg, Virginia, during Christmas 1862, Confederate John Dooley's father sent him more than a quart of whiskey for the holidays. He remarked that "a great many" of the soldiers in the regiment received similar gifts.[39] These packages arrived despite General Robert E. Lee's attempts to rid the Army of Northern Virginia of liquor.[40]

Union soldiers also received spirituous packages—although perhaps not as easily as their Confederate counterparts. While the 44th Massachusetts was still encamped in Readville in 1862, the regiment received wine from Boston friends during a visit.[41] But for the most part, once Union soldiers moved away from their home states, they had to rely on mails to receive packages. John Chase of the 1st Massachusetts Light Artillery relied on his brother, Samuel, to send him whiskey that was "a much better kind than the *Busthead*." He drank the whiskey for his health, and he relied on couriers from the Christian Commission (USCC) to deliver the boxes from Washington to White Oak Church.[42] Officers were allowed to keep private stores of liquor, but they had to retrieve their packages quickly in order to keep them from falling into the possession of enlisted men. In December 1863, the Army of the Potomac ordered its officers to pick up their spirits from the sutler within a day of its delivery. Sutlers who kept the spirits longer would be assumed to be selling it to soldiers (which was forbidden because of the "Wilson bill").[43]

While family suppliers of enlisted men certainly annoyed officers who wanted to keep liquor out of the camps, the amounts were small enough that the flow was somewhat controllable through the inspection of barrels and crates arriving from relatives. Encamped near Falmouth for the winter of 1862–63, soldiers in the 141st Pennsylvania knew that all the liquors arriving in their care packages would be confiscated before it ever reached their tents.[44] Confederates tended to confiscate family-supplied spirits as well. After M. L. Kendrick heard that his brother was sick in camp near Fairfax Court House, he and a friend loaded up a wagon with four gallons of whiskey and headed over from Leesburg for a visit. Unfortunately, after Kendrick sold two pints of whiskey to soldiers, both men were arrested on suspicion of disloyalty (neither having enlisted) and confined for several months. General J. E. B. Stuart, having no use for whiskey, had the liquor destroyed.[45] The Virginians' punishment was unusually harsh. For the most part, civilians who shipped liquor to their soldier-relatives were spared military justice. Nevertheless, that Stuart conflated selling with disloyalty speaks to Confederate officials' suspicion of civilians who supplied soldiers.

Whether military officials allowed soldiers or officers to send and receive liquor did not necessarily prevent soldiers from acquiring spirits by other means, including smuggling. Soldiers smuggled most successfully when their efforts were coordinated with other men and civilians outside of the camps. Early in the war, when General George B. McClellan attempted to cut off access to liquor by prohibiting the trade in the Army of the Potomac, "unprincipled men in and out of the army" began smuggling spirits into the ranks. According to Black correspondent (and subsequently lieutenant) George Stephens, the soldiers of Joseph Hooker's Division resorted to all manner of chicanery—filling butter tubs and potato sacks with whiskey to sneak past the inspectors. One soldier figured out that the barrel of his musket held a pint of whiskey. The man "straightway gets a pass, has himself and his musket filled, and comes into camp, and fills a famished comrade." Others disguised the whiskey as pickles, hair tonic, and—perhaps less subtly—as Schniedam Schnapps. One inventive fellow even buried casks of rum so that he could pump it out and dispense it "from the bowels of the earth."[46] Despite Stephens's disapproval, he recognized that soldiers' smuggling was an attempt to mimic the luxuries of officers.[47] In at least a few cases, enemy soldiers helped smuggle whiskey. While on opposing picket lines near Edsall's Hill in Virginia during the war's first Christmas, the Irish Brigade made arrangements with rebel soldiers to exchange whiskey along with coffee, sugar, and tobacco. Officers tacitly approved.[48] Like the soldiers that George Stephens observed smuggling whiskey for their holiday, these fraternizers use spirits to claim a bit of space amid the rigid discipline of military life.[49]

By 1862, however, it became clear that the smuggling efforts were becoming more coordinated. Chaplain Joseph Twichell noticed a systemic smuggling problem when his soldiers began working at a wharf near Yorktown, Virginia. Because a large volume of supplies came to the Union troops by way of the Chesapeake Bay, "cunning ... rumsellers" were able to sneak enormous quantities of rum to the soldiers by concealing it in sloops. The bay was so crowded and the profits so "enormous" that putting a stop to the trafficking was nearly impossible.[50] Chaplain J. Chandler Gregg blamed the "connivance of high officials" for the constant funneling of whiskey into the camps.[51] For the night watchman at a Union camp near New Orleans in 1864, the supplementary income seemed to be the draw. He devised a scheme to sell liquor in exchange for clothing. He kept his whiskey under the floorboards of his tent, but a loose plank gave him away.[52]

While chaplains and sober-minded officers wrung their hands at the unstoppable flow of liquor, plenty of soldiers believed that smugglers (unlike sutlers) provided an invaluable patriotic service. Yorktown, Virginia, truly was a hub of whiskey trafficking, and soldiers in the Irish Brigade regularly did business with a woman near Ship Point. She "always kept on hand a generous supply of bottled commissary," which she watered down ("for fear it would be too strong and hurt the boys") and sold it "on the sly for three dollars per bottle" (a more reasonable price than sutlers). Known affectionately as the "supernumerary quartermaster or commissary assistant," the woman was not the only one of her type serving in the Union army.[53] The Carter brothers were fascinated by a similar woman they read about in the Pennsylvania newspapers. The wife of Colonel Max Einstein of the 27th Pennsylvania accompanied her husband to war and supposedly served as a vivandiere (a woman peddler) to the men while participating in battles at Bull Run, Fair Oaks, Richmond, and Fredericksburg. Nothing could "dampen her patriotism," and when the woman was not "under fire," she purchased and sold luxury goods such as tobacco, ham, and cigars to the soldiers. When it came to contraband whiskey, her patriotism paid off—she sold her liquor to the soldiers at five dollars a pint.[54] Unlike commanding officers, who regarded smuggling as a systemic problem, soldiers viewed these individual women as heroes whose sex allowed them to smuggle contraband into the ranks undetected. Equally interesting, soldiers believed that they provided a valuable service to the war effort. Though soldiers got testy when their sutlers' whiskey was of poor quality and prices were high, soldiers seemed to be of the opinion that civilian sellers—especially women—did their patriotic duty by providing much-needed liquor to thirsty troops. Perhaps the notion that women could have self-interested motives never occurred to them.

Union soldiers often assumed that African Americans had a similar duty to supply them with liquor, but they were far less charitable in their dealings with Black civilians. As they headed toward Hagerstown, Maryland, in 1862, Louis Richards and his comrade inquired of "an old negro whom we picked up by the way" where to buy "a couple of bottles of good whiskey."[55] Because whiskey was prohibited among the rank and file, exasperated officers at times targeted African Americans who were supposedly selling to their men. Michigan soldier Ira Gillespie noted that his Sergeant Twichell along with about half a dozen other soldiers invaded "an oald negro den whare they kept whiskey to sell to the soldiers in their posesion." When the sellers refused to divulge the location of their stash to the Union authorities, Twichell and others strung them up by their necks and then poured the whiskey over their heads and into their eyes.[56] Whether they were blamed for providing whiskey to white troops or perceived to act more brutishly under the influence of alcohol, Black men were seen in the eyes of white Northerners and Southerners as being prone to drunkenness, disorder, and beastly behavior. Rather than afford Black sellers formal access to military justice, soldiers and officers simply resorted to vigilantism. White men—both Union and Confederate—conveniently justified their own brutal behavior by arguing that they were merely protecting white people from the influence of Blackness and whiskey.

WHEN SOLDIERS RECEIVED CARE PACKAGES or smuggled liquor into camps with the help of civilians, it created isolated problems for military officials. But when Union soldiers gained more systematic access to civilian sellers along roads and in urban areas, the drunken violence and disorder became more acute, challenging military efforts to keep peace as armies moved through or occupied cities and towns. Secluded cottages and roadside taverns offered plenty of opportunities for soldiers to snag liquor for themselves and their buddies as they moved through the Confederacy, and when soldiers had access to larger communities, the problems increased substantially. Groups of rowdy drunken men had plagued cities in antebellum decades, but the war brought a new problem: the drunken soldier. In contested border regions, soldiers managed to rustle up liquor when they passed through towns, contributing to disorder. When troops occupied Southern towns, soldiers and civilians clashed, and alcohol exacerbated tensions, leaving Union officials scrambling to extend their authority to curb civilian sales.

As troops gathered near towns throughout the North, supportive civilians rushed to make sure the men were plenty refreshed as they mustered and trained. When the 7th New York disembarked for a few hours in Camden, New Jersey, on its way to Maryland in 1861, the men were greeted warmly by citizens of the town. In an effort to prevent chaos, Federal guards were "posted at the door of every neighbouring rum-hole." Still, the men managed to circulate a few bottles from well-meaning citizens. Union chaplain Joseph Twichell concluded that such "mistaken liberality" could have had incredibly dire consequences if the regiment had been allowed to drink all that was offered. As it was, before the night ended, "a man was seriously wounded in the face by a cannon fired in our honor."[57] Twichell seems to have wished that the good folk would have displayed their patriotism in a less liquid form. The Federal guards took a limited approach to controlling access. About 150 miles to the west, the 77th Pennsylvania encountered spirits before ever making it to their mustering. While waiting in the rain to board a train from Chambersburg to Pittsburgh, many of the men in the regiment "supplied themselves" (presumably from civilian shops) "with mean whisky." The officers only partially restored order as the men boarded the train, and on the journey, one soldier jumped from the cars and became "terribly mangled" when he was run over.[58] Though civilians provided the liquor as a gesture of support, the resulting accidents were more than the army could afford.

As thousands of volunteers arrived in Washington, D.C., in the spring and summer of 1861, bacchanalian excess descended along with them. The federal capital teemed with soldiers, served as a supply depot, and hosted massive hospitals—expanding more rapidly than its municipal government. But unlike Northern cities, D.C. was threatened by its proximity to enemy forces, and disloyal citizens lurked. British observer William Howard Russell noted in July 1861 that Union officers made copious purchases from a "wine and spirit store" near his lodging, and as the night wore on, there was "a good deal of tumult" when a group of Zouaves wrecked a brothel. One private was murdered, and there were "no police, no provost guard" to control the crowd.[59] Drinking establishments and entertainment houses "had sprung up like mushrooms." Perhaps the "most prolific" was a variety theater known as the "Canterbury Hall," which had entertainment so "marvelous" that soldiers encamped near the city would sneak off as often as possible to enjoy its distractions.[60] When soldiers arrived in the city, the more sober-minded, such as Charles B. Haydon, quenched their thirst in moderation with a glass or two of lager-beer.[61] Most men did not exercise Haydon's restraint. The Union military took an active role in curbing the disorder by punishing soldiers who roamed the streets intoxicated but focused on liquor trafficking as a discrete problem.[62] In the weeks following the first Battle of Bull Run, Captain Robert Goldthwaite Carter, who served with the city guards, spent his day patrolling Canterbury Hall and other establishments, rounding up drunken soldiers. Carter's duties are emblematic of the Union army's initial response to drunkenness—punishing the individual soldiers. But as early as August 2, 1861, Provost Marshal General Andrew Porter recognized that such a piecemeal approach was not going to work.

Porter attempted to establish order in the city by issuing General Orders, No. 1, which provided for the arrest of any soldier absent without a pass, but also, importantly, called for the "suppression of gambling-houses, drinking houses, or bar-rooms, and brothels."[63] Following the example of the federal government, which had already called on the military to protect federal authority in border cities, such as Washington and Baltimore, with large disloyal populations, Porter took matters into his own hands. Significantly, Porter's order did not target disloyal sellers; instead, it targeted civilians whose businesses interfered with military discipline. The problems, however, did not completely abate with Porter's order—at least not in the outlying neighborhoods. Assigned to Provost Guard in August 1861, Massachusetts private Rufus Robbins was tasked with "report[ing] liquor sellers" and capturing wayward soldiers and rebels in Georgetown.[64] Although William Howard Russell commented that Georgetown was "much more respectable and old-world looking than its vulgar, empty, overgrown, mushroom neighbor, Washington," he observed that the soldiers merely moved their drunkenness within its bounds after the provost guard cracked down in Washington. To make matters worse, the soldiers drank with the tacit approval of their officers. In one instance Russell saw a captain take a long swig of bourbon out of a bottle secreted in a soldier's pocket. By October 1861, Russell was aghast after nearly being run down by drunken soldiers and officers who had been "riding full gallop down the streets, and as fast as they can round the corners" in Washington and its neighboring communities. Russell himself nearly took a saber to the head while waiting for a ferry at Georgetown, and at least two officers—a colonel and a major—were killed "by falls from horseback, in furious riding in the city." Only by placing mounted guards in the streets could the Union army keep its men under control.[65] A few miles away in Brightwood, Private Robbins still had his hands full with his duties as a provost guard—inspecting "market men" who returned from Washington to ensure that they did not smuggle any liquor into camp unless they had permits from General Darius Couch.[66] Clearly Porter did not have the full support of Union officers when he passed his general orders, which did not entirely curtail sales to soldiers within D.C. or its surrounding neighborhoods.

Alexandria, Virginia, offered all the moral entrapments of Washington with the addition of even greater numbers of disloyal citizens, a combination that greatly exasperated Union military officials. In a February 1862 letter to Secretary of State William Seward, Special Government Agent S. W. Morton warned that the city was not only full of secessionist sympathizers but also abounded with "the vilest of whisky dens and rum holes and other vile places of corrupt debauch to demoralize the soldiers." The road leading to the camps outside of town were "filled with staggering, drunken soldiers, poisoned and rendered unfit to serve their country." They "disgraced" the Union army with their conduct. Moreover, Morton feared that the unruly environment of the city, along with alcohol's undoubtedly bad influence, facilitated a rebel spy network. He advised the military to govern the city with "more stringent measures" in the interest of the Union.[67] Morton expressed the need for an expansion of military authority more clearly than Porter: civilian liquor dealers rendered soldiers unfit to serve. Morton also clearly linked whiskey-selling with disloyalty, and in doing so he legitimized the Union army's expansion of authority. In his mind, securing the city and keeping soldiers disciplined required closing the shops. Other Federal officials were less convinced that such stringent measures were the way to go.

Morton's rhetoric is more moralistic than empirical, but courts-martial records for the Civil War era indeed suggest that D.C., Alexandria, and the roads between them had a problem. More than 11 percent of all cases involving alcohol occurred in D.C. or Alexandria. No other metropolitan area came close to that percentage.[68] Of course, the region's huge population of troops contributed to its high number of cases. But if Morton's dire warnings prompted Seward to authorize the Union army to enact more forceful policies to control vice, the measures never took hold. Eighteen months later, Indiana soldier Elijah Cavins described the city as "a perfect Sodom." Being close to the city had its perks—Cavins was eating fresh fruit of all varieties—but the "rowdyism and drunkenness" made him wish to be "farther off from town." There were "bawdy houses" everywhere, and women made "indecent advances" toward soldiers and watched them bathe. Cavins found the experience "disgusting."[69] Despite the trouble, no Union authority effectively curbed civilian-enabled vice.

When Union soldiers entered Confederate territory, spirits continued to follow the Army of the Potomac (suggesting that most civilians were motivated by profits more than patriotism). In the early months of 1863, civilians in Stafford County filled apple barrels with whiskey bottles for soldiers at

Belle Landing, and a teamster from Stoneman's Switch sneaked a canteen of whiskey to men of the 11th Corps (which supplemented the illegal whiskey sales of the sutler of the 82nd Ohio).[70] The Virginia sellers seemed unfazed by Union soldiers' political proclivities, and instead seized on the opportunity to earn some money with so many soldiers encamped near their homes. There is little evidence that Federal officials attempted to enact sweeping measures to control these rural sellers (even though they punished soldiers for drunkenness). Undoubtedly, this in large part stems from the Union not having firm control over territory in northern Virginia. But it also serves as evidence of Federal policy in the war's first half that focused on treating Southern civilians gingerly in hope of cultivating feelings of reconciliation (or at least avoiding greater animosity).[71]

Access to willing civilian suppliers increased as Union soldiers moved closer to Confederate cities, further complicating officers' attempts to keep order. When Union soldiers under Colonel Albert L. Lee entered Somerville, Tennessee, in January 1863, Confederate sympathizers "treated the soldiers well, and offered them in singular profusion wines and liquors of all kinds." Beyond what the townspeople provided, Lee found fourteen barrels of whiskey in a Confederate storehouse. He posted a captain to guard the door, but the Union soldiers, who had eaten nothing all day after spending the night outside in a "pelting storm," drank heavily and became "somewhat exhilarated" on the liquor provided by civilians. The intoxicated soldiers attempted to break into the storehouse and shot the captain when he refused to let them pass. Lee was aghast at the violence. The South was known for its "proverbial" whiskey shortage, and he had never thought to develop a policy for preventing rampant drunkenness among his men.[72] Though his men behaved poorly, he gave no indication that the Confederate civilians purposefully provoked the men by providing liquor.

It seems more likely that Somerville's proximity to Memphis colored the soldiers' experiences. Memphis's location on the contested Mississippi River makes it an excellent example of how access to liquor had as much—if not more—to do with soldiers' location than with the loyalties of the sellers. Before Federal forces occupied Memphis in mid-1862, Confederate troops used the city for recreation. After chasing a steamer up the Mississippi River in October 1861, Confederate surgeon Junius Newport Bragg and the Camden Knights of the 1st Arkansas disembarked at Memphis for the night. Bragg had looked forward to being in the city, but quickly decided that it offered too many opportunities for officers to become "jovially tight."[73]

After Union forces occupied Memphis, the city provided similar opportunities for refreshment and (subsequent) handwringing. Union soldiers kept the roads to and from their camps crowded with drunks. After Lieutenant Augustus Ayling and his comrades in the 29th Massachusetts passed through Kentucky enjoying "cake and wine" and conversing with "nice girls," the regiment stopped in Memphis on its way to join Union forces at Vicksburg. Although Ayling had ridden in an ambulance much of the time—complaining of sore heels—he found that once he arrived in Memphis, his feet were rested enough that he could join other officers for a night on the town. After enjoying "juleps" and "cobblers," the men treated themselves to a showing of *The Drunkard*, which was, ironically, a temperance play. Not surprisingly, Ayling declared the play "Not very interesting!" and "went with the crowd around town and did not get to bed until about two."[74] Jenkin Lloyd Jones spent his New Year's Eve near Memphis, during which time "nearly two-thirds of the soldiers were *drunk*," though he was more amused than appalled."[75] Jones's experience was not a holiday anomaly but rather an "everyday occurrence." John Quincy Adams Campbell found the constant stream of men returning from Memphis drunk to be abominable.[76]

Plenty of Union soldiers saw little reason not to imbibe, and when no one could sell or dispense whiskey within a city, Federals simply stole it. In late 1862, Nashville, Tennessee's *Dispatch* reported that soldiers were "breaking into some stores, drinking whiskey, and afterward robbing them of such articles as they could carry off, and destroying property promiscuously." That there was a provost guard nearby made little difference.[77] These problems continued throughout the war. Near Chico Pass, Louisiana, Massachusetts soldiers "broke open" a bar.[78] In Jackson, Mississippi, soldiers ransacked closed shops in search of rum.[79] When Union troops entered Columbia, South Carolina, in February 1865, an "almost wild soldiery" roamed the streets "under the control of no one" after finding "plenty of spirituous liquors." In this case, Colonel Oscar Lawrence Jackson believed that the men were asking citizens for the spirits, who obliged.[80] Whether those citizens were coerced or willingly acquiesced, Jackson does not say. Despite liquor shortages throughout the Southern states, there always seemed to be enough supply in urban areas to make soldiers drunk, and, regardless of the intentions of the civilian suppliers, the liquor often had a disruptive effect and complicated Federal attempts at occupation.

Yet Union military officials hesitated to close shops with sweeping orders, even though they sought out individual dealers who caused trouble by selling to soldiers. Instead, Union generals tended to focus on large-scale liquor trafficking.[81] After General Ulysses S. Grant captured Forts Henry and Donelson, the Department of the Missouri prohibited commerce in whiskey on both the Cumberland and Tennessee Rivers.[82] In part, these orders may have been intended to prevent chaos ahead of Union gunboats. But in December 1861, Grant had suggested that his concerns about the illicit whiskey trade along the rivers had little to do with preventing drunkenness. After Union troops intercepted eighty barrels of whiskey being shipped to Hickman, Kentucky, from New Madrid, Missouri, Grant expressed his worry that the barrels actually did not contain whiskey but were filled with supplies for Confederates.[83] Grant's worries were not off-base. Located along the Mississippi River, Hickman—filled with Confederate sympathizers—served as a prime smuggling point throughout the war. In August 1863, Union soldiers intercepted twenty-five wagons on the road from Jackson, Tennessee, to Hickman. The wagons contained not only plenty of whiskey (which by 1863 was increasingly scarce in the Confederacy and vital to its medical department) but also valuable supplies.[84] In short, for Union officials the flow of valuable supplies through the contested border regions presented a greater threat to their war aims (in this case, keeping Missouri and Kentucky secured) than preventing civilians from conducting business in occupied towns.

This is not to say that Union commanders were satisfied to let their soldiers gallivant drunkenly through towns. Rather, when it came to keeping soldiers sober, Federal officers were reluctant to enact stringent prohibitory measures. For example, even though General Benjamin Butler was notorious for his intolerance of drunken soldiers and officers, he typically did not prohibit civilian sales across the board. The closest Butler came to enacting widespread control over civilian drinking was in May 1862 with his General Orders, No. 25 in occupied New Orleans. He stated that the duty of the Union army was to "feed and protect" the women and children. This protection required, among other things, that Federal officials remove "a whisky-drinking mob" from the city.[85] Butler did not suggest that Union soldiers constituted the drunken mob. But he suggested that women and children were vulnerable when drunken hoards roamed a city already in a state of wartime disorder. Keeping order, in this particular instance, required sobering up an occupied city. In cases later in the war, however, Butler distributed licenses and regulated quantity. As long as sellers steered clear of soldiers, he allowed liquor to flow in small amounts.[86] Even after learning that Baltimore dealers loaded up Union recruits with "bad whiskey" while they lingered in the city, Butler ordered the provost marshal of the 8th Army Corps to "keep them [recruits] under close guard" to prevent them from becoming drunk before they were transported to Fort Monroe.[87] These later actions illustrate that he much preferred to keep order by using provost guards to control soldiers' drinking rather than by targeting civilians.

Butler's habit of using provost guards to patrol streets and keep soldiers in order was similar to the policies the Federals used in Washington, D.C., and other occupied cities. Much of the time, however, these guards were ineffective because soldiers were able to leave camp and the provost guards themselves had little interest in remaining sober. For example, the 29th Massachusetts assigned Company H to be its provost guard, but this included the julep-guzzling Lieutenant Ayling.[88] Ayling claimed to have kept order, but he was no temperance crusader, and neither were most of the other men who served as provost guards. In September 1864, Jenkin Lloyd Jones encountered problems while serving guard duty near Allatoona, Georgia. A sergeant "went out with a squad on pass," and they returned from town "too drunk to take care of themselves."[89] A month later, John Quincy Adams Campbell complained about being assigned "officer of the day" in Louisville. The soldiers "were allowed to go out in town as they choose," and he had the task of keeping them corralled. He "managed to get along," but noted that "a number of the men came to quarters very drunk during the evening."[90] If men had passes, guards were largely powerless to stop them.

While controlling drunkenness by punishing soldiers presented obvious shortcomings, Union officers often hesitated to close shops in occupied towns outright, especially early in the war. In contested regions, however, Union authorities were more likely to regulate civilians as they tried to preserve order over vast territory.[91] Missouri's liquor dealers experienced varying Union approaches to controlling their businesses. St. Louis had a burgeoning beer industry before the war, and its location at the confluence of the Mississippi and Missouri Rivers and on the border between the North, the South, and the West meant it was filled with soldiers. Though Union officials banned liquor, they permitted soldiers to drink lager beer (because it was less intoxicating) and contracted agreements with local brewers to supply lager to troops stationed in the area.[92] The resulting atmosphere dismayed John Vance Lauderdale. St. Louis could not "boast much for its morality.... *Everybody*—almost—drinks." Lauderdale credited the many beer gardens to the "mixed population" of German and French Americans coupled with the "floating population."[93]

But if cities elsewhere in the nation were bastions of revelry, in Missouri, the rural regions were more susceptible to whiskey's ravages. Throughout the state, high levels of guerrilla violence did not preclude civilians from selling liquor to soldiers—in fact, in some cases, it seems to have facilitated the exchange. North of St. Louis, in Lincoln County, guerrillas stole horses from citizens, although there were "no threats or acts of violence toward anyone." Citizens notified Federal officials that most disturbances occurred as a result of "bad whisky," and they suggested extending the "same regulations in regard to dram-shops as exist in Saint Louis" to the rest of the state in order that "the peace of the country generally would be better preserved." The regulations that they suggested were that "no permits to dram sellers or liquor dealers in any town or village" be given "unless recommended by a majority of the citizens through the committee of safety."[94] These measures, presumably, would ensure that only reliable (loyal) citizens opened dram shops. Though the regulations were facilitated by Union officials, the measures in St. Louis and Lincoln County left control of the shops within the hands of civilians. Yet in other cases, Federal officials awarded licenses to sell liquor to dealers who were willing to take oaths of loyalty.[95] Sometimes, sellers had to agree additionally not to sell to soldiers and only to provide liquor to loyal citizens.[96] In these cases, permits to sell liquor were clearly integrated into the Union army's plan to keep order by working with civilians and by rewarding loyalty with the ability to conduct business. Of course, one could argue that these licensed dealers' patriotism was pragmatic rather than authentic. Nevertheless, in Missouri, the performance of loyalty and selling liquor were linked.

At the same time that the Federals were willing to dole out licenses to loyal sellers in parts of the state, other Missourians were subjected to harsher policies. In March 1862, Callaway County resident Austin Brewner found himself in trouble when he sold whiskey and brandy to Federal troops in violation of martial law. He was court-martialed and fined twenty-five dollars.[97] The problem was not isolated. The Missouri State Militia struggled to maintain order farther south in Wayne County, as well, when men "lurking in the woods" sold and gave "whisky . . . to the soldiers indiscriminately." The soldiers were subsequently drunk and under guard during a skirmish.[98] These sellers, it seems, were not necessarily loyal citizens attempting to support soldiers encamped in their midst. Rather, sowing disorder—and thereby exacerbating tensions between the Federals and guerrillas—seems to have been the purpose of the sales.

Just east in Tennessee, civilians experienced similarly shifting policies when it came to liquor sales. During a brief occupation of Tullahoma in March 1862, Colonel John Kennett of the 4th Ohio Cavalry assured the citizens that the soldiers sent by the Union government had only "kind intentions." If rebel citizens were to be brought back into the national fold, kindness was imperative. But to maintain good relations with the townspeople, Kennett also had to hunt down whiskey dealers. He found two shops and "threatened to burn them down if the inmates retailed a single dram."[99] Drunkenness created chaos that would prevent conciliatory policies from working. When Federal forces returned to Middle Tennessee in 1863 for a more permanent occupation, General Eleazer Paine had less patience than Kennett. Kennett had construed closing shops as a part of conciliatory policy toward secessionists, but Paine was convinced that selling liquor was an act of overt disloyalty. If the dispatches of Union soldier Stephen F. Fleharty are to be believed, Paine threatened not only to burn down the businesses of liquor dealers but also to tie them up by their thumbs for two days. The problem, as Paine put it, was not simply that dealers might sell to soldiers but that as soon as civilian men began drinking whiskey, they were converted into rebels.[100] By arguing that whiskey was connected to disloyalty, Paine could justify his harsh military-esque punishment for civilians. Although Paine was not the only Union general to conflate whiskey with disloyalty, his harsh physical punishments of civilian sellers were a bit anomalous.

In fact, by 1863, military arrests of civilians for selling liquor to soldiers had come under fire in many locations, both in the North and in occupied cities. After Federal officials in Indiana broadly prohibited the sale of liquor to soldiers and threatened to arrest civilian shopkeepers who violated the order, the Indiana Supreme Court ruled that the Union army did not have the power to subject civilians to martial law in areas where civil courts were still operating.[101] This case had more to do with pushing back against the expansions of martial law of the Lincoln administration by articulating the parameters for enacting martial law than it had to do with liquor sales. Nevertheless, it demonstrates that Federal officials did not have carte blanche when dealing with civilian sellers, even in contested regions where sales to soldiers could threaten stability.

Back in Missouri, 1864 reports indicate the dram shops remained a problem for Federal forces trying to suppress guerrilla bands. But unlike Paine in Tennessee, Union officers on the ground in Missouri shied away from tying up whiskey dealers by their thumbs. Near the western border in the town of Weston, General James Craig tried to organize companies to guard the towns and relieve the Union soldiers for other duties. But liquor "shops were running under the highest kind of pressure, and very many of the people [were] excited." In this case, Union officials closed all the shops and tried to disperse the crowds, but they seemed less than optimistic about keeping the militia units sober and fit for duty.[102] A few months later, the struggle in Platte County continued. Confederate officers were "prowling about," contributing to disorder, as liquor shops continued to sell despite being fined.[103] Elsewhere, in Central Missouri (which had moderate amounts of guerrilla unrest), Federal officials pled with the Calhoun Citizen Guards to police civilian sellers themselves. As soon as civilians agreed to "cease their exertions to demoralize the troops by giving them whisky," the Union army would step up its protection of the town from guerrilla attacks.[104] In these cases, Federal forces at times closed and fined shops, just as they enacted other measures to control civilians throughout the state. But when it came to liquor shops, policies varied from county to county, and officials continued to work with local authorities to attempt to control disorder caused by drunken soldiers.[105] Their approach to keeping order in a contested but nonseceded state combined civil and military control over liquor shops.

By the war's final months, Union officers argued that completely closing liquor shops was the only way to ensure that rowdy Union soldiers would not disrupt order in the occupied Confederacy. In March 1865, General Edward R. S. Canby issued General Orders, No. 32 for the Military Division of West Mississippi that, among other things, prohibited the sale of all intoxicating liquors—including wines, beers, and ales—"in the vicinity of any place occupied by our troops, either on the march or stationed."[106] These orders, which predominately applied to New Orleans, were similar to those that Federal occupiers would implement in Richmond in the following months. The orders strongly suggested that Federal officials believed the Union soldiers could not act as a disciplined occupying force if allowed to consume liquors. Nevertheless, Union generals took a more limited approach to using military authority to control civilians when it came to liquor sales. When they closed shops, it overwhelmingly involved keeping troops disciplined during occupation rather than trying to crack down on disloyal or immoral behavior.

LIKE THEIR UNION COUNTERPARTS, Confederates understood that preventing clashes between drunken soldiers and civilians was paramount to their military success. Yet they were also plagued with civilian sellers who were more than willing to accommodate thirsty soldiers. Confederate troops had the advantage (generally) of fighting in regions surrounded by supportive civilians, although plenty of sellers seemed to be at least as motivated by profit as by patriotism. Regardless of the sellers' intentions, Confederate soldiers, like their Union counterparts, managed to become drunk and disorderly from roadside distilleries and urban shops. But unlike Federal officials, Confederate commanders were more likely to resort to sweeping measures to close shops to curtail urban sales, despite the fact that they tended to operate in Confederate, rather than hostile, territory.

In the Confederate capital, both military and civilian authorities targeted sellers regardless of whether they sold to soldiers or civilians (unlike Washington, where military authorities focused on soldiers and the shops they patronized).[107] The Richmond city council struck first, suggesting that the problems associated with public drunkenness increased almost immediately after the war began. Less than two weeks after Virginia seceded, the council cracked down on liquor sales. Every evening at ten o'clock, all establishments "where ardent spirits, porter, beer, or cider" was "sold or given away" would close and violators would be fined twenty dollars each day they stayed open too late.[108] Simply placing a curfew on liquor shops did little to curb access—at least from the perspective of Confederate officers. By September 1861, Captain George C. Gibbs was calling for more stringent measures. Charged with commanding the prison guard at the Confederate States Prison, Gibbs was frustrated because his sentries had a habit of stepping away from their posts to fill their canteens. They returned drunk and allowed prisoners to escape. He pled with General John H. Winder to close all the grog-shops near the prison.[109]

This need to close shops to keep discipline within their ranks but also to control civilians spread beyond Virginia by the fall of 1861. When it came to keeping soldiers away from sellers and out of the town rum holes, some officers attempted to move their men as far away from the shops as possible. Shortly after becoming a brigade commander in the Confederate Army of Central Kentucky, Colonel S. A. M. Wood determined to keep liquor out of reach of his 7th Alabama and other soldiers by moving his camp more than fifteen miles away from Chattanooga at Tyner's Crossroads. Even had the soldiers determined to hoof it to town, they would have found the road's bridges burned out. As a result, Wood reported, his camp and its surrounding country were "perfectly quiet." As an extra precaution, Wood also declared martial law, closed all the groceries in the nearby town, and prohibited anyone from coming or going. His goal seemed to be twofold: to control soldiers and clamp down on civilians "who were talking Lincolnism."[110] This second component is noteworthy: liquor and Unionism among civilians presented a threat to the stability of the infant Confederate nation.

Martial law, which included closing shops, spread quickly through Tennessee in the following months. When the Confederacy's Army of Mississippi was headquartered in Jackson, Tennessee, in March 1862, General Braxton Bragg instituted General Orders, No. 2. The orders not only declared martial law in Memphis but also recognized the spirituous temptations that lurked along the roads. All shops within a mile of the highways and within five miles of Confederate stations were closed. Any liquor—except that used for medicinal purposes—would be destroyed.[111] In eastern Tennessee, Confederates shuttered shops in Kingston and Cleveland, mimicking General Bragg's orders in the western parts of the state.[112] In short, when it came to controlling liquor,

Confederate generals did not shy away from enacting sweeping measures that placed civilians under military authority.

Back in Virginia, Winder worked to close shops throughout Richmond, ushering in an era of intermittent wartime prohibition on spirits. Charged with enforcing the law throughout the capital city, Winder, in February 1862, placed the entire community under martial law.[113] Winder's prohibition was a part of much broader measures that severely curtailed civilians' actions within the city. Winder's actions did not happen in a vacuum. While he was clamping down broadly on disorder in Richmond, President Jefferson Davis attempted to control the flow of liquor throughout the Confederate military. In January 1862, Davis enacted General Orders, No. 3, which sought to keep all liquors from Confederate camps (Davis's orders followed practices that had already been adopted by General Braxton Bragg).[114] On March 1, 1862, Davis extended these regulations by issuing General Orders, No. 8, which declared martial law in Richmond, closed the liquor shops, and prohibited distilling within ten miles of the city.[115] While Davis's General Orders, No. 3 reflected, in many ways, Porter's General Orders, No. 1 in Washington because it targeted troops, with his General Orders, No. 8, Davis extended Confederate military authority beyond what Union authorities enacted—passing prohibition as a part of a sweeping declaration of martial law.

By March 1862, Confederates were putting more stringent prohibitory laws into place wherever soldiers were stationed in Virginia. General Stonewall Jackson tried to keep ardent spirits out of reach of his troops, at times ordering that wagons be searched and barrels shattered and drained to keep young soldiers from drinking the contents.[116] After Confederates occupied Harpers Ferry in May 1862, Jackson had the liquor seized and dumped over the bluff into the river (while enterprising soldiers waited at the bottom to catch it in buckets).[117] Civilians praised Jackson's efforts and hoped his tactics would spread to Confederate cities in the Deep South.[118] In Norfolk and Portsmouth, the sale of any intoxicating beverage was strictly prohibited. Beyond that, the army ordered all "places where liquors are kept for sale or use" closed and promised to arrest any person—man or woman—found to be drunk, disorderly, or disloyal.[119] General Joseph Johnston followed suit. At Orange Court House, he had Colonel Thomas H. Taylor of the 1st Kentucky named provost-marshal and ordered him to "regulate the town." Specifically, Taylor and his regiment were to ensure that "perfect order is preserved" by "closing all stores and shops where liquor is sold."[120] That Confederate officers wanted to control soldiers is clear, but the inclusion of civilians who were drunk or disloyal provides additional evidence that Confederates in Virginia were also worried that civilians' political unrest could be exacerbated by free-flowing liquor.

When closing shops, Confederate officers often acted with the blessings of civilians. Only a few months after Davis and Confederate officials had declared martial law in Richmond and other Virginia cities, inhabitants of Charlottesville implored Captain John Taylor to "declare martial law so far as selling liquor is involved." The "cases of drunkenness and fights are of such frequent occurrence that ladies are afraid to go into the streets." Taylor asked Secretary of War George Randolph to give him the authority to close shops in order to prevent "poisoned whisky" from turning "the thoughtless soldier" into "a madman" and risking public safety.[121] Confederate women's willingness to call on government authorities to protect them from the threat of rowdy soldiers could be considered surprising, considering white Southerners' emphasis on private property and states' rights. Nevertheless, these women articulated that drunken Confederate soldiers (not invaders) threatened their safety. If the army was thought to embody the ideals of the young nation, its members could not endanger women in loyal cities.[122]

Outside of urban areas, however, martial law had limited effect. In the mountains of Virginia, Confederate soldiers easily found civilians willing to sell them apple brandy, which they loved. Nestled in a valley near Virginia's Hawksbill peak on the road leading over the Blue Ridge were Kite's still-house and apple orchard. During the Valley Campaign in the summer of 1862, Stonewall Jackson's men had discovered the apple brandy, and in November, as the soldiers marched toward Fredericksburg, the men decided to pay Kite another visit. At a brief rest stop, company commander James Cooper Nisbet of the 21st Georgia Regiment asked Captain A. S. Hamilton if he could send a detail to fill the canteens "for all that wanted" the refreshing apple brandy. After receiving permission from Hamilton, Nisbet and others set off for the orchard, only to be stopped at the entry to the still-house by a cavalry guard who informed them that General Jubal Early (commanding Ewell's division) had prohibited Kite from selling liquor to the soldiers. After learning of Early's order, Captain Hamilton took matters into his own hands, inquiring whether or not the general had procured any of the spirits for himself. Not surprisingly, he discovered that Early had filled his canteen along with a keg he was hauling behind his ambulance. Hamilton wasted no time disregarding Early's orders. His men purchased the apple brandy and spent the rest of the afternoon enjoying themselves, happily singing "very *risqué* couplets" within earshot of Stonewall Jackson as they headed toward Madison Court House on their way to Fredericksburg.[123] Clearly commanders were not making sobriety a priority on this march, despite the threats that drunken soldiers potentially posed to civilians.

Soldiers who imbibed Kite's spirits had a humorous experience, but at other times, transactions got ugly. In the summer of 1862, farmers near Camp Kellyville along the Rapidan River traded with Confederate soldiers in the 16th Mississippi by providing chicken, bread, and an apple brandy that "packs a wallop."[124] Mississippi soldiers in the Army of Northern Virginia acquired a taste for the stuff, which led to an altercation with one opportunistic seller the following summer. After soldiers began flocking to his secluded location about two miles from camp to fill their canteens at a dollar a drink, the "old countryman" decided to increase profits. First he doubled and tripled the price, and he found thirsty soldiers willing to shell out the money for it. But when he raised the cost to five dollars per shot, the angry Mississippians knocked him over the head and stole his brandy. When the moonshiner marched into camp, seeking compensation for his stolen goods, the officers, no doubt tipsy from their fresh supply of his liquor, threatened to arrest him for violating General Lee's orders by selling to soldiers. They chased the Virginian into the woods and kept his brandy for themselves.[125] General Lee's attempt to prohibit sales from the top down apparently only had limited effect, in part because lower-ranking officers only haphazardly enforced his orders.

Even in Richmond, martial law was not completely effective. At least one Richmond saloon-keeper at first considered prohibitory measures largely a formality due to supply shortages that diminished profits. Longtime resident John Gottfried Lange received his lager beer from Redding, Pennsylvania, and found himself forced to close his saloon after the Union blockade prevented his supplies from traveling up the James River. Other beerhouses were, apparently, less affected by the blockade. The preacher of one German congregation, John Heyer, spent so much time in the saloons in the early weeks of the war that his congregation stopped showing up for worship. But Davis's declarations of martial law had a mixed long-term effect. When the city calmed down in fall of 1862, German brewers began serving again. But Lange and other brewers hardly seemed the villainous predators that the press made dealers out to be. Rather than taking advantage of soldiers to rake in tremendous profits, Lange struggled to make ends meet. Even when sales were legal, the licenses and taxes were expensive, and keg prices rose with Confederate inflation. Lange gardened and made shoes to supplement his income, and he expressed frustration when the Confederate government declared martial law—shutting his shop after he had paid for licenses.[126] This expanding and contracting of martial law continued through most of the war.

Yet the tendency to close liquor shops entirely began to abate shortly after Federal forces occupied Richmond. In May 1865, Union chief of staff Henry Halleck refused to provide licenses to sell liquor within the boundaries of Richmond (although he authorized commanding officers in other parts of Virginia to "exercise their own discretion").[127] By June, General Frederick Dent relaxed the prohibitions ever so slightly—allowing large hotels to serve wine and beers to their guests. The provost marshal, as well, granted at least one proprietor, a Mr. Ziegler from New York, a license to keep a liquor shop at the corner of Broad and Ninth Streets. Dent's successor General Alfred Terry was content to slacken the restraints even further, issuing General Orders, No. 6, which allowed vendors to obtain licenses, provided they did not sell to enlisted men. Terry seemingly had no problem with beer, in general, as he and his staff held at least one meeting at John Lange's saloon, despite Lange's willingness to defend his loyalty to the Confederacy.[128] With these regulations, focused on controlling soldiers' access rather than civilians' shops, Richmond's Union occupiers put in place regulations that more closely mimicked Union policy in other occupied towns.

BOTH UNION AND CONFEDERATE AUTHORITIES recognized that when soldiers interacted with civilian liquor dealers, chaos ensued, especially in towns and regions with high concentrations of troops. While generals and provost marshals sought to limit soldiers' access to civilian sellers, their approaches to expanding military authority differed in important ways.

For Union authorities, the approach was almost always localized and focused on the specific problem of soldier drinking. In loyal and border states, they controlled sutlers and civilian sellers through licensing and partnerships with civil authorities and widely relied on provost guards to round up drunken men to prevent them from harassing civilians. In the instances when Union officers stretched military authority to curtail civilian sales, they targeted those who sold to soldiers. Only in limited instances did Federal occupiers close shops entirely, arguing that the problem of public drunkenness was so acute that it directly threatened the war effort—by compromising soldiers or the occupation. So while the Union army embraced the notion that it had the ability to extend its authority over civilians, when it came to controlling liquor, the military exercised restraint. Importantly, as cases in Missouri illustrate, Federals tried to work with civilian authorities to keep order rather than impose harsh prohibitions on occupied (even hostile) populations.

On the other hand, Confederate authorities were much more comfortable enacting widespread closings of shops as part of sweeping declarations of martial law. This was especially true in embattled regions like Virginia and Tennessee. Moreover, whereas Federals only sometimes argued that they were extending their authority over occupied persons, Confederates could not. Their actions often referenced Unionists and disloyalty, but the measures to control sales made no distinctions between loyal sellers and suspected Unionists. Moreover, the threat posed by drunken soldiers and disloyal citizens even prompted Confederate civilians to praise the expansion of martial law. In short, military responses to civilian sellers represent yet another instance of Confederates tolerating a wide expansion of martial authority while their Federal counterparts relied on mixed martial-civil solutions.

In the few cases in which Federal officials passed sweeping orders that curtailed drinking in cities, they suggested that more was at stake than simply keeping order in their own barracks. Butler not only desired to protect the women and children of New Orleans from drunken mobs in 1862, but in February 1864, Colonel R. B. Palmer of the 73rd Regiment Enrolled Missouri Militia observed that whiskey dealers prospered at the expense of women and children. Not only were vulnerable civilians starving, but soldiers who purchased the liquor became drunk and enacted "vengeance on any whom they may choose to look on as personal or political enemies."[129] This was antithetical to the Federals' responsibilities, as Palmer saw it. The Union military had a duty to use its authority to prevent liquor from harming women and children.

Confederate generals concurred. On the same day that General Braxton Bragg had issued his orders prohibiting the supplying or selling of liquor to soldiers within the 2nd Grand Division of the Army of Mississippi, General P. G. T. Beauregard connected the war's goals to protecting civilians. Upon assuming command, he argued that the soldiers serving with him were fighting for a "defense of our homes and liberties," and that their "mothers and wives, our sisters and children, expect us to do our duty even to the sacrifice of our lives." By being "true" to their "just and sacred" cause, Beauregard believed that his soldiers would garner the "continued protection of the Almighty" in order to "triumph." It is difficult to separate Beauregard's perception that the war was fought to protect women and children from Bragg's orders that soldiers ought to conduct themselves soberly.[130]

Both Butler's and Beauregard's statements provide insight into the fundamental aims of Union and Confederate control of liquor sales through martial authority. For the Federals, restoring the Union was at stake, and protecting civilians and keeping order in occupied cities was a central component of their war aims. Controlling some sales of liquor fit pragmatically within their goals, but working with civilian authorities and continuing to issue business licenses where appropriate also supported federal aims of keeping the occupied South operating smoothly for civilians. Confederates, on the other hand, despite fighting the war in friendly territory, acted as though liquor presented a much more serious existential threat to their war aims. Beauregard invoked the Almighty and suggested that Confederate soldiers who endangered civilians undercut Providential support for the war. Other Confederate authorities suggested not only that drunk soldiers caused an internal threat but also that liquor could increase domestic unrest among Unionists. In other words, while drunkenness complicated Union occupation, it directly threatened Confederate survival.

CHAPTER FIVE

Controlling the Traffic in the Union and Confederate States

In early 1862, Virginia state senator James M. Whittle found himself in hot water. The legislature had recently voted to prohibit distilling because it wasted grain, and Whittle had voted in support of the measure.[1] He received angry letters from his constituents—the farmers of Pittsylvania County—for his trouble. Writing to a friend and political supporter, Whittle explained that though he had been encouraged "to support the stills"—specifically those Virginians who distilled grains for their own private use—he believed that the prohibition on distilling could be borne stoically and patriotically. The problem with distilling during a time of war was twofold: the state was running out of grain and "the army has been demoralized by liquor." If distilling continued, Whittle pointed out, there was no way for the Confederacy to sustain its war effort. "Certainly some will lose money" by being unable to distill, he acknowledged, "but we all lose money by the war & no one ought to complain on that account." Instead, Whittle insisted, all patriotic Virginians must embrace the financial hardships caused by the war. Even Whittle was willing to adjust his habits. Knowing that whiskey "has killed more than the Yankee," he vowed "to take not a drop ... to save the cause of the country." He insisted that he was "no temperance man & had no such view in my vote."[2] His teetotalism, as he understood it, was a patriotic gesture.

Whittle's exchange illustrates that debates over liquor and the war extended far beyond simply controlling drunken soldiers who passed through towns. Not only did civilians in both the Union and Confederacy support efforts by military authorities to control soldiers' behavior, but many also believed that the war necessitated additional state or federal regulation or prohibition of manufacturing and selling liquor. That the scope of the problem required systemic solutions is perhaps not surprising. But ironically, the calls for prohibition came much more loudly from civilians in Confederate states than from their Northern counterparts. This marked a shift in public attitudes toward prohibition from the antebellum era. Before the war, when many Northern states were swept up in the enthusiasm for Maine Laws, Southern states were much less inclined toward statewide prohibition.[3] The war changed the stakes. Controlling drunken soldiers, especially in the Confederacy, required controlling the manufacturing and trafficking of liquor as well. More than that, because Americans on both sides believed fervently that morality and military victory were intertwined, preventing the sordid liquor traffic became imperative.

In the North, the public was somewhat divided over how best to regulate the liquor traffic during a time of war. Temperance reformers decried spirit rations and sellers (especially sutlers), arguing that saving the Union required ending the traffic. Reformers held enough sway to prompt Congress to act to control liquor in the ranks. But when it came to prohibition, reformers found themselves in the minority. Most Northern civilians favored regulation in the form of excise taxes and license laws rather than prohibition. Practically, it made sense to regulate liquor and use the revenue to fund the war. After all, concerns about soldiers' drunkenness were not acutely felt in most Northern communities (save those few large cities in which soldiers were constantly encamped).

For Confederates, however, the problems created by drunken soldiers and liquor traffickers were much more severe and immediate. Because the war was fought primarily in the South, Confederate civilians experienced soldiers' drunken revelry more directly than most of their Northern counterparts. More problematically, Confederates faced severe food shortages, which made distillers, who diverted grain from bread production into liquor, appear wasteful. That distillers were thought to make immense profits from their liquors made the distillers seem unpatriotic, putting their personal profits ahead of the war effort. While prohibition-favoring Northerners believed, in abstract, that traffickers' sins endangered the Union, Confederates concretely feared that distillers' sins threatened their national survival by wasting resources while simultaneously incurring God's judgment due to their selfishness. Confederates not only supported the military's intervention to curb soldiers' drunkenness in their towns but also asked civilian authorities to pass prohibition. While the Richmond government never entertained the notion of national prohibition, several Confederate states prohibited distilling, fomenting an unwinnable battle between state and national authority.

WHEN THE WAR BEGAN, Northerners had spent a decade debating prohibition. In 1851, the state of Maine passed prohibition. By 1855, twelve additional Northern and Midwestern states had followed suit. According to historian Ian Tyrrell, pro-prohibition sentiment was even more widespread. In all states north of the Ohio River, prohibition found support among Democrats and Whigs, even if the states did not vote to go dry. Despite prohibition's seeming popularity, the issue proved divisive in both political parties—neither was willing to fully incorporate prohibition into its platform for fear that it would alienate pro-liquor voters.[4] By the late 1850s, a series of court cases struck down portions of the various state laws, and most early supporters lost their zeal for prohibition when they realized that it was simply unenforceable. Membership in the American Temperance Union (ATU) declined (in part because Americans were not consuming as much alcohol), but hardline supporters of prohibition doubled down and became angry when the Republican Party refused to incorporate support for prohibition into its state and national platforms in the 1850s. Members of the American Temperance Union, for example, did not understand that prohibition had simply lost public support.[5] Thus, when war began, Northerners' memories of failed prohibition crusades shaped their understandings of liquor's role in the crisis. For temperance reformers, the war made the liquor traffic even more evil because it put soldiers and the nation at risk. But for most Northern communities, the debates over controlling liquor continued outside of the context of war, with many states and towns continuing to discuss the best methods of regulating the traffic.

Taxes were another matter. Even before the first Battle of Bull Run, Northerners were debating how much liquor dealers should contribute to the war's costs. The members of the New York–centered American Temperance Union publicly exclaimed that they were not willing to pay higher war taxes unless the government ramped up its efforts to enforce existing license laws. In 1861, there were more than ten thousand dram shops in New York City, and most of them were unlicensed. An article published in the New York Times estimated that the city could tap into more than half a million dollars in revenue simply by collecting license fees and fines. Comparing rum-sellers to secessionists, the New York Times maintained that the city "can't afford to have [laws] defied in New-York" while "we are fighting to enforce the laws in Dixie Land." The unregulated liquor traffic had been burdening the citizens of New York with crime and extra taxes for years, but during wartime, when coffee, tea, and sugar were being taxed, citizens were aghast that "the rum-trade" was largely exempt. Liquor dealers "must pay in war time" to keep "the privilege of making paupers and tipplers."[6] With its statements on the civilian tax burden, the ATU was merely rearticulating its opinion that liquor dealers burdened society.

The U.S. Congress may not have been overly concerned about the societal burden of the liquor traffic, but using excise duties on alcohol to generate income certainly appealed to the federal legislators. While the Federal army sought to control liquor rations and sutlers among the soldiers, Congress was keen to take advantage of the vast amounts of capital available in the Northern states by raising both income and excise taxes.[7] In July 1861, the federal government began the process of instituting an excise tax on alcohol that it would maintain and raise throughout the war. The tax was the first federal regulatory measure placed on alcohol in more than four decades. Only twice previously, for brief periods—1791–1802 and 1814–17—had the federal government taxed distilling in order to pay off debts incurred during the Revolution and the War of 1812.[8] After months of debate, in July 1862, Congress placed duties of twenty cents per gallon on all distilled spirits and one dollar per barrel on "all beer, lager beer, ale, porter, and other similar fermented liquors, by whatever name such liquors may be called." Congress raised the duties on distilled liquors to sixty cents per gallon in March 1864, one dollar and fifty cents per gallon in July 1864, and two dollars per gallon in January 1865.[9] While both houses agreed on the necessity of a duty on alcohol, when it came to determining how to apply a regressive tax on distilled and fermented beverages that were aged (where their volume changed over time) or "on hand" when the legislation was passed, congressmen disagreed. The House of Representatives decided not to tax liquor (especially foreign) retroactively, but when it came to lager beer, Congress found itself engaged in a struggle against the increasingly powerful Liquor Dealers' Association. When the excise laws were passed in 1862, Congress made provisions for the aging process and exempted beers that had been placed in storage in February and March 1862 that would not be ready for consumption until September 1862. All beer removed after September 1 would be taxed. In 1865, the Liquor Dealers' Association decided, however, that any beer placed in storage before February 1862 should be exempt from the tax regardless of whether or not it was removed by September 1862. Congress refused to refund their taxes.[10]

Congress's concerns were pragmatic, but Northern temperance reformers found the excise taxes difficult to stomach. On the one hand, Northern reformers hoped that the heavy tax burden might put liquor dealers out of business. On the other hand, reformers maintained that taxation made it seem as though the federal government was tacitly giving its approval for drinking. Reformers not only found the taxes troubling, but they argued that existing state license and Sunday prohibitions needed strengthening in order to protect Northern communities and soldiers from bacchanalian chaos. In Congress, Representatives Josiah Grinnell (Iowa, Union Party) and John Law (Indiana, Democrat) argued that tax rates had moral implications. As Law saw it, reducing the taxes on fermented beverages would encourage Americans to consume more beer and less liquor. When the use of hard spirits decreased, the country would sober up.[11] Thus, when Congress raised duties on distilled liquors in 1864, taxes on fermented drinks remained at just one dollar per barrel.[12] Attempts in 1865 to increase the tax to one dollar and fifty cents per barrel were voted down in the Senate.[13] The American Temperance Union certainly did not argue for lowering taxes on any form of alcohol, but it retreated slightly from its stance that any tax or license law legitimized the traffic. In 1863, the ATU urged the federal government to scale back citizens' general tax burden by imposing higher taxes on liquor dealers. Higher taxes would make alcohol prohibitively expensive for consumers. The trade might cease altogether. The ATU created a petition for its subscribers and encouraged reformers to send it in from all parts of the North. They urged Congress, "in justice and for the benefit of the country," that liquor dealers "should be made to bear more heavily than others the burdens of war." The extra duties would "in some degree compensate for the immense evils" caused by the traffic.[14]

But as the *Journal of the American Temperance Union* acknowledged, the goal of the excise tax was not to put liquor dealers out of business but to use their goods to raise revenue, and the Union therefore benefited from American tippling. In an ironic article reprinted from an exchange paper, the *JATU* somewhat light-heartedly shared the story of "a 'loyal' man" who "got a little heavy about the head." Sensing that a crowd of people were casting silent judgment on him for his drunkenness, the man pointed out that every man who "drinks taxed lickers" was a patriot. "Every blessed drop of licker he swallers is taxed to pay the salaries of them big officers at Washington and support the war," he explained. If "all was to quit a drinking why the war must stop and the Government fail." He, personally, would "rather drink buttermilk, or ginger-pop, or soda-water."[15] Of course, drinking for the good of the war effort was not what reformers had in mind, and the transcriptions of slurred speech and use of quotations around the adjective "loyal" reveal the ATU's true position on licensed liquor. Even so, taxing liquor heavily, they believed, mitigated a few of the harmful effects of alcohol if it relieved Northern civilians of some of their personal tax burdens.

When the conversation moved beyond excise taxes, however, most Northern civilians did not use the war to make a renewed push for prohibition, even in states that had supported prohibition in the 1850s. Rather, many states continued to debate the best way to regulate the flow of liquor. The state of Iowa provides of a good example of the context in which Northern civilians debated prohibition and regulation. Although Iowa shared a border with Missouri and supplied many volunteers to the Union army, the state itself was spared most of the war's acute devastation. As a result, its inhabitants voiced their concerns about liquor without worrying about its role in the conflict. Like many Northern states, Iowa had passed statewide prohibition in 1855, but by 1860, the law had been amended to allow the buying and selling of liquor for "mechanical, medicinal, culinary, and sacramental purposes."[16] This strict licensing law left Iowans divided. By early 1862, Iowa citizens had presented a petition to the state legislature asking it to consider passing more stringent prohibitory measures.[17] In the ensuing debate, state legislators discussed their "duty as men—as members—as Christian men, to do anything ... to aid the community to aid those who cannot help themselves," but they earnestly weighed whether or not prohibition was "utterly inefficient." While the 1855 law had been effective in the interior portions of the state, legislators pointed out that it simply did not work in the river towns. License laws, perhaps, could be better enforced.[18] In an effort to find a workable solution, the Iowa legislature passed "Smith's Civil Damages Liquor Bill"—a law that "empowers parties aggrieved by the sale of liquor to hold the vendor responsible for damages." Without resorting to complete (and unenforceable) prohibition, the legislature had found a way to protect the innocent, which in this case included grown men who purchased liquor, from the evils of the predatory liquor traffic.[19] Iowa's more zealous reformers scoffed. The liquor traffic was "a grievous wrong, a heinous sin, a wanton crime," and such "a fundamental irregularity cannot be regulated." Liquor was so "destructive to the health and morals of the community" and such "a great moral cancer that emollients [in the form of licenses and civil damage laws] cannot remove." Only "extirpation" could be sufficient.[20]

Although Iowans did not reference the war, their prohibition debate offers a good window into the world of Northern temperance reform in the 1860s. Clearly, legislatures were wary of enacting statewide prohibition in the wake the Maine Law failures of the previous decade. Yet it is equally evident that enthusiasm for total abstinence and legal impediments to drinking had not disappeared. That the liquor traffic was sinful—a danger to the physical and moral health of Iowa's communities—was evident. And that the state had a responsibility to protect its citizens from the sale (through prohibition, strict licensing, or civil damage law) was the conclusion Iowans reached.[21]

Throughout the North, folks debated liquor's consequences for the moral health of their communities, often with a nativist bent. A few states, such as Michigan and Massachusetts, continued to debate strenuous license laws throughout the 1860s, with Michigan expanding its laws to heavily regulate the sale of fermented beverages in early 1861, a statute that targeted German American brewers.[22] In other states, discussions of Sunday Laws targeted

German Americans more directly. For decades, native-born Protestants had used Sunday Laws to target religious and ethnic minorities whom they believed threatened the cultural and religious status quo. Nativists glommed on to Sunday Laws as part of their larger crusade against immigrants, arguing specifically that German- and Irish-owned houses of public amusement facilitated crime and threatened American democracy.[23] In the midst of the secession crisis, New Yorkers reopened their debates over amending or repealing their Sunday Laws. Multiple proposals circulated. Christian Woodruff, a member of the State Assembly and part of the Select Committee on Sunday Laws, proposed amending the laws to allow the sale of fermented beverages on Sundays.[24] The state's German American community was truly divided over how to respond. More than a decade of nativist attacks had left German-speaking communities unsure of the best strategy for proving their belonging in American society. Because brewing and spending Sundays at beer gardens were central to German culture, the German Republican Committee suggested repealing Sabbath restrictions altogether. In doing so, they doubled down on preserving a Pan-German identity. But in March 1861, more than four thousand German Americans and other New Yorkers met at the Cooper Institute to speak on the immorality of Sunday drinking, arguing that it would "undermine our free, self-governing institutions." Their opponents decried the Sunday Laws as an assault on their "Liberty." But while the *New York Times* reported that "the Germans are divided in sentiment," the paper also claimed that "Americans are not." Native-born "citizens," according to the paper, "cling to the institution [of Sunday Laws]." That the German Republican Committee, which supported repeal of Sunday Laws for all the working classes, "assumes that the bottle and the theatre are indispensable to the 'enjoyment' of the people on Sunday" appalled the paper's editors, who countered with "the fact that the day of rest is a day of peculiar temptation, unless specially guarded from perversion."[25] Ultimately, when pro-repeal candidates were defeated in New York City's fall elections, the *Vermont Chronicle* rejoiced that the city and state had been "emancipated" from the "social evils" that accompanied Sunday drinking.[26]

Elsewhere in the Union, Sunday Law debates continued throughout the war years. In Chicago, Republican infighting over Sunday sales upended C. N. Holden's candidacy for mayor in early 1862. Holden was both an abolitionist and a prohibitionist, but the city's large bloc of German Republicans swung the election for Democrat Francis Cornwall Sherman, supposedly because they believed he would oppose Sunday restrictions. Whereas Germans considered beer gardens essential to their neighborhoods, other Chicagoans regarded the "saloons and public dance gardens" to be sources of "wide spread demoralization." Although Sherman seemingly cared little about Sunday Laws, he was regarded as "one of the strongest Union men in Chicago." Of course, the reporter never considered that German Americans might have been motivated by his support of the Union, as much as, if not more than, his support for Sunday beer drinking.[27]

By the war's midpoint, however, Sunday Law proponents had more explicitly linked the protection of the Sabbath with the war effort. At a Sabbath Convention in Saratoga, New York, in August 1863, a nativist crowd argued that defending the Sabbath was "essential . . . to the maintenance of public morals, to the progress of our civilization, and to the preservation of our national life, and our civil liberties; and that to guard and defend it against latitudinarian indifference, against the evil influences of civil war, against the assaults of irreligion and vice, and against the corrupting agencies of an immigrant population, unaccustomed to its sacredness and hostile to its restraints, is a clear and irresistible duty of every Christian and of every patriot." Union soldiers must have a guarded Sabbath in order to fight successfully.[28] The implication, of course, was that immigrant civilians and soldiers could compromise the Union war effort with their Sunday drinking.

This hodgepodge of Sunday, license, and civil damage laws is quite emblematic of the state of temperance reform in Northern communities during the 1860s. To say that Northerners had entirely lost their zeal for temperance would be inaccurate. But any effort to affect municipal and state laws had to contend with large German-American voting blocs—which naturally made Republicans wary of supporting prohibition. Nevertheless, when Northerners advocated for restrictions on liquor trafficking, they linked sobriety and morality to American nationalism, and at times, as the New York examples illustrate, argued that temperance, Sunday laws, and the war effort were intertwined.

THE VAST MAJORITY OF NORTHERNERS' conversations about temperance focused on controlling local drunkenness, but the American Temperance Union emphasized the danger the liquor traffic posed to the Union army. Crusaders persuaded soldiers to voluntarily stop drinking by signing pledges and joining camp temperance societies. But, from years of experience, reformers knew who their real targets were: liquor traffickers. Individual men, including soldiers, held some limited responsibility for their actions. But the real sinners, when it came to the liquor problem, were those who supplied it. In the Union, temperance reformers worried about spirit rations, sutlers, and, to an extent, civilian traffickers. Anticipating pushback from other Northerners, the ATU argued that the peacetime arguments against controlling the liquor traffic (that laws should protect property but not control morality) did not apply during wartime. Citing concerns about national stability, reformers concluded that "moral suasion is good in the family, the school, the church; but when we come to the army there, there must be law. Prohibition then, is a right principle sometimes. . . . Shall [society] be deprived of its only defense, because it interferes with the self-indulging humors of men who are resolved in doing as they please, or with the pockets of men who cry out 'By this craft we have our wealth?'"[29] To profit at the expense of the nation was anathema.

Of course, the ATU's first obstacle in convincing the military to combat liquor dealers using martial law was the fact that the army and navy supplied liquor rations. These spirit rations, reformers charged, served no legitimate purpose. Citing claims from the army that whiskey was necessary as a stimulant in cases of fatigue, they pointed out that this was a slippery slope—"the army are always fatigued."[30] Presumably, men would use this excuse to drink all the time (reformers were not wrong about this). Daily rations were the "most dangerous to the physical and moral man."[31] When Generals George McClellan, Benjamin Butler, and Henry Halleck abolished liquor rations in various army departments in the summer of 1862, reformers rejoiced.[32] By September 1863, they were dismayed that rum rations had been restored on the premise of keeping the army healthy.[33] Aghast, reformers continued to decry the risks of whiskey rations. A Pennsylvania woman expressed through poetry Northerners' desires that the military would "Withold [sic] the whisky rations," so that their "cherished ones" would "fall nobly, facing rebel guns" as "good men, and 'temperance sons.'" Whiskey rations compromised a soldier's ability to die a good death. It was not worth the risk.[34]

The ATU wanted to see rations abolished not only in the army but in the navy as well. Of course, reforming the navy was nothing new in the 1860s. During the first half of the nineteenth century, the U.S. Navy had undergone a series of reforms—especially regarding the use of flogging and other forms of corporal punishment—in an attempt to make the institution more palatable to recruits. The abolition of the grog ration fit neatly within this context of reform.[35] By the start of the war, however, the grog ration had reappeared. In the fall of 1861, a U.S. steamer, *R. B. Forbes*, "ran ashore twice near the mouth of the Potomac, and most strangely fired upon a passing ship" (according to the synopsis reported in the *Journal of the American Temperance Union*). Its captain, undoubtedly, was drunk, as it was his habitual state. Such recklessness pointed to the need for the abolition of the spirit ration in the navy and for the ousting of all drunken officers from its ranks.[36] Unlike in the army, where the distribution of rations was left to commanding officers, in the case of the navy, Congress stepped in, abolishing the grog ration in summer 1862. Naval officers decried the action, arguing that Congress acted without knowledge of how the grog ration acted to promote health on the ships.[37] But temperance reformers rejoiced.[38] They had assurances from a naval officer, who wrote to the *New York Tribune*, that drunkenness in the navy was indeed on the wane and had been for some time. For years, most sailors had opted to take bonus pay instead of their daily grog ration (one of the navy's antebellum reforms), and at present, tippling officers had been dismissed from the service.[39]

Beyond abolishing spirit rations in the navy, the ATU wanted civilian authorities to put an end to the liquor trade—especially in areas where it affected soldiers. It not only pressured Congress to take control of liquor rations but also requested that the federal government close shops—at least in areas close to troops. After hearing that drunken soldiers had harassed travelers on the roads between Alexandria and Arlington, reformers argued that "nothing will be of any avail to save our armies but martial law against the traffic."[40] When soldiers acted to destroy rum shops themselves, reformers rejoiced at the effectiveness of "military suasion" and the ad hoc "Maine Law in the Army."[41] Closer to home, reformers implored New York governor Edwin D. Morgan to use his power "as head of the forces of the State" to declare that "military necessity" gave him power to make selling liquor to soldiers an offense punishable with prison time.[42] They also campaigned during the war for statewide prohibition in New York.[43] By the election of 1864, the American Temperance Union announced the need for both a temperance-supporting governor and also "a President and a Congress that shall protect our armies and navies from the alcoholic curse, and set an example which shall be for the salvation of the land."[44]

The ATU may have dreamed of prohibition, but practically, temperance reformers had to settle for controlling sutlers through civil or martial measures. One army correspondent condemned sutlers for robbing soldiers with their "exorbitant prices" and also for "robbing them of their manhood and ruining them forever" by selling them liquor.[45] The Democratic *New York Herald* went even further than the temperance paper, comparing sutlers to extortioners. The paper accused the "unprincipled" peddlers of causing serious problems for the Union soldiers, including deadly battlefield disasters.[46] New Yorkers, joined by Senator Henry Wilson of Massachusetts, called for the federal government to "drive the devils" from Union camps. Not only were they miring soldiers in debt and debauchery, but they represented a more dangerous political foe. The ATU pointed out that sutlers were asking Northern businessmen ("every seller of gingerbread and grog") to raise funds to protect their interests.[47]

The way reformers saw it, any trafficker in spirituous beverages was a political and national liability. Nothing captured their concerns better than when General George Meade placed the sutler system in the Army of the Potomac under the control of Provost Marshal General Marsena Patrick. Though reformers believed they could trust Patrick on some level, they doubted that his personal morality would overcome the problems caused if sutlers were allowed to sell the "deadly poison." Drawing on the historical notion that "men of good moral character" should be the only ones given the privilege of selling ardent spirits, the ATU pointed out the fundamental flaw with the entire system of regulating sutlers. "Thousands" of soldiers would be "ruined because they bought of good men." A moral liquor dealer was nonexistent. Sutlers' laws, like all attempts at regulation, would "prove a failure." Reformers, knowing that the stakes were high—military success and national salvation hung in the balance—implored Northerners to come by "common consent" to suppress the liquor trade.[48]

Beyond the temperance circles, however, Northerners had less to say about controlling the liquor traffic the farther away from the armies they lived. For example, Washington's *Evening Star* diligently reported arrests of those who sold liquor to soldiers and reported on the work of the provost guard to keep order. For the most part, though, the paper offered no commentary on the traffic to soldiers—except to point out that the liquor laws were largely unenforceable, resulting in "high glee" among the liquor dealers.[49] The *Chicago Daily Tribune* concluded in similar fashion, "Proper control of the sutler is scarcely maintained in volunteer regiments," which resulted in about 30 percent of them selling liquor legally and a good many more smuggling it in. Even so, the paper reported that "there is very little dram-drinking except shortly after pay-day, and the volunteers are believed to be more temperate than any European army."[50] In other words, while Northerners may have surmised that the traffic was poorly controlled among the soldiers, with the exception of the temperance reformers, they devoted little newspaper space to calling for stronger regulations of sutlers and liquor traffickers. Moreover, temperance reformers' pleas received little serious attention from Congress. While certainly the abolishment of naval rations and the passing of Wilson's Bill put some limits on supply in the army, for the most part (as illustrated in chapter 4), sutlers continued to ply their trade in the army without much interference from civilian authorities.

FOR NORTHERNERS, wartime regulation of the liquor traffic proceeded much as it had in the late 1850s (much to the consternation of temperance reformers), but Confederates experienced significant changes in the way they regarded the traffic. Before the war, white southerners' biggest concerns related to the liquor traffic were fears that drunken enslaved populations would ravage the country. Southern states thus prohibited enslaved people from drinking in the antebellum era.[51] While there is plenty of evidence that Southern white women continued to fear enslaved men's access to liquor, during the war, Confederate civil authorities shifted their focus away from enslaved men's drinking to focus on controlling distillers, and they turned to prohibition.

While most Northerners (outside of the circles of temperance reform) were far enough removed from the war that they were not acutely concerned with the liquor traffic's effect on the armies, Confederate civilians perceived that they saw the evils of liquor firsthand, and they focused their wrath on distillers and sellers in their neighborhoods. In this way, Southern civilians shared the concerns of commanding officers about the nearly unstoppable liquor trade. In 1863, the Ten Islands Baptist Association of Calhoun County, Alabama, strongly urged citizens to "strike with terror and dismay the sordid retailers of the hellish poison" in order to save them and their customers from hell, but they stopped short of connecting the sin of liquor trafficking to Confederate soldiers and their well-being.[52] Other Confederates made the connection explicitly. In August 1861, the *Richmond Daily Dispatch* suggested that if the "Black Republicans" really wanted to subdue the Confederacy quickly, they could start by removing the blockade "so far as lager beer and whiskey are concerned." Liquor dealers lurked throughout the South, waiting to undercut the war effort from within. Knowing "that intoxicating beverages do more mischief to mankind than any other agency of evil," the editor concluded that the North could do the Confederacy no "greater injury than to let in the liquor." By cutting off the supply, the North was transforming the Confederacy into "a great Tee-total Maine Liquor Law Temperance Society"—inadvertently saving "the souls and bodies of the whole Southern people."[53]

Despite civilians' concerns, in the war's early months, liquor regulation in the Confederacy progressed somewhat like it had in the North, with states moving quickly to tax alcohol to raise revenue. Within six months of the war's beginning, North Carolina, Texas, and Georgia imposed taxes on liquor, with Georgia taxing distillers up to three hundred dollars per year, although the laws varied in their contents and enforcement from county to county.[54] These taxes were components of larger revenue-raising schemes put in place by the states in the war's first years. Financing the war was more important than regulating the liquor traffic.[55] Nevertheless, Southern temperance reformers welcomed the tax laws, arguing that the distilleries were "springing up like dragon's teeth" and becoming a public nuisance. The way reformers saw it, the "degrading and demoralizing affects [sic]" of liquor alone should have been "sufficient to justify a heavy tax." But war made the moral stakes even higher: distillers used up enormous quantities of grain and lined their own pockets while women, children, and even livestock bore the burdens of war.[56] Using the vivid imagery of the antebellum temperance movement, the *Spirit of the Age* accused distillers of letting "down a *pump into hell*" and pouring "over our land, into our houses, over human hearts, over human souls a burning tide of sin and misery and anguish." Through the liquor flowed "widow's tears and orphans' sighs," and money-grubbing distillers promoted "profaneness, indecency, pauperism, madness, suicide, misery, and woe." These men—who put private gain ahead of the public good—could hardly be considered good Confederates.

Significantly, this critique of distilling in the South was not confined to temperance reformers. Confederates quickly decided that taxation was insufficient to control the traffic, and by early 1862, many Southern state legislatures were considering moving beyond taxation and regulation to prohibition. Cutting off soldiers from liquor was certainly one concern, but Confederates were also attempting to mitigate the effects of the Union blockade and shortages caused by a lack of domestic food production. By December 1861, the coasts of North Carolina, South Carolina, and Georgia were closed (and the Mississippi River, likewise, had been closed to traffic since the late summer).[57] The blockade contributed to food shortages but also made whiskey a scarce commodity.[58] These shortages seemingly prompted distillers to raise their prices significantly, and they became more than a nuisance—they were grain-wasting speculators. North Carolina adopted price controls—seventy-five cents a gallon—that would limit profits for distillers with the intention of making the business less lucrative.[59] Other legislation required distillers to register with magistrates in their counties.[60]

At the national level, however, Jefferson Davis and the Confederate Congress were slow to respond to the blockade's transformation of the liquor traffic. The Confederate government certainly tried to crack down on smugglers and blockade runners, but by and large, it overlooked the effects of the blockade on domestic manufacturing.[61] Civilians had a complicated relationship with the blockade. Writing to his wife in 1864, John Bratton lamented that their supply of brandy "had given out," and "whiskey did not answer the purpose" of treating illness. They were desperate, and money should be of no concern. The trick, though, would be to find a blockade runner to sell "two or three bottles of fine French Brandy."[62] People were desperate for spirits, and the Confederate government knew that blockade runners could make significant profits by sneaking luxury items into the starving Confederacy. Congress passed laws in early 1864 that made it illegal to import most alcoholic beverages—including beer, rum, brandy, cider, and wine—for any purpose other than medicinal use.[63] Once there were no guaranteed profits to entice potential smugglers to take the risk, Congress hoped that the liquor flow would ebb significantly.

By the time the national government acted against smuggling in 1864, however, many Confederate states had already passed prohibition to curb domestic manufacturing. The early price controls that North Carolina and other Southern states adopted proved quickly to be ineffective. Not only was Lincoln's blockade contracting the food supply, but the war also decimated the Confederate food-producing regions of Virginia, Kentucky, and Tennessee.[64] In response, by spring of 1862, Tennessee, North Carolina, Virginia, and Alabama had prohibited distilling.[65] In Georgia, Governor Joseph E. Brown flexed his executive muscles to enact prohibition (the state legislature affirmed his proclamation in November 1862).[66] In the fall, South Carolina, which had already placed a moratorium on new liquor licenses, made plans to criminalize the possession of ardent spirits.[67] By January 1863, Mississippi had followed suit, prohibiting distilling, albeit with the caveat that citizens were allowed to produce and sell wine made from native grapes.[68] In short, Southern state legislators who had represented a rural society largely uninterested in temperance prior to the war had come to support prohibition. In doing so, they expanded state authority to regulate business and behavior.

State legislatures defended prohibition as a wartime measure of practical necessity. Politicians, most certainly fearing backlash from rural constituents, explained that the prohibitory measures were practical rather than moral. For example, North and South Carolinians asserted that distillation contributed to an "unnecessary consumption" of cereal grains, such as corn, wheat, rye, and barley.[69] Georgia's Governor Brown likewise recognized that because the farmlands of the upper South had been trampled, the states of the lower South had to abandon cash crops and grow as much food as possible.[70] The governor, however, went a step further than preserving grain when he argued for prohibition. "Gun metal," he continued, was "composed of ninety parts of copper and ten of tin." By happy coincidence, the stills of Georgia were made of copper. Surely, Brown concluded, they could be put to more productive use if they were "manufactured into cannon ... to be turned against the enemy."[71]

Support for prohibition extended well beyond the halls of the state capitols into the rural counties of the states. In Virginia, concerned citizens of the Shenandoah Valley and the southwestern counties organized public meetings and sent petitions to Richmond.[72] They urged the state to prohibit the distillation of grain for the duration of the war, insisting that they were not temperance reformers. In fact, the editor of the *Staunton Spectator* deemed Maine Laws–type prohibition "improper and odious," arguing that this situation was altogether different. "In times of great public emergency," he explained, "the sale of ardent spirits ought to be suppressed as a measure of public safety and military discipline."[73] Many white Southerners who supported prohibition purposefully set themselves apart from the temperance community, which they considered to be meddlesome. Nevertheless, when Confederates debated prohibition—in legislative journals, government records, and newspapers—they often couched their wartime concerns in the same moral arguments against distilling and liquor consumption that temperance reformers had used in the antebellum decades. In other words, in the context of war, support for government regulation of behavior was growing well beyond the confines of the organized temperance movement.

For example, when Georgia's Governor Brown issued his February 1862 proclamation banning distilling, he framed his concerns in moral terms. Brown argued not only that potential foodstuffs and war materiel were being wasted but that the whiskey being manufactured instead was sent to soldiers where Brown believed it "degrades and demoralizes our troops and causes them to be slaughtered, and our flag to train in the dust before the enemy." His language strongly emphasized the moral risk Georgians took if they continued to allow distilling. Brown declared that "the distillation of corn into ardent spirits has grown to be an evil of the most alarming magnitude" because he knew "that about seventy stills" in one county alone were "constantly boiling," daily wasting the grain that could have fed the county's entire population.[74] Like other Confederates, Brown believed that his decision to melt down the stills had Providential, in addition to practical, significance. By converting copper into weaponry, Brown believed that Georgians would merit "God's blessing" for their crusade. If the copper continued to be used for distilling, however, Georgians could expect God's "Curse."[75] For Brown, distilling was so profoundly immoral—because it wasted food and resources and caused soldiers to fight poorly—that continuing to allow it risked God's willingness to fight on the side of Confederates. Because white Southerners (like their Northern counterparts) believed that God would aid whichever nation he has chosen, moral behavior was paramount to the Confederacy's success.

In addition to being concerned about Providence, however, Brown also seemed to allude to the Declaration of Independence in his proclamation. In justifying his executive decision, Brown asserted that the state government—or, in this case, the executive specifically—had the duty to use "its strong arm of power" to "protect the rights" and "promote the happiness" of its citizens.⁷⁶ That it was the duty of the government to facilitate its citizens' pursuits of happiness was certainly an American idea that stretched back to the earliest days of the Republic. It suggests that Brown was doing his part—like so many Confederates—to ensure that Georgia recaptured its dreams of becoming a republican society. Significantly, however, even as Brown imagined a virtuous Georgia working to bring about God's blessings on the Confederacy, he also expressed that Georgians would not behave as proper republicans and Christians unless the state used "its strong arm of power" to compel them. Put simply, while Brown might have chafed at the expansion of the national government in other contexts, he clearly had no difficulty with the concept of the state of Georgia expanding its own authority to regulate morality.⁷⁷

Brown's prohibition laws were seemingly quite popular among certain classes of Georgians, who echoed their governor's moral condemnation of distillers. Decrying distillers for their "moral *crime*" and their "utter lack of *patriotism*," the "sober" and "intelligent masses" of Milledgeville sang the governor's praises.⁷⁸ Brown even claimed that most distillers "acquiesced cheerfully."⁷⁹ The problem, as most citizens understood it, was the profiteers. Georgians declared speculative distilling to be an "evil greater than Yankee invasion" and "wickedly waste[ful]."⁸⁰ Distillers were "bloodsuckers who fatten on the distresses of mankind," who not only did not enlist to fight the Union army, but also "aggravate[d] the poor soldier's burden and suffering" by snatching food out of the mouths of women and children.⁸¹

Throughout the Confederacy, civilians reiterated that the state had a duty to protect women and children from liquor's harm. Virginians urged Richmond to act because they argued that the commonwealth had a duty not only to prevent the soldiers from becoming demoralized by liquor but also to "provide for the families of the absent [soldiers]" by protecting the food supply from greedy distillers.⁸² In South Carolina, for example, the breadstuffs confiscated from unlawful distilleries were given to the soldiers' families who waited "helpless" and "suffering" while their "poor and patriotic men are exposed in defence of our homes."⁸³ In this way, Confederates' arguments in favor of prohibition fit squarely within the tradition of temperance reform, whether they recognized the connection or not. Temperance reformers had long identified women and children as the ultimate victims of the liquor traffic. More than that, though, advocates of prohibition were among those Confederates who believed that the state needed to reenvision its role in order to protect vulnerable women and children in the absence of their husbands.⁸⁴ In other words, Joe Brown was not an anomaly. Confederates' perceptions of the role of the government were shifting and widening.

In practice, creating laws that prohibited speculative distilling was difficult because so many farmers distilled excess grains and fruits for personal use. When it came to prosecuting distillers in Georgia, Brown had urged the legislature to enact stiff penalties and force local officials to enforce them.[85] But the laws were complicated and constantly changing. For example, in the spring and summer of 1862, Brown prohibited the distillation of peaches into brandy—a measure that hurt the state's farmers who sought to preserve their produce and to make medicinal spirits. He revised the law to allow private distillation in cases where drying fruit would not suffice. Still, citizens wanted clarification.[86] Vague laws made it difficult for farmers to determine if they could brew lager beer or distill fruits, potatoes, and molasses privately, and more unscrupulous profiteers found that they could dodge the prohibitions on grain and still make a profit distilling everything else.[87] Likewise, the need to make exceptions for medicinal spirits contributed to the environment in which distilling laws were being "evaded in every way that ingenuity can devise," local authorities hesitated to make arrests, and judges were uncertain that laws passed by the legislature gave them the authority to fully prosecute distillers.[88]

Similar tensions existed in Virginia, where civilians experienced shortages acutely and balked at the notion that they distilled unscrupulously. Men from Rappahannock and Pittsylvania Counties expressed their concern that private citizens would not be able to distill excess grain for their own consumption under the new laws. Pointing out that men were never intended to "live by bread alone," one Virginian urged the legislature to use "common sense" when regulating alcohol. Farmers needed to drink it, and more than that, hogs grew the plumpest on slop left over after the distilling process. Allowing for the private distillation of whiskey, therefore, would help increase the food supply.[89] Even state senator James Whittle, who voted in favor of prohibition, would have preferred a law that allowed farmers to distill their own grain for personal use. Many of his constituents opposed the bill entirely.[90] In the Southwest, supporters of the bill urged legislators to act, despite knowing that there would be "violent opposition to the measure" in rural counties. Politicians who failed to vote for prohibition could be expected to be accused of acting cowardly to "further some miserable personal aims" at the expense of a starving nation.[91] This was the conundrum: any politician or local official who supported legal distilling earned a reputation as a war profiteer, but in reality, many rural Confederates needed to distill their excess grains and fruits in order to survive.

It was hardly the case that Virginia's private distillers were working purposefully to undermine the Confederacy.

North Carolinians, as well, experienced acutely the practical difficulty of enforcing prohibition and distinguishing between farmers and illicit distillers. After North Carolina passed prohibition in 1862, Governor Zebulon Vance received numerous letters from citizens regarding distilling. More than half of those letters were requests from farmers and physicians who wanted permits to distill medicinal spirits.[92] These requests speak to the centrality of distilling in agriculture. At least one North Carolina distiller chose to fight back against prohibition by using the same imagery that his opponents had employed. In January 1863, S. W. Wallace of Coddle Creek asked Governor Vance for a permit to distill some whiskey. The corn crop, he explained, was "scanty" and "unfit for Bread" or hog slop. To prove that he was not interested in profiting, Wallace emphasized that this was not even his corn. The corn in question had been raised by a "worthy lady a soldiers wife with a large family of children" who was running the farm while her husband was at war. Stilling the ruined corn was the only way the woman would have enough money to buy bread to keep her children from starving. This, of course, was the precise problem prohibition was supposed to prevent. Neither Wallace nor the woman was a speculator; both were trying to survive the war.[93] This was the conundrum for Confederate states. On the one hand, legislatures responded to civilian demands that they put an end to the needless and immoral wasting of foodstuffs by speculative distillers. But at the same time, the feasibility of passing prohibition in large agrarian regions was limited. Rural Confederates relied on distilled grains to feed their livestock. Even with popular support, statewide prohibition had its glitches.

THE BIGGEST WEAKNESS OF STATE-LEVEL PROHIBITION was that it pitted Confederate governors against the Confederate military and national authorities in Richmond. The Richmond government had to strike a delicate balance between prohibiting speculation and regulating the scarce food supply while also keeping the military medical departments stocked with alcohol. The laws that the Confederate Congress had passed in early 1864 had made it illegal for blockade runners to smuggle luxury items, such as beer, rum, brandy, cider, wine, and other liquors for anything but medicinal use.[94] This series of laws did little to curtail starvation, but nevertheless made whiskey incredibly expensive, and distilling became more difficult for states to regulate, creating additional problems for the Confederate government. The risk of confiscation and stiff fines deterred the smuggling of ardent spirits, but the

Confederate government also had to act to prevent grain being consumed by distillers. Here the government had to negotiate a middle position, allowing grain to be distilled for medicinal purposes while forbidding its distillation for general consumption. In June 1864, the Confederate Congress passed an act to allow the surgeon and commissary generals to contract with distillers for whiskey, brandy, and other spirits to be used in the army and its hospitals. Authorized manufacturers could set up distilleries and hire laborers but were not allowed to distill more grain than specified by the terms of the contract with the army.[95] This amounted to licensing and trumped any state law that prohibited distilling.

When it came to regulating these contracts for medicinal spirits, most state authorities had little idea of where their jurisdiction began and ended, and in fact often expected the Davis administration to support state prohibition laws. In Georgia, Governor Brown became angry that military contractors had the right to make private arrangements for the production of alcohol while he was attempting to preserve food for his state. Despite statewide prohibition, Brown permitted the contracts, but by November 1862 he had determined that it was "very difficult to prevent abuses of the system."[96] Specifically, Brown clashed with Captain S. G. Cabell, who had made a contract with the Confederate medical purveyor to distill medicinal whiskey in Georgia. Although Brown gave Cabell permission to work with one distiller in one location, Cabell forged copies of his agreement with Brown in order to work with multiple distillers, tripling the amount of whiskey in his possession. If that were not criminal enough, Cabell paid only one dollar and fifty cents per gallon of whiskey, which he then sold to the Confederate army at two dollars and fifty cents a gallon.[97] This type of speculation flourished given the Confederate army's disorganized contract system, and it angered Georgians, who believed that the military was stealing their bread.[98] Brown requested that the Confederate government centralize its distilling operations to one or a few locations in the state so it could be better controlled.[99] Brown continued to butt heads with Confederate commissary-general J. F. Cummings, who was stationed in Atlanta, throughout the war.[100]

Brown begrudgingly acquiesced (more or less), but in Virginia, state officials directly challenged Confederate distilling contracts. Although the General Assembly made provisions for government contracts in 1862, later in the war, Virginia's legislators decreed that no whiskey be distilled in the commonwealth—not even by those under contract to the Confederate government. By January 1864, the *Staunton Spectator* predicted a battle between the Confederacy and the state of Virginia over the matter. As soon as state authorities caught their first distiller, Virginians would learn whether the state "has a right to regulate her own domestic police, or whether she is... a mere municipal corporation subject to the paramount authority of the Confederate Government."[101] In November 1864, the showdown occurred. Congress had stipulated in June that the surgeon and commissary generals could distill ardent spirits for medical purposes and that they would be allowed to erect distilleries. But when the Confederate army began distilling in Botetourt County, the sheriff shut down the operations and brought criminal charges against the officer managing the still. The incident elicited a furious response from Attorney General George Davis, who assured the secretary of war James Seddon that the state of Virginia did not have the power to usurp the authority of the Confederate government. The states were not allowed to interfere with the manufacture of medical supplies any more than they could "prohibit the manufacture of powder, arms, and all the munitions of war, and the enlistment of men." If the national government acknowledged state sovereignty on prohibition, then "the whole war power of the Confederate Government would prostrate at the feet of the State Legislatures."[102]

When it came to distilling, however, Secretary Seddon was engaged in a multiround fight to keep the Confederate government upright. In North Carolina, he and Governor Zebulon Vance had no shortage of disagreements about contracted distillers. On December 31, 1863, Vance sent Seddon an angry letter regarding distilleries in Charlotte and Salisbury, which he believed had contracts to distill thirty thousand bushels of grain for medicinal whiskey. Vance believed the grain should be reserved for the poor, but more importantly, he pointed out to Seddon that the laws of the state of North Carolina prohibited distilling. According to the governor, "no person can under authority of the Confederate Government violate State laws with impunity."[103] Seddon disagreed. North Carolina had "no power to interfere with the Confederate Government in the manufacture or even contracting for such supplies."[104] In fact, North Carolina's own attorney general Sion H. Rogers agreed with Seddon. The Confederate government could continue to distill despite state prohibition laws.[105] For the remainder of the war, Vance, like Brown, was left firing off angry letters to no avail.

While Georgia, Virginia, and North Carolina tussled with the Confederate government over supplying whiskey, the state of Mississippi organized a central whiskey dispensary system that allowed it to control the distillation of grain, provide medicinal spirits for its citizens, and keep Confederate troops supplied with hospital stores. Although Mississippi's legislature had prohibited distilling in 1863, a year later it amended the law to dismantle all distilleries in the state but allow Governor Charles Clark to establish two state-owned distilleries to manufacture and dispense medicinal spirits.[106] The Mississippi legislature hoped the distilling bans, along with cooperation from neighboring Alabama to control rural distilling, could take full effect and preserve food. By August, Clark had set up a system of dispensaries that would facilitate the distribution of this state-produced alcohol.[107] Each Mississippi county not occupied by Union forces appointed a dispenser of whiskey who used county tax money to distill whiskey and distribute it to the residents. By keeping careful records of prescriptions, as well as tables of spirits dispensed and prices, Mississippi kept tabs on alcohol distribution.[108] Prescription records show that in addition to white men, white women and enslaved persons received prescriptions for whiskey, which was often dispensed by the quart. Moreover, through this system, the Mississippi auditor's office controlled—to an extent—the amount of whiskey available to the Confederate army. Confederate soldiers' and officers' names appear regularly in the log books of the county dispensers, indicating that the state of Mississippi, not the Confederate army, held much of the whiskey.[109] Likewise, Clark appointed Major William A. Strong as a dispensary agent, and he produced one hundred gallons of whiskey a day to send at least a portion of it to the Confederate forces. By 1865, Mississippi's state distilleries had sent 3,777 gallons to the rebel army.[110]

With its dispensaries, the state of Mississippi supplied Confederate armies but also addressed its own pressing welfare needs. When drafting the initial legislation, Mississippi's lawmakers provided that the revenue each county generated through the selling of medicinal whiskey would be kept with the counties and used to provide relief for impoverished soldier families, especially families of those soldiers killed or wounded.[111] Aside from aiding soldiers' families, the dispensary system supposedly satisfied medical needs. Physicians writing prescriptions and vouchers for whiskey made special notes when the women needing the alcohol were "destitute soldiers' wives." One physician in Jones County authorized providing one "poor soldier's widow" with free whiskey.[112] By centralizing and limiting distilling, the state of Mississippi tried to simultaneously address food shortages, alcohol production, social welfare, and even medical treatment. Like other states and the military, Mississippi made itself responsible for the well-being of its citizens, particularly vulnerable women and children. Yet unlike Virginia, North Carolina, and Georgia, Mississippi avoided showdowns with the central government.

WHILE CONFEDERATE STATE AUTHORITIES argued they were protecting women and children from speculative distillers who would cause their starvation, Confederate women expressed different concerns in their calls for prohibition, including fears of drunken slaves. White Southerners had often harbored fearful images of African Americans threatening the racial social order as soon as they became drunk. Less than a year before the war in September 1860, Louisianan Sarah Lois Wadley expressed this fear when one enslaved man, Jim Burke, became especially "insolent" after "many of the negro men had gotten drunk." Burke was generally "an excellent servant" when he was sober, but in the midst of his drunken spree the overseer took a stick to him and beat him until he ran off into the woods.[113] The fear of drunken mobs of African Americans hung over the port city of Savannah, Georgia, as well. Echoing the concerns of the Northern temperance reformers, the men of the Jones family complained that the Savannah police were not enforcing the "Sunday ordinance," and as a result, the city's "rum shops are filled with Negroes drinking at all hours of the day and night. Gambling is rampant," and to restore order the city needed "an effective mayor" who could force the police to keep control over the liquor dens. To solve the problem, young Charles Jones ran for the office himself, becoming mayor of Savannah in 1860. But the problem was not simply that gambling and drinking disrupted peaceful Sabbaths for the soberminded.[114] After his election, Charles Jones wrote to his mother that "the present political status of the county" made the "conduct of the Negro population" particularly troubling. Free Black sailors and other "scoundrels" were "attempting to induce [the enslaved population] to leave the state." The rules governing the Black population, both free and enslaved, were not properly being enforced, and as a result, "they have forgotten their places—are guilty of gambling, smoking in the streets, drinking, and disorderly conduct in general." Rum-sellers, all of "foreign birth," were "demoralizing" and "ruining" the enslaved population with their intoxicating beverages.[115]

Once the secession crisis devolved into war, preserving the institution of slavery necessitated keeping whiskey out of the hands of an increasingly restless enslaved population.[116] At least some slaveholders succeeded. When visiting Southern plantations early in the war, William Howard Russell noted the strange relationship between enslaved men and whiskey. On one plantation, many enslaved people were raising poultry on their own time and selling the eggs and meats to white masters. This additional income was "spent in purchasing tobacco, molasses, clothes, and flour," but not liquor. Russell noted that alcohol, despite being slaves' "great delight," was prohibited. While other luxuries were permitted, whiskey—that marker of masculine privilege—was kept out of reach.[117] Drunkenness threatened the order of the plantation household. South Carolinian Mary Chesnut recounted one instance where

Caroline Preston (presumably because of her husband's absence) had to wrest the butcher knife from the hands of her drunken footman, who "was keeping everybody from their business" by "threatening to kill any one who dared go into the basement." As the rest of the kitchen staff ran about, "screaming and shouting," Preston approached the footman, who 'was bellowing like a bull of Bashan," took the knife from him, locked him in an "empty smoke-house," and returned to her dinner guests, having restored order to her kitchen. Her ability to prevent the drunken man from destroying her dinner party earned her the title of "heroine" in upper-crust Richmond.[118] That being said, that her enslaved footman had access to liquor and took advantage of the absence of male slaveholders validates the observation Charles Jones had made the year before: political upheaval undercut slavery and left enslaved men feeling more empowered to drink (and challenge white women's authority). As traumatic as a spoiled dinner party might have seemed in 1862, by the war's later years, Southern slaveholders had bigger worries. Lincoln's Emancipation Proclamation, coupled with the encroachment of the Federal army, had white Southerners on the home front in a constant state of panic.

Throughout the South, the presence of whiskey and the Union army heightened white Southerners' fears of disorder among enslaved peoples. In 1864, Virginian Judith McGuire worried that the arrival of Union forces and the availability of alcohol would inspire her slaves to make a run for freedom. When Union soldiers invaded McGuire's plantation, the enslaved people found the mix of whiskey and "Abolition preachers" too much to resist. When the Northern soldiers finally left, McGuire remarked somewhat sarcastically that all the enslaved people had "gone to Canaan, by way of York River, Chesapeake Bay, and the Potomac." Of course, from her perspective, the aspirations of freedom brought about by Union soldiers and alcohol were nothing more than delusions. McGuire pitied her former servants whom she had once regarded "as humble friends and members" of her family. While they had "gone with blissful hope of idleness and free supplies," once they sobered up and found themselves in the cold North, they would live in poverty and disease, and "many of them [would] die without sympathy."[119]

White Southerners may have believed that alcohol led their slaves down the road to ruin, but at the same time, they feared free African Americans might use alcohol to assert their freedom. Late in the war, plenty of enslaved Southerners had all but concluded that slavery was doomed, and in Montgomery, Alabama, a "crowd of colored gentlemen" took "possession of a grog shop" one January night. These men consumed large amounts of whiskey, according to the *Daily Mail*, and an altercation broke out between them and the city marshal. The enslaved men were arrested and convicted of unlawful assembly and received thirty-nine lashes.[120] That white Southerners feared drunken Black men was evident in the South Carolina Lowcountry as well. In March 1865, Charlotte Ravenel and her neighbors in St. John's Parish became caught in the middle of raids between local scouts and Union soldiers. "Four Yankee negroes" who had drunk "a quantity of wine" roused up support among "a good many plantation negroes." Armed and "mounted on anything they could find," the men rode through the parish "in a drunken state," raiding plantation homes.[121]

The image of the drunken Black Yankee soldier weighed heavily on many white Southern minds. After the battle of Brice's Crossroads in June 1864, the *Atlanta Appeal* sprang to the defense of Confederate soldiers who had routed the Union soldiers and had murdered Black troops rather than taking them prisoner. From the Atlanta paper's perspective, the Union soldiers serving under General Samuel Sturgis deserved "their instant execution." As Sturgis and his men moved through Tennessee and Mississippi, local whites reported gruesome atrocities committed by the "drunken brutes" who sought to avenge the massacre of their comrades at Fort Pillow. Confederates charged the "negro mercenaries" with raping white women, using descriptive words such as "a dozen fiends," "savage lusts," and "remorseless fiends in human shape." Their supposed beastly inhumanity wreaked havoc on the "poor frightened people" who became their victims. The "sufferings" of the white Southerners, according to the *Appeal*, were "such as never before were inflicted upon human creatures." The Black men's purported beastly behavior, instigated by white officers, left "humanity . . . appalled."[122] Foreshadowing the archetype of the Southern Black beast rapist that would gain prominence in the postwar decades and serve as an excuse for lynching, the *Atlanta Appeal* juxtaposed the image of the helpless white woman against the drunken brutish Black soldier. By arguing that African American soldiers could not control their violent lust while intoxicated and angry, they not only justified the killing of Black soldiers by General Nathan Bedford Forrest but also set the tone for postwar race relations: Black men who violated the social order by drinking and becoming soldiers could be killed.[123]

Although the Confederate military found justification for executing (or enslaving) Black soldiers, Confederate civil authorities did not include undermining slavery on the list of distillers' sins. In fact, when it came to seeking protection from drunken slaves or Black or white Union soldiers, white Southern women turned to their Union occupiers. After Federal forces occupied Murfreesboro, Tennessee, in the spring of 1862, Kate Carney and other women enthusiastically declared their support for the Confederacy and

Jefferson Davis. An intoxicated soldier became "so enraged" that he "jumped over the fence [and] rushed into the house saying he considered the ladies under arrest." The outraged women then sent for Federal guards, who hauled the drunkard off to jail.[124] Although they laughed off the incident, these Confederate women laid claim to protection from Union troops and requested guards to remove disorderly soldiers from their presence. When Yankee soldiers poured into Richmond after the fall of Petersburg, Judith McGuire and other women were terrified and did not sleep as "Federal soldiers were roaming about the streets; either whiskey or the excess of joy had given some of them the appearance of being beside themselves." When the unruly Yankees occupied the lawn of one of her neighbors, McGuire wasted no time requesting that the provost-marshal place a guard at her house, demanding Federal protection.[125]

For some Confederate women, the threats of drunken Union soldiers and freedpeople were intertwined. Shortly after the Confederate surrender at Appomattox, Eliza Frances Andrews heard about the "depredations" the Union soldiers were committing as they took "peaceable possession" of her Georgia county. In one instance, they broke into a neighbor's cellar and consumed "as much of his peach brandy as they could hold." What they could not drink, they ruined with their spit, and then they "strut about the streets of Washington with negro women on their arms ... sneak[ing] around into people's kitchens [and] tampering with the servants and setting them against the white people."[126] From Andrews's perspective, conditions deteriorated over the summer, as the town became increasingly "crowded with 'freedmen' every day." To add to the chaos the women felt, Mary Semmes and Andrews had been "almost knocked down" when two intoxicated Union soldiers had seemingly charged them in the street while "whooping and yelling with all their might." Whether the men had purposefully targeted the women or were simply running wild is hard to know, but from the women's perspective, the men were acting aggressively and whiskey was in large part responsible.[127] Southern white women seemed comfortable turning to Union military authorities when Confederate military and civil authority collapsed.[128]

THE VARIED RESPONSES TO CONTROLLING LIQUOR in the Union and Confederacy illustrate the state of transition of Americans' strategies for policing the liquor traffic. Northerners, having experimented with statewide prohibition in the 1850s, were more apt to use license laws and excise taxes to regulate and profit from the selling of liquor. Although temperance reformers called for more stringent measures to protect soldiers and save the nation, other Northerners who lived away from the war's effects did not so readily connect license laws and the war effort. Nevertheless, when it came to debating Sunday Laws, tensions reveal that Northerners were very much actively debating the relationship between drinking and good citizenship. Sunday Law debates that pitted immigrants and working-class Americans against the native-born (and seemingly more affluent) suggests that Northerners had conflicting notions of masculinity and its relationship to patriotic duty. These conflicts over the morality of Sunday Laws continued in the decades following the war, as would heated debates between the merits of taxation and regulation versus outright prohibition.[129]

But if the Union positions on prohibition during the war showed continuity with the late 1850s, for Confederates, the war brought a shift in public attitudes toward prohibition. Whereas before the war, white Southerners had been most concerned with controlling Black Southerners' access to liquor, during the war, state authorities shifted their focus almost entirely to controlling white men, especially soldiers and distillers. Controlling the population and resources were suddenly paramount. As their Northern counterparts had discovered in the 1850s, Confederates found statewide prohibition nearly impossible, especially given liquor's medicinal uses and a national government not interested in prohibition. Despite wartime prohibition's shortcomings, white Southerners emerged from the war much more comfortable with state control over the liquor traffic, similar to the ways in which they accepted the other far-reaching and centralized aspects of Confederate government authority.

Taken together, Northern and Southern states' responses to the liquor problem during a time of war foreshadowed the approaches states (and eventually the federal government) would take to controlling the liquor traffic in the late nineteenth century. Southern states pivoted toward state control, and dispensaries, licenses, and excise taxes emerged as profitable mechanisms for controlling the flow of spirits that were (perhaps) more amenable to both the general population and liquor dealers. In fact, Mississippi's dispensary system, despite being an anomaly during the war, was simply a precursor to the postwar state dispensaries that balanced regulation and revenue.[130] Regardless of how states sought to control liquor, distillers, traffickers, and drinkers were becoming increasingly conflated with disloyalty. While the fiery rhetoric often originated with temperance reformers, both Unionists and Confederates beyond the membership rolls of the temperance societies argued that their political opponents were drunks, that distillers threatened national well-being, and that drunken soldiers and officers endangered the nation.

CHAPTER SIX

Drinking, Duty, and Disloyalty

On May 24, 1861, Elmer Ellsworth, colonel of the 11th New York Volunteers, crossed the Potomac River with his Zouaves to take down a Confederate flag that had been hoisted in Alexandria, Virginia, and could be seen from the White House. After capturing the flag, Ellsworth was shot and immediately became a hero for the Union. His death became a rallying cry as Northern men enlisted. Northern temperance reformers lauded Ellsworth as "a perfect model" of a sober soldier and officer. Despite Zouaves' reputation for disorderly behavior, Ellsworth's soldiers—rugged firefighters from New York—were prohibited from drinking, smoking, or visiting grog shops. Ellsworth never drank, reformers pointed out, and as a result had "remarkable health of body," "vigor," and "controlling power of mind"—traits that would benefit all Union troops.[1] His death, they assured themselves, would not end his influence, but his legacy of "manly effort" and "virtuous self-denial" would encourage other young men to act bravely and responsibly in the face of war.[2] With the fate of the nation hanging in the balance, temperance reformers quickly drafted pledges to engage Ellsworth's memory for useful purposes and encouraged young officers and enlistees to sign as they went off to war. Only sober officers and soldiers could rescue the country from the unprincipled secessionists. In the eyes of many Americans, especially temperance reformers, Ellsworth became a symbol of the ideal patriot and manly leader. He was sober, disciplined, and courageous.

The worship of Ellsworth's self-denial was largely a Northern phenomenon—in fact, Confederates perceived Ellsworth's Zouaves as cutthroats who ruthlessly invaded Virginia's soil—but Southern temperance reformers nevertheless believed that winning the war required the same traits of self-discipline and sobriety that their Northern counterparts had.[3] The South Carolina Tract Society assured its young readers that "strict temperance" would directly influence *"the health and vigor of both mind and body"* and cited Martin Luther and Isaac Newton as examples of great temperate minds. As men marched off to fight the enemy, they were reminded that Samson's strength rested with his sobriety. Even with such historical examples, reformers worried that the soldiers would drink at least moderately. Teetotaling Confederates knew that consuming ardent spirits was often a marker of privilege in Southern communities. To try to dissuade young officers from becoming enamored with the privileges their military rank afforded them, reformers reminded the men that most kings and princes, men in the highest positions of leadership, avoided "strong drink"; furthermore, they added, liquor had become increasingly "disparaged in the most moral and intelligent circles." These young "gentlemen" would become "martial heroes" when they went off to battle, but whether they became "moral heroes" was yet to be determined, for "moral heroism" required "fortitude and self-denial." The Confederacy required moral, not just martial, heroes "not to sully or sink her cause by surrendering [themselves] to so ignoble a foe as Whiskey."[4]

With these examples, Northern and Southern civilians set out very clearly the masculine characteristics they believed were vital to winning the war. It was up to all men—inside and outside of the ranks—to perform this restrained and self-sacrificing version of manly behavior to fulfill their patriotic duty. Although this definition of masculine patriotism was rooted in prewar republican ideals that mostly reflected the values of middle-class evangelicals, during the war, these values became a measuring stick by which to determine which men were good patriots and which were not.[5] Generals down to the rank and file had their service and masculinity judged by the extent of their sober patriotism. Immigrant and African American men were forced to prove they belonged in society based on these sober, masculine ideals. Ultimately, civilians such as distillers, businessmen, and politicians had their wartime behavior judged based on how much whiskey they consumed or trafficked.

CONCERN THAT DRUNKEN MEN ENDANGERED the cause provoked anxieties about generals who civilians worried were intoxicated during engagements. Generals who drank, it was thought, were responsible for defeats in battle. Civilians freely speculated about the morals of men in high command, especially in the wake of losses. At the same time that they worried about drunkenness, however, civilians also tended to assume that sober generals would be successful in their martial endeavors. Both the Union and Confederate publics looked for men they could hold up as examples of moral heroism. Civilians, especially temperance reformers, were quick to conflate moral health, physical fitness, and martial success; the generals themselves pushed back against this notion.

Northern temperance reformers lamented the ruinous effects of whiskey on the war effort, and they praised generals who kept it out of the ranks. The *Journal of the American Temperance Union* claimed that drunkards were a worse problem than disloyalty: "treason can be punished with death, while drunkenness secures all the results of treason, and goes unpunished."[6] Two months later, in December 1862, the editorial staff continued its lament. Drunkenness had worsened the "present national calamity" by creating a group of officers so incompetent that they presided over the "grossest blunders in the management, and the most disheartening and murderous defeats in battle."[7] The rebels, it seemed, were not the only enemy; the Union army defeated itself with its drinking.[8] Northern temperance reformers celebrated when two men, Generals Neal Dow and Oliver Otis Howard, who had been soldiers in the battle against alcohol for decades, received commissions in the Union army. Dow and Howard became moral heroes instantly, and temperance reformers overlooked their less-than-sterling performances on the battlefield.

When Neal Dow, the architect of the Maine Law of 1851, was appointed colonel of the 13th Maine in the fall of 1861, he seemed the perfect example of moral manhood. His men of "true temperance principles" would be prompt, efficient, and orderly.[9] Maine reformers even likened the regiment to one of Oliver Cromwell's—the men had "united *faith and works*" in their noble struggle against "outraged tyranny."[10] Under Dow's leadership, these sober soldiers would find success. For his part, Dow became the eyes and ears of the *Journal of the American Temperance Union*, corresponding regularly with updates on the state of morality among the troops. He applauded their efforts and encouraged them as they worked diligently to rid the Union army of that "terrible enemy to the soldier," which "kills far more of them than fall on the battlefield."[11] Temperance reformers were not surprised when Dow was promoted to brigadier general. But when he was relegated to a command at Ship Island, Mississippi, they complained about the lack of opportunity the position offered him, and they concluded that "wine and brandy drinking officers" had colluded to "thrust him into the back ground" (away from major military action) because they hated "his temperance principles."[12] Even after Dow was captured and imprisoned in Richmond, reformers worried, for undoubtedly his imprisonment was "humiliating" and trying. Dow's "strong anti-slavery principles exposed him to the deep hatred of the rebels; his temperance principles to the cold shoulder of many officers."[13] Dow became an invaluable representative for the temperance cause, and he fought two enemies: the rebels and the Northern drunkards. Any misfortunes he experienced came from those threatened by his unwavering temperance, rather than any personal or professional shortcoming.

Another general from Maine rivaled Dow in popularity among teetotalers. Oliver Otis Howard, commander of the 3rd Maine who eventually took command of the Army of the Tennessee in 1864, hated two things: drunkenness and profanity. Those two vices were "the worst enemies" Union soldiers would encounter. Profanity would "set us as rebels against God, and drunkenness makes us worse than rebels at home."[14] His intolerance for both made him a useful ally of chaplains and reformers in the field, who had little trouble convincing him to prohibit the commissary from selling any more of the rum which was "probably" full of "poisonous strychnine."[15] Howard also won plaudits from abstainers on the home front, who overlooked his military shortcomings. Early in the war, Howard gained some notoriety for fighting bravely, first at the Battle of Fair Oaks, where he was seriously wounded, and then at Fredericksburg. Howard earned the confidence of Union officials and replaced Franz Sigel as commander of the 11th Corps shortly before the Battle of Chancellorsville. After the disastrous Union performance, many Northerners blamed the German American soldiers, including division commander General Carl Schurz, for being routed during Stonewall Jackson's famous flank attack at Chancellorsville.[16] But temperance reformers took little notice of Howard's involvement with the Chancellorsville disaster. They criticized General Joseph Hooker, but their only mention of Howard's role in the battle came near the end of the war when they noted that his name was "brilliantly associated" with Chancellorsville, as well as every other engagement with which he had been involved. Reformers were more enthralled with his "cosummate [sic] bravery and intrepidity upon a field of action," "established integrity," "Christian fortitude," and "natural imperturbation." The general had been stamped "as one of God's own men."[17] That neither Howard nor Dow commanded sober soldiers to decisive victories registered with temperance reformers, who blamed the suspected drunken men around the generals for all their shortcomings.

For generals whose commitment to teetotalism was not well documented, temperance reformers looked to their record in battle for evidence of their morality. And in their quest to save the Union, reformers kept their rumor mill working around the clock. Reports of drunken incompetence began to circulate shortly after the disastrous Federal performance at Bull Run in July 1861. Commanding general Irvin McDowell insisted the men were too inexperienced to fight, but Lincoln ordered the advance. Northerners blamed McDowell for the catastrophe and accused him of drunkenness although he had "never tasted anything stronger than a water-melon in all his life."[18] In fact, some soldiers in German regiments even considered him "obnoxious" because he "objected to the barrels of lager and the cases of wines and liquors which increased the wagon trains and delayed movements."[19] So committed was McDowell to temperance that after he fell off his horse one day while reviewing troops in 1862, the "staff surgeon endeavored to get some brandy into his mouth, but his teeth were rigidly set and the effort was unsuccessful." When McDowell regained consciousness, he proudly noted that "brandy could not be forced down his throat," even when he was not in control of his faculties.[20] Nevertheless, this veteran of the Mexican War had been accused of drunkenness in the past, mostly due to his clumsy mannerisms and his knack for blushing when he was nervous.[21] After the defeat at Bull Run, Northerners needed to blame someone, and so they accused McDowell of drunkenness. There was no truth to the accusation, but Northerners seemed unwilling to accept the notion that the rebels had won the battle because of superior military prowess. Instead, the Federals could only have defeated themselves by putting their army under the leadership of a man who they concluded must have been drunk.[22] The rumors flew again after McDowell's failure at Second Bull Run. Soldiers blamed him for the losses, calling him a traitor.[23] The rumors from soldiers and civilians held enough weight that a court of inquiry convened to investigate McDowell's conduct.[24] It concluded that the charges were unfounded, and McDowell cleared his name. Yet the controversy revealed the power of suspicion and the assumption that a losing general was likely intoxicated. A man who did not measure up—who experienced failure—could be accused of drunkenness and treachery, without any hard evidence, and then the rumor could exist on its own and plague the officer throughout the war.

Whatever problems Northerners thought they had with McDowell, they paled in comparison to those that accompanied General Joseph Hooker, whose drinking was well known and much discussed. After taking command of the Army of the Potomac in December 1862, Hooker issued an order allowing whiskey rations for the soldiers, much to the consternation of chaplains and temperate officers.[25] More troubling than the whiskey rations were Hooker's own habits. When, in early 1863, rumors of his tippling had spread, Confederates had a field day. The Richmond press suspected that his surname originated from his ability to hook a bottle. So talented a drinker was he that "Temperance Society people once talked of employing him to destroy all the ardent within fifty miles around.... Precious little liquor would have been left for any other drunkard after Joe had gotten a swig at the bottles." This, concluded the *Dispatch*, was the reason he had been given command of the Army of the Potomac. The Union soldiers, much demoralized by heavy drinking, would be restored to sobriety with Hooker in command. The general would drink "all the whiskey himself."[26]

Northerners were understandably less amused, and after Chancellorsville, rumors spread in and out of the ranks that Hooker had been too drunk to command effectively. "Nearly all are very bitter on Hooker," wrote artillery officer Charles Wainwright on May 7, 1863, "and many accuse him openly of being drunk." Wainwright, for his part, thought Hooker had shown no signs of intoxication during the battle, but that did not keep "every tongue in the army" from "wagging its fastest."[27] Francis Adams Donaldson thought that, like so many commanders, promotion to general "overcame" Hooker and he "commenced that infernal tippling." Donaldson swore that he witnessed the general, "during the heat of battle, guzzling (I can call it by no other name) wine instead of attending to his duties." The Union defeat at Chancellorsville would "be placed among the other thousands of disasters wrought by rum." More than that, Donaldson reasoned that Hooker was "of no further use to the cause" because the soldiers had lost confidence in his ability to lead them into battle without needlessly risking their lives.[28] Military physician John Vance Lauderdale agreed. While working at New York's Bellevue Hospital, Lauderdale heard the news that the army had "been whipped by the Rebels again!" Lauderdale dismissed Hooker as useless for "conducting an attack while his brain was stupefied with liquor."[29] The gossip reached Gideon Welles, who spent weeks after the battle trying to determine whether or not Hooker was drunk during the fight. No one in the War Department could corroborate the stories, but Welles expressed much relief when Hooker was replaced by George Meade in June 1863, as Welles had suspected that "liquor" was the cause "of the sudden paralysis which befell the army" at Chancellorsville.[30]

Hooker's removal did not squelch suspicion surrounding his character. Americans needed a place to lay blame for the defeat, and prolific temperance reformer Henry Ward Beecher cranked up the rumor mill at a meeting of the National Temperance League in England by accusing Hooker of drunkenness. His comments were subsequently picked up by the *New York Independent*, and Congress launched an inquiry into the matter. When pressed for more information, Beecher became cagey, refusing to reveal his sources and leaving Congress to question the Union officers about Hooker's frame of mind during the battle. If Hooker had been intoxicated, his fellow generals either did not know it or were not willing to admit it. Daniel Sickles, Alfred Pleasonton, and Daniel Butterfield all testified to his sobriety, although Pleasonton noted that "his whole manner was that of a sick person." Butterfield went further, comparing the allegations that trailed Hooker to those that had plagued McDowell. The accusations had to be based in "malice; upon the general principle that when a man attains a high position people are always found to carp at him and endeavor to pull him down."[31] Whether the officers were closing ranks or being truthful is impossible to know, but independent accounts by George Meade and Carl Schurz both indicate that Hooker, despite his colorful past, had indeed sobered up before Chancellorsville. In April 1863, Meade assured his wife that he could "bear testimony of the utter falsehood of the charge of drunkenness." Hooker had been sober since Meade had known him.[32] Schurz thought, though, that Hooker's sobriety was a novelty, and even blamed that sick look that Pleasonton had noticed on the fact that Hooker's "brain failed to work because he had not given it the stimulus to which it had been habituated."[33] With Hooker, no one reached any definitive conclusions about his character. Nevertheless, the accusations hurled at him and McDowell speak to the ability of military defeat to shape the narrative about a man's morality, if there was no long public record of temperance pledges.

Perhaps no Union general's drinking came under so much scrutiny as Ulysses S. Grant's. Rumors of intoxication dogged his military career, beginning with a supposed bout of drunkenness while he was stationed on the Pacific Coast in the 1850s that was reported to have resulted in his resignation from the U.S. Army under threat of court-martial. Nearly ten years later, when Grant began to move up in the ranks of the Union army, his suspected drinking once again became fodder for gossip. Even before the Battle of Shiloh, Stephen Minot Weld was distressed to hear that Grant had been promoted to major general. He had heard that the general was "a man of great energy and a laborious worker," but he also knew from another (unnamed) general that Grant was "just as likely to be drunk in the gutter as to be sober."[34] Questions surrounding Grant's drinking swirled throughout the war. Rumors were spurred on, in part, by conflicts with Generals Henry Halleck and John McClernand. Grant also suffered from migraine headaches and drank to control the pain. When he drank, he could not hold his liquor well, but his wife, Julia, and close friend John Rawlins successfully encouraged him to avoid spirits. Often during the war, Julia stayed with him at his headquarters, where she not only nursed him through his headaches but also quieted the rumor mill. Under his wife's domestic influence, civilians believed, the general could not become intoxicated.[35]

Nothing could completely stop people from speculating about his habits. After businessman John Murray Forbes voiced his suspicions of Grant's drunkenness, *New York Evening Post* editor William Cullen Bryant insisted that Grant was "a temperate man," and that he had "a batch of written testimonials to that effect." No one close to the general had seen him drink.[36] After being sent by Edwin Stanton to monitor Grant's progress with the Army of the Tennessee in 1863, Charles A. Dana concluded, despite the accusations of McClernand, that the general was sober, a claim he would maintain throughout and after the war.[37] Whether they were true or not, Dana's observations of Grant carried significant weight. After hearing from Dana in August 1863 "that Grant doesn't drink," diarist George Templeton Strong found himself increasingly convinced of Grant's sobriety. By the end of 1864, Strong and his fellow Sanitary Commission officers, who were stationed near Petersburg, were firmly convinced that Grant had a "singleness of purpose," an "entire devotion to his work," and a remarkable ability to work well with other officers.[38]

Northern temperance reformers needed convincing; they were nervous about Grant. If a patriotic leader had to be sober to achieve victory and national salvation, a drunkard at the head of the army signaled disaster. Grant perplexed them. When it came to figuring out his drinking habits, reformers relied on eyewitness accounts and battlefield evidence. According to staff member Major E. D. Osborn, whose assessment of Grant's character was printed in the *Journal of the American Temperance Union* a few months after the capture of Vicksburg, Grant looked "more like a chaplain than a general" when he sat with his wife and children. The general embodied middle-class virtues: he was "brave," "cool to excess," "always hopeful," and "more pure and spotless in his private character than almost any man" Osborn had ever known.[39] Another correspondent offered a similar assessment in August 1864: "Grant does not drink, does not swear, does not tell his plans, and does not have his picture taken!" He was a model patriot, sharing hardship with his men, avoiding vices, possessing many of the "qualifications necessary in a good General."[40] If the assurances of those close to Grant did not convince Northern teetotalers of Grant's temperance, his military record spoke for itself. Remembering Shiloh, a contributor to the *Journal* concluded that Grant had not been drunk during the battle "as alleged," because if he had been intoxicated, "he never would have gained a victory." He had also been "assured by one who was present with him all the time" that the general had not allowed "a drop of liquor to pass his lips."[41] Those assurances were important, to be sure, and set reformers' minds at ease, but his conclusions about Grant's character are important. When civilians had doubts about a man's drinking habits, they looked for proof of morality in victory. Using the argument often made by factory owners in the new industrial age, reformers addressed Grant directly and pointed out that he was tasked with guiding the "vast machine" of the army—a machine more complicated than any of the industrial factories that moved "with perfect regularity," a machine composed entirely of "living, intelligent, conscious and voluntary agent[s]." Grant's job, as commander, was to make the machine work to bring about victory.[42] Unlike McDowell and Hooker, Grant passed the test by winning battle after battle. Therefore, he had to be sober.

Confederates looked for moral heroes who would turn the tide of war in their favor, but in the war's early months, they had to work diligently to turn shady characters into upright officers who fought valiantly for a moral cause. An interesting example of their recrafting efforts was General John B. Floyd, the former secretary of war under James Buchanan who had been accused of fraud and treason against the United States during the 1850s. Although Floyd might not have fit the bill as a hero in the eyes of most Americans, shortly after the war began, the *Richmond Dispatch* published a piece lauding his "bravery and military sagacity." He had "not ma[d]e a single mistake" in fighting at the Battle of Carnifex Ferry; as for his personal habits, Floyd "neither drinks, nor gambles, nor uses profane language." He treated his soldiers and officers with respect and care, and he did not allow them "to injure any private or public property." Virginians, the editors believed, should look on Floyd as a "protector" and a patriot who would be successful, in time, "in driving the enemy from their soil."[43] John Floyd turned out to be a poor choice for a military hero. Less than a year later, in February 1862, Floyd turned tail and ran with several of his regiments when the Confederate surrender of Fort Donelson was imminent. Had Floyd surrendered, he risked being charged with and hanged for treason for his prewar antics, so he and General Gideon Pillow left their comrade General Simon Bolivar Buckner to bear the responsibility of surrender while they escaped safely up the Cumberland River.[44] The *Richmond Dispatch* continued to laud the bravery of the Confederate soldiers who defended their homes while condemning the savage Yankee murderers. Still, the day after the surrender, the paper reported a Washington news source that let Virginians know that when "the fact of Floyd having ran was announced [in the House of Representatives], it was greeted with applause and laughter." Virginia's hero had become a laughingstock.[45]

Floyd fell short of the mark, but Confederates quickly replaced him with better models of military and moral manhood: Generals Thomas "Stonewall" Jackson and Robert E. Lee. To be certain, images of Jackson and Lee have been manipulated by hagiographers since the war's end, and both generals' moral characteristics have been amplified by Lost Cause enthusiasts bent on presenting Confederate heroes as morally upright. Nevertheless, both men's aversion to alcohol has been well noted by historians, and soldiers and civilians praised the generals and took pains to follow their examples.[46] Jackson's fervent Presbyterian faith and strong penchant for cold water—both as a beverage and as a curative—were well known among Confederates. From the time he was a young man at West Point, Jackson had avoided liquor. Partly for health reasons, he followed a bland diet and drank mostly water. According to a few friends, though, Jackson reportedly liked the taste of whiskey quite a bit and avoided it because he feared he would turn into a drunkard if he imbibed too regularly.[47] Confederates were captivated by his dietary oddities, and rumors circulated. A friend's encounter with Jackson left Charles Minor Blackford, an officer in the Army of Northern Virginia, fascinated. Although the man had offered the general "every variety of strong drink," Jackson accepted only buttermilk. According to Blackford, "his refusing to take something stronger did not lower him in his [friend's] estimation." Instead it "emphasized his admiration."[48]

Lee avoided the bottle as well. From the time he was a young man, Lee seems to have purposefully set out to dodge some of his father Light Horse Harry Lee's misfortunes, consciously choosing to emulate his mother's evangelical habits rather than his father's reckless ones. But even though he chose a life of self-control, his conversion to teetotalism was a gradual evolution. In the decades before the war, Lee, though a nondrinker himself, continued to follow Virginian patterns of hospitality, serving wine and spirits to house guests. Over time, Lee had decided that providing alcohol merely facilitated bad habits, so he stopped.[49]

Lee especially believed that spirituous liquors and military service were a volatile mix. Two years before the war began, Lee stressed the dangers of consuming alcohol to his son, Fitz Lee, who was preparing to depart for military service. The deprivations of army life would increase temptations to drink, at least in part because there would be nothing else to pass the time. He feared that soldiers thought of ardent spirits as "a substitute for every luxury." The elder Lee knew that strong drink would often be offered as a form of hospitality, but he urged his son to avoid whiskey altogether because "its temperate use is so difficult."[50] In this regard, Lee was not unlike Jackson, and their belief that an occasional drink of whiskey would eventually lead a man down the slippery slope to drunken ruin put them firmly in the camp of other temperance reformers. Confederate soldiers listened to Lee and used him for inspiration in their own attempts to practice self-restraint. On the inside cover of his diary, Confederate soldier John Baxter Moseley fastened a newspaper clipping featuring a quotation from Robert E. Lee: "Whisky—I like it, I always did—and that is the reason I never use it." Moseley, committed to remaining sober throughout the conflict, seemingly kept the quotation to remind him daily to follow the example of Lee, the great Confederate leader.[51] Moderation was difficult, many soldiers and civilians agreed. And in the ranks, a soldier could best do his duty if he avoided whiskey altogether. Having high-ranking officials to emulate made the goal of abstinence easier to achieve, and an army of teetotaling soldiers led into battle by a sober general would certainly bring about victory.

Other Confederate officers fell short of moral perfection, and among them, Jubal Early was notorious. Early was a colorful character—he liked women, strong drink, and strong language. Rumors of heavy drinking dogged him throughout the war: some officers complained about his behavior; soldiers noted his fondness for apple brandy.[52] By 1864, Early's habits had caught up with him, and after Confederates under his command were defeated at the third Battle of Winchester, politicians throughout the South began to call for an investigation into the general's drinking habits. Hard evidence of his drunkenness proved difficult to find, but Early nevertheless launched an impassioned defense of his character and his skills as a commander.[53] Early implored his friend, Colonel Alexander R. Boteler, to publish a letter in the *Richmond Enquirer* refuting the charges that his being "very drunk at Winchester" had caused "disaster." "God only knows," emphasized Early, "how ... faithfully I have labored for success in this campaign."[54] The accusation may have shaken the usually hard-living Early. A month later, fellow Confederate general Clement Anselm Evans reported that Early "lately refused to receive a barrel of whiskey as a present!" and that the general had been seen accompanying "a lady to church." Evans concluded that the changes in Early's behavior would "humanize" him and would also allow him to keep his command.[55] It was too little, too late. With rumors of Early's drunken defeat swirling through the Virginia countryside, Lee had no choice but to relieve him of his command in March 1865.[56] The Early hullabaloo illustrates clearly the power of rumor to shape civilian perceptions of generals' character, perceptions that could wreak havoc—justly or unjustly—with their careers.

NORTHERNERS AND SOUTHERNERS not only perceived that liquor had the power to compromise generals and decide battles but also claimed that intoxicants were the greatest enemy threatening the rank and file. Americans on both sides of the conflict worried that their own soldiers would succumb to liquor's temptations and would lose battles or transform from upstanding men and citizen-soldiers into marauding guerrillas who threatened their own civilians. Civilians—and some soldiers—believed that drunkenness signified a lack of manliness and moral courage, so even as Unionists and Confederates worried that whiskey might bring down their own armies, they also looked for evidence that their enemies were drinking. Drunken enemy soldiers signified low morale and a meaningless cause.

At the root of these concerns about liquor's ability to undermine the war effort was that it literally carried significant risks in both its pure and adulterated forms. Few laws existed in the mid-nineteenth century to regulate the ingredients of distilled and fermented beverages. While most distilleries and breweries were small family operations, rogue distillers took various shortcuts during the manufacturing process to create cheap, adulterated beverages.[57] At best, consumers purchased rotgut spirits; at worst, they died. This lurking fear bothered Americans during the war. A belief that liquor might be mixed with unknown substances and, therefore, poisonous, formed the basis for their concerns about its harmful effects.

Southern men were warned that they were heading off to fight not simply Northern men but also *"yankee* rum," *"Ohio* buckeye whiskey," "Cincinnati whiskey," and the "counterfeit Cognacs" of New York and Philadelphia. The implications were twofold. Being near the Northern border would expose innocent young Southerners to Northern vice. More than that, the reference to "counterfeit Cognac" implied a particular deviousness. Southern temperance reformers were convinced that their Northern enemies would concoct extraordinarily potent and even poisonous beverages "especially for the work of sending death and destruction among Southern men." Liquor itself could become a weapon in the war.[58]

Northerners expressed similar worries. After an engagement in Pike County, Kentucky, in November 1861, one Union soldier recalled that rebels in the area had felled numerous trees across the road to make it difficult for the Federal troops to pass through. While the soldiers removed the trees, they "came across two barrels of apple brandy," which commanding officer Major Alexander McCook immediately ordered destroyed for fear his men might be poisoned, "as the rebels had been inquiring for arsenic along the road."[59] McCook's suspicion was no isolated fear.[60] In February 1862, forty-two Union soldiers and officers "were poisoned in Mud Town," Missouri, after "eating rebel food or drinking rebel liquor." One officer died. General Samuel R. Curtis concluded that the poisoning was almost certainly intentional.[61] These instances explain, to some degree, why so many commanders were bent on destroying confiscated spirits despite wails of protest from their tired and thirsty men.

Beyond fearing poisoned spirits, both Federals and Confederates worried that liquor literally made their soldiers poor fighters. After the Battle of Bull Run in 1861, reformers in Raleigh and Richmond warned that "King Alcohol"—a more "intimate enemy"—might accomplish what the Yankee could not:

vanquishing the Confederacy. They defined "national sin" as "the gross and continued swilling of liquors, largely adulterated, and which, even when pure, contain too much alcohol to be compatible with the sound mind in the sound body."[62] Plenty of Confederates were convinced that liquor would be the downfall of the infant nation. If the "Black Republicans" really wanted to subdue the Confederacy quickly, the Richmond *Daily Dispatch* recommended that they start by removing the blockade "so far as lager beer and whiskey are concerned." Knowing "that intoxicating beverages do more mischief to mankind than any other agency of evil," the editor concluded that the North could do the Confederacy no "greater injury than to let in the liquor." By cutting off the supply, the North was transforming the Confederacy into "a great Tee-total Maine Liquor Law Temperance Society"—inadvertently saving "the souls and bodies of the whole Southern people." And while the North was accidentally fortifying the South with cold water, the Confederates hoped that Union secretary of state William Seward would "draw the corks of his lager beer bottles" and "roll over a few of his brandy casks." From civilians' perspective, the victor of the war would be the side that drank the least.[63]

Northerners and Southerners thought that soldiers who fought under the influence were careless and cowardly, and they relished coming across drunken enemies. During the Peninsula Campaign, correspondents with the *New York Herald* "noticed"—and reported enthusiastically—"that the secesh prisoners were all *drunk*—a fact which was observed in the battle of Gaines' Hill [sic] last Friday."[64] If the rebels were already relying on bottled motivation after only a year of fighting, certainly the Union would soon be victorious. At Cold Harbor in 1864, Levi Bird Duff commented that attacking rebels had undoubtedly been made drunk before being "repulsed with heavy loss." There was no other way the men could have been convinced to make such an attack. Their morale was too low (the Federals presumed).[65] Confederate soldiers who attacked Federal gunboats while "excited by liquor" were so deranged that they charged foolishly and "were shot down like sheep."[66]

Confederates offered similar blasts against the Yankees—commenting that whiskey made them poor shots and prone to surrender. Palmetto Sharpshooters fighting near Spotsylvania in 1864 found themselves being attacked by a Union regiment "so crazy and drunk they never hit a man" but instead surrendered as soon as the Confederates fired on them.[67] In other cases, Confederate captors noted that their Northern prisoners "had canteens of mean whisky" in their possession. They assumed that the booze had been issued to help the men "get up a little Dutch courage."[68] Confederate Reverend Moses Drury Hoge thought he noticed similar tendencies among Grant's men. Not only were they drunk when they were captured, but many of the Yankees surrendered "with their guns loaded declaring they would rather come to Richmond as prisoners." Unlike Confederates, who were imbued with the manly "self-sacrificing spirit" of "self-possession" and "Noble heroism," the Yankees' literal self-sacrificing tendencies could be credited not to patriotic zeal but to the overindulgence of liquor, which made them abandon their cause and their manhood.[69]

If some soldiers supposedly laid down their weapons when they were drunk, Federals and Confederates also argued that their enemies' masculine courage was so lacking that they would only fight if they were bribed with liquor. The *Richmond Whig* published revised "Yankee Doodle" lyrics in 1861 that mocked Union soldiers for always being drunk on brandy—or some combination of brandy and gunpowder—during battles.[70] The gunpowder-and-whiskey cocktail proved a common myth on both sides. Kentucky Unionist Frances Peter had heard that Confederates "crazed" by drink would "rush into the thickest of the fray, screaming and yelling and fight[ing] like fiends, regardless of any danger, and seemingly uncon[s]cious of any."[71] In Atlanta, Chauncey Herbert Cooke observed that the Confederates who charged Union batteries under heavy fire were "crazed with gunpowder and whiskey given them to make them brave."[72] Peter and Cooke reached the same conclusion about their enemy's bravery: only a man "crazed" by liquor would be foolish enough fight for the Confederacy. More than that, they implied that Confederate soldiers fought recklessly, without the restrained conduct needed to successfully complete maneuvers. Frances Peter went even further, concluding that the typical rebel soldier had to be completely "ignorant." No man in his right mind would sign up to fight for the rebels willingly, and the gunpowder whiskey a Confederate soldier drank in his canteen made him "a perfect slave to his officers." Peter asserted that drunkenness robbed Confederate soldiers of their independence and manhood and made them unthinking "abused creatures" who were tricked into fighting for a bad cause. The proof of their cowardice and their enslavement became especially apparent upon their deaths. According to Peter, the "proof" was that "the bodies of the rebel soldiers killed in battle turn black, or lurid purple in face and sometimes all over."[73]

So closely associated with cowardice was drunkenness that most soldiers bristled at any intimation that their courage and "superhuman" edge came from whiskey. Yankee soldier Charles Wright Wills offered a sharp retort when he found out that Confederates reported that the Federals "were all drunk and fought more like devils than men." Wills emphasized that he and his fellow soldiers were in "splendid spirits," and despite their exhaustion, they had "made the woods ring with their Fourth of July cheers." Patriotism, not drunkenness, had shored up their fighting spirit.[74] Brigadier-General Robert S. Granger noted a similar phenomenon near Athens, Alabama, when the men of the 18th Michigan and 102nd Ohio drove back an entire brigade of Nathan Bedford Forrest's men. After the surrender, Confederates had "accused the officers of making their men drunk, insisting that no men would fight with such desperation unless under the influence of liquor." This was not true, claimed Granger. Confederates had simply never witnessed men who fought as "boldly" and "determinedly" in the face of danger as the brave Union soldiers.[75] In short, even though soldiers used whiskey rations to fortify themselves against fatigue and exposure, they stiffened at the idea that liquor's stimulating properties motivated them to fight. When it came to charging, they were motivated by masculine courage and love of country.

Pious Confederates feared that too many soldiers were not sober (and, by extension, not victorious). That "fiend of intemperance" (which was worse in the army) had "slain more of our brave soldiers than has the sword of our enemy." The future of the Confederacy, "a nation just entering on its young life," was at stake. During the General Assembly of the Presbyterian Church of the Confederate States of America, the delegates concluded that "the moral character not only of those who sit in its high places, but of its population at large, is of the very first importance." Sober soldiers (and citizens) could bring "glory" to the new nation, but drunkards would bring nothing but "shame."[76]

This idea that liquor undercut soldiers' ability to fight as disciplined men is evident in the ways that civilians and military authorities described the link between liquor and guerrilla warfare. In northern Missouri, Union general Clinton B. Fisk urged his subordinate officers to consider that liquor was "a great enemy." They would have to "treat it as you would a guerrilla."[77] Although guerrillas played important roles in contested regions of the Confederacy and Border South, their irregular tactics made both civilians and regular officers uncomfortable. Confederate general Joseph Shelby complained about bands of rogue drunken soldiers, who were roaming the countryside in central Arkansas engaged in "cotton speculating, horse stealing, [and] illicit and pernicious trading with the Federals." They were supposed to be guarding civilians from Union soldiers, but instead they were joy-riding through the countryside, inflicting additional damage on Arkansan families, all while "sweltering in the hot fumes of Memphis whiskey." Shelby was determined to sober them up, restore order, and "kill . . . like excommunicated felons" any soldier who refused to be whipped into shape.[78] But even Shelby was not immune from accusations that his raiders behaved worse than Yankees when drunk. When his own intoxicated officers turned their soldiers into a disorganized mob that ravaged the Arkansas countryside, Confederate colonel Cyrus Franklin complained to President Jefferson Davis. As Franklin saw it, the "cause" suffered whenever civilians, particularly women, were "insulted or robbed" by drunken raiders who "transferred to the Confederate uniform all the dread and terror which used to attach to the Lincoln blue."[79]

As Yankees marched through Virginia in October 1864, the *Richmond Enquirer* went on its own tirade against drunkenness among the Confederate cavalry. Despite containing "the very flower of the land, dashing, enthusiastic young men, full of ardor and esprit du [sic] corps," the cavalry was disorganized and undisciplined and a threat to Confederate security. "We have two enemies to contend with in the valley," reported the paper, "the Federal Army and John Barley Corn." For the moment, it seemed that John Barley Corn was gaining the upper hand. The Shenandoah Valley was "running with apple brandy," and the responsibility for Confederate reverses lay with the "officers of high position" who had been "too drunk to command themselves, much less an army, a division, a brigade, or a regiment." Furthermore, "when officers in high command are in the habit of drinking to *excess*, we may be sure their pernicious example will be followed by those in lower grades." Most egregious were Confederate cavalrymen, who had been "flitting hither and thither along the Potomac and Shenandoah," terrorizing and robbing women who had already been widowed and demoralized by years of war.[80] The *Enquirer*'s position was clear: as liquor trickled down through the ranks, it undercut the restrained manhood of officers to such an extent that the men ended up terrorizing the very women and children they were supposed to be protecting.

THIS PERVASIVE TENDENCY TO LINK DRINKING with a lack of proper masculinity or patriotism had significant ramification for Irish and German Americans, who spent the war years justifying their dual identities as they served. Nativist attacks on German and Irish immigrants had long included condemnation of drinking culture, and temperance reformers targeted immigrants with Sunday Laws and licensing restrictions in their attempts to assimilate immigrant workers into a more "American" Protestant culture. Simultaneously, nativists blamed drunken immigrants for all the social ills plaguing their communities. These accusations did not disappear when the war began but instead were repackaged to suggest that Irish and German Americans did not possess the proper masculine traits to defend their countries.

Irish Americans in both the Union and the Confederacy used the war to solidify both their Irish and American identities, and in doing so, they butted up against nativist attacks on their motives and fighting abilities.[81] In 1861, English visitor William Howard Russell portrayed Irish Americans as lazy opportunists whose allegiances depended on the size of their paychecks and who shirked their duties whenever possible.[82] To many nativists, Irishmen made unreliable and unruly soldiers. When Texan John Camden West was too injured to write a letter to his wife, an Irish comrade helped him out. Despite the favor, West had the Irish soldier transcribe that he was "afraid that the Irishman will get drunk and lose this, so I have no heart to write you as fully as I would wish." Nevertheless, the soldier completed the transcription and sent the letter to West's wife.[83] Beyond making disparaging comments about Irishmen's character, soldiers believed that Irish soldiers deserved violent punishments when drunk. Charles Wainwright encountered an Irish American soldier so drunk one evening in Alexandria that the man had to be bound and sent to the city guard. Once there, he stripped and had to be knocked unconscious so the guard could dress him again.[84] The Carter brothers from Massachusetts had a similar experience shortly after they enlisted. On their train ride through Pennsylvania, they and the other passengers were annoyed by a man whom they perceived to be "a burly, drunken Irishman, overflowing with bad whiskey and pugilistic ambition." The man was so intoxicated he was bent on harassing everyone in the cars until the brothers grabbed him, knocked him out, emptied his flask, and left him to sleep it off.[85]

White Southerners feared that Irish Yankees had a particularly violent streak.[86] Confederate civilian Mary Mallard likened Irish soldiers in the Army of the Tennessee to guerrillas. As General William T. Sherman's men marched toward Savannah in 1864, she found her Montevideo home under threat from men in Kilpatrick's Cavalry. Mallard specifically described a "stalwart Kentucky Irishman" who spoke "in a very rough voice" as he demanded to know where whiskey was kept. These men then searched the premises from top to bottom.[87] Confederate soldier Edmund DeWitt Patterson worried that the "drunken Irishman" who stumbled upon his wounded body during the Battle of Seven Pines would bayonet him after presenting a "most fiendish look" and threatening to put him "out of [his] misery." In Patterson's mind, the Irish American soldier in his drunken state would not spare the life of a rebel prisoner. Only after a native-born officer stepped in was Patterson convinced he would not be murdered.[88] South Carolinian J. J. McDaniel did not notice any particular penchant for violence among Irish Yankees at Fredericksburg, but he observed that Brigadier-General Thomas Meagher's men, "half drunk with liquor," tried foolishly to overtake the rebel batteries. Instead, the "liquor had led them into the 'slaughter pen.'" As they fled through the streets, McDaniel hoped that their lopsided bloody defeat would "be the fate of all the beastly, drunken, thievish foreigners who pollute our Southern soil in the company of their employers, the Yankees."[89] Like native-born Union soldiers, McDaniel doubted that the Irish were capable of any purely patriotic bravery. Historians have argued that these constant nativist critiques ultimately undercut Irish American support for the war, to an extent. But when it came to cultural drinking habits, such as celebrating Christmas and St. Patrick's Day, evidence suggests that Irish American soldiers continued to embrace their Irish heritage even as they fought for inclusion in their adopted countries.[90]

German American soldiers and civilians encountered similar prejudice, as native-born citizens questioned their patriotism and fortitude. At times, nativist Americans used German-speaking soldiers as scapegoats for defeats, most notably in the Union loss at Chancellorsville, and their beliefs that German American soldiers lacked that masculine composure needed to fight is evident in the way Anglo-American soldiers described their German counterparts' drinking. Anglo soldiers simply assumed that German soldiers had a taste for alcohol, particularly lager beer. An account of a raid against Confederates near Webb's Cross Roads in Kentucky offered several stereotypical descriptions of German behavior. Upon storming the fortification, the Union forces discovered a barrel of apple brandy. Quickly, twelve German American soldiers filled their canteens despite warnings from other Union soldiers that the alcohol might have been poisoned by Confederates. "I tells you vat I do," responded one soldier, "I trinks some, and if it don't kill me, den you trinks."[91] The manner with which the author describes the soldiers' drinking—reckless and hasty—along with the supposed dialogue illuminates his perceptions of German soldiers as less careful and more prone to drunkenness. Union physician John Vance Lauderdale offered similar criticisms. German Americans, in his mind, were "an indifferent race" who "care[d] for no other happiness" than "tobacco and beer."[92] Among nativists, there was no notion that German Americans could rally behind more significant values like duty and patriotism.

Native-born soldiers' accusations that their German American counterparts had a proclivity for drunkenness stemmed, at least in part, from jealousy. Because lager beer was so central to German culture and dining habits, enlisted men in largely German regiments received extra rations of lager beer and permission to drink. The *New York Times* noted that German soldiers stationed at Camp Jessie in Virginia were rewarded with glasses of lager after a day of hard work.⁹³ At other times, German American soldiers relied on both patriotic citizens at home to send whiskey and beer to the camps and their own knack for finding saloons.⁹⁴ Union soldiers seethed when German regiments received extra beer.⁹⁵ In May 1863, Lewis Bissell wrote to his father that German soldiers alone were allowed lager beer at Fort Lyons, Virginia. The sober Bissell listened to the "Dutchmen" singing "like so many black birds chattering" because, presumably, they consumed "a good deal of lager beer." Union officers could stroll into the fort at will and drink the beer, but the enlisted men encamped outside the walls were prohibited from entering. This "makes the men mad," Bissell noted with considerable understatement.⁹⁶ As much as Anglo-Americans may have pointed to German American drinking as a character flaw, it was fairly clear that they would have guzzled equal, if not greater, amounts of lager beer if given access.

Still, these charges left German Americans angrily defending their loyalty against the accusations that they were unpatriotic, draft-dodging drunks. Even so, they did not go so far as to change their cultural practices in hopes of assuaging Anglo-American distaste. Instead, and perhaps ironically, some shared the notion that excessive drinking threatened the war effort, but they argued instead that native-born Americans were careless drinkers. Wilhelm Franchsen, a Wisconsin soldier, explained. The "common man" in the United States "goes into a saloon, drinks a lot, and pays for drinks for other people who have to drink with him but don't have anything to do with him otherwise." The ensuing drunkenness usually led "to killing and murder." Franchsen was frustrated with the sensational partisan press, "the arrogant *Yankees*," and the native-born Americans' penchant for treating immigrants with "less respect than a Negro." Rather than endangering sacred white American traditions like sober Sundays, Franchsen thought that the German community "had done the most to cultivate Americans," and he viewed the Northerners he encountered as drunken scoundrels.⁹⁷ It was only by learning how to drink with self-control that native-born American men could become decent citizens.

Out of the ranks, German American professionals had to fend off charges that they did not enlist in the military quickly enough. For some men, the concerns about fighting seemed to be almost entirely pragmatic: they had businesses to run and families to support. Emilé Dupre paid a friend to serve as a substitute so he could stay with his wife in New York City. Philadelphian Carl Hermanns expressed relief to his German parents that he had not become an American citizen yet and could not be drafted. The teacher was tired of the "wretched war" by 1862, and he loathed the "*Conskription*" that snatched fathers "away from their families."⁹⁸ Albert Augustin was similarly nervous about the possibility of leaving his wife when he informed his family in August 1861 that a "horrible war has broken out between North and South ... and soldiers are being signed up every day." Augustin and his wife were saloon-keepers in Champaign, Illinois, and Augustin expressed quite a bit of anxiety that he might have to leave her alone in a strange country and fight because he lived so close to enemy territory. His anxiety did not seem to be tied to a lack of patriotism, as he noted that "every single citizen ... is willing to give his last drop of blood for freedom," and he wished for "eternal damnation to the slave traders!"[99]

Confederate saloon-keeper John Gottfried Lange expressed his patriotism similarly, even as he complained bitterly that excise taxes and wartime prohibition interfered with his business.[100] The verbose diarist and German immigrant expressed his frustration with martial law that kept him from supporting his family with his lager-beer saloon in Richmond. Until the secession crisis, Lange's business had prospered, and although he occasionally had run afoul of Sunday Laws, he and his wife assimilated into Richmond's cultural life. Lange expressed his patriotism openly, dressing as a continental guard for Carnival balls and after John Brown's raid in 1859 serving beer and snacks to Virginia militiamen. When Virginia seceded, Lange treated his customers with free beer and penned impassioned letters criticizing Northern wage labor. "Old and young were called upon to help defend the fatherland," remembered Lange, a devoted Confederate, and he himself, although too old to join the regular army, volunteered to serve in the home guard. Patrolling the streets of Richmond, Lange lambasted the myriad "Germans who had fought at home for their freedom in 1848" but now fought for the Union "to suppress our freedom and our states [sic] rights." In Lange's view, Confederates fought firmly within the tradition of the 1848 nationalistic revolutions in Europe. White Southerners were fighting against tyranny.[101]

Lange's business took repeated hits throughout the war, as supplies of beer dwindled, the war disrupted customers' routines, and prohibitory measures and license fees cut into profits. Through it all, Lange remained an active member of the home guard and fought to provide for his family, even though he found it increasingly hard to make ends meet. After the First Battle of Bull Run, Lange joined in the patriotic fervor sweeping through Richmond. Schoolchildren used his saloon to collect and cut rags for use as bandages. When local laws allowed, Lange and other Germans sold beer to soldiers. When the war finally ended, the German Confederate rebuilt his business mostly from scratch in a city under Union occupation. Strict laws governed sales to soldiers and African Americans, but Lange remained a proud Confederate, who at times clashed with Federal authorities and insisted on hanging a portrait of Jefferson Davis on the wall of his saloon. Even when Union officers patronized his saloon, Lange openly avowed that he "had been a rebel."[102]

Lange and his Unionist counterparts in the North passionately denied that they were unpatriotic drunks who threatened the war effort. Like other businesses, saloons supported the war effort by refreshing soldiers or, perhaps more importantly, participating in wartime volunteer activities. They insisted that their trade in ardent spirits did not force native-born Americans to guzzle alcohol. In short, Germans maintained that they brought stability to American society, and they insisted that they were loyal citizens who made important contributions to the war effort.

AS THE WAR PROGRESSED, many African Americans found themselves in a similar situation as immigrants, trying to justify through their actions that they belonged in the American community. White Americans, North and South, assumed that African American men had a predilection for strong drink, but African Americans worked diligently to disprove the theory. Unlike German and Irish Americans, who were content to keep their drinking habits as part of their distinct culture, African Americans, especially those from the Black middle class, adopted mainstream evangelical temperance principles during the antebellum decades. They relied on these ideals of sober, restrained masculinity to guide their wartime behavior.[103]

Early in the war, African American civilians argued that they were more sober (and thereby more self-disciplined and more manly) than white secessionists. In December 1861, enslaved "Negro Jack" escaped from a "Mr. Cox" by entering Union lines, and subsequently informed some New York troops of his master's "Secessionist sympathies." Cox followed him there, and with the help of slave catchers and agreeable Union soldiers, he reclaimed his slave and beat him senseless while in a drunken stupor. When on trial, the jury found Cox innocent by concluding that Jack had died of "exposure and excitement" (excitement being a euphemism for drunkenness), even though Jack was whipped to death. Responding in outrage, the *Liberator* pointed out in a letter addressed to Horace Greeley of the *New York Tribune* that none of the Union soldiers had ever seen Jack "*drunk publicly*" while he was within their lines, and that furthermore, he would have had no means for acquiring whiskey. Jack had provided "patriotic and valuable services" to the Union army by reporting on the disloyal behavior of his—not coincidentally—drunken master. Jack was promised asylum in the Union lines, and instead, soldiers had returned him to his master, and civilian courts had stripped him of his patriotism and relabeled him a drunken slave. The *Liberator* was clear on this point: the drunken, violent slaveholder was the disloyal citizen, and the sober Black man who risked his life to serve his country was the patriot.[104]

After emancipation, the conversation of Black drinking heightened. Many white Northerners and Southerners assumed that African Americans were naturally predisposed to abuse liquor. Southern whites, especially, worried that liquor would incite rebellion among enslaved people whom they believed were normally docile when sober. In the antebellum South, access to liquor was a marker of freedom and whiteness. Occasionally, white masters offered liquor to their enslaved workers as a reward for a successful harvest or for a Christmas celebration, but in those cases, the meaning was clear: that drinking was a privilege generally belonging to white people that could be given to people of color only as a reward for good behavior.[105] White Northerners, for their part, worried similarly that emancipation would lead to drunken chaos in Black neighborhoods. In Franklin County, Pennsylvania, local citizens worried that free Black people would be prone to drunkenness, crime, and disorder unless reformers intervened. In 1859, the *Valley Spirit* described an "abode of crime and wretchedness of destitute and degraded humanity," where "fourteen women and six children" crammed into tiny, dimly lit apartments. Poverty stricken, "drinking whisky and inhaling tobacco smoke," free Black people reveled in "licentious and blasphemous orgies" because American "society" had not educated them to be moral citizens. If white Americans wanted to prevent such moral decay from encroaching on their cities, they needed to make "a generous donation to the Foreign Missionary Society."[106] Reformers believed that rescuing the newly freed population from the perils of drunkenness would become their burden.

Black civilians and soldiers knew they had to counter these white perceptions to prove their eligibility for citizenship, and evidence indicates that Black soldiers resisted alcohol's temptations more successfully than their white counterparts. The middle-class Black community, for its part, lauded sobriety, and Black temperance reformers, like their white counterparts, argued that abstinence was a marker of progress.[107] Highly critical of drunkenness among Union soldiers and officers, African American soldier and abolitionist George E. Stephens argued that there were "two great sins of the nation which threaten its very existence, the upper and nether millstones which threaten to grind into atoms all its elements of goodness and greatness": slavery and drunkenness. Stephens condemned white soldiers whose camps were "more like that of bacchanals"—full of "brawls, riots, and midnight orgies." McClellan had done little to stop the flow of liquor, in his opinion. And Stephens further touted his moral and masculine superiority by arguing that with "ten thousand sober troops," he could "subdue the whole [white] Army of the Potomac."[108]

The idea that an army of temperate Black men could fight better than white soldiers was echoed in other parts of the North. After the New York Draft Riots in 1863, U.S. Colored soldier Junius Albus complained that white civil and military authorities had not been able to protect Black New Yorkers from violent attacks at the hands of white immigrants. Striking a nativist tone, Albus questioned why "a white foreigner, ignorant of our polity, our religion, our laws, and even our language, is permitted to settle here, and ... enjoy all the common advantages of a citizen ... , and yet a peaceable and educated colored man cannot even enjoy unmolested, the most common rights of an ordinary citizen?" Albus believed white authorities could not prevent similar riots in his own city of Philadelphia and proposed that Black men "organize for their own defence." The "colored population" was "much inferior in numbers, but in intelligence, coolness, temperance, and courage, they are much superior to their bloody antagonists."[109] Intelligence, temperance, and courage: all traits required for citizenship and to win the war. Albus and others in the African American community believed that Black men possessed them in greater quantities than their white counterparts, especially those of foreign birth.

White Northerners expressed some surprise whenever Black men showed a preference for sobriety. In the aftermath of the Emancipation Proclamation, temperance reformers had determined that keeping the freedpeople away from alcohol was going to be one of their new responsibilities. Under slavery, they knew, white slaveholders had kept their enslaved people sober out of necessity because it "was a loss of a thousand dollars to have slave become a drunkard." But liberty offered "no such protection" to a Black man, as he was now free to visit "the grogshop and get far worse fetters put upon him than he ever had before." It was up to the American Temperance Union to prevent this from happening through, among other methods, the dissemination of tracts.[110] But even as white Northerners were preparing to step up their reform efforts, civilian and military officials decided it was unnecessary. Civilians living near Camp Delaware noted that the U.S. Colored Troops encamped in their midst were "more orderly and more honest than white soldiers." They did not harass the local population, and there had been "less drunkenness." Temperance reformers patted themselves on the back for improving the condition of the freedmen after so little time "under instruction."[111] Union military authorities in charge of the Port Royal experiment concluded that the Black "race is not addicted to intemperance," like their white counterparts, after noticing that enslaved Southerners did not drink. Perhaps in slavery

Black men had been "cut off from [alcohol's] temptation," but Superintendent Captain Edward Hooper noted that he "never saw a negro drunk" and had only ever heard of one case where a Black worker was given whiskey by nearby whites.[112]

Neither the military nor the American Temperance Union was ready to bestow equal citizenship on sober African Americans, but in April 1865, the *New York Times* remarked that there was something "irrepressible" about African Americans, and sobriety had much to do with it. Despite the ability to "smuggle whisky easily" into camp, Black soldiers were seldom, if ever, observed to be "the worse for liquor." The reason, quite plainly, was because a "colored soldier feels himself to be 'every inch a man,' whenever he has exchanged his old rags for military blue, and shouldered his musket for the first time." And it went beyond the military. Even among the civilian population, the paper noted that the number of Black Northerners selling and drinking whiskey "is far below that of their fair-skinned neighbors."[113] There was simply no evidence to show that the end of slavery brought with it the long-feared disorder and drunkenness among the free populations of color.

YET THE FEAR THAT DRUNKEN MEN undermined the war spread throughout the Union and Confederate home fronts. Many civilians believed that King Alcohol lurked behind every devious activity. At a time when individuals were urged to show their support for the war effort through self-sacrifice, anyone who appeared to be drunk risked being accused of unpatriotic activities. Likewise, anyone who appeared to be profiting from the conflict or dodging service was suspected of drunkenness. Civilians noted that alcohol was always bound up with illicit trading. Ultimately, they believed so strongly that alcohol threatened the democratic process that they accused political rivals of using alcohol to gain political advantage.

Confederates believed that liquor threatened their infant nation's very survival. As a part of their efforts to mobilize the Southern white population and encourage civilians to accept deprivations as part of their patriotic duty, Confederate politicians, clergymen, and newspaper editors blasted unscrupulous civilians working as profiteers.[114] In the midst of the secession crisis, Thomas Atkinson, bishop of North Carolina, lamented that the Southern states had not withstood the temptations that accompanied prosperity—drunkenness, fraud, bribery, and speculation, among other things. As men prepared "to march to the uncertain issues of the siege, or the battle-field," Southerners needed to fight the temptation to sin. The war and its burdens were tests from God. Southerners needed to bear them righteously.[115] Virginia reverend

James B. Ramsey echoed Atkinson's sentiments, reminding Confederates of 1 Corinthians 6:10: that sinners, including "drunkards" and "extortioners," could not "inherit the kingdom of God."[116] On their list of extortionists, Confederates included smugglers, blockade runners, cotton speculators, and barkeepers. Not coincidentally, all were involved in some aspect of the liquor traffic. Almost as soon as the war began, saloon-keepers in Richmond raised prices, much to the consternation of the *Dispatch*. For "two cents worth of distilled corn juice and a lump of rice, well shaken in a tumbler," barkeepers were charging an exorbitant fifteen cents. The only possible good that might arise would be an inadvertent victory for the temperance cause.[117] Of more serious consequence were Confederates engaged in what Jefferson Davis referred to as "the villainous traffic" of blockade-running, liquor trafficking, and cotton speculating. Blockade runners not only brought "rum and gin" into the country instead of "arms or munitions of war" but also drove up cotton prices, which encouraged Southern farmers to plant the lucrative cash crop in place of much-needed grains.[118] Confederate pleas for civilians to change their ways did not keep many Southerners from engaging in illicit trading with equally profit-minded Northerners.[119] By 1863, cotton speculators plied the Mississippi River between Memphis and Helena, Arkansas, where the Union government exchanged clothing, food, and whiskey for cotton. The cotton was much needed, but the whiskey and provisions were going, by the barrel load, to Confederate guerrillas and other "public enemies."[120]

Despite not facing acute shortages, Northerners asserted that unscrupulous liquor dealers and those who dealt with them worked to undermine the war effort and the Lincoln administration. In April 1863, the American Temperance Union cried that "rum"—rather than slavery—riled "the bad passions of men against law and order, destroys all moral sensibilities, and fits the villainous for carnage and the rending of the nation.... There is not a grogshop in the North that is a supporter of government. There is not a press which advocates secession that does not advocate the trade of rum."[121] Other Northerners made the connection between liquor and Copperheads more explicit. In April 1863 in Franklin County, Pennsylvania, the Republican *Transcript*'s war correspondent labeled Copperheads "the lowest, meanest, dirtiest, draggle tailed, whisky drinking, card-playing, horse-racing, hell-defying... characters... arrayed against their country." The rival Democratic *Valley Spirit* countered that the correspondent was a "blatant and slanderous abolitionist" who was likely to "find a considerable quantity of copperhead boot-leather inserted somewhere about the lower end of his spinal column" the next time he rode into town.[122] But two years later, Hoosiers echoed the *Transcript*'s remarks, charging local Copperheads with becoming "gloriously drunk" at news of the war's end and "cursing black Republicans, preachers, and the damned [n—er]." In this case, alcohol loosened the tongue and revealed treachery.[123]

Northern Republicans further linked Democrats, immigrants, and liquor with draft resistance. After the war began, native-born Northerners grew increasingly suspicious of German and Irish immigrants who did not enlist at the first call for volunteers.[124] After Congress began conscripting men in the spring of 1863, Republicans charged that Democrats in New York City plied Irish immigrants with alcohol to spark violence. In the weeks following the Union victories at Gettysburg and Vicksburg in 1863, working-class men in New York City, Boston, and other cities violently resisted the draft. For four days in July, working men, many of whom were Irish immigrants, rioted against the federal government, which they believed was conscripting them to fight in a war not of their making.[125] While working in Bellevue Hospital in New York City, John Vance Lauderdale encountered "a drunken man" who shared with him "the sentiments of the mob." New Yorkers were "infuriated" because "a poor man had to be drafted and go to the war, but a rich man could pay his money and stay home." Lauderdale knew that certain members of the press (presumably Democrats) encouraged the rioters, whose grievances he suggested were legitimate. Still, he argued, people had been "made furious by liquor," and so many thieves and rabble-rousers wreaked so much havoc with the city that Lauderdale feared venturing outside.[126]

Rioters might have considered their violent actions to be a justifiable rebellion against an unfair system that favored the wealthy, but Union officers diverted from the front lines in Pennsylvania to enforce the draft considered the violence subversive. Colonel Robert Nugent of the 69th New York Volunteers estimated that he would need more than fifteen thousand additional men to restore law and order because the rioters—some of whom were "thieves and gamblers that infest this metropolis"—were joined by Democrats and had been made even more unruly "by the copious supply of liquor." The problem, in Nugent's view, was not simply that such men could not control themselves, but rather that they had been egged on by liquor deviously supplied by the Democratic Party. Nugent echoed the view of many middle-class Americans on this point. He (and others) thought the laboring classes incapable of independent political action and instead suspected that Democratic politicians, who actively opposed the Lincoln administration, were "at the bottom of this riot." Not even New York's governor Horatio Seymour could be trusted. Nugent questioned the "loyalty" of the state's leaders, accusing them of using liquor to incite working-class resistance against the federal government.[127]

Union officer William Wheeler, on the other hand, placed the blame on the shoulders of Irish rioters rather than on Democrats. He remarked that while he had not paid much attention to the events, he still "wished that they would send me with my Battery to the city for a couple of weeks" because he "would much rather fire canister into those drunken Irish rowdies, than into the secesh brethren." He explained that Confederates, "although deluded," were "worth all the Paddies that ever had a brogue."[128] Politically deluded white men, he reasoned, were not as dangerous as drunken Irishmen.

Most Northerners stopped short of fantasizing about shooting immigrants instead of rebels, but many expressed deep reservations about immigrants' political allegiances. Heavy drinking supposedly corrupted the democratic political process.[129] As the heavily contested 1864 election neared, both Democrats and Republicans accused each other of drunkenness. Wisconsin soldier Guy C. Taylor told his wife that "you cannot find a irish man nor a drunkard scurisely [sic] but what is a McClynon [sic] man."[130] But McClellan supporter Daniel Robinson Hundley accused Republicans of buying votes. While casting a vote in Illinois, Hundley "witnessed the desecration of the ballot-box—drunken foreigners voting, who could not speak a word of English, and whose tickets were changed in my presence without their knowledge—as well as made sick from the fumes of tobacco-smoke, lager beer, whisky, etc."[131] Just as nativist soldiers questioned whether their immigrant comrades were fit to fight, Union men also used xenophobic arguments to undercut immigrants' claims to participation in politics. Drunkenness, nativists believed, made immigrants unfit for American citizenship.

Northerners conflated drunkenness and the desecration of democracy with barbarity, and they argued that secessionists were predisposed to all of it. John B. Farr, a man arrested in January 1862 and tried for disloyalty, was a violent secessionist and a member of a band of guerrillas headquartered in Dranesville, Virginia. Farr and his cronies robbed and murdered Union soldiers, leaving them "unburied on the field to be eaten up ... by the rebels' hogs," all while "being made jolly with whisky." The report went further, describing the acts as "savage barbarity," "bestial joy," and "sacrilegious." Although Farr claimed to be a Unionist, reports of these inhuman acts against Union soldiers, committed while he was amid "intoxicated madness," proved that he was disloyal.[132]

Confederates similarly tended to assume that drunkards and distillers were disloyal—especially in disaffected regions. When Sergeant E. R. Norton found distilling implements stashed in hollow trees near the South Carolina border while commanding Scout Thomas's Legion, he surmised that the tools "belong to deserters."[133] When hungry Confederate soldiers entered her home looking for food, Georgian Eliza Andrews determined that they "were drunk, or stragglers from some of the conscript regiments" after they threatened to burn down the property.[134] It is important to note that Norton and Andrews conflated drunkenness with desertion, straggling, and conscription. Neither stragglers nor conscripts behaved according to the imagined ideals of Southern manhood. They were unpatriotic men (perhaps cowards) who shirked their duties. Andrews put drunks in the same category. They were all men who cared so little about the Confederate cause that they would burn down the homes of loyal Confederates. Likewise, in Montgomery, Alabama, locals were so disgusted with intoxicated soldiers that they demanded the guilty men *"be sent to the front, and forced to remain there; for as long as they are permitted to remain in this city, they are perfectly useless in the service."*[135] In January 1865, Alabama needed men who expressed their masculinity through military service, not drunken disorder.

In North Carolina, distilling became a tool to sort out who was loyal to the Confederacy and who was not. In the Piedmont region, Pittsboro residents noted correctly that there was much distilling "in the disaffected region of Moore & Chatham."[136] In fact, more than 30 percent of the letters addressed to Governor Zebulon Vance concerning distilling came from Yadkin, Davidson, Forsyth, Davie, Moore, Chatham, Alamance, Guilford, Surry, and Wilkes Counties—all of which were heavily populated by Unionists. More interestingly, 75 percent of the letters from that region reported illicit distilling, unlike the majority of letters from the rest of the state, which dealt with requests for permits for personal and medicinal distilling.[137] Because distilling was so commonplace in rural North Carolina and because the citizens of those counties were not always invested in the Confederate war effort, it is likely that plenty of the charges of distilling had merit (although it is doubtful that these Piedmont distillers were raking in heavy profits). To a certain extent, however, the validity of the charge is not necessarily important. What is clear is that in a region filled with rancorous political divisions, hurling a charge of distilling at a neighbor was not uncommon and served as an effective way to imply that a personal enemy was also disloyal.

More broadly, when it came to describing distillers, Confederates did not mince words. Rather than portray distillers as farmers trying to preserve their grains and fruits, they characterized distillers as "profiteers," who, enticed by rising prices, continued to churn out alcohol at the expense of the war effort. These abstract definitions of good Confederates set absolute standards of loyal behavior and left little room for Southerners whose practical behavior might not fit the established paradigm of loyalty.[138] By characterizing all distillers as profiteers, Confederates argued that distillers were bad men who made profits immorally and subsequently caused other men (in this case, soldiers) to sin and behave unpatriotically by becoming drunk. Confederates juxtaposed the morality of soldiers' patriotic sacrifice against the distillers' selfish greed. As early as February 1862, the *Richmond Dispatch* claimed sensationally that distillers were raking in $4,000 to $5,000 per day, prices that would raise the cost of corn five dollars per bushel unless the government interceded.[139] These prices were surely exaggerated, but similarly panicked rhetoric appeared throughout the state of Virginia. In Floyd County, along the Roanoke River, the "smoke of more than fifty distilleries blackens the horison [sic]" as profiteers rushed to take advantage of the high prices. One Virginian estimated that the distilleries in Floyd County alone would consume enough grain to feed six hundred families for a year.[140] In other words, much like the drunken soldier, the speculative distiller was more than a personal failure; he was a danger to the nation because he put personal profit ahead of the public good and loyalty to the cause.

BY AND LARGE, NORTHERNERS AND SOUTHERNERS believed that patriotism and duty required sober, self-sacrificing masculinity. Men who wanted to assimilate into mainstream society (in either the Union or the Confederacy) had to fit into a specific mold of Americanness. African Americans were expected to model a specific brand of sober masculinity in order to be considered for citizenship by their white counterparts. Immigrants, because liquor and beer were central to their cultures, often found themselves on the outside looking in, justifying their heritage and claiming that they were patriotic despite their lack of interest in teetotalism.

Ironically, though, this conflation of sobriety with national duty and patriotic masculinity often left out the soldiers who were literally fighting to save their respective nations. Soldiers may have chafed at the notion that their patriotism came from a bottle. Nevertheless, that officers and soldiers drank often is clear because liquor was part of their health regime to guard against sickness, exposure, fatigue, and mental exhaustion. As such, when civilians argued that drinking was anathema to proper soldiering and patriotism, officers and soldiers responded by arguing that their service justified their drinking.

Epilogue

On June 5, 1865, Alexander Downing and the soldiers of the 11th Iowa gathered at their camp headquarters near Washington, D.C., as they were being mustered out of service. Their train for Louisville would leave in a few days. But, before they departed, they gathered for a temperance speech. Blank pledges from the Washington Temperance Society circulated "and a good many of the boys signed the blanks after they were filled out." With fresh promises to remain sober, the soldiers began their journey home.[1] The pledges given to Downing's comrades were part of a concerted effort by Northern reformers to prevent veterans from becoming drunkards when they returned to their homes. Thus began the postwar temperance crusade.

A month before the Confederate surrender at Appomattox, the war's imminent end set reformers to thinking about the future. "Let temperance men through the land wake up," commanded the *Journal of the American Temperance Union*. Hundreds of thousands of soldiers who had "learned a wandering life" would be returning to their families shortly. The Union had much work to do. Lamenting that they had been unable, during the war, to smote "the grog-shop nuisance from the land, as we expel[led] slavery, before our armies came home," reformers vowed not to let veterans head down the road to ruin. Their bodies were wounded, and for so long the men had existed only on "hard-tack and salt beef." When they came in contact with colorful shops filled with goods and carts of "refreshments" on board trains, the returning soldiers would be too weak to resist temptation. Reformers determined to "get public sentiment aroused" and redouble temperance efforts in the camps. Now was the time to begin fighting postwar drunkenness by reminding soldiers about the importance of sobriety before they ever left the ranks.[2]

Temperance reformers had some reason to be hopeful that they would be able to restart their crusade—to save not only veterans but also the rest of the nation—in the wake of the war. The conflict had not brought reformers the push for prohibition that they had hoped, but over the course of the war Northerners became willing to condemn drunken officers, soldiers, and civilians and to suggest that chronically intoxicated men were unpatriotic. If reformers hoped to gain momentum for prohibition campaigns, a national conversation about the danger of drinking to the nation's survival (or, in this case, its reconstruction) would provide the proper atmosphere. Moreover, Northern reformers emerged from the war believing that the conflict had added legal sanction to their moral crusade for prohibition. The Emancipation Proclamation and subsequent outlawing of slavery with the Thirteenth Amendment reshaped the relationship between law and morality, from the perspective of reformers. Slavery, like liquor, had been a national sin. By eliminating it, the federal government signaled its commitment to using the legislative process to purge the nation of immorality.[3] As abolitionists celebrated, teetotalers believed their triumph would be next. "We shall celebrate our jubilee when the sun of the world's last long millennial day is higher in the heaven than now.... A great revival is to take place in the interests of this cause." Not only in New England but also throughout the western parts of the United States, support for prohibition was spreading—reformers were certain.[4] The Templars expanded as well, as new lodges sprung up in California, New Mexico, and even Missouri—"where the Order but barely survived the shock of war."[5] The movement was reawakening after four years of disruption.

Evidence of momentum appeared in the former Confederacy as well. Of course, to a much greater extent than Northerners, white Southerners had championed prohibition during the war years. While pragmatic concerns about food shortages may have provided the final impetus for state legislators to prohibit distilling, moral arguments emerged as well. The state had a duty to protect women and children. Men who distilled and drank excessively hurt their families and the nation as a whole. Wartime prohibition faltered, but the notion that the state could expand and regulate behavior persisted. In Virginia, the Friends of Temperance recovered from the war quickly, and it was holding semiannual meetings in October 1866, though it remained officially severed from Northern organizations and specified that membership could be extended to only white men and women.[6] In the years following the war, other white Southerners followed suit. They may have chafed at federal enforcement of excise taxes on home distilling, but at the local and state level, controlling liquor became a useful means of controlling the social order after the end of slavery. Virginians were not alone in demanding that temperance be a whites-only movement. Stringent license laws and prohibition measures, such as through Black Codes, became useful tools in policing Black Southerners' access to liquor during and after Reconstruction.[7]

North and South, lodges formed and reformed. The goals of the postwar temperance movement, according to the Good Templars of Kentucky, were threefold: that liquor dealers would "be driven out of society"; that "moderate drinkers will be compelled to quit their cups"; and that "many drunkards" would be "saved from the gaping grave."[8] Over the next three decades, myriad regional and national organizations such as the National Temperance Society, the Women's Christian Temperance Union, and the National Prohibition Party gained support in Northern, Southern, and Western states. Prohibition trumped moral suasion as the reforming mechanism of choice after the Civil War. For decades, prohibitionists attempted to convince state legislatures that drunkenness threatened their families and was anathema to the American masculine values of hard work, thrift, and sobriety.[9]

Yet prohibitionists' goals of unilaterally defining the terms of appropriate American masculinity fell short as an entire generation of men emerged from the war physically and emotionally scarred. To an extent, reformers recognized what they were up against. The ATU acknowledged that many soldiers not only were returning wounded but also had been "away from the restraints of friends" for so long that they had undoubtedly "been exposed to the temptations of life in the camp." These men had "passed through the terrible storm of shot and shell, and hurricanes of flame and smoke." And while soldiers had "fought and conquered" the rebels, reformers worried that a veteran would "find it difficult to conquer himself."[10] The Independent Order of Good Templars noted, too, that both Union and Confederate soldiers had abandoned temperance principles in the army, where camp temptations and surgeons' prescriptions had left them on "the precipice of ruin."[11] Whether civilian reformers fully understood all these problems is unclear, but they were certainly sympathetic to the soldiers' plight. With calls for a renewed national focus on temperance, they argued that it was the job of the nation to step in and save veterans from strong drink because the trauma of war had seriously weakened their ability to refuse that glass of whiskey.

To be sure, plenty of American men living in the postwar decades found that a masculinity that blended sobriety with virility and athleticism suited them quite well. Many people—especially white men and women—monitored their diets carefully because they believed that consuming excessive amounts of liquor, meats, and other rich foods could endanger their health. Even as men shifted their focus away from moral restraint and toward athletic prowess, close attention to diet remained central to their goals of developing a carefully crafted and disciplined human body. As the United States expanded its imperialistic pursuits in the late nineteenth and early twentieth centuries, virile and athletic men exemplified the moral and national superiority of American values on a global stage.[12] While this conception of masculinity was perhaps more secular in its orientation than the one to which nineteenth-century temperance reformers adhered, temperance crusaders certainly championed the relationship between sobriety, physical health, and national well-being.

Significantly, however, Civil War veterans could not and did not buy into this conception of masculinity. During the war, they had adopted conceptions of masculinity that allowed plenty of space for drinking. When they returned home, the definitions of appropriate drinking they had adopted during their days in camp—drinking for health, to stave off exposure and fatigue, and to combat emotional trauma—continued to work well as veterans attempted to treat chronic physical and psychological pain. In other words, when reformers predicted that veterans would prove tough to convert to the ranks of the teetotaling army, they were correct. Both Union and Confederate veterans found themselves unable to readjust to civilian life. Many were financially unstable and persistently pained by physical and emotional wounds; rocky relationships with their families were often exacerbated by dependence on alcohol. When many aging veterans moved into homes, they continued to drink as they tried to cope with the physical and emotional pain left by the war.[13] Despite identifying the problem correctly in 1865, temperance reformers never convinced veterans to give up alcohol. Because of this—at least in part—aging soldiers found themselves increasingly marginalized in American society.

That does not mean, of course, that veterans were the only men opposed to stringent prohibitory measures. Irish and German Americans, as evidenced by their wartime commitment to their cultural traditions, continued to consume liquor. German brewers organized politically to lobby against prohibition, and by doing so contributed to Republican and Democratic hesitancy to adopt prohibition as parts of their platforms.[14] African Americans, likewise, were of no single mind on the liquor question. Plenty of Black men continued to espouse the virtues of temperance, linking sobriety with freedom and arguing that temperance was required for racial uplift. Yet Black Americans, especially in the South, also clearly recognized the connections between prohibition and white supremacy and joined with wet campaigns to preserve the privilege of drinking among their rights as free people.[15] These men joined the ranks of plenty of others who continued to visit saloons, consume liquor, and oppose prohibition.[16]

In short, prohibitionists had their work cut out for them. It is true and significant that reformers were able to mobilize in the years after the Civil War, to build on the momentum of the 1850s Maine Laws, Confederate prohibition, and the abolition of slavery in order to mount campaigns for local option laws and statewide prohibition in states across the North, South, and Midwest. Nevertheless, tens of thousands of veterans, along with German and Irish Americans and the many rural and working men for whom complete sobriety made little sense, illustrate the significant limits of temperance reform, enthusiasm for prohibition, and adoption of sober masculinity. Though reformers faced challenges, they worked at the local and state levels, sometimes pitting Democrats and Republicans against each other, in order to court moderate supporters and move toward more radical positions. Nevertheless, despite the increasing efforts of the state to regulate and control behavior through legislation, governments from the local and state level only experienced limited success in influencing the contours of men's behavior.[17]

In fact, the prohibition movement did not garner enough national support to pass the Eighteenth Amendment, which prohibited the manufacturing and selling of alcohol at the federal level, until 1917, when the United States was involved in World War I. Once again, the zeal for prohibition became more popular nationally as Americans linked sobriety to wartime patriotism. As the nation mobilized resources for the war, food took on immense moral significance. Suddenly, it became important to save the best provisions for soldiers fighting abroad. Americans on the home front who wanted to perform their patriotism became very conscious of the foods they put in their bodies, not unlike Civil War–era civilians and soldiers who believed that consuming liquor could lead to sickness and death or prevent vulnerable civilians from having enough food.[18] In an atmosphere in which Americans were already primed to conflate food, morality, and patriotism, German American brewers became easy targets during World War I. To an even greater extent than during the Civil War, nativist Americans suspected German Americans of disloyalty. Lashing out at breweries seemed a natural extension of the fight against the Kaiser. Just as the Civil War over half a century earlier had increased American civilians' conflation of sobriety with patriotism, World War I provided prohibitionists with the boost they needed to gain support for nationwide prohibition. In the process, the Eighteenth Amendment defined sobriety as a moral behavior that was most appropriately American. Federal law then condemned and criminalized the culture of workers, immigrants, and people of color.[19]

While it took World War I to ultimately push the United States to federal prohibition, in many ways the Civil War foreshadows the extent to which armed conflict provided momentum to reformers who wanted to combine state power and public opinion to assert cultural control when it came to drinking and the liquor traffic. The Civil War invigorated temperance reformers who had been frustrated that their movement had seemingly plateaued. It enabled them to link their cause to patriotic duty and mobilize popular support for the notion that liquor threatened the war effort. Wartime hardships even caused enthusiasm for prohibition to spread through Southern states.

But if the Civil War provided a preview of the factors required to ultimately pass federal prohibition, it also foretold the Eighteenth Amendment's downfall. On one level, the Civil War demonstrated that attempting to prohibit or significantly limit the liquor traffic was nearly impossible in a society in which liquor had important medicinal value. More importantly, however, the war illustrated how many Americans—especially men—were not only uninterested in prohibition but considered drinking an important part of their masculine cultural expression. Prohibition, which required Americans to be of one mind culturally and morally, was practically impossible.

Acknowledgments

In the process of writing this monograph, I have incurred many debts. From the time I began my journey as a historian, I have benefited from the generous support of faculty and colleagues. While I was at the University of Alabama, George Rable was an ideal adviser: full of experience and advice and capable of making clear his expectations with kindness and patience. He has continued to serve as a dear mentor. Joshua Rothman, Lisa Lindquist-Dorr, and Andrew Huebner enabled me to shape (and reshape) my project by reading drafts and engaging in plenty of casual discussions about drinking and soldiers and Americans. Before I ever arrived at Alabama, professors at Purdue University cultivated my love of history and research. Whitney Walton and Karl Brandt taught me to think critically and globally. I almost accidentally landed in a course with Carrie Janney during my final year at Purdue. Carrie not only provided guidance through my graduate career, but she has continued to be a mentor and a friend over the years. Words cannot quite express my level of gratitude. For many years, my friends and colleagues within the Society of Civil War Historians and beyond have provided much-needed camaraderie and advice. To Becky Bruce, Jill Cooley, Colin Chapell, John Mitcham, Allison Huntley, Mark Johnson, Laura Mammina, Lindsay Privette, Angela Elder, Lauren Thompson, Laura June Davis, Jonathan Lande, Evan Rothera, and Dave Thomson: thank you for reading drafts and conversing over beers.

Since arriving at Missouri Southern State University (MSSU) in 2014, I have enjoyed tremendous support from my colleagues. Veteran historians Paul Teverow, Steve Wagner, and Virginia Laas welcomed me to MSSU and began immersing me into the world of Jasper County history. My colleagues in the Social Sciences Department have been generous with their time, helping me to workshop multiple chapters of this project. Their interdisciplinary perspectives have been incredibly valuable. Supportive administrators Ree Wells-Lewis, Marsi Archer, and Paula Carson enabled me to successfully balance teaching and revising the project. Undergraduate researchers Deanna Smith and Ashley Thomas spent many hours transcribing and organizing medical supply ledgers as a part of their Mapping Alcohol in the Civil War project. Friendships with Bill Fischer, Becca Shriver, Nicole Shoaf, Will Mountz, Steve Smith, Leslie Smith, Rebecca Mouser, Emily Larson, Michael Pyle, Karen Kostan, Dustin Faulstick, Jordan Wilson, Adrian Ramos, Andrea Cullers, and Amber Carr have made these past years in Joplin truly rich.

This project has been supported by generous financial support and library assistance throughout its development. MSSU has provided support for research and travel. Support from the University of Alabama, particularly a Graduate Council Fellowship and a Graduate Research Assistantship, enabled me to lay the foundations for the project. Travel grants and fellowships from the Missouri State Archives, the Filson Historical Society, and the Virginia Historical Society provided support while I researched. I also have relied on the helpfulness and expertise of librarians at the National Archives and Records Administration, the State Archives of North Carolina, the Southern Historical Collection at the University of

North Carolina, the State Historical Society of Iowa, the Wisconsin Historical Society, the Library of Virginia, Small Special Collections at the University of Virginia, the Virginia Historical Society (VHS), the Museum of the Confederacy (MOC), the Mississippi Department of Archives and History (MDAH), and the Filson Historical Society. Katherine Wilkins at the VHS, Teresa Roane at the MOC, Clinton Bagley at the MDAH, and Mike Veach at the Filson all deserve special thanks for sharing the knowledge of their collections. At the University of Alabama, Brett Spencer guided me to many digital archives, and Patricia Causey brought many valuable materials to me in Tuscaloosa through Interlibrary Loan. At MSSU's Spiva Library, Kayla Reed and Whitney Hamm have answered questions about collections and fielded many requests for loans.

The process of turning this project into a book manuscript has benefited from the expertise of the editors at the University of North Carolina Press. Early conversations with Mark Simpson-Vos helped me to reframe the project's narrative and argument. Aaron Sheehan-Dean spent many hours over the years helping me to fine-tune my ideas to better fit my project into the Civil War America series. The anonymous readers, as well, offered valuable suggestions for sharpening and hammering home my arguments in the final version of the manuscript. Many others at UNC Press have patiently fielded my questions and provided their expertise as I moved through the process of publication.

My family has supported me for many years. My grandparents, Wendell and Eva Bever and Gloria and Dois Nix, instilled in me an appreciation for family and American history at an early age. Shannon and Shawn Nix, Erin Nix, Kathryn Presley, Kelsey Nix, and Haley and Scott Proctor all opened their homes to me while I traveled for my research. They, along with Janice and Bascom Ratliff, James Delehanty, Ryan Bailey, Dennis, Gladys, and Joshua Bever, the Jarvises, the Hulls, and the Matukewiczes, have provided support and respite from work throughout the years. Evan and Breanna Bever are not only my brother and sister-in-law but also dear friends. Rich conversations with them have shaped my scholarship and my teaching. My nephew Isaiah provides joy and creative insight about life. Atticus has provided constant companionship and (in his own furry way) research assistance since I began my graduate career long ago. Hedy is less helpful with work but is still cute enough.

While writing this book, my life has undergone immense changes. When I began working at MSSU, I met a quiet political scientist, Will Delehanty. Over the years, we became friends. Eventually, we got married. Will has provided wonderful support for my research, and his insights have helped me immensely—especially with my copious data sets, which are more his purview than mine. When I married Will, I gained a daughter, Lilly, who fills our home with laughter and sometimes joins me for writing sessions, during which she points out that her stories, unlike mine, include original illustrations. The imminent arrival of our son, Benjamin, gave me the motivation I needed to push through to the end of the project. His smiles and coos enrich every day.

Finally, I owe a tremendous debt to my parents, David and Kelly Bever. My mother died while I was working on the book, but throughout my childhood and young adulthood she and Dad instilled in me a deep love and appreciation for the past. Dad and Linda Bever continue to provide love and support for Will and me as we research and teach. I am grateful for family that never questions the value of studying history and the humanities.

Notes

List of Abbreviations

FHS	Filson Historical Society
JATU	*Journal of the American Temperance Union and New York Prohibitionist*
LVA	Library of Virginia
MDAH	Mississippi Department of Archives and History
MOC	Museum of the Confederacy
MOSA	Missouri State Archives
NARA	National Archives and Records Administration
OR	*Official Records of the Union and Confederate Armies*
ORN	*Official Records of the Union and Confederate Navies*
SANC	State Archives of North Carolina
SHC	Southern Historical Collection
SHSI	State Historical Society of Iowa
UVA	University of Virginia Libraries
VHS	Virginia Historical Society
WHS	Wisconsin Historical Society

Introduction

1. [No title], *JATU* 23 (December 1860): 184. Although Lincoln and Hamlin had both publicly espoused some personal temperance habits, there was no indication that the Republican Party was set to make temperance a central component of its platform, despite what ATU members perceived.

2. The *Templars' Magazine* (Cincinnati) quoted in the *JATU* 23 (December 1860): 188.

3. Quoted in "What Next?," *JATU* 23 (December 1860): 184.

4. It is difficult to find hard data to determine how many subscribers the *JATU* had in the 1860s. Millions of temperance pamphlets, tracts, and periodicals circulated throughout the Northeast in the antebellum decades, and the American Temperance Society and American Temperance Union had more than a million members in their heydays. See Rorabaugh, *Alcoholic Republic*, 197–202. Frank Luther Mott lists the *JATU* as the only temperance journal to publish throughout the Civil War, but he does not provide subscriber information for the journal or any other temperance publication; see Mott, *History of American Magazines, 1741–1930*, 2:210. Clifford S. Griffin estimates that thousands of Union troops read the *JATU* while serving in the ranks; see Griffin, *Their Brothers' Keepers*, 247.

5. "Mr. Delavan has forwarded to us the following letter from James Black, Esq., of Pennsylvania, for publication, which we give with pleasure, Lancaster, Pa, 25, July, 1860," *JATU* 23 (September 1860): 130. Ian R. Tyrrell notes similar complaints from 1850s temperance reformers in *Sobering Up*, 306.

6. Studies of temperance and prohibition often focus on either the antebellum or the postbellum decades, and the Civil War period is often overlooked or too often characterized as the nadir of the temperance movement, a view I believe overlooks the complex conversations about liquor that took place during the war. My study builds on the work of Holly Berkley Fletcher, whose gendered analysis of nineteenth-century temperance reform provides perhaps the best analysis of the war years. Fletcher argues that the Civil War was a period of transition for the temperance movement in the North and that Northern reformers often found themselves at odds with the military and the growing brewing industry as they tried to win a war against alcohol. See Fletcher, *Gender*, 58–78. Paul Boyer mentions the New York Draft Riots only in passing in his important work on moral reform in the long nineteenth century. See Boyer, *Urban Masses and Moral Order*, 69–70, 96–97. Elaine Frantz Parsons touches on the Civil War in passing in her study on alcohol and nineteenth-century manhood by briefly mentioning that liquor was considered an enemy and a form of enslavement worse than Southern slavery; see Parsons, *Manhood Lost*, 26, 135.

7. Boyer, *Urban Masses and Moral Order*; Dorsey, *Reforming Men and Women*; Parsons, *Manhood Lost*; Fletcher, *Gender*.

8. Cary, *Historical Sketch*, 3–4; *Constitution and By-Laws of Harrod Division*; Tyrrell, *Sobering Up*; Dorsey, *Reforming Men and Women*, 124–31; Sellers, *Prohibition Movement in Alabama*, 22–23; Pearson and Hendricks, *Liquor and Anti-Liquor in Virginia*, 91–110; Blocker, *American Temperance Movements*, 50–51.

9. Thompson, *Most Stirring and Significant Episode*, 15–44.

10. Blocker, *American Temperance Movements*, 14. For comparison, membership in the American Anti-Slavery Society hovered around 5–10 percent of the population in middle and Northern states. See Sinha, *Slave's Cause*, 252–53.

11. Tyrrell, *Sobering Up*; Griffin, *Their Brothers' Keepers*; Blocker, *American Temperance Movements*, 1–60.

12. Conlin, "Dangerous *Isms*." Joe L. Coker contends that although evangelical temperance organizations existed in the antebellum South, the legal prohibition movement gained little traction in the region before the 1880s; see Coker, *Liquor*, 13–36.

13. Tyrrell, "Drink and Temperance"; Eslinger, "Antebellum Liquor Reform"; Carlson, "'Drinks He'"; Huebner, "Joseph Henry Lumpkin"; Stewart, *Moonshiners and Prohibitionists*, 9–60; Lebsock, *Free Women of Petersburg*, 229; Wells, *Origins*, 89–132; Willis, *Southern Prohibition*, 15–66.

14. Willis, *Southern Prohibition*, 17; Coker, *Liquor*, 24.

15. "Boston, December 11, 1860," *JATU* 25 (February 1861): 24; Tyrrell, *Sobering Up*, 290–309; Dannenbaum, *Drink and Disorder*, 69–175.

16. "Report, of the Executive Committee of the Vermont State Temperance Society," *JATU* 26 (January 1862): 2.

17. For studies of moral reform and national vision, see Abzug, *Cosmos Crumbling*; Morone, *Hellfire Nation*. Historians argue that many Americans understood the war in providential terms; see Woodworth, *While God Is Marching On*; Rable, *God's Almost Chosen Peoples*; Wright and Dresser, *Apocalypse and the Millennium*.

18. For scholarship on camp life and troop discipline, see Wiley, *Life of Johnny Reb*; Wiley, *Life of Billy Yank*; Glatthaar, *General Lee's Army*; Foote, *Gentlemen and the Roughs*; Ramold, *Baring the Iron Hand*.

19. Ural, *Harp and the Eagle*, 28; Christian B. Keller, *Chancellorsville and the Germans*, 11–15.

20. Historians debate the extent to which sectional definitions of masculinity shaped Northern and Southern men's experiences as soldiers. Recently, Peter S. Carmichael has argued that while both Union and Confederate soldiers adopted a pragmatic approach to dealing with the war's carnage, Northern soldiers understood better the consequences of their actions in the midst of war than their Southern counterparts. Despite identifying regional differences, however, Carmichael also argues that class status and education affected soldiers' behavior and understanding of their role in the conflict. See Carmichael, *War for the Common Soldier*. Reid Mitchell also argues for regional differences between Northern and Southern soldiers, noting that Southern men had an even more difficult time than their Northern counterparts in accepting military discipline because they associated it with slavery; see Mitchell, *Civil War Soldiers*, 58. That being said, other scholars have shown that not all Northern soldiers brought with them to war the notion that self-control was an important component of masculinity; see Foote, *Gentlemen and the Roughs*; Mitchell, *Vacant Chair*, 3–18. Definitions of masculinity were clearly fluid. This study argues that when it came to drinking and masculinity, class status and urban/rural divides played a much bigger role than region in shaping men's ideas. Moreover, this study argues that wartime experiences reshaped their definitions of masculinity, building on the work of scholars such as Gerald F. Linderman, who argues that Northern and Southern soldiers similarly prized courage as a cornerstone of their masculinity when the war began, but the terror of war led to disillusionment as men recognized that courage and morality resulted in death, and more recently, Lauren K. Thompson, who argues that men ignored and adapted military regulations to suit their physical and emotional needs in the midst of dehumanizing carnage. See Linderman, *Embattled Courage*; Lauren K. Thompson, *Friendly Enemies*.

21. Paul D. Escott argues that Confederates gave military officers a wide berth to define "military necessity" and allowed them to curtail civilians' rights as a result. See Escott, *Military Necessity*. Mark Neely Jr. has had perhaps the most substantive discussion of Confederate prohibition in his study of martial law, and he asserts that morality absolutely played a role in Southern states' willingness to curtail the liquor trade. See Neely, *Southern Rights*, 29–42. Scholars have shown that Lincoln flexed the power of the federal government to control civilian behavior through suspending the writ of habeas corpus or authorizing martial law. For discussions of the expansion of the Union government, see Paludan, *People's Contest*; Bensel, *Yankee Leviathan*. For discussions of the Lincoln administration's expansion of martial law, see Neely, *Fate of Liberty*; Blair, *With Malice toward Some*.

22. The arguments between the national and state governments over distilling represent yet another example of the expanding Confederate state—at multiple levels—and the conflicts over sovereignty it created. For scholarship on the expansion of the Confederate state and national governments, see Thomas, *Confederate Nation*; Thomas, *Confederacy as a Revolutionary Experience*; Blair, *Virginia's Private War*; McCurry, *Confederate Reckoning*.

23. Scholars have argued that the Civil War necessitated the development of new ideas of patriotism and national duty. Northerners and Southerners embraced new notions of loyalty and patriotism that required individuals to embrace a particular vision of the nation and act it out through service and personal sacrifice; see Lawson, *Patriotic Fires*; Faust, *Confederate Nationalism*, 41–57; Gallman, *Defining Duty*.

24. Christian G. Samito argues that the Civil War allowed communities—such as African Americans and Irish immigrants—who had previously been considered outsiders in American political society to claim citizenship through their wartime service and sacrifice. Loyalty was demonstrable through behavior. See Samito, *Becoming American under Fire*. Studies on German, Irish, Jewish, African, and Native Americans have broadened this discussion further. See Ural, *Civil War Citizens*.

25. Scott C. Martin has attempted to tackle this topic. He argues that the Union and Confederate armies had inconsistent alcohol policies, that alcohol was available to soldiers, and that it undoubtedly caused serious blunders on the battlefield. See Martin, "Soldier Intoxicated."

26. For scholarship on Grant and his drinking, see Catton, *Grant Moves South*; Catton, *Grant Takes Command*; Simpson, *Ulysses S. Grant*; Waugh, *U. S. Grant*.

27. Foster, *Moral Reconstruction*; Coker, *Liquor*; Willis, *Southern Prohibition*.

Chapter One

1. "Return to the Spirit Ration," *JATU* 24 (November 1861): 169.
2. "Spirit Ration in the Army," *JATU* 25 (July 1862): 106.
3. Marsh, *No. 90*, 19. This tract retold the biography (in shortened form) of British imperial solder Vicars, who relied on cold water to survive the Crimean War. Another tract similarly cites British experiences in the Crimean War to argue that liquor endangered Southern soldiers; see Physician, *Liquor and Lincoln*, 1–2.
4. Tripler, *Manual*, 17–18.
5. Ramold, *Baring the Iron Hand*, 126; Vargas, "Progressive Agent of Mischief."
6. Conroy, *In Public Houses*, 57–156; Salinger, *Taverns and Drinking*, 151–209.
7. Flannery, *Civil War Pharmacy*, 36–39.
8. Hammond, *Treatise on Hygiene*, 534.
9. Hammond, *Treatise on Hygiene*, 543–45.
10. Warren, *Epitome of Practical Surgery*, 70.
11. Ledger records from Mobile, Alabama's Ross General Hospital show liquor amounts approximately seven times greater than those of Richmond, Virginia's Moore Hospital during the summer and fall of 1862. But whereas Moore Hospital's supply remained relatively steady throughout the war, Ross General Hospital's whiskey supply took a nosedive by the winter of 1863 and never quite rebounded. A comparison between Georgia's and Virginia's medical requisition records shows similar shortages in the summer and fall of 1863. But while both states revived their medical supply in 1864, Virginia never quite reached Georgia's levels. Vols. 24, 36, 122½, 320, 336, 355, 374, 383, 388, 433, 469, 470, 471, 536, 542, 567, 568, 569, 571, 574, 575, 577, 580; chap. 6, RG 109, NARA. I compared information for medical records from Georgia, Virginia, and Alabama because of diligent work by research assistants Deanna Smith and Ashley Thomas, who worked with me on a Mapping Alcohol in the Civil War project at Missouri Southern State University. Comments from commanding officers indicate that outside the Medical Departments, supplies of whiskey rations were even scarcer, although their availability followed the similar pattern: whiskey was more available in the Deep South than it was in Virginia. See *OR*, ser. 1, 33:1065; *Rebellion Record*, 11:Doc. 153.

12. Warren, *Epitome of Practical Surgery*, 70.

13. The surgeons do not specifically mention the strength of the liquors when discussing which settled best in patients' stomachs. But in the nineteenth century, brandies tended to range from 80 to 110 proof, whereas whiskey was generally 150 proof. Michael R. Veach, email to author, September 24, 2020; Raitz, *Bourbon's Backroads*, 7.

14. Porcher, *Resources*, 65, 157, 160, 162, 166, 222, 266, 280, 386, 522.

15. United States War Department, *Revised Regulations for the Army of the United States, 1861*, 244. For comparison, a single shot in the United States is approximately 1.5 fluid ounces. If these men received a full ration of whiskey, they received more than a modern double-shot of alcohol. *Regulations for the Subsistence Department of the Confederate States of America* (1861), 45; *Regulations for the Subsistence Department of the Confederate States* (1862), 13; *Regulations for the Medical Department of the C. S. Army*, 11, 47. For scholarship on Confederate medical supply, see Cunningham, *Doctors in Gray*, 134–62; for alcohol, see 151–52.

16. Billings, *Hardtack and Coffee*, 139–41; *OR*, ser. 1, 42(2):70; Bellard, *Gone for a Soldier*, 77; Ramold, *Baring the Iron Hand*, 150–52.

17. Chisolm, *Manual of Military Surgery*, 128.

18. Chloroform was the preferred anesthetic. See Chisolm, *Manual of Military Surgery*, 128–29; Warren, *Epitome of Practical Surgery*, 93, 242.

19. Warren, *Epitome of Practical Surgery*, 98–99.

20. Warren, *Epitome of Practical Surgery*, 168. In cases where primary amputation was unwarranted, patients, again, were to be stimulated with "cool water, then wine, brandy or food if possible." Warren, *Epitome of Practical Surgery*, 85–86.

21. Chisolm, *Manual of Military Surgery*, 114, 110–11. For carrying brandy among battle supplies, see also "General Orders, No. 53," April 5, 1863, *OR*, ser. 1, 14:883.

22. Chisolm, *Manual of Military Surgery*, 249.

23. Scholars have found that the Union army was much better supplied than its Confederate counterpart, and in general, the Confederacy and its subsistence department suffered from chronic food shortages and economic mismanagement. Even so, Union supply fluctuated based on location and depended on Union control of roads, railways, and rivers. See Earl J. Hess, *Civil War Supply and Strategy*; Goff, *Confederate Supply*; Donald, *Why the North Won*; Andrew F. Smith, *Starving the South*. Provision ledgers for the Commissary General of Subsistence detail the amount of whiskey by location (and usually by regiment). Although NARA does not have complete ledgers for all years of the war, the existing volumes illustrate clearly that during the war's first two years, Maryland and Virginia received 98,620 and 67,670 gallons of whiskey, respectively, and the District of Columbia received 6,360 gallons. Beyond the eastern theater, supply was significantly less. For example, Minnesota and Tennessee received approximately 14,000 gallons, South Carolina received 13,200, and Florida, Missouri, and Illinois received between 11,000 and 12,000. All remaining states in the Union received fewer than 10,000 during the first two years of the war. (The average of all states was 7,950 gallons). See Volume 191: Records of the War Dept., Office of the Commissary General of Subsistence, Selections from Provision Book, 1854–1861; Volume 192: 1861–1862; and Volume 193: Issues to Indians and Destitute Citizens in Entry 36, RG 192, NARA. In September 1862, U.S. Army medical inspector Richard H. Coolidge assured the surgeon general that essential supplies reached wounded troops in Centreville. Among the hospital stores being requisitioned were whiskey, brandy, and wine: *OR*, ser. 1, 19(2):260. Reports from

the spring of 1864 indicate that supplies varied from corps to corps: *OR*, ser. 1, 36(1):214, 223, 237; *OR*, ser. 1, 22(2):524. Reports from November 1864 state that supplies delivered by boat to Union soldiers stationed at Little Rock contained plenty of groceries and dry goods, and even some ale, but "no large shipments of liquor": *OR*, ser. 1, 41(4):571.

24. *OR*, ser. 1, 15(1):398. Union medical director Jonathan Letterman likewise stipulated that hospital wagons in the Army of the Potomac should carry twelve pints of alcohol, twenty-four bottles of whiskey, and six bottles of brandy. Letterman, *Medical Recollections*, 40, 53–54.

25. *OR*, ser. 1, 5:102.

26. *OR*, ser. 1, 31(1):100.

27. *OR*, ser. 1, 46(1):695. There is an additional example where the 3rd US Colored Troops are accused by Acting Ensign James H. Berry of not providing for his men, but Lieutenant D. P. Yates and Colonel I. G. Kappner maintain that the sailors of the steamer were rescued and cared for, and noted that the injured received "medical attendance, and all whisky, coffee, meat, and bread." So, like the other examples, whiskey is provided right alongside rations and medical care to fortify the wounded. See *OR*, ser. 1, 48(1):222.

28. Chisolm, *Manual of Military Surgery*, 199; Warren, *Epitome of Practical Surgery*, 129–30; Chisolm, *Manual of Military Surgery*, 14–15.

29. Shively, *Nature's Civil War*, 18–21; George Worthington Adams, *Doctors in Blue*, 218–19.

30. Headrick, *Tools of Empire*, 58–79.

31. *Sanitary Commission No. 31*; *OR*, ser. 1, 5:83–84.

32. *OR*, ser. 1, 5:261; *OR*, ser. 1, 16(2):62.

33. Bellard, *Gone for a Soldier*, 74, 77 (May 1862); Corby, *Memoirs of Chaplain Life*, 82–83.

34. *OR*, ser. 1, 11(3):577.

35. Walters, *American Reformers*, 147–73; Shprintzen, *Vegetarian Crusade*.

36. W. J. Rorabaugh argues that temperance advocates had been encouraging Americans to stop drinking to promote their health since the late eighteenth century. See Rorabaugh, *Alcoholic Republic*, 41–47.

37. "Medical Reaction against Stimulants," *JATU* 24 (March 1861): 46; "Poison in Liquors," *JATU* 24 (April 1861): 49.

38. "Medical Use," from the *Maine Journal* quoted in the *JATU* 24 (April 1861): 63.

39. James Black, "The True Temperance Platform," *JATU* 27 (July 1864): 100.

40. "Alcohol as a Medicine," *JATU* 28 (April 1865): 52.

41. "Liquor as a Medicine," *JATU* 24 (June 1861): 95.

42. "The Testimonies of Experience," *JATU* 26 (September 1863): 131.

43. F. Vivian, President of Torquay Temperance Society, "Medical Action of Alcohol: From the Torquay Directory," *JATU* 27 (February 1864): 19.

44. "The Temperance Cause," *Herald of Health and Water-Cure Journal* 1 (January 1863): 13.

45. "Temperance Cause," 16. For additional discussion of the alliance with Delevan and the temperance movement against the medical profession, see also "Popular Lectures in the College," *Herald of Health and Water-Cure Journal* 1 (January 1863): 23; "Showers of Compliments," *Herald of Health and Water-Cure Journal* 1 (February 1863): 72; "The Muddle of the Teetotalers," *Herald of Health and Water-Cure Journal* 1 (March 1863): 105; "The Herald for the Doctors," *Herald of Health and Water-Cure Journal* 1 (May 1863): 209.

46. "Water the Drink for Soldiers," *JATU* 24 (September 1861): 131.
47. "Water," *Spirit of the Age* 13 (November 20, 1861), 1.
48. "The Use of Intoxicating Drinks," *Spirit of the Age* 14 (March 16, 1863), 1.
49. "The Sick Soldiers," *Spirit of the Age* 13 (September 25, 1861), 2.
50. *OR*, ser. 1, 24(3):577 [General Orders, No. 105] (Memphis, TN, August 5, 1863).
51. *OR*, ser. 1, 36(3):74; *OR*, ser. 1, 42(1):192. (Petersburg, August 1864).
52. McClellan issued General Order No. 136 on June 19, 1862; Butler issued General Order No. 7 on March 28, 1862; Halleck issued General Orders No. 4, on September 25, 1862. The *JATU* reported when officers passed these orders. See "Spirit Ration Discontinued," *JATU* 25 (July 1862): 112; "Gen. Butler's Order," *JATU* 25 (August 1862): 116; "Gen. Halleck's Army," *JATU* 25 (August 1862): 116.
53. Bircher, *Drummer-Boy's Diary*, 111–12. For an additional example, see *OR*, ser. 1, 37(1):339.
54. *OR*, ser. 1, 46(3):646.
55. Shively, *Nature's Civil War*, 18–21.
56. *Lynchburg Republican*, n.d., in *Daily Dispatch* (Richmond, VA), September 27, 1861.
57. *OR*, ser. 1, 28(2):534.
58. Brown, *Diary of a Line Officer*, 16. For an additional example involving U.S. Colored Troops (USCT), see Wilder, *Practicing Medicine*, 142–43.
59. Campbell, *Union Must Stand*, 40–41.
60. *OR*, ser. 1, 40(3):784–85.
61. Jones, *Artilleryman's Diary*, 208. For additional examples, see Day, *My Diary*, 96; Weld, *War Diary*, 57–59.
62. Dexter, *Seymour Dexter, Union Army*, 14; Butler, *Private and Official Correspondence*, 5:168; Seth James Wells, *Siege of Vicksburg*, 93; Stevens, *"Dear Carrie"*, 316. Kathryn Shively has analyzed the relationship between mental and physical health extensively. She argues persuasively that even though nineteenth-century physicians believed that mental capacity and physical health were related, medical departments during the war did not keep close records on mental illness. Nonetheless, there is plenty of documentation that morale and physical health were intertwined. Shively, *Nature's Civil War*, 59–64.
63. Stotelmyer, *Bivouacs of the Dead*, 5. For scholarship on burying the dead, see Neff, *Honoring the Civil War Dead*, 16–65.
64. *OR*, ser. 1, 42(2):70, 552–53.
65. *OR*, ser. 1, 5:110.
66. Day, *My Diary*, 60.
67. Ford, Adams, and Adams, *Cycle of Adams Letters*, 1:203–5.
68. *OR*, ser. 1, 14:350. Letterman reiterated his policy in March 1863: *OR*, ser. 1, 11(1):213.
69. Howe, *Passages*, 42. For an additional example, see Jackson, *Colonel's Diary*, 93.
70. Day, *My Diary*, 37.
71. Rorabaugh, *Alcoholic Republic*, 95–122.
72. "The Health of the Army," *New York Times*, August 1, 1861. Attempting to ward off scurvy with fermented beverages was not unheard of in the nineteenth century, although it may not have been as effective as the *New York Times* and others perceived it to be. See Stubbs, "Captain Cook's Beer."
73. *OR*, ser. 1, 52(1):621.

74. *OR*, ser. 1, 39(2):275–76.

75. Alonzo Miller, *Diaries and Letters*, 104. For more context on Union supply during Sherman's campaigns in Georgia, see Earl Hess, *Civil War Supply and Strategy*, 139–204.

76. Donaldson, *Inside*, 323.

77. Day, *My Diary*, 96.

78. Robert Goldthwaite Carter, *Four Brothers in Blue*, 458.

79. Hubbs, *Voices from Company D*, 61.

80. Goff, *Confederate Supply*.

81. *OR*, ser. 3, 5:423.

82. Dixon, *Blues in Gray*, 91–92.

83. *OR*, ser. 1, 29(1):76.

84. *OR*, ser. 1, 22(2):287.

85. Reinhart, *German Hurrah!*, 129.

86. *Regulations for the Medical Department of the C. S. Army*, 13–14.

87. *OR*, ser. 2, 7:119.

88. Cumming, *Kate*, 255.

89. Wilder, *Practicing Medicine*, 221, 214.

90. Emerson, *Life of Abbey Hopper Gibbons*, 2:90.

91. Kamphoefner and Helbich, *Germans in the Civil War*, 161.

92. Haupt, *Reminiscences of General Herman Haupt*, 118, 126–27.

93. Frederick Hess, *Letters to Tobitha*, 186; Eugene Forbes, *Diary of a Soldier*, 38. Political prisoner Lawrence Sangston had his private stores of blackberry brandy confiscated by a Colonel Burke. His medicinal brandy bottle was found empty the next morning "with several others on the wood pile outside the fort." All the confiscated medicinal spirits had been consumed by the prison staff. See Sangston, *Bastiles of the North*, 53.

94. *OR*, ser. 2, 5:562.

95. Blackford, *Letters from Lee's Army*, 261.

96. Pember, *Southern Woman's Story*, 47–48. Pember's assumption that women were more reliable (and more sober) than their male counterparts had at least one notable exception. One English nurse—a veteran of the Crimean war with fourteen years of hospital experience—was reputedly unqualified to do her job and nearly immediately removed from her ward "dead drunk and swearing like a trooper." See von Olnhausen, *Adventures*, 44–45.

97. Northern and Southern women participated in hospital work during the war. Some women chose to view their work as nurses as a patriotic extension of their domestic relief work. In the Confederacy, women nurses faced hostility from men who believed that hospitals were too gruesome for women. Nurses in the South also confronted organizational and moral chaos from their male colleagues. For scholarship on nursing, see Rable, *Civil Wars*, 121–28; Faust, *Mothers of Invention*, 92–113; Cutter, *Domestic Devils, Battlefield Angels*, 154–95; Silber, *Daughters of the Union*, 194–221.

98. Von Olnhausen, *Adventures of an Army Nurse in Two Wars*, 182–87.

99. Von Olnhausen, *Adventures of an Army Nurse in Two Wars*, 193–94.

100. David Bagley to James D. Robison, undated, and James D. Robison to David Bagley, undated, James D. Robison with David Bagley Letters, Section 19, Conrad (Holmes) Papers, VHS.

101. Circular... [concerning issue of alcoholic stimulants], (Charleston, SC: 1863); Circular... [concerning the administration of alcoholic stimulants], (Charleston, SC: 1864); Circular no. 10 ... [relating to abuse of administration of alcoholic stimulants], (Richmond, VA: 1864).

102. Cumming, *Kate*, 203.

103. *OR*, ser. 2, 5:881.

104. Cummins, *Give God the Glory*, 79.

105. Tyler, *Recollections of the Civil War*, 268–69.

106. Wilder, *Practicing Medicine*, 145–46, 77.

107. Warren, *Epitome of Practical Surgery*, 19.

108. Pender, *General to His Lady*, 210.

109. Humphreys, *Marrow of Tragedy*, 170–71.

110. Surgeon-General's Office, Confederate States of America, *Guide for Inspection of Hospitals and for Inspector's Report*, 2.

111. For excerpts from the temperance sections of Union hospital newspapers, see Spar, *Civil War Hospital Newspapers*. For quotations, see 177 (first quotation), 55 (second quotation).

112. "The Wounded Soldier," *JATU* 25 (October 1862): 145.

113. "The Sick Soldier," *JATU* 26 (July 1863): 101.

114. "The Soldier Needs and Must Have Liquor," *JATU* 27 (January 1864): 8.

115. Clifford S. Griffin briefly explores the conflict between the various volunteers who promoted temperance and the U.S. Sanitary Commission, which provided medicinal rations, in *Their Brothers' Keepers*, 248–55. For more scholarship on the USSC, see Maxwell, *Lincoln's Fifth Wheel*; Giesberg, *Civil War Sisterhood*.

116. Tyler, *Recollections of the Civil War*, 298.

117. Surgeon M. W. Robbins, Articles Necessary for the Hospital, 4th Regiment Iowa Volunteers, December 19, 1861, Document 39, folder 6, box 1; Annie Winterborham to Annie Wittenmyer, January 20, 1862, Document 51, folder 7, box 1; C. D. Allen to Mrs. Strong, February 29, 1862, Document 63, folder 8, box 1; Mrs. M. A. Allison to Annie Wittenmyer, May 2, 1862, Document 85, folder 10, box 1; Anna Me. P. Dillon to Annie Wittenmyer, September 21, 1862, Document 130, folder 13, box 1; From the Glasgow Ladies Soldiers' Aid Society, April 21, 1862, Document 187, folder 17, box 1; A list of the articles in the box of Hospital Stores sent by the ladies, April 22, 1862, Document 190, folder 17, box 1; Wa. M. Milford to Annie Wittenmyer, July 12, 1862, Document 207, folder 19, box 1; Rantau [?] to Annie Wittenmyer, no date, Document 207, folder 2, box 17; Mrs. N. L. Price to Mrs. Wittenmyer, June 26, 1863, Document 123, folder 12, box 2; Annie Wittenmyer Papers, 1861–1901, Manuscripts Collection, Des Moines Historical Library, SHSI.

118. Holmes, *Diary of Miss Emma Holmes*, 229.

Chapter Two

1. Stott, *For Duty and Destiny*, 195.

2. "They Sacrificed in Many Ways: Here's Five Madison County Soldiers Who Made Their Marks in Civil War," *Herald Bulletin* (Anderson, IN), July 23, 2017, http://www.heraldbulletin.com/community/they-sacrificed-in-many-ways/article_6c4227a8-c9fe-524f-ac22-6a179632bf35.html (accessed April 6, 2020).

184 *Notes to Chapter Two*

3. Dorsey, *Reforming Men and Women*; Bederman, *Manliness and Civilization*.

4. Mitchell, *Vacant Chair*, 19–37; Foote, *Gentlemen and the Roughs*, 17–65; Bledsoe, *Citizen-Officers*, 1–24; Broomall, *Private Confederacies*, 12–31.

5. Tyrrell, *Sobering Up*; Ownby, *Subduing Satan*; Tyrrell, "Drink and Temperance"; Eslinger, "Antebellum Liquor Reform"; Carlson, "'Drinks He'"; Huebner, "Joseph Henry Lumpkin"; Stewart, *Moonshiners and Prohibitionists*, 9–60; Willis, *Southern Prohibition*, 15–66.

6. MacDonald, *Sons of the Empire*; Mosse, *Image of Man*; Beattie, *Tribute of Blood*.

7. Mitchell, *Vacant Chair*, 39–54; Foote, *Gentlemen and the Roughs*, 67–170; Glatthaar, *General Lee's Army*; Ramold, *Baring the Iron Hand*.

8. Bledsoe, *Citizen-Officers*.

9. Jones, *Artilleryman's Diary*, 79.

10. Jones, *Artilleryman's Diary*, 348.

11. Wheeler, *Letters*, 293.

12. Kinsley, *Diary of a Christian Soldier*, 140–41.

13. Trobriand, *Four Years*, 707–8.

14. *History of the 127th Regiment Pennsylvania Volunteers*, 167–69.

15. Gregg, *Life in the Army*, 94–96. The story is recounted in the regimental history, although presumably it is based off of Gregg's memoir, which was published thirty years earlier. See *History of the 127th Regiment Pennsylvania Volunteers*, 181.

16. Russell, *My Diary North and South*, 206, 214.

17. Russell, *My Diary North and South*, 568.

18. Reminisco, *Life in the Union Army*, 16, 72, and 60 (for quotation).

19. Kamphoefner and Helbich, *Germans in the Civil War*, 281–82.

20. Donaldson, *Inside*, 268–70.

21. Conyngham, *Irish brigade*, 234.

22. Ayling, *Yankee at Arms*, 124.

23. Morse, *Letters*, 35–36.

24. Wainwright, *Diary of Battle*, 271, 433.

25. Shively, *Nature's Civil War*.

26. Robert Manson Myers, *Children of Pride*, 208, 210, 279–81.

27. Myers, *Children of Pride*, 363, 384, 387–88.

28. Myers, *Children of Pride*, 857, 861, 906, 915–17.

29. Johansson, *Widows by the Thousand*, 214.

30. Petty, *Journey to Pleasant Hill*, 81.

31. Robert A. Moore, *Life for the Confederacy*, 38.

32. Patterson, *Yankee Rebel*, l, 101.

33. David Holt, *Mississippi Rebel*, 118.

34. Reinhart, *German Hurrah!*, 51.

35. Foroughi, *Go If You Think*, 92.

36. Ayling, *Yankee at Arms*, 58–59, 61.

37. Susan J. Matt argues that the antebellum celebration of family life and homes created difficulties for soldiers who were far away from their families for the first times in their lives. Soldiers were supposed to fight for their homes—their countries—but Matt finds that homesickness had a crippling physical and emotional effect on many young men. See Matt, *Homesickness*, 75–101.

38. Shively, *Nature's Civil War*, 63.
39. Donaldson, *Inside*, 196.
40. Bragg, *Letters of a Confederate Surgeon*, 149.
41. Haydon, *For Country, Cause, and Leader*, 332–33.
42. Gerald F. Linderman has argued that soldiers became disillusioned with notions of moral courage and duty and that they found themselves isolated from the civilian population by the horrors they witnessed. See Linderman, *Embattled Courage*.
43. Jones, *Artilleryman's Diary*, 90.
44. Bellard, *Gone for a Soldier*, 28–29.
45. Howe, *Passages*, 26.
46. Nelson, *Ruin Nation*.
47. Glatthaar, *General Lee's Army*, 220–41; Bell Irvin Wiley, *Life of Billy Yank*, 152–91; Bell Irvin Wiley, *Life of Johnny Reb*, 59–67, 151–73.
48. Wainwright, *Diary of Battle*, 172; Petty, *Journey to Pleasant Hill*, 257–58.
49. Ayling, *Yankee at Arms*, 210; Wainwright, *Diary of Battle*, 473.
50. Haydon, *For Country, Cause, and Leader*, 322.
51. Ownby, *Subduing Satan*, 21–99.
52. Glatthaar, *General Lee's Army*, 221.
53. Chauncey Herbert Cooke, *Soldier Boy's Letters*, 15.
54. Welch, *Confederate Surgeon's Letters*, 52; Ayling, *Yankee at Arms*, 189.
55. Patterson, *Yankee Rebel*, 69.
56. Dexter, *Seymour Dexter, Union Army*, 11–12. Antebellum colleges, especially in New England, noted that young men were particularly susceptible to drinking, and faculty formed clubs to promote temperance among students, see David R. Huehner, "'Water Is Indeed Best,'" in Blocker, *Alcohol, Reform and Society*, 69–100.
57. Haines, *In the Country*, 58–59.
58. Quoted, "Intemperance in the Camp," *Spirit of the Age* 12 (June 26, 1861): 2.
59. Gregg, *Life in the Army*, 86–87.
60. Dooley, *John Dooley, Confederate Soldier*, 173.
61. Conyngham, *Irish brigade*, 514.
62. Reinhart, *German Hurrah!*, 87–88.
63. Bellard, *Gone for a Soldier*, 267.
64. Stevens, "*Dear Carrie . . .*," 228–29.
65. Reinhart, *German Hurrah!*, 47.
66. *OR*, ser. 2, 4:124.
67. Tenney, *War Diary*, 2 [July 4, 1862].
68. Kinsley, *Diary of a Christian Soldier*, 177.
69. Campbell, *Union Must Stand*, 79.
70. Nissenbaum, *Battle for Christmas*.
71. George C. Rable, "Hearth, Home, and Family in the Fredericksburg Campaign," in Cashin, *War Was You and Me*, 85–111.
72. Conyngham, *Irish brigade*, 39–40.
73. Stephens, *Voice of Thunder*, 219. For additional accounts of commissary rations near Fredericksburg, see Bellard, *Gone for a Soldier*, 189; Rable, *Fredericksburg! Fredericksburg!*.
74. Kamphoefner and Helbich, *Germans in the Civil War*, 263–64.

75. Stephens, *Voice of Thunder*, 219.
76. Boyd, *Belle Boyd*, 2:179–80; Frank Moore, *Rebellion Record*, 4:Poetry 23.
77. David Holt, *Mississippi Rebel*, 221.
78. Petty, *Journey to Pleasant Hill*, 117.
79. Robert A. Moore, *Life for the Confederacy*, 126.
80. Dooley, *John Dooley, Confederate Soldier*, 82.
81. Baptist chaplain William Taylor Stott of the 18th Indiana was quite "sorry ... that quite a number of our company are drunk" on Christmas Day 1861. See *For Duty and Destiny*, 88.
82. Dooley, *John Dooley, Confederate Soldier*, 82; Donaldson, *Inside*, 429.
83. Petty, *Journey to Pleasant Hill*, 29.
84. Patterson, *Yankee Rebel*, 10–11.
85. Kamphoefner and Helbich, *Germans in the Civil War*, 81.
86. Reinhart, *German Hurrah!*, 192.
87. Higginson, *Army Life*, 38.
88. Kamphoefner and Helbich, *Germans in the Civil War*, 123.
89. Jackson, Bryant, and Wills, *Three Rebels Write Home*, 81.
90. Ford, Adams, and Adams, *Cycle of Adams Letters*, 1:215.
91. Robert A. Moore, *Life for the Confederacy*, 90; Toalson, *Mama*, 4; Watson, *Southern Service*, 91.
92. December 26, 1864, John Baxter Moseley Diary, VHS.
93. Richard Lewis, *Camp Life*, 38.
94. Bell Irvin Wiley, *Life of Billy Yank*, 48–49; Bell Irvin Wiley, *Life of Johnny Reb*, 136.
95. Dwight, *Life and Letters*, 82.
96. Haydon, *For Country, Cause, and Leader*, 96–97; Wheeler, *Letters*, 359.
97. Cavins, *Civil War Letters*, 70.
98. *OR*, ser. 1, 17(2):188.
99. Holly Berkley Fletcher, *Gender*, 7–29.
100. Haydon, *For Country, Cause, and Leader*, 96–97.
101. Henry Warren Howe, *Passages*, 62.
102. John C. Myers, *Daily Journal*, 15.
103. Wheeler, *Letters*, 359.
104. Kamphoefner and Helbich, *Germans in the Civil War*, 361.
105. Faust, *Mothers of Invention*; Rable, *Civil Wars*; McCurry, *Confederate Reckoning*; Silber, *Daughters of the Union*; Giesberg, *Army at Home*.
106. Daniel M. Holt, *Surgeon's Civil War*, 98–99.
107. Reminisco, *Life in the Union Army*, 19.
108. Alonzo Miller, *Diaries and Letters, 1864–1865*, 90. Miller had a taste for coffee, to be certain, but he also used coffee as currency in at least once instance to buy pies. See 13, 73.
109. William Wiley, *Civil War Diary*, 153.
110. Corson, *My Dear Jennie*, 31.
111. Hubbs, *Voices from Company D*, 358.
112. Larimer, *Love and Valor*, 243.
113. Elliot H. Fletcher, *Civil War Letters*, 36.
114. Stott, *For Duty and Destiny*, 188.

115. Thompson and Wainwright, *Confidential Correspondence*, 2:78.
116. Butler, *Private and Official Correspondence*, 1:184.
117. Butler, *Private and Official Correspondence*, 3:181.
118. Brewster, *When This Cruel War*, 267.
119. Tyler, *Recollections of the Civil War*, 270.
120. "Document 104: Capture of Union City, TN, Correspondent, March 31, 1862," *Rebellion Record*, 4:Doc. 346.
121. Cumming, *Kate*, 201–2.
122. Reminisco, *Life in the Union Army*, 98.
123. Watson, *Southern Service*, 152–53.
124. McIntyre, *Federals on the Frontier*, 136; for more context, see Monaghan, *Civil War on the Western Border*, 252–60.
125. Kamphoefner and Helbich, *Germans in the Civil War*, 458.
126. Hess, *Letters to Tobitha*, 222.
127. Patrick, *Reluctant Rebel*, 151–52, 159–61, 166; For other accounts of soldiers left hungry while under the command of drunken officers, see Robert A. Moore, *Life for the Confederacy*, 68.
128. *OR*, ser. 1, 42(3):442.
129. Temperance reformers made connections between officers' responsibilities and fatherhood by suggesting all the ways that soldiers were dependent on their officers and how enlisted men's own fathers would certainly be hesitant to turn over their sons to the care of such reckless drunks. "Drunken Officers," *Journal of the American Temperance Union and New York Prohibitionist* 27 (December 1863): 185–86.
130. Nathan W. Daniels, *Thank God*, 121.
131. Hosmer, *Color-Guard*, 240–41.
132. Linderman, *Embattled Courage*; Lauren K. Thompson, *Friendly Enemies*.

Chapter Three

1. Beaudry, *War Journal of Louis N. Beaudry*, 80; Boudrye, *Historic Records*, 88–89.
2. Ramold, *Baring the Iron Hand*; Foote, *Gentlemen and the Roughs*, 119–70; Glatthaar, *General Lee's Army*, 174–85.
3. Rable, *Fredericksburg! Fredericksburg!*, 410–19; Martin, "'Soldier Intoxicated.'"
4. West, *Texan*, 90–91.
5. *OR*, ser. 1, 43(1):580–81. For other examples, see Welles, *Diary of Gideon Welles*, 2:75; Alonzo Miller, *Diaries and Letters, 1864–1865*, 99.
6. Jonathan Huntington Johnson, *Letters and Diary*, 136.
7. Pate, *When This Evil War*, 74.
8. Bellard, *Gone for a Soldier*, 169.
9. Russell, *My Diary North and South*, 301–2.
10. "Soldiers in the Cars," *JATU* 24 (November 1861): 171.
11. Patrick, *Reluctant Rebel*, 64.
12. *OR*, ser. 1, 22(1):668.
13. *OR*, ser. 1, 46(2):167; 46(3):1240.
14. Bellard, *Gone for a Soldier*, 32–33.

15. Howe, *Passages*, 73.
16. *OR*, ser. 1, 5:370.
17. *OR*, ser. 1, 11(2):333.
18. *OR*, ser. 1, 40(1):782.
19. *OR*, ser. 1, 51(1):1209.
20. Brown, *Diary of a Line Officer*, 79.
21. Bledsoe, *Citizen-Officers*; Linderman, *Embattled Courage*.
22. *OR*, ser. 1, 25(2):93.
23. Gregg, *Life in the Army*, 94–96.
24. William Wiley, *Civil War Diary*, 17.
25. William Wiley, *Civil War Diary*, 69–70.
26. Robert A. Moore, *Life for the Confederacy*, 67.
27. Watson, *Southern Service*, 152.
28. Conyngham, *Irish brigade*, 110.
29. Jones, *Artilleryman's Diary*, 79.
30. *OR*, ser. 1, 22(2):1058–60.
31. Duff, *To Petersburg*, 27–28.
32. Reinhart, *Two Germans*, 24, 20–21.
33. Trobriand, *Four Years*, 398–401.
34. Jones, *Artilleryman's Diary*, 91.
35. Chauncey Herbert Cooke, *Soldier Boy's Letters*, 33.
36. Jones, *Artilleryman's Diary*, 29.
37. Hubbs, *Voices from Company D*, 365.
38. Nisbet, *Four Years*, 26.
39. Gregg, *Life in the Army*, 86–87; Haydon, *For Country, Cause, and Leader*, 96–97.
40. Haydon, *For Country, Cause, and Leader*, 96–97.
41. Patrick, *Reluctant Rebel*, 51.
42. Perry, *Letters*, 100.
43. Thomas N. Stevens, *"Dear Carrie . . .,"* 187.
44. Fremantle, *Three Months*, 67.
45. Twichell, *Civil War Letters*, 93.
46. Wills, *Army Life*, 87. Wills also writes that his court-martial duty included "occasionally a shooting or cutting affair among some drunken men." See 224.
47. Weld, *War Diary and Letters*, 362.
48. George Gilbert Smith, *Leaves from a Soldier's Diary*, 85.
49. Hancock, *Hancock's Diary*, 131; Weld, *War Diary and Letters*, 265; Wainwright, *Diary of Battle*, 490.
50. Robert A. Moore, *Life for the Confederacy*, 79, 85.
51. Robert Goldthwaite Carter, *Four Brothers in Blue*, 217; Matthew Cook to Martha Winn, August 24, 1864, Winn-Cook Family Papers, 1861–1875 (Transcriptions), FHS.
52. Lusk, *War Letters*, 72–76.
53. Fleming, *Life and Letters*, 129, 261; Fullam, *Our Cruise*, 23.
54. Duff, *To Petersburg*, 51–52.
55. "Bellum, Horridum Bellum," *JATU* 24 (May 1861): 65; "Editorial Pride," *JATU* 24 (June 1861): 93; "Bellum, Horridum Bellum," *Spirit of the Age* 12 (15 May 1861): 2.

56. "Temperance in the Army," *JATU* 24 (June 1861): 89.

57. "Bellum, Horridum Bellum," *JATU* 24 (May 1861): 65; "Editorial Pride," *JATU* 24 (June 1861): 93.

58. Parsons, *Manhood Lost*; Ownby, *Subduing Satan*; Walters, *American Reformers, 1815–1860*; Holly Berkley Fletcher, *Gender*; Dorsey, *Reforming Men and Women*; Boyer, *Urban Masses*; Stewart, *Moonshiners and Prohibitionists*, 9–60; Willis, *Southern Prohibition*, 15–66.

59. "Patriotism and Temperance," *Spirit of the Age* 12 (May 8, 1861): 2.

60. *JATU* 24 (June 1861): 95.

61. "Capital Lodge 1: Minutes of Meetings, 1864, April 28–1875, May 22," vol. 1, box 2, Register of the Independent Order of Good Templars: Madison Lodge Records, 1864–1923, WHS. In 1861, sixty-one (45 percent) of the new members have flags (out of 115 male and 19 female new members). In 1862, eighty (58 percent) of the new members have flags (out of 124 male and 14 female new members).

62. "Sons of Temperance," *Daily Dispatch* (Richmond, VA), January 13, 1862.

63. "Temperance in War," *Spirit of the Age* 12 (May 15, 1861): 2.

64. Nina Silber has argued that women lost domestic authority over men after the men became soldiers. I would posit that in many cases, when women had authority before the war, they kept it. See Silber, *Daughters of the Union*, 96–98.

65. Brewster, *When This Cruel War*, 31.

66. Foroughi, *Go*, 157. For an additional example, see 232.

67. Harriet Jane Thompson, "Civil War Wife," 222.

68. McFall and McFall, *Civil War Correspondence*, 31.

69. Larimer, *Love and Valor*, 216, 83, 209.

70. Powers, *Hospital Pencillings*, 124.

71. John C. Carter, *Welcome*, 21.

72. Seth James Wells, *Siege of Vicksburg*, 25.

73. Cummins, *Give God the Glory*, 27, 64, 122.

74. Cavins, *Civil War Letters*, 8.

75. Cavins, *Civil War Letters*, 123.

76. Foroughi, *Go*, 232.

77. *JATU* 24 (June 1861): 84.

78. "Tracts for the Army," *JATU* 24 (July 1861): 105; "Tracts for the Army," *JATU* 24 (August 1861): 121.

79. "Tracts for the Army," *JATU* 24 (August 1861): 121.

80. The *JATU* published its donation information monthly, from August 1861 to August 1865. The donation lists, which included the name of the donor along with the amount of the donation, typically appeared on the last page of the journal. In 1861, the *JATU* raised approximately $990; in 1862, $2,100; in 1863, $6,500; in 1864, $6,000; in 1865, $2,500. The *JATU* reported that it could send a package of one thousand tracts for two dollars and fifty cents. Based on this estimate, I have concluded that if the money reportedly raised to send tracts to the army was used for such purposes, the ATU sent more than seven million tracts to the Union army.

81. *No. 26: Are You Ready [For the Soldiers]*, 3.

82. South Carolina Tract Society, *Descriptive List of Tracts*, 3–17.

83. Faust, *This Republic of Suffering*.

84. *No. 26: Are You Ready [For the Soldiers]*; *No. 87: A Word of Warning for the Sick Soldier*; *No. 44: Advice to Soldiers*, 5. For another example, see South Carolina Tract Society, *No. 84: Appeal to the Youth*, 3–6.

85. "The Lobster Bite: A Tract for the Army by the American Temperance Union," *JATU* 26 (April 1863): 51; "Another Tract for the Army," *JATU* 25 (January 1862): 1. For another example, see "Another Tract for the Army: The Returned Soldier," *JATU* 25 (November 1862): 161–62.

86. Marsh, *No. 90*.

87. "The Wounded Soldier: A New Tract for the Army," *JATU* 25 (October 1862): 145–46.

88. Bell Irvin Wiley, *Life of Billy Yank*, 153–57; Bell Irvin Wiley, *Life of Johnny Reb*, 161–62.

89. Robert Winn to sister, August 20, 1863; Robert Winn to Sister, March 22, 1864; Robert Winn to sister, January 8, 1863; Robert Winn to sister, January 15, 1864, Winn-Cook Family Papers, 1861–1875 (Transcriptions), FHS.

90. Taylor, *Letters Home to Sarah*, 63, 65, 73, 79, 81, 206.

91. U.S. Christian Commission, *First Annual Report*, 126.

92. U.S. Christian Commission, *First Annual Report*, 70–73.

93. U.S. Christian Commission, *First Annual Report*, 63, 73.

94. U.S. Christian Commission, *First Annual Report*, 42.

95. U.S. Christian Commission, *First Annual Report*, 178.

96. U.S. Christian Commission, *First Annual Report*, 216.

97. Fuller, *Chaplain Fuller*, 193–94.

98. Dexter, *Seymour Dexter, Union Army*, 63.

99. Beaudry, *War Journal of Louis N. Beaudry*, 26, 31, 93–110.

100. See "Correspondence of the Richmond *Dispatch*, affairs in Lynchburg," *Daily Dispatch* (Richmond, VA), March 8, 1861; *Daily Dispatch*, May 25, 1861; *Daily Dispatch*, December 27, 1861.

101. "From Norfolk," *Daily Dispatch* (Richmond, VA), January 27, 1862.

102. "Temperance," *Daily Dispatch* (Richmond, VA), February 19, 1862.

103. Sheeran, *Confederate Chaplain*, 57.

104. Robert to Priscilla, November 11, 1863, Letters of Robert, an unidentified soldier in the 14th Massachusetts, Heavy Artillery of Lynn, Mass., to his wife, Priscilla, MSS 1242, UVA.

105. Chauncey Herbert Cooke, *Soldier Boy's Letters*, 35.

106. Robert Winn to Martha Winn, March 25, 1864, Winn-Cook Family Papers, 1861–1875 (Transcriptions), FHS.

107. Letter, Matthew Cook to Martha Winn, December 31, 1861, Winn-Cook Family Papers, 1861–1875 (Transcriptions), FHS.

108. Kamphoefner and Helbich, *Germans in the Civil War*, 139.

109. McAllister, *Civil War Letters*, 389.

110. "HIGH IMPORTANT EVENTS," *New York Herald*, July 1, 1862.

111. Larimer, *Love and Valor*, 243.

112. McAllister, *Civil War Letters*, 388.

113. Bissell, *Civil War Letters*, 202–3.

114. Beaudry, *War Journal*, 93–110; McAllister, *Civil War Letters*, 385–90.

115. Blocker, *American Temperance Movements*, 14.

116. Fullam, *Our Cruise*, 63.

117. For these numbers, I used the Beverly and Tom Lowry Database of Civil War Courts-Martial, which catalogs the courts-martial contained in RG 153 at the National Archives and Records Administration in Washington, DC. Using sorting functions in the database, I identified 12,402 cases that involve alcohol. Of those, the primary charge was conduct prejudicial in 2,820 cases; drunkenness in 2,670; AWOL in 770; disobedience in 525; 45th article of war in 415; quitting/leaving/sleeping on post in 300; and neglect in 150. These numbers are approximations—there is variability both in the military's recording of the charges and in the Lowry Database's transcription of the record. These cases are also overwhelmingly Union.

118. Robert A. Moore, *Life for the Confederacy*, 28; Larimer, *Love and Valor*, 20.

119. Because the Lowry Database lists punishments discursively, it can be difficult to assess the entire body of cases. In a sampling (unscientific) of data from cases contained in RG 153 (for which I also often have case files), I found 499 cases in which the primary charge was conduct prejudicial, a violation of article 45, AWOL, disobedience, quitting or sleeping on post, drunkenness, or neglect. Of those cases, 286 (57 percent) involve fines and/or pay reductions and 233 (47 percent) involve hard labor (many with a ball and chain). Another 95 (19 percent) cases include some type of public and/or corporal punishment in addition to the ball and chain. Many men, of course, received multiple punishments for their crimes.

120. Day, *My Diary*, 14.

121. Brown, *Diary of a Line Officer*, 87.

122. Robert Winn to sister, March 22, 1864, Winn-Cook Family Papers, 1861–1875 (Transcriptions), FHS.

123. Ayling, *Yankee at Arms*, 126; Dwight, *Life and Letters of Wilder Dwight*, 82. A drunken fellow in the 13th Connecticut was "'seized' up in the rigging" while traveling from New York to Ship Island, Louisiana. See George Gilbert Smith, *Leaves from a Soldier's Diary*, 1.

124. Peter, *Union Woman*, 90–91.

125. Bissell, *Civil War Letters*, 225.

126. Powers, *Hospital Pencillings*, 168; Armstrong, *Letters*, 12.

127. Dwight, *Life and Letters*, 113.

128. Chase, *Yours for the Union*, 13; Wills, *Army Life*, 220.

129. Weld, *War Diary and Letters*, 352; Bissell, *Civil War Letters*, 219.

130. Evans, *Intrepid Warrior*, 56.

131. In crimes involving alcohol, desertion accounts for 1,789 in the Lowry Database. This is 14 percent of the cases overall and 37 percent of the more serious charges. In the smaller sample used to tabulate punishments, there were sixty-three desertion cases, forty-five (71 percent) of which received fines and/or reduced pay and twenty-five (40 percent) that received hard labor. Again, men usually received more than one punishment.

132. Robert A. Moore, *Life for the Confederacy*, 36.

133. Robert A. Moore, *Life for the Confederacy*, 76. In another instance, Moore reports that he had two men arrested, 66; Jon C. Myers reported ten men under guard for theft and drunkenness; see John C. Myers, *Daily Journal*, 77. Henry Warren Howe had twenty-two soldiers to look after who were confined either for drunkenness or for being absent without

leave; see Howe, *Passages*, 66. "Several members" of the 21st Virginia were arrested for drunkenness; see December 28, 1864, John Baxter Moseley Diary, VHS.

134. In my sample of punishments, there were seventy-one men charged with violence toward an officer or the 9th article of war, mutiny, manslaughter, or murder. Thirty-nine men (55 percent) received hard labor; 44 percent received fines or reduction in pay; nine were executed, but that number includes five of fourteen men convicted of mutiny.

135. Dwight, *Life and Letters*, 93.

136. "Civil War Journal of S. O. Bereman," Garth Hagerman Photo/Graphics, [http://garthagerman/com/fambly/bereman.php], accessed August 31, 2012.

137. Watson, *Southern Service*, 106.

138. Wills, *Army Life*, 27; Bellard, *Gone for a Soldier*, 33–34.

139. Donaldson, *Inside*, 365–67.

Chapter Four

1. Ellis, *Leaves*, 16.
2. Ellis, *Leaves*, 19–20.
3. Ford, Adams, and Adams, *Cycle of Adams Letters*, 1:97.
4. "Disgraceful Conduct of Soldiers," *New York Times*, October 15, 1861.
5. Ellis, *Leaves*, 19–20; Ford, Adams, and Adams, *Cycle of Adams Letters*, 1:97.
6. For an in-depth discussion of Confederate expansions of martial law, see Escott, *Military Necessity*; Neely, *Southern Rights*. For scholarship on the federal government's willingness to extend military jurisdiction to civilians, see Neely, *Fate of Liberty*; Blair, *With Malice toward Some*; Bray, *Court-Martial*, 121–46.
7. Most scholarship on sutlers focuses heavily on the Federal army. See Lord, *Civil War Sutlers*; Tapson, "Sutler and the Soldier"; Murphy, "Pistol's Legacy," 44–57.
8. Kamphoefner and Helbich, *Germans in the Civil War*, 48–49.
9. Haydon, *For Country, Cause, and Leader*, 63–64, 76.
10. Reinhart, *August Willich's Gallant Dutchmen*, 25.
11. Confederate soldiers clearly had sutlers at times. See Bell Irvin Wiley, *Life of Johnny Reb*, 41, 100, 196–97; Lord, *Civil War Sutlers*, 90–92; and Delo, *Peddlers and Post Traders*, 103–27; *OR*, ser. 2, 5:335–36. But in forty-five references to sutlers I have in personal accounts, newspapers, and the OR, only five are Confederate. Of those, one refers to a sutler who may have had a license, two reference dealers near camp, one refers to the rumor of sutlers, and the final reports the capture of Union sutlers' stores. See *OR*, ser. 1, 45(1):1259; "Document 26: Summer Campaign of 1862, Confederate—Report of Brigadier-General Trimble of Capture of Manassas Junction (Charlottesville, January 6, 1863)," *Rebellion Record*, 9:Doc. 651; [correspondence of the *Richmond Dispatch*], *Daily Dispatch* (Richmond, VA), November 7, 1861; "Military grievance," *Daily Dispatch* (Richmond, VA), July 28, 1863; "Document 26: Summer Campaign of 1862, Confederate—Report of General Jackson of Operations from 15th August to 5th September 1862—Headquarters Second Corps, Army of Northern Virginia, April 27, 1863," *Rebellion Record*, 9:Doc. 577.
12. Robert A. Moore, *Life for the Confederacy*, 65 (October 8, 1861).
13. Pender, *General to His Lady*, 105–6 (December 4, 1861).
14. Blair, *Virginia's Private War*, 39; Faust, *Creation of Confederate Nationalism*, 22–57.

15. "Sanitary Commission," *JATU* 25 (January 1862): 7. In 1861, contracts were granted by a variety of individuals.

16. *OR*, ser. 1, 50(1):640.

17. Bellard, *Gone for a Soldier*, 39.

18. "Document 1: Military Measures of Congress," *Rebellion Record*, 10:Doc. 24–27. "Wilson's Bill," passed March 19, 1862, placed regimental sutlers' appointments in the hands of commissioned officers, but left post sutler appointments under the control of the secretary of war. See Murphy, "Pistol's Legacy," 50.

19. Fleming, *Life and Letters*, 261. For an additional example of a commissary-turned-sutler, see Gregg, *Life in the Army*, 88.

20. William Wiley, *Civil War Diary*, 8 (August 24, 1862).

21. Tapson, "Sutler and the Soldier," 175; Lord, *Civil War Sutlers*, 56–63.

22. McAllister, *Civil War Letters*, 209. McAllister was not specifically referring to selling liquor but to the tremendous opportunities that generally awaited camp merchants.

23. *OR*, ser. 1, 10(2):14.

24. Bircher, *Drummer-Boy's Diary*, 73 (September 8, 1863).

25. Whiskey prices seem to have been irregularly affected by inflation. Andrew F. Smith notes that inflation increased by about 10 percent per month in the Confederacy; see Smith, *Starving the South*, 39. On the home front, whiskey prices seem to have increased on pace with other goods in the first year of the war, only to steady from 1863 to 1865. In Virginia, for example, shopkeepers' records show that the cost of whiskey went from approximately one dollar to one dollar and fifty cents per gallon in 1861 to five dollars per gallon in 1862. Bottles of whiskey cost two to three dollars per gallon. Farther south in North Carolina, whiskey cost approximately a dollar to one dollar and twenty-five cents per gallon in 1860 and 1861 but was three dollars per gallon in 1862. Kentucky prices rose similarly, from one dollar and twenty cents per gallon in 1860 to four dollars in 1865. For 1861 prices in Virginia, see David Holmes Morton Daybook and Journal, 1861–1865, Charlotte County Court Records; Unidentified Daybook F, 1861–1876, New Kent County Court Records; for 1862 prices, see Account Book, 1861–1865, Charlotte County Court Records, Local Government Records Collection, LVA. For North Carolina prices, see J. W. Cook Account Book, 1845–1861, SANC; and Benjamin Hickman Bunn Account Book, 1861–1862, 1877–1889, 1892, folder 36, ser. 1, Nash County Historical Association Collection, 1806–1928, #5480, SHC. For Kentucky (Laurel County), see Ledger, vol. 1 (1859–1860), folder 2; Ledger, vol. 3 (1862–1869), folder 4; Ledger, vol. 4 (1865), folder 5; box 1, Business Records of Jonathan McNeill and Elbert S. McNeill, 1810–1890, no. 3915, SHC.

26. Confederate reports in the *OR* consistently list prices at three to four dollars per gallon in Virginia, Kentucky, and Texas up to January 1864. See *OR* ser. 1, 26(2):207; *OR* ser. 1, 34(2):812; *OR* ser. 2, 4:822; *OR* ser. 4, 2:418, 560–61, 653, 744, 837, 843, 1050; *OR* ser. 4, 3:55. In October 1861, the *Daily Dispatch* (Richmond, VA) reported sutlers selling whiskey for as much as ten dollars per quart at Camp Barlow near the Greenbriar River in Virginia, "[correspondence of the Richmond Dispatch]," *Daily Dispatch*, November 7, 1861. In Maryland, political prisoner Lawrence Sangston reported paying ten dollars per gallon in November 1861 at Fort Lafayette, but undoubtedly prisoners paid a markup for access to luxuries. Lawrence Sangston, *Bastiles of the North*, 78 (November 9, 1861). In March 1863, Union officers complained of sutlers selling whiskey at nine dollars per gallon near Cairo, Illinois.

OR ser. 1 10(2):14. Near Fort Fauntleroy in New Mexico, sutlers (whose loyalty was questionable) sold whiskey for ten dollars per gallon and sixteen dollars per gill. But these price reports are so isolated it is difficult to determine the extent to which the markup is atypical for western forts. OR ser. 1 50(1):640.

27. Larimer, *Love and Valor*, 243 (November 20, 1863).

28. Robert A. Moore, *Life for the Confederacy*, 126 (December 27, 1861); Petty, *Journey to Pleasant Hill*, 117 (December 24, 1862).

29. In February 1864, the Confederate congress fixed impressment prices for whiskey (at twenty-five dollars per gallon) and apple and peach brandies (at fifteen dollars per gallon), which provides a reference for liquor prices across the Confederacy. OR, ser. 4, 3:1171–72. Other pricing schedules used by the Confederate armies list whiskey and brandies at ten to thirty dollars per gallon. Confederate States of America, War Department, *Message of the President: Richmond, Va., Jan. 6, 1865*, 7; OR ser. 1 42(3):1350–51; OR ser. 1 40(30):767; Quartermaster Dept. Day Book, vol. 201, chap. 5, RG 109, NARA. In one instance, a Union soldier encamped in Virginia reports paying three dollars for a bottle of whiskey (equivalent to eighteen dollars per gallon) from a sutler, which puts the prices that Union soldiers paid fairly well in line with Confederate prices. Molyneux, *Quill of the Wild Goose*, 180 (April 24, 1864).

30. Brown, *Diary of a Line Officer*, 17 (April 13, 1864).

31. Reinhart, *Two Germans in the Civil War*, 84 (April 20, 1864).

32. Nisbet, *Four Years*, 315.

33. Alonzo Miller, *Diaries and Letters, 1864–1865*, 8 (February 14, 1864).

34. Molyneux, *Quill of the Wild Goose*, 180; OR, ser. 1, 41(4):726; OR, ser. 1, 25(1):632.

35. Taylor, *Letters Home to Sarah*, 84–85, 200 (August 5, 1864, January 25, 1865).

36. Robert A. Moore, *Life for the Confederacy*, 51 (August 18, 1861).

37. Hubbs, *Voices from Company D*, 14 (July 12, 1861).

38. Marx Mitteldorfer to parents, August 7 [1861], and Marx Mitteldorfer to Moses Hutzler, March 10, 1862, both in Mitteldorfer Letters, Soldier Letters Collection, MOC. These letters were retrieved by the author in the summer of 2012; the collection has since been rehoused in the Virginia Museum of History and Culture. See secs. 1 and 2, Mitteldorfer Family of Richmond, Virginia, Papers, 1860–1940, Mss2 M6977, Confederate Memorial Literary Society Collection, Virginia Museum of History and Culture, Richmond, VA. For an additional example, see William McFall's repeated letters to his family requesting brandy from South Carolina. McFall and McFall, *Civil War Correspondence*, 13, 16 (June 27 and October 25, 1863). For additional example, see Bratton, *Letters of John Bratton*, 51 (January 8, 1862).

39. Dooley, *John Dooley, Confederate Soldier*, 79, 82.

40. David Holt, *Mississippi Rebel*, 221.

41. Haines, *In the Country*, 38 (September 6, 1862).

42. Chase, *Yours for the Union*, 222–23 (April 10, 1863).

43. OR, ser. 1, 40(3):155–56.

44. Molyneux, *Quill of the Wild Goose*, 67 (February 5, 1863).

45. OR, ser. 2, 2:1456, 1458.

46. George E. Stephens, *Voice of Thunder*, 149, 156 (November 30, 1861; January 4, 1862).

47. George E. Stephens, *Voice of Thunder*, 150–51 (December 6, 1861).

48. Conyngham, *Irish brigade*, 87 (December 25, 1861). For additional examples late in the war, see Kamphoefner and Helbich, *Germans in the Civil War*, 422 (January 12, 1864); Reinhart, *Two Germans*, 135 (July 6, 1864).
49. Lauren K. Thompson, *Friendly Enemies*.
50. Twichell, *Civil War Letters*, 123 (May 4, 1862).
51. Gregg, *Life in the Army*, 95.
52. Kinsley, *Diary of a Christian Soldier*, 144.
53. Conyngham, *Irish brigade*, 120.
54. Robert Goldthwaite Carter, *Four Brothers in Blue*, 281–82.
55. Richards, *Eleven Days*, 33.
56. Gillaspie, *Diary*, 23–24.
57. Twichell, *Civil War Letters*, 47 (July 27, 1861).
58. "Departure of the Troops," *Semi-Weekly Dispatch* (Franklin County, PA), October 11, 1861.
59. Russell, *My Diary North and South*, 390 (July 6, 1861).
60. Robert Goldthwaite Carter, *Four Brothers in Blue*, 29–30.
61. Haydon, *For Country, Cause, and Leader*, 63–64 (July 27, 1861).
62. While federal officials sometimes used police and the military to curb civilian disloyalty within DC and defend the capital against invasion, disciplining soldiers and keeping them from liquor were dealt with as a problem of urban disorder (and military discipline) rather than an issue of national security. See Winkle, *Lincoln's Citadel*.
63. Robert Goldthwaite Carter, *Four Brothers in Blue*, 30.
64. Robbins, *Through Ordinary Eyes*, 48.
65. Russell, *My Diary North and South*, 482, 561.
66. Robbins, *Through Ordinary Eyes*, 85.
67. *OR*, ser. 2, 2:218.
68. The Beverly and Tom Lowry Database of Civil War Courts-Martial lists DC or Alexandria in the charge or description of at least 1,408 cases involving alcohol (of which they found 12,402). DC (with at least 1,156 cases) had the larger problem than Alexandria (with at least 252 cases).
69. Cavins, *Civil War Letters*, 182.
70. Dexter, *Seymour Dexter, Union Army*, 131 (February 15, 1863); *OR*, ser. 1, 25(1):632.
71. On Union rosewater policies of conciliation (which turned out to be ineffective in most cases), see Grimsley, *Hard Hand of War*; Ash, *When the Yankees Came*, 25–37.
72. *OR*, ser. 1, 24(3):141–43.
73. Bragg, *Letters of a Confederate Surgeon, 1861–65*, 18 (October 11, 1861).
74. Ayling, *Yankee at Arms*, 133–34; 138–39; for information on *The Drunkard*, a temperance play first performed in 1844 that told the tale of a drunkard's family, see Krout, *Origins of Prohibition*, 254–55.
75. Jones, *Artilleryman's Diary*, 24 (December 30–31, 1862).
76. Campbell, *Union Must Stand*, 77 (February 9, 1863).
77. "General News," *New York Times*, November 12, 1862 (page 4).
78. Howe, *Passages*, 60 (January 23, 1864).
79. *OR*, ser. 1, 24(1):754 (May 15, 1863).
80. Oscar Lawrence Jackson, *Colonel's Diary*, 183–84 (February 17, 1865).

81. In the Beverly and Tom Lowry Database of Civil War Courts-Martial, there are 336 alcohol-related cases involving citizens. Of those, at least ninety-eight civilians were charged with selling liquor to soldiers or a violation of orders that involved selling liquor. Approximately thirty charges deal with smuggling or blockade running. But while more civilians were tried for selling to soldiers, widespread prohibitions (in the form of general orders) seem to focus more on smuggling operations.

82. *OR*, ser. 1, 8:595.

83. *OR*, ser. 1, 8:404.

84. *OR*, ser. 1, 30(3):146.

85. *OR*, ser. 1, 15:425.

86. Butler, *Private and Official Correspondence*, 3: 597, 5:20 (August 8, 1864).

87. Butler, *Private and Official Correspondence*, 4:91 (April 18, 1864).

88. Ayling, *Yankee at Arms*, 134.

89. Jones, *Artillerymen's Diary*, 244 (September 1, 1864).

90. Campbell, *Union Must Stand*, 189 (October 28, 1864).

91. Neely, *Fate of Liberty*, 32–50, 75–92.

92. Ogle, *Ambitious Brew*, 1–85, 42–45.

93. Lauderdale, *Wounded River*, 85.

94. *OR*, ser. 2, 1:224.

95. F1139, F1147, F1162, F1165, F1184, F1188, Missouri Provost Marshal Records, MOSA.

96. "Charles Brandan," F1139; "Karle Huber," F1146; "Henry Huhn," F1147; Missouri Provost Marshal Records, MOSA.

97. *OR*, ser. 2 1:480. For an additional example of soldiers seeking out distillers, see Downing, *Downing's Civil War Diary*, 29.

98. *OR*, ser. 1 13:169–70.

99. *OR*, ser. 1, 10(1):48. Kennett's policy exemplifies what Mark Grimsley has termed "conciliatory policy," which guided the Union military's actions toward civilian populations in 1861 through the summer of 1862. The purpose of conciliation was to treat Confederate civilians kindly in order to possibly bring them back into the Union. See Grimsley, *Hard Hand of War*.

100. Fleharty, *Civil War Dispatches*, 148–49.

101. Neely, *Fate of Liberty*, 86–90.

102. *OR*, ser. 1, 41(2):100.

103. *OR*, ser. 1, 41(4):726.

104. *OR*, ser. 1, 34(4):509. For information on which counties in Missouri experienced high levels of guerrilla violence, I consulted Fialka, *Of Methods and Madness*, http://ehistory.org/projects/of-methods-and-madness.html, published April 2015, accessed August 14, 2019.

105. Blair, *With Malice toward Some*, 55–57; Fellman, *Inside War*.

106. *OR*, ser. 1, 48(2):1093.

107. In Richmond, where authority was divided between the city council, the Virginia state legislature, and the Confederate government, efforts to curb drunkenness and control the liquor traffic were swept up with other measures to place the city under military authority. See Thomas, *Confederate State of Richmond*. The Confederate government, much more than its Union counterpart, was willing to use martial law to control its civilian populations; see Escott, *Military Necessity*; Neely, *Southern Rights*.

108. "Local Matters: Closing the Liquor Shops," *Daily Dispatch* (Richmond, VA), April 24, 1861.

109. *OR*, ser. 2, 3:718.

110. *OR*, ser. 1, 4:248–49.

111. *OR*, ser. 1, 10(2):297–98.

112. *OR*, ser. 1, 10(2):369; *OR*, ser. 2, 2:1423.

113. General John Winder enacted prohibition in Richmond in late February 1862 when he placed the city under martial law. See Blakey, *General John H. Winder, C.S.A.*, 121–22.

114. *OR*, ser. 4, 1:835.

115. "By the President of the Confederate States of America. A Proclamation," *Daily Dispatch* (Richmond, VA), March 3, 1862.

116. Robertson, *Stonewall Jackson*, 328.

117. Robertson, *Stonewall Jackson*, 231.

118. Robert Manson Myers, *Children of Pride*, 857.

119. *OR*, ser. 1, 51(2):491.

120. *OR*, ser. 1, 51(2):504–5.

121. *OR*, ser. 2, 3:900.

122. For more scholarship on the Confederate army—specifically, the Army of Northern Virginia—as the embodiment of Confederate nationalism, see Gallagher, *Confederate War*.

123. Nisbet, *Four Years*, 117–19.

124. Riley, *Grandfather's Journal*, 75.

125. David Holt, *Mississippi Rebel*, 184–88 (May 1863).

126. John Gottfried Lange Memoirs, "The New Name or the Shoemaker in the Old and New World, Thirty Years in Europe and Thirty Years in America," vol. 1 (typescript translated into English), VHS.

127. *OR*, ser. 1, 46(3):1121.

128. John Gottfried Lange Memoirs, "The New Name or the Shoemaker in the Old and New World," 276, 280, 282.

129. *OR*, ser. 1, 34(2):412.

130. *OR*, ser. 1, 10(2):297.

Chapter Five

1. "An act to prevent the unnecessary Consumption of grain by Distillers and other Manufacturers of Spirituous and Maltliquors—passed March 12, 1862," *Daily Dispatch* (Richmond, VA), March 17, 1862.

2. James M. Whittle to Zach L. Finney, March 20, 1862, Accession 41447, Personal Papers Collection, LVA.

3. Prohibition had less support in Southern states, but it is worth noting that many Southerners joined the anti-liquor crusade in some form or fashion. Tyrrell, "Drink and Temperance"; Eslinger, "Antebellum Liquor Reform"; Carlson, "'Drinks He to His Own Undoing'"; Stewart, "'This County Improves in Cultivation'"; Stewart, "Select Men"; Stewart, "'Forces of Bacchus.'"

4. Tyrrell, *Sobering Up*, 260–69.

5. Tyrrell, *Sobering Up*, 290–309.

6. "A Revenue Placer," *New York Times*, June 16, 1861.

7. Paludan, *People's Contest*, 105–26.

8. Veach, *Kentucky Bourbon Whiskey*, 63.

9. "An Act to provide Internal Revenue to support the Government and to pay Interest on the Public Debt," *U.S. Statutes at Large*, 12:432–89; "An Act to amend an Act entitled 'An Act to provide Internal Revenue to support the Government and pay Interest on the Public Debt,' approved July 1, 1862, and for other Purposes," 12:713–31; "An Act to increase the Internal Revenue, and for other Purposes," 13:14–17; "An Act to provide Internal Revenue to support the Government, to pay Interest on the Public Debt, and for other Purposes," 13:223–306; "An Act to amend an Act entitled, 'An Act to provide Internal Revenue to support the Government, to pay Interest on the Public Debt, and for other Purposes,' approved June thirtieth, eighteen hundred and sixty-four," 13:469–70. For context surrounding the passing of the laws, see 37th Cong., 1st Sess., *Journal of the Senate of the United States of America*, 53:110–11; 37th Cong., 2nd Sess., *Journal of the Senate of the United States of America*, 54:598–602, 748; 37th Cong., 1st Sess., *Journal of the House of Representatives of the United States*, 58:145, 201; 37th Cong., 2nd Sess., *Journal of the House of Representatives of the United States*, 59:148. For scholarship on the whiskey tax, see Hu, *Liquor Tax*, 37–38.

10. "House of Representatives: The Internal Tax Bill," *New York Times*, April 22, 1864; "Internal Revenue Decisions," *New York Times*, July 2, 1865.

11. "House of Representatives: The Internal Tax Bill," *New York Times*, April 22, 1864.

12. "From Washington: Dispatches to the Associated Press," *New York Times*, April 16, 1864.

13. "Thirty-Eighth Congress: Second Session—House of Representatives, The Internal Revenue Bill," *New York Times*, February 19, 1865.

14. "Taxing of Liquors," *JATU* 26 (February 1863): 17.

15. From an exchange paper, "Patriotic Drinking," *JATU* 27 (September 1864): 134–35.

16. "Chapter 64: The Sale of Intoxicating Liquors," *Revision of 1860, containing all the Statutes of a General Nature of the State of Iowa*, 265.

17. "Iowa Legislature," *Muscatine (IA) Weekly Journal*, February 14, 1862.

18. "Des Moines Correspondent," *Tipton (IA) Advertiser*, March 13, 1862.

19. "The New Liquor Law" and "Legislative Summary," *Daily Democrat and News* (Davenport, IA), March 17, 1862. Elaine Frantz Parsons has analyzed at length the shift in culpability for chronic drunkenness. Although drinkers would eventually be held responsible for their own choices, Parsons contends that in the mid-nineteenth century, most reformers believed that the trafficker, not the drinker, was responsible for the resulting drunkenness. For her detailed analysis on Smith's Civil Damage Liquor Law, see "Slaves to the Bottle."

20. "Regulation or Prohibition," *Tipton (IA) Advertiser*, May 14, 1863.

21. Ohio passed a similar law in 1869, allowing a drunkard's relatives to sue liquor dealers for damages. In the early 1870s, other Northern states, including Michigan, Illinois, Wisconsin, Missouri, and Minnesota, debated passing similar laws. See Meyer, *We Are What We Drink*, 56–57.

22. Before the war began, in 1859, Massachusetts revised and strengthened its license laws, stipulating that all sales had to go through a commissioner. See "Chapter 86: Of the Manufacture, Sale, &c. of Intoxicating Liquors," *General Statutes of the Commonwealth of Massachusetts*, 437–38. For Michigan's law, see "Amendment to the Prohibitory Liquor Law—The Ale, Beer and Cider Clause Restored," *Grand Haven (MI) News*, March 20, 1861.

23. Volk, *Moral Minorities*, 37–100; Ritter, *Inventing America's First Immigration Crisis*, 105–47.

24. "Assembly," *New York Times*, March 25, 1861.

25. "Political Lager Beer," *New York Times*, April 4, 1861; "The Sunday Law Controversy," *New York Herald*, March 11, 1861; "Lager-Bier-Dom in a Ferment," *New York Times*, March 16, 1861. This Sunday Law debate of 1861 is emblematic of the struggles that New York's German community would continue to face over the course of the war, as they coordinated their responses to nativist attacks on their service to the Union. Yet as the Sunday Law debate illustrates, German Americans were by no means a monolithic bloc. See Christian B. Keller, *Chancellorsville and the Germans*, 117–22.

26. "Gotham Emancipated," *Vermont Chronicle* (Bellows Falls), December 10, 1861.

27. "Affairs in Chicago," *New York Times*, April 27, 1862.

28. "Sabbath Convention," *Vermont Chronicle*, August 25, 1863.

29. "Should the Government Interfere with Intemperance in the Army," *JATU* 24 (July 1861): 106–7.

30. "Excursion to Washington," *JATU* 24 (July 1861): 106.

31. "Whiskey Rations," *JATU* 25 (May 1862): 73.

32. "Spirit Ration Discontinued," *JATU* 25 (July 1862): 112; "Gen. Butler's Order," *JATU* 25 (August 1862): 116; "Gen. Halleck's Army," *JATU* 25 (August 1862): 116.

33. "The Rum Ration Restored," *JATU* 26 (September 1863): 129.

34. Myra Myrtle, "Whisky Rations," from the *Northern Christian Advocate*, reprinted in *JATU* 27 (November 1864): 173. The last stanzas are: "Withhold the whisky rations, we entreat; / Let every other comfort be replete, / But give no deadly drink, however sweet. / Give not this serpent to our cherished ones, / They may fall nobly, facing rebel guns, / But let them fall good men, and 'temperance sons.'" For scholarship on the "good death" and the war, see Faust, *This Republic of Suffering*.

35. Langley, *Social Reform*.

36. "Drunkenness in the Navy," *JATU* 24 (October 1861): 157.

37. "Chapter 164: An Act Making Appropriations for the Naval Service . . . ," *Public Acts of the Thirty-Seventh Congress of the United States*; ORN, ser. 1, 7:650–52.

38. "Congratulations for the Navy," *JATU* 25 (August 1862): 113; "Spirit Ration in the Navy," *JATU* 25 (November 1862): 170.

39. "Intemperance in the Navy," *JATU* 25 (December 1862): 179. The number of officers who had been dismissed was apparently contentious. Other sailors countered the report in the *Tribune* by arguing that very few officers had been dismissed for drunkenness because very few naval officers were drunkards. The reputation of a hard-drinking navy was undeserved. See "Intemperance in the Navy," *JATU* 26 (January 1863): 14.

40. "Drunkenness in Camp," *JATU* 24 (October 1861): 157.

41. "Military Suasion," *JATU* 24 (August 1861): 119; "Maine Law in the Army," *JATU* 25 (March 1862): 43–44.

42. "To His Excellency, Gov. E. D. Morgan," *JATU* 25 (September 1862): 136.

43. "Prohibition: Action of the Last Senate," *JATU* 24 (September 1861): 144; "The Liquor Dealers of this state . . . ," *JATU* 24 (November 1861): 170; "Proposed Amendment to the Constitution," *JATU* 24 (December 1861): 184; "Prohibition," *JATU* 25 (February 1862): 17, and (March 1862): 33; "Sons of Temperance on the Convention," *JATU* 25 (March 1862): 35; "New York Legislature," *JATU* 25 (April 1862): 59–60.

44. "The Presidential Election," *JATU* 27 (November 1864): 161–62.

45. "Lancaster Co. Regiment," *JATU* 25 (February 1862): 28; for an additional example, see "Army Correspondence: Letter from Joseph Little, Chaplain 5th Virginia," *JATU* 26 (May 1863): 78.

46. Oscar G. Sawyer, Correspondent, "Important from Charleston," *New York Herald*, August 3, 1863.

47. "Lancaster Co. Regiment," *JATU* 25 (February 1862): 28; "Sutlers in the Camp," *JATU* 25 (January 1862): 11.

48. "Gen. Meade and the Sutler System," *JATU* 27 (February 1864): 25.

49. "The Magistrates and the Liquor Law," *Evening Star* (Washington, DC), October 8, 1861; "The Provost Guard," *Evening Star* (Washington, DC), December 10, 1862; for examples of reports for arrests for selling to soldiers, see "Another Habeas Corpus," *Evening Star* (Washington, DC), October 8, 1861; "Police Reports," *Evening Star* (Washington, DC), December 20, 1862; "More than He Bargained For," *Evening Star* (Washington, DC), August 8, 1863; "Georgetown Liquor Dealers Fined," *Evening Star* (Washington, DC), April 11, 1864; "Liquor Sellers Fined" and "SEIZURE OF LIQUORS—OFFICER FIRED ON," *Evening Star* (Washington, DC), March 15, 1864; "Selling Liquor to Soldiers," *Evening Star* (Washington, DC), March 28, 1865.

50. *Chicago* (IL) *Daily Tribune*, January 13, 1862.

51. Willis, *Southern Prohibition*, 17; Coker, *Liquor*, 24.

52. Ten Islands Baptist Association, *Minutes of the Proceedings . . .*, 1863, 6.

53. "Blockade of Liquor," *Daily Dispatch* (Richmond, VA), August 6, 1861. For an additional example, see A. B., "[correspondence of the *Richmond Dispatch*]," *Daily Dispatch* (Richmond, VA), February 5, 1862.

54. *. . . Ordinance upon distilled spirits*, November 1861; "An Act to amend an act . . . to raise revenue by taxation," April 8, 1861, *Laws of the Eighth Legislature of the State of Texas: Extra Session*, 52; "No. 92: An Act to authorize the Commissioners of the Town of Spring Place, in Murray county, to issue license for the retail of Spirituous Liquors, and to fix the amount of the license for the same, and to punish for selling without license," and "No. 93: An Act to amend the several laws theretofore passed incorporating the city of Rome, in the county of Floyd; and to enlarge the powers of the City council of the City of Rome, in relation to the granting of license to retail and sell liquors," *Acts of the General Assembly of the State of Georgia . . .*, 1861, 96–97.

55. While the national government was slow to implement tax policies (waiting until 1863), Confederate states began almost immediately increasing taxes on income, land, and luxury goods in a desperate attempt to raise revenue to fight the war. Ringold, *Role of the State Legislatures*, 89–93; Thomas, *Confederate Nation*, 197–99.

56. "The Memorial," *Spirit of the Age* 13 (November, 20, 1861): 2.

57. Andrew F. Smith, *Starving the South*, 12–15.

58. Patterns in Union confiscation reports show a marked decline in the amount of whiskey circulating through the Confederacy by 1864. Early in the war, Union officers regularly reported capturing Confederate supplies containing fifty to eighty barrels of whiskey, but by 1865, reports included only one to twelve barrels. Confiscation reports, not surprisingly, follow the movement of the Union army through the border and Deep South regions, so 1863 and 1864 offer the best comparisons. In 1863, Union army sources from Virginia, North

Carolina, Kentucky, Tennessee, and Louisiana show that Federals captured approximately twelve thousand gallons of liquors. By 1864, however, sources from Virginia, Kentucky, Tennessee, Missouri, Louisiana, Mississippi, Alabama, Georgia, and South Carolina show that Federal forces captured only about three thousand gallons of liquors. Again, although these numbers are not completely comprehensive, they nevertheless show that the decimation of Confederate grain-producing (and distilling) regions by 1863, coupled with increasing Union occupation of the Confederate heartland by 1864, led to a noticeable decrease in whiskey and other spirits in the South. I derived my numbers from close to fifty references to confiscated liquors contained in the *Official Records*, newspapers, and personal accounts of the war. When specific units—barrels, demijohns, tierces, and so on—are available, I converted the measures to gallons to obtain the amount. Often, the liquor is referenced more generally. In those cases, I have taken what I think are conservative estimates of the number of gallons. See *OR*, ser. 1, 2:624 [1861, supply train with whiskey]; "Movements of Patterson's Column," *Daily Dispatch* (Richmond, VA), July 9, 1861 [distillery emptied]; *OR*, ser. 1, 8:404 [1861, 80 barrels]; *Rebellion Record*, 4:Poetry 75, D72, D86 [1862, barrel of apple brandy, smuggled whiskey, whiskey on steamers]; *OR*, ser. 1, 11(2):336 [1862, liquor in warehouses]; *OR*, ser. 1, 13:132 [1862, 2 barrels]; *OR*, ser. 1, 16:124 [1862, several tierces of whiskey]; *OR*, ser. 1, 20(1):21 [1862, 20 barrels]; *OR*, ser. 1, 21:16 [1862, 2 barrels]; *OR*, ser. 1 20(1):76 [1862, wagon-load of whiskey]; *OR*, ser. 1, 18:124 [1863, whiskey in a storehouse]; Zenas T. Haines, *Letters from the 44th Regiment M.V.M.*, 76 [1863, barrel of cider]; *OR*, ser. 1, 25(1):12 [1863, 50 barrels]; *OR*, ser. 1, 23(1):215 [1863, 40 casks]; *OR*, ser. 1, 15:344, 368 [1863, 50 barrels]; *OR*, ser. 1, 23(1):263 [1863, 100 barrels]; *OR*, ser. 1, 27(2):779 [1863, 80 gallons]; *OR*, ser. 1, 23(1):537 [1863, some whiskey]; *OR*, ser. 1, 24(2):675 [1863, 30 barrels]; *OR*, ser. 1, 30(3):146 [1863, 25 wagons of whiskey and supplies]; *OR*, ser. 1, 35(2):40 [1864, whiskey on a blockade runner]; *OR*, ser. 1, 32(1):297 [1864, large amount of commissary whiskey]; *OR*, ser. 1, 33:162 [1864, whiskey stores]; Nancy E. Moore, *Journal of Eldress Nancy*, 191 [1864, 2 barrels]; *OR*, ser. 1, 34(4):237–38 [1864, whiskey on a steamer]; *OR*, ser. 1, 38(2):775 [1864, 4 barrels]; *OR*, ser. 1, 38(2):868–69 [1864, 9 train cars with whiskey]; *OR*, ser. 1, 41(3):281 [1864, "barrels of whiskey"]; *OR*, ser. 1, 41(1):882 [1864, 12 barrels]; "The expedition into Luray Valley," *Daily Dispatch* (Richmond, VA), October 25, 1864 [1864, 30 stills destroyed]; *OR*, ser. 1, 45(1):952 [1864, smuggler with whiskey]; *OR*, ser. 1, 45(1):637 [1864, canteens of whiskey]; *OR*, ser. 1, 44:330 [1864, wine and whiskey]; *OR*, ser. 1, 44:238 [1864, 2 barrels]; *OR*, ser. 1, 44:259 [1864, 1 barrel]; *OR*, ser. 1, 44:219 [1864, 3 barrels]; *OR*, ser. 1, 47(1):589 [1865, 96 gallons]; *OR*, ser. 1, 47(1):239 [1865, 5 barrels]; *OR*, ser. 1, 47(1):323 [1865, two distilleries]; Sarah Lois Wadley, Diary, August 8, 1859–May 15, 1865 (digitized manuscript), SHC, 318 [1865, whiskey confiscated from distillery]; *OR*, ser. 1, 46(1):543 [1865, several barrels of apple jack]; *OR*, ser. 1, 49(1):504 [1865, whiskey stores].

59. ... *An ordinance to restrict the distillation of grain, and to raise revenue*, February 1862, 1–2. North Carolina's early measures to control the prices of liquor foreshadow the price controls that civilians demanded from the Richmond government in 1863, as food shortages and impressments sent prices soaring the eastern Confederacy. Hurt, *Agriculture and the Confederacy*, 157–62.

60. ... *An ordinance for the suppression of distilleries*, February 1862.

61. *OR*, ser. 4, 2:487.

62. Bratton, *Letters*, 155.

63. "An act to prohibit the importation of luxuries, or articles not necessaries or of common use," February 6, 1864, in Matthews, *Public Laws*, 179–81; C. G. Memminger, [Regulations "prescribed for the government and directions of all officers of the Revenue, to carry into effect the provisions of the Act to prohibit the importation of luxuries, or of articles not necessary or of common use, approved February 6th, 1864"], March 12, 1864.

64. For scholarship on Lincoln's blockade and food shortages in the Confederacy, see Andrew F. Smith, *Starving the South*, 9–71; Blair, *Virginia's Private War*, 73–76, 93–100.

65. "An Act to prevent the Waste of Grains," *Fayetteville* (TN) *Observer*, February 6, 1862; "Facts for consideration," *Daily Dispatch* (Richmond, VA), February 17, 1862. Although newspaper sources indicate that Tennessee acted first, prohibiting distilling shortly before the capture of Nashville by Union troops, other historians point to Virginia as the first Confederate state to prohibit distilling. See Gates, *Agriculture and the Civil War*, 97; Hurt, *Agriculture and the Confederacy*, 58. For other states, see . . . *An ordinance for the Suppression of Distilleries*, February 1862; "An act to prevent the unnecessary Consumption of grain by Distillers and other Manufacturers of Spirituous and Maltliquors—passed March 12, 1862," *Daily Dispatch* (Richmond, VA), March 17, 1862; "No More Whisky," *Southern Recorder* (Milledgeville, GA), April 8, 1862.

66. Joseph E. Brown, Governor of Georgia, "A Proclamation" (February 26, 1862), in Candler, *Confederate Records of the State of Georgia*, 2:202–7; "An Act to prevent the unnecessary consumption of grain by distillers and manufacturers of spirituous liquors in Georgia," November 22, 1862, *Acts of the General Assembly of the State of Georgia . . .*, 1862, 25–26.

67. . . . *A bill to prohibit the sale of spirituous liquors in small quantities during the war, first read on December 15, 1862*, 1–2; . . . *A bill to suppress the undue distillation of spirituous liquors from the cereal grains of this state, first read on December 3, 1862*, 1–3; "An Act to Suppress the Undue Distillation of Spirituous Liquors from the Cereal Grains of This State," December 18, 1862, *Acts of the General Assembly of the State of South Carolina, Passed in December, 1862, and February and April, 1863*, 113–14.

68. "An Act to prohibit the distillation of spirits from grain, molasses, and sugar," January 3, 1863, *Laws of the State of Mississippi, Passed . . . Dec. 1862 and Nov. 1863*, 95–96; "An Act to encourage the manufacturing of Wine from the native grape," December 9, 1863, *Laws of the State of Mississippi*, 146.

69. *Ordinance to Restrict the Distillation of Grain, and to Raise Revenue*; "An Act to Suppress the Undue Distillation of Spirituous Liquors from the Cereal Grains of This State [South Carolina]," December 18, 1862; "An Act to Prevent the Unnecessary Consumption of Grain by Distillers and Other Manufacturers of Spirituous and Malt Liquors–Passed March 12, 1862," *Daily Dispatch* (Richmond, VA), March 17, 1862; "An Act to prevent the unnecessary consumption of grain by distillers and manufacturers of spirituous liquors in Georgia," November 22, 1862.

70. "The Chief Danger of the South," *Daily Dispatch* (Richmond, VA), March 10, 1862.

71. Joseph E. Brown, Governor of Georgia, "A Proclamation" (February 26, 1862), in Candler, *Confederate Records of the State of Georgia*, 2:202–5. Mark Neely notes that Tennessean Albert G. Graham made a similar suggestion about melting copper stills to Jefferson Davis. See Neely, *Southern Rights*, 36.

72. The state received petitions from Roanoke, Shenandoah, Montgomery, Floyd, and Patrick Counties. See *Journal of the House of Delegates of Virginia, for the Session of 1861–62*, 62, 89, 94, 128, 137.

73. "Petitions-Distilleries," *Staunton (VA) Spectator*, February 18, 1862.

74. Joseph E. Brown, Governor of Georgia, "A Proclamation" (February 26, 1862), in Candler, *Confederate Records of the State of Georgia*, 2:202–3.

75. Candler, *Confederate Records of the State of Georgia*, 2:204–5.

76. Joseph E. Brown, Governor of Georgia, "A Proclamation" (February 26, 1862), in Candler, *Confederate Records of the State of Georgia*, 2:204–5.

77. Thomas, *Confederate Nation*, 154; Rable, *Confederate Republic*, 141–43. Although Brown opposed conscription rather vehemently, Mark Neely points out that when it came to controlling liquor, Brown acquiesced, in at least one instance, to the military imposing martial law on the town of Savannah. See Neely, *Southern Rights*, 38.

78. "Whiskey Distilleries," *Southern Recorder* (Milledgeville, GA), March 11, 1862. For more context, see T. H. Moore, "Gov. Brown's Correspondence with T. H. Moore, Esq.," from the *Atlanta Intelligencer*, repr. in *Southern Federal Union* (Milledgeville, GA), July 15, 1862; "Sumter County," *Southern Federal Union* (Milledgeville, GA), March 18, 1862; "Planters' Meeting," *Southern Recorder* (Milledgeville, GA), April 1, 1862.

79. "Gov. Brown and Peach Brandy," *Southern Recorder* (Milledgeville, GA), July 15, 1862.

80. "Whiskey Distilleries," *Southern Recorder* (Milledgeville, GA), March 11, 1862; "Cultivate Wheat and Corn," *Southern Federal Union* (Milledgeville, GA), April 8, 1862.

81. "Justice to the Yankees," *Southern Recorder* (Milledgeville, GA), March 18, 1862; Rev. J. R. Thomas, "Our Future if Defeated in the Struggle," from the *Southern Confederacy*, repr. in *Southern Recorder* (Milledgeville, GA), April 15, 1862.

82. "The Whiskey Business—Voice of the People," *Daily Dispatch* (Richmond, VA), February 14, 1862.

83. F. W. Pickens, Governor's Message No. 1 to the South Carolina General Assembly, November 25, 1862, *Journal of the Senate of South Carolina: Being the Session of 1862*, 10–37 (quotations on 15).

84. Stephanie McCurry explores the changing relationship between women and the state in *Confederate Reckoning*, 85–217.

85. Joseph E. Brown, Governor of Georgia, "A Proclamation" (February 26, 1862), in Candler, *Confederate Records of the State of Georgia*, 2:202–7; "An Act to prevent the unnecessary consumption of grain by distillers and manufacturers of spirituous liquors in Georgia," November 22, 1862.

86. "No Peach Brandy," *Southern Federal Union* (Milledgeville, GA), May 6, 1862; [no title], *Southern Recorder* (Milledgeville, GA), May 6, 1862; [no title], *Southern Federal Union* (Milledgeville, GA), July 15, 1862; "Gov. Brown and Peach Brandy," *Southern Recorder* (Milledgeville, GA), July 15, 1862.

87. Joseph E. Brown to the Georgia General Assembly, March 25, 1863, in Candler, *Confederate Records of the State of Georgia*, 2:367–95, esp. 370–72; Joseph E. Brown to the Georgia General Assembly, March 10, 1864, *Journal of the Senate at an Extra Session of the General Assembly of the State of Georgia, Convened . . . March 10,1864*, 5–46.

88. *Journal of the Senate at an Extra Session of the General Assembly of the State of Georgia, Convened . . . March 10,1864*, 7–8.

89. "Distilling—how it is Useful," *Daily Dispatch* (Richmond, VA), February 20, 1862.

90. James M. Whittle to Zach L. Finney, March 20, 1862, Accession 41447, Personal Papers Collection, LVA.

91. "Facts for consideration," *Daily Dispatch* (Richmond, VA), February 17, 1862.

92. Of sixty letters written to Vance on the topic of distilling/alcohol, thirty-two letters requested permits and asked for clarification about the laws. Boxes G.P. 161–G.P. 184, Vance Governor's Papers. For the North Carolina laws, see "An Ordinance to Prohibit, for a Limited Time, the Manufacture of Spiritous [sic] Liquors from Grain," February 21, 1862, *Ordinances and Resolutions of the State Convention of North Carolina, Third Session in January and February, 1862*, 119–20; and "An Act to Prohibit the Distillation of Spirituous Liquors," December 17, 1862, *Public Laws of the State of North-Carolina, Passed by the General Assembly, at Its Session of 1862–'63*, 20–21.

93. S. W. Wallace to Zebulon B. Vance, January 6, 1863, box G.P. 161, Vance Governors Papers.

94. *An act to prohibit the importation of luxuries, or articles not necessary or of common use,* 1–11; *Regulations prescribed for the government and directions of all officers of the revenue . . .,* approved February 6th, 1864, 1–6.

95. "An Act to authorize the manufacture of spirituous liquors for the use of the army and hospitals," June 14, 1864, in Matthews, *Statutes at Large*, 271; Robinson, "Prohibition in the Confederacy," 50–58; Gates, *Agriculture and the Civil War*, 96–100; Hurt, *Agriculture and the Confederacy*, 58–59.

96. "Governor's Annual Message," *Confederate Union* (Milledgeville, GA), November 11, 1862.

97. "A Whiskey Speculator—Tries to Impose on Gov. Brown and Disregard his Proclamation against the Manufacture of Whiskey," from the *Atlanta Intelligencer*, repr. in the *Confederate Union* (Milledgeville, GA), November 4, 1862.

98. "Gov. Brown and the Whisky Speculation," *Confederate Union* (Milledgeville, GA), October 28, 1862.

99. "Governor's Annual Message," *Confederate Union* (Milledgeville, GA), November 11, 1862.

100. Major J. F. Cummings to Col. L. B. Northrop, February 13, 1864, in Candler, *Confederate Records of the State of Georgia*, 2:467–71. It is difficult to gain a sense from incomplete medical purveyor's records how much contracted distillers were producing. But the records of the Medical Purveyor's Office for District 4 in Macon, Georgia, for early 1865 list five contracted distillers who supplied the Confederate armies. Between February and April 1865, G. F. and H. E. Oliver supplied 1,581 gallons of whiskey and alcohol; A. I. Simmons supplied 810.25 gallons; Hussy and Williams supplied 103.5 gallons; Carr, Glenn, and Wright supplied 3,609 gallons; and I. A. Taylor supplied 33.5 gallons. These numbers indicate that distillers—at least near the war's end—actually supplied around 2,000 gallons per month, rather than the 3,000 gallons Cummings requested. Brown's worries may have been overblown. Medical Department, Account of Whiskey and Alcohol Received, Medical Purveyor's Office, Macon, GA Department, 1865, chap. 6, vol. 626, RG 109, NARA.

101. "An Important Question," *Staunton* (VA) *Spectator*, January 26, 1864.

102. George Davis to James Seddon, November 30, 1864, Accession 26101, Personal Papers Collection, LVA.

103. Zebulon B. Vance to James A. Seddon, December 31, 1863, in Johnston and Mobley, *Papers of Zebulon Baird Vance*, 2:360.

104. James A. Seddon to Zebulon B. Vance, January 12, 1864, in Johnston and Mobley, *Papers of Zebulon Baird Vance*, 3:44–45. Seddon's response to Vance does indicate that significant disorder existed on the ground. Seddon asserted that no civilians in North Carolina had contracts to distill because they manufactured poor whiskey. The Salisbury distillery, in fact, was owned and operated by the Confederate Medical Department (and "should not be interfered with or the supply of grain cut off"). As to the distillery in Charlotte, Seddon knew nothing about it. Either Vance was hearing rumors or distillers in Charlotte and other parts of the state were forging contracts.

105. Zebulon B. Vance to Sion H. Rogers, January 22, 1864, in Johnston and Mobley, *Papers of Zebulon Baird Vance* 3:65; Zebulon B. Vance to Sion H. Rogers, January 16, 1865, in Johnston and Mobley, *Papers of Zebulon Baird Vance*, 3:384; Sion H. Rogers to Zebulon B. Vance, January 18, 1865, in Johnston and Mobley, *Papers of Zebulon Baird Vance*, 3:386–87.

106. "An Act to prevent the distillation of spirituous liquors, and to declare the distilleries to be a public and common nuisance, and to authorize the same to be abated, and for other purposes," *Laws of the State of Mississippi, Passed at a Called Session of the Mississippi Legislature, held in Macon, March 1864*, 63–68.

107. *Journal of the House of Representatives of the State of Mississippi, Called Session at Macon, August 1864*, 34–36.

108. Hundreds of receipts and expense reports are filed in boxes 2704, 3414, 12850, 12851, and 12852, Whiskey Dispensary Records, 1861–1869, Mississippi Office of the State Auditor, Mississippi Auditor of Public Accounts, ser. 333 (RG 29), State Government Records Collection, MDAH.

109. *Journal of the House of Representatives of the State of Mississippi, Called Session at Columbus, February and March, 1865*, 35; Captain Abram Adams prescription, Noxubee County folder (1 of 2); Captain D. G. Cooper prescription, Rankin County folder (1 of 6); Rankin County folder (6 of 6), box 12850; J. C. Albion prescription, Winston County folder (2 of 2), box 12851, Whiskey Dispensary Records, 1861–1869, Mississippi Office of the State Auditor, Mississippi Auditor of Public Accounts, ser. 333 (RG 29), State Government Records Collection, MDAH.

110. *Journal of the House of Representatives of the State of Mississippi* (1865), 50.

111. "An Act in relation to Distilleries, and the Distillation of Ardent Spirits," Governor's and Auditor's Papers, 1861–1865, undated folder, box 2704, Whiskey Dispensary Records, 1861–1869, Mississippi Office of the State Auditor, Mississippi Auditor of Public Accounts, ser. 333 (RG 29), State Government Records Collection, MDAH.

112. G. M. Porter prescriptions, November 20 and 30, 1864, Tallahatchie County folder, box 12851; Vouchers for Harriet Valentine, M. H. Ainsworth, and Mrs. Margaret Thompson, Jasper County folder; Voucher for Elisabeth McGee, Jones County folder, box 3415, Whiskey Dispensary Records, 1861–1869, Mississippi Office of the State Auditor, Mississippi Auditor of Public Accounts, ser. 333 (RG 29), State Government Records Collection, MDAH.

113. September 23, 1860, Sarah Lois Wadley Diary, August 8, 1859–May 15, 1865 (Electronic Edition), 63, SHC.

114. Robert Manson Myers, *Children of Pride*, 524.

115. Robert Manson Myers, *Children of Pride*, 624.

116. Faust, *Mothers of Invention*, 53–79; Rable, *Civil Wars*, 114–21; McCurry, *Confederate Reckoning*, 218–62.

117. Russell, *My Diary North and South*, 258.

118. Chesnut, *Mary Chesnut's Civil War*, 348–49.

119. McGuire, *Diary*, 278–79.

120. "Local Intelligence," *Daily Mail* (Montgomery, AL), January 6, 1865.

121. Ravenel, *Two Diaries*, 37–38.

122. "Document 89: The Murder of Negro Troops—*Atlanta Appeal*, July 1864," *Rebellion Record*, 11:Doc. 526.

123. The notion that Black men were beastly in nature and incapable of self-control gained traction in the eighteenth century. For scholarship, see Jordan, *White over Black*. During and after the Civil War, the notion was used by white people to falsely accuse African American men of rape and to justify white violence and lynching. See Rosen, *Terror in the Heart of Freedom*, 194–202; Hale, *Making Whiteness*, 85–119.

124. May 25, 1862, Kate Carney Diary: April 15, 1861–July 31, 1862 (Electronic Edition), SHC.

125. McGuire, *Diary*, 346–48.

126. Andrews, *War-Time Journal*, 259.

127. Andrews, *War-Time Journal*, 365–66.

128. Historians have shown that Northern and Southern women became increasingly comfortable petitioning the state with their grievances during the war. Giesberg, *Army at Home*; Silber, *Daughters of the Union*; Rable, *Civil Wars*; Ash, *When the Yankees Came*; Faust, *Mothers of Invention*; McCurry, *Confederate Reckoning*. My study of Southern women and drunken Union soldiers benefits from conversations with Laura Mammina, whose own work in progress explores wartime interactions between Northern soldiers and Southern women. Laura Mammina, "Home Front."

129. Kleppner, *Third Electoral System, 1853–1892*; Foster, *Moral Reconstruction*.

130. Michael Lewis, *Coming of Southern Prohibition*.

Chapter Six

1. "Ellsworth and his Zouaves: The Temperance Home Guard on the Death of Col. Ellsworth," *JATU* 24 (June 1861): 96.

2. Memor. (Worcester, June 20), "Honor to Col. Ellsworth," *JATU* 24 (July 1861): 102.

3. "News from the Seat of War," *Spirit of the Age* 12 (June 5, 1861): 2.

4. South Carolina Tract Society, *No. 84: Appeal to the Youth*, 2, 3, 11, 15.

5. As other historians have shown, debates about duty, republicanism, and appropriate masculinity abounded in both the Union and the Confederacy, and personal behavior was a key expression of commitment to one's respective cause. See Gallman, *Defining Duty*; Rable, *Confederate Republic*; Bledsoe, *Citizen-Officers*.

6. "General Order, Spirituous Liquors," *JATU* 25 (October 1862): 152.

7. "Ecclesiastical Action," *JATU* 25 (December 1862): 179.

8. C. N. Nichols, "A Solemn Fact," *JATU* 25 (November 1862): 163; "A Dangerous and Disgraceful Exception," *JATU* 26 (February 1863): 29.

9. "The Hon. Neal Dow," *JATU* 24 (November 1861): 169.

10. From *Maine Journal*, "Col. Neal Dow's Regiment," *JATU* 24 (December 1861): 182.

11. "Letter from Col. Neal Dow," *JATU* 25 (February 1862): 29.

12. "Army Items," *JATU* 25 (July 1862): 99; "Gen. Neal Dow," *JATU* 25 (November 1862): 161.

13. "Gen. Neal Dow's Return," *JATU* 27 (April 1864): 57.

14. "Gen. O. O. Howard's Address on Temperance," *JATU* 26 (August 1863): 123.

15. Gregg, *Life in the Army*, 88.

16. Carpenter, *Sword and Olive Branch*, 23–58; Christian B. Keller, *Chancellorsville and the Germans*.

17. From the *Times*, "Gen. Oliver Otis Howard," *JATU* 27 (December 1864): 187–88.

18. Russell, *My Diary North and South*, 500.

19. Haupt, *Reminiscences of General Herman Haupt*, 303.

20. Haupt, *Reminiscences of General Herman Haupt*, 63.

21. Longacre, "Fortune's Fool," 22.

22. Russell, *My Diary North and South*, 500, 506–7.

23. Longacre, "Fortune's Fool," 22–31.

24. *OR*, ser. 1, 15:65–66, 94.

25. Gregg, *Life in the Army*, 85.

26. "Fighting Joe," *Daily Dispatch* (Richmond, VA), February 14, 1863.

27. Wainwright, *Diary of Battle*, 202.

28. Donaldson, *Inside*, 226–27.

29. Lauderdale, *Wounded River*, 158–59.

30. Welles, *Diary of Gideon Welles*, 1:348–49.

31. The record of Beecher's comments appear in the text of the congressional investigation published in the *Report of the Joint Committee on the Conduct of the War, at the Second Session Thirty-Eighth Congress*, xli–lv, 15, 31, 84. Walter H. Herbert provides a similar account of the rumor surrounding Hooker in his biography, but he credits the Beecher rumor with influencing Welles, when, in fact, Welles's diary entry predates the Beecher gossip by a week and indicates that rumors were already flying before Beecher made his comments. See Herbert, *Fighting Joe Hooker*, 225.

32. Meade, *Life and Letters*, 1:365.

33. Schurz, *Reminiscences of Carl Schurz*, 2:431.

34. Weld, *War Diary and Letters*, 61.

35. Dana, *Recollections of the Civil War*, 72–73; Simpson, *Ulysses S. Grant*; Waugh, *U. S. Grant*; John Y. Simon, "A Marriage Tested by War," in Bleser and Gordon, *Intimate Strategies*, 127–29; chap. 1 deals at length with domesticity and its effects on soldiers' sobriety.

36. John Murray Forbes, *Letters and Recollections*, 1:336.

37. Charles Dana's biography of Grant published in 1868 praises the general for his temperance and argues that he was not a drunk, despite sometimes appearing so due to illness and exhaustion. See Dana and Wilson, *Life of Ulysses S. Grant*, 28, 401–5.

38. George Templeton Strong, *Diary*, 3:352, 533.

39. "Gen. Grant's Character," *JATU* 26 (October 1863): 156.

40. "Grant neither Drinks nor Swears," *JATU* 27 (August 1864): 124.

41. "Massachusetts Men," *JATU* 27 (September 1864): 132.

42. "Address: To Lieut. Gen. Grant, U.S.A.," *JATU* 27 (April 1864): 56.

208 Notes to Chapter Six

43. "From the West," *Daily Dispatch* (Richmond, VA), September 30, 1861.

44. Earl J. Hess, *Civil War in the West*, 37.

45. "The Fall of Fort Donelson," *Daily Dispatch* (Richmond, VA), February 19, 1862; "Latest from the North. surrender of Fort Donelson. Official reports. Great losses on both sides," *Daily Dispatch* (Richmond, VA), February 20, 1862.

46. For examples of early biographies of Jackson that celebrate his character, see John Esten Cooke, *Life of Stonewall Jackson*; Daniel, *Character of Stonewall Jackson*. For scholarship on the myth-building surrounding both generals, see Hettle, *Inventing Stonewall Jackson*; Connelly, *Marble Man*.

47. Robertson, *Stonewall Jackson*, 130, 299, 418.

48. Blackford, *Letters from Lee's Army*, 88–89.

49. Pryor, *Reading the Man*, 1–38; Thomas, *Robert E. Lee*, 30–55, 78.

50. Robert E. Lee to William Henry Fitzhugh Lee, May 30, 1858, sec. 26, George Bolling Lee Papers, VHS.

51. John Baxter Moseley Diary, VHS.

52. Osborne, *Jubal*, 75; Nisbet, *Four Years*, 117–19.

53. Osborne, *Jubal*, 349–98; specifically 354, 381, 383.

54. Jubal Early to Alexander R. Boteler, October 19, 1864, Jubal Early (Lt. Gen.) box, Confederate Military Leaders Collection, Eleanor S. Brockenbrough Library, MOC.

55. Evans, *Intrepid Warrior*, 518.

56. Osborne, *Jubal*, 390–92.

57. Temperance reformers discuss the danger of liquor poisoned during the fermenting and distilling process in their own literature. See Rev. Dr. E. Nott, "No. 13: Temperance Lecture No. XI," in Delavan, *Temperance Essays*, 187–88; Veach, *Kentucky Bourbon Whiskey*, 45–61.

58. "Patriotism and Temperance," *Spirit of the Age* 12 (May 8, 1861): 2.

59. "Account by a Participant," *Rebellion Record*, 3:Doc. 341.

60. During the Rappahannock Expedition, Union sailors were warned when they entered the town of Tappahannock in April 1862 that they should not drink any liquor because it had been poisoned. When the town's inhabitants offered it, the soldiers refused. See "Document 132: Rappahannock Expeditions, Correspondent, April 16, 1862," *Rebellion Record*, 4:474.

61. *OR*, ser. 1, 8:68.

62. "Our Intimate Enemies," from the *Richmond Examiner*, repr. in *Spirit of the Age* 8 (September 11, 1861): 1.

63. "Blockade of Liquor," *Daily Dispatch* (Richmond, VA), August 6, 1861. For an additional example, A. B., "[correspondence of the *Richmond Dispatch*]," *Daily Dispatch* (Richmond, VA), February 5, 1862.

64. "McClellan's Army," *New York Herald*, July 9, 1862.

65. Duff, *To Petersburg*, 200.

66. *OR*, ser. 1, 24(3):153.

67. Richard Lewis, *Camp Life*, 95.

68. *OR*, ser. 1, 30(1):924–25.

69. Moses Drury Hoge to William G. Crenshaw, June 3, 1864, sec. 2, Crenshaw Family Papers, 1807–1977, VHS.

70. "Another Yankee Doodle," *Rebellion Record*, 3:Poetry 8–9.
71. Peter, *Union Woman*, 170–71.
72. Chauncey Herbert Cooke, *Soldier Boy's Letters*, 89.
73. Peter, *Union Woman*, 170–71.
74. Wills, *Army Life*, 273.
75. *OR*, ser. 1, 39(1):514.
76. *Minutes of the General Assembly of the Presbyterian Church in the Confederate States of America*, 1:37, 27.
77. *OR*, ser. 1, 48(1):1253.
78. *OR*, ser. 1, 34(1):924–25.
79. *OR*, ser. 1, 22(2):1058–60.
80. "Our Cavalry," *Richmond Enquirer*, October 18, 1864.
81. Ural, *Harp and the Eagle*, 42–81; Gleeson, *Green and the Gray*, 41–72.
82. Russell, *My Diary North and South*, 284–85, 345.
83. West, *Texan in Search of a Fight*, 68.
84. Wainwright, *Diary of Battle*, 89.
85. Robert Goldthwaite Carter, *Four Brothers in Blue*, 76–77.
86. Gleeson, *Green and the Gray*, 73–111.
87. Robert Manson Myers, *Children of Pride*, 1222–24.
88. Patterson, *Yankee Rebel*, 49–50.
89. McDaniel, *Diary of Battles*, 18–19.
90. Gleeson, *Green and the Gray*, 80–93, 221–24; Ural, *Harp and the Eagle*, 136–232.
91. "Incidents of Webb's Cross-Roads," *Rebellion Record*, 4:Poetry 75.
92. Lauderdale, *Wounded River*, 85.
93. The article notes that at first some soldiers declined the beer but assumes that because they were German, they only turned it down temporarily. See "The Mountain Department: Gen. Fremont in the Field—The Obstacles which he has Overcome—Camp Jessie—New-Creek (VA)," *New York Times*, May 10, 1862.
94. Reinhart, *German Hurrah!*, 37; Kamphoefner and Helbich, *Germans in the Civil War*, 310.
95. Christian B. Keller, *Germans at Chancellorsville*, 32–34.
96. Bissell, *Civil War Letters*, 118.
97. Kamphoefner and Helbich, *Germans in the Civil War*, 141. Maureen Ogle argues that these rapid-fire drinking patterns forced German brewers to adapt their recipes to suit American chugging, so to speak. See Ogle, *Ambitious Brew*, 85.
98. Kamphoefner and Helbich, *Germans in the Civil War*, 44, 115.
99. Kamphoefner and Helbich, *Germans in the Civil War*, 77, 79.
100. Andrea Mehrländer argues that Germans in wartime Richmond were, much like their Northern counterparts, targets of discrimination. Native-born Confederates charged them with disloyalty. See "'With More Freedom and Independence than the Yankees': The Germans of Richmond, Charleston, and New Orleans during the American Civil War," in Ural, *Civil War Citizens*, 57–97.
101. John Gottfried Lange Memoirs, "The New Name or the Shoemaker in the Old and the New World, Thirty Years in Europe and Thirty Years in America," vol. 1, typescript translated into English, VHS, 171–92, 194, 197, 199, 203, 206.

102. John Gottfried Lange Memoirs, 211–12, 226, 275, 280, 285.

103. Roberts, *Evangelicalism*, 109–27; Pease and Pease, *They Who Would Be Free*, 124–43.

104. "Mr. Cox and the Slave who was Whipped to Death," *Liberator* (Boston, MA), April 4, 1862.

105. Genovese, *Roll, Jordan, Roll*, 577–78, 643–44.

106. "How Our Negroes Live," *Valley Spirit* (Franklin County, PA), March 30, 1859.

107. For scholarship on military service and citizenship, see Samito, *Becoming American under Fire*, 45–102, 134–71.

108. Stephens, *Voice of Thunder*, 156.

109. Junius Albus, "Colored Troops, No. 5," *Christian Recorder*, August 1, 1863.

110. "A new class to be cared for," *JATU* 27 (June 1864): 91; Charles A. Carleton, Adjutant 4th N. H. Volunteers to John Marsh, *JATU* 26 (November 1863): 164.

111. "Camp for Colored Soldiers," *JATU* 26 (October 1863): 158.

112. *OR*, ser. 3, 3:436.

113. "'The Irrepressible Negro': The Border States after the War: Ninth Letter" *New York Times*, April 16, 1865.

114. Faust, *Confederate Nationalism*, 41–57.

115. Atkinson, *Christian Duty*, 9–10.

116. Ramsey, *No. 3 How Shall I Live?*, 2.

117. "Aid from the enemy," *Daily Dispatch* (Richmond, VA), July 15, 1861; "Definition of Billiards," *Daily Dispatch* (Richmond, VA), July 14, 1862.

118. *OR*, ser. 4, 2:487.

119. Michael Thomas Smith, *Enemy Within*, 154–74.

120. *OR*, ser. 1, 22(2):15.

121. *JATU* 26 (April 1863): 56.

122. "The Blood-thirsty Knight," *Valley Spirit* (Franklin County, PA), April 15, 1863.

123. "Wheatland Correspondence," *Weekly Vincennes* (IN) *Gazette*, April 15, 1865.

124. For scholarship on Northern German American enlistment and the perception among nativists that Germans did not volunteer quickly enough, see Stephen D. Engle, "Yankee Dutchmen: Germans, the Union, and the Construction of Wartime Identity," in Ural, *Civil War Citizens*, 11–55; Christian B. Keller, *Chancellorsville and the Germans*, 24–30. For Irish American enlistment, see Susannah J. Ural, "'Ye Sons of Green Erin Assemble': Northern Irish American Catholics and the Union War Effort, 1861–1865," in Ural, *Civil War Citizens*, 99–129; Samito, *Becoming American under Fire*, 103–33.

125. For broader historical context surrounding the New York Draft Riots, see Bernstein, *New York City Draft Riots*.

126. Lauderdale, *Wounded River*, 162–63.

127. *OR*, ser. 1, 27(2):903–4.

128. Wheeler, *Letters*, 417.

129. Lydia Child worried about "drunken foreigners" at the polls. See Child, *Letters of Lydia Maria Child*, 153.

130. Taylor, *Letters Home to Sarah*, 107. Two years before the election, Levi Bird Duff, who strongly disliked McClellan, had charged him with looking "like a German of ample means who makes free use of Lager & the pipe." Duff seems to have tied together immigrants, alcohol, and anti-McClellan sentiment earlier than others. See Duff, *To Petersburg*, 54.

131. Hundley, *Prison Echoes*, 176–77.

132. *OR*, ser. 2, 2:1289–91.

133. E. R. Norton to Zebulon B. Vance, September 27, 1864, Correspondence: September 25–27, 1864, C. P. 180, Vance Governors Papers, SANC.

134. Andrews, *War-Time Journal*, 200.

135. "Local Intelligence," *Montgomery* (AL) *Daily Mail*, January 6, 1865.

136. J. J. Jackson to Zebulon B. Vance, February 3, 1863, Correspondence: February 1–4, 1863, G.P. 162, Vance Governors Papers. As other historians have shown, these counties had significant Unionist populations. See Bynum, *Unruly Women*, 136; Barton A. Myers, *Rebels against the Confederacy*. Myers argues, overall, that closely examining these Unionists reveals significant fissures in Confederate society. The conflict over distilling in North Carolina confirms his point. Unionists and disaffected Southerners distilled, undoubtedly, because they did not buy into notions of "good" Confederate behavior.

137. Of sixty letters written to Vance on the topic of distilling and/or alcohol, twenty-eight letters reported incidents of illicit distilling (the rest request permits and ask for clarification about the laws). Significantly, of the twenty letters sent to Vance from the Unionist counties, fifteen of them reported illicit distillers. See G.P. 162–184, Vance Governors Papers; William A. Graham to Zebulon B. Vance, March 7, 1863, #161, box no. 15.2; Thomas F. McKesson to Zebulon B. Vance, February 8, 1865, #788, box no. 15.6, Personal Papers of Zebulon Baird Vance (PC 15.1–15.49), SANC.

138. This is an example of the tension between protective nationalists and ordinary Confederates that Jarret Ruminski has found extensively in his study of wartime Mississippi. See Ruminski, *Limits of Loyalty*.

139. "The consumption of grain by distilleries—necessity of Legislation," *Daily Dispatch* (Richmond, VA), February 13, 1862.

140. "Facts for consideration," *Daily Dispatch* (Richmond, VA), February 17, 1862. Rand Dotson identifies Floyd County, Virginia, as an area in which loyalty to the Confederacy faded over the course of the war. He cites illicit distillers who wasted scarce resources as one of the factors contributing to citizens' demoralization. See Dotson, "'Grave and Scandalous Evil,'" 403.

Epilogue

1. Downing, *Downing's Civil War*, 280.

2. "What is to be the Future of our Soldiers?," *JATU* 28 (March 1865): 40.

3. For scholarship on the Civil War as a catalyst for state-sanctioned reform movements, see Morton Keller, *Affairs of State*, 122–61; Foster, *Moral Reconstruction*.

4. "Twenty-Ninth Anniversary," *JATU* 28 (June 1865): 83.

5. Independent Order of Good Templars, *Journal of the Proceedings*, 7.

6. The 1869 proceedings reference meetings as early as 1866. See Office of the Secretary of the State Council, *Proceedings of the Fourth Semi-Annual Session*, 9; *Constitutions of the Supreme, State, and Subordinate Councils, of the Friends of Temperance*, 14–15.

7. Mississippi's Black Codes, for example, specifically prohibit Black and white people from selling liquor to Black people. See BlackPast, *(1866) Mississippi Black Codes*; Fahey, *Temperance and Racism*; Coker, *Liquor*; Stewart, *Moonshiners and Prohibitionists*; Charles D.

Thompson, *Spirits of Just Men*; Willis, *Southern Prohibition*; Michael Lewis, *Coming of Southern Prohibition*.

8. *Proceedings of the Called Session, held at Skilesville*, 13.

9. Bordin, *Woman and Temperance*; Holly Berkley Fletcher, *Gender*.

10. "'When Johnny Comes Home," *JATU* 28 (May 1865): 77.

11. Independent Order of Good Templars, *Journal of the Proceedings*, 392–93.

12. Historians have long included excellent analyses of body reformers in their studies of the American reform tradition. For example, Walters, *American Moral Reformers, 1815–1860*, 147–73; Abzug, *Cosmos Crumbling*, 163–82. More recently, Adam D. Shprintzen's study of vegetarianism has provided an in-depth examination of how physical and moral reform became closely related as the nineteenth century progressed. See Shprintzen, *Vegetarian Crusade*. Other historians argue that virile and athletic masculinity was intertwined with American imperialism; see Bederman, *Manliness and Civilization*; Hoganson, *Fighting for American Manhood*.

13. McClurken, *Take Care of the Living*, 66, 96, 126; Marten, *Sing Not War*. Although Sarah Handley-Cousins does not explore drinking among veterans, her study argues persuasively that disabled veterans had their masculinity compromised by the war and were left coping for decades with chronic pain and a loss of identity. See Handley-Cousins, *Bodies in Blue*.

14. Mittelman, *Brewing Battles*, 23–70; Kleppner, *Cross of Culture*, 112, 144–45.

15. Fahey, *Temperance and Racism*, 105–25; Mark A. Johnson, *Rough Tactics*, 51–86; H. Paul Thompson, *Most Stirring and Significant Episode*.

16. Veach, *Kentucky Bourbon Whiskey*, 63–90; Wilbur R. Miller, *Revenuers and Moonshiners*; Ownby, *Subduing Satan*.

17. For an analysis of local gradualism and the slowly radicalizing prohibition movement, see Szymanski, *Pathways to Prohibition*, 153–217.

18. Veit, *Modern Food, Moral Food*.

19. McGirr, *War on Alcohol*.

Bibliography

Manuscript Collections

Filson Historical Society, Louisville, Kentucky
    Winn-Cook Family Papers
Library of Virginia, Richmond, Virginia
    Local Government Records Collection
    Personal Papers Collection
Louis Round Wilson Library, University of North Carolina,
      Chapel Hill, North Carolina
    Southern Historical Collection
Mississippi Department of Archives and History, Jackson, Mississippi
    State Government Records Collection, RG 29
Missouri State Archives, Jefferson City, Missouri
    Missouri Provost Marshal Records
Museum of the Confederacy, Eleanor S. Brockenbrough Library, Richmond, Virginia
      (now housed at the Confederate Memorial Literary Society Collection,
      Virginia Museum of History and Culture)
    Confederate Military Leaders Collection
    Soldier Letters Collection
National Archives and Records Administration, Washington, DC
    Records of the Office of the Commissary General of Subsistence (RG 192)
    War Department Collection of Confederate Records (RG 109)
State Archives of North Carolina, Raleigh, North Carolina
    Governors Papers–Zebulon Baird Vance
    J. W. Cook Account Book, 1845–1861
    Personal Papers of Zebulon Baird Vance
State Historical Society of Iowa, Des Moines Historical Library
    Annie Wittenmyer Papers, 1861–1901, Manuscripts Collection
University of Virginia Libraries, Charlottesville, Virginia
    Albert and Shirley Small Special Collections
      Letters of Robert, MSS 1242
Virginia Historical Society, Richmond, Virginia
      (now the Virginia Museum of History and Culture)
    Conrad (Holmes) Papers
    Crenshaw Family Papers
    John Gottfried Lange Memoirs
    George Bolling Lee Papers
    John Baxter Moseley Diary

Wisconsin Historical Society, Madison, Wisconsin
  Register of the Independent Order of Good Templars: Madison Lodge Records, 1864–1923 (Archives)

Newspapers and Periodicals

Chicago (IL) *Daily Tribune*
Confederate Union (Milledgeville, GA)
The *Daily Democrat and News* (Davenport, IA)
Daily Dispatch (Richmond, VA)
Daily Mail (Montgomery, AL)
Evening Star (Washington, DC)
Fayetteville (TN) *Observer*
Grand Haven (MI) *News*
Herald Bulletin (Anderson, IN)
Liberator (Boston, MA)
Muscatine (IA) *Weekly Journal*
New York Herald
New York Times
Richmond (VA) *Enquirer*
Semi-Weekly Dispatch (Franklin County, PA)
Southern Federal Union (Milledgeville, GA)
Southern Recorder (Milledgeville, GA)
Staunton (VA) *Spectator*
Valley Spirit (Franklin County, PA)
Vermont Chronicle (Bellows Falls, VT)
The Tipton (IA) *Advertiser*
Weekly Vincennes (IN) *Gazette*

REFORM PERIODICALS

Christian Recorder
Herald of Health and Water-Cure Journal
Journal of the American Temperance Union and the New York Prohibitionist
Spirit of the Age (Raleigh, NC)

Temperance Publications

Constitution and By-Laws of Harrod Division, No. 105, Sons of Temperance, Harrodsburg, KY. Harrodsburg: Ploughboy Print, 1852.
Constitutions of the Supreme, State, and Subordinate Councils, of the Friends of Temperance, adopted at the First Meeting of the Supreme Council of the Order, held in Petersburg, June 25, 26, 27, and 28, 1867. To which is appended the Rules of Order for the Supreme and State Councils. Petersburg, VA: Index Job rooms, 1868.
Delavan, Edward C., ed. *Temperance Essays, and Selections from Different Authors.* Albany, NY: Van Benthuysen's Steam Printing House, 1865.
Independent Order of Good Templars. *Journal of the Proceedings of the Eleventh Annual Session of the Right Worthy Grand Lodge of North America held at London, C. W., May 23, 24, 25, 1865.* Chicago, IL: Jameson and Morse, 1865.
Marsh, Catherine. *No. 90: A Sketch of the Life of Capt. Hedley Vicars, the Christian Soldier.* Raleigh, NC: s.n., 1863.
No. 26: Are You Ready [For the Soldiers]. Raleigh, NC: s.n., between 1861 and 1865.
No. 44: Advice to Soldiers. Raleigh, NC: s.n., between 1861 and 1865.
No. 87: A Word of Warning for the Sick Soldier. Raleigh, NC: s.n., between 1861 and 1865.
Office of the Secretary of the State Council. *Proceedings of the Fourth Semi-Annual Session of the State Council of the Friends of Temperance of the State of Virginia, Held at Harrisonburg, Va., April 27, 28, and 29, 1869.* Norfolk, VA: Journal Office, 1869.

Physician. *Liquor and Lincoln*. Petersburg, VA?: s.n., between 1861 and 1865.
Proceedings of the Called Session, held at Skilesville, on the 11th and 12th of April, 1866. Owensboro, KY: Thos. S. Pettit, Printer, Monitor Office, 1867.
South Carolina Tract Society. *Descriptive List of Tracts published by the South Carolina Tract Society*. Charleston, SC: Evans and Cogswell, 1863?.
South Carolina Tract Society. *No. 84: Appeal to the Youth, and especially to the Soldiers of the Confederate States*. Charleston, SC: Evans and Cogswell, n.d.

Church Reports

Presbyterian Church in the Confederate States of America. *Minutes of the General Assembly of the Presbyterian Church in the Confederate States of America*. Vol. 1. Augusta, GA: Steam Power Press Chronicle and Sentinel, 1862.
Ten Islands Baptist Association. *Minutes of the Proceedings of the Ten Islands Baptist Association. Held with the Church at Post Oak Spring, Calhoun County, Alabama, on the 26th, 27th and the 28th Days of September, 1863*. Alabama?: s.n., 1863?.

Sermons

Atkinson, Thomas, Right Reverend, Bishop of North Carolina. *Christian Duty in the Present Time of Trouble: A Sermon Preached at St. James' Church, Wilmington, N. C., on the Fifth Sunday after Easter, 1861*. Wilmington, NC: Fulton and Price, Steam Power Press Printers, 1861.
Ramsey, James B., Reverend, Lynchburg, VA. *No. 3 How Shall I Live?*. Richmond, VA: Presbyterian Committee of Publication, between 1861 and 1865.

Medical Publications

Chisholm, John Julian. *A Manual of Military Surgery: For the Use of the Surgeons in the Confederate Army: With an Appendix of the Rules and Regulations for the Medical Department of the Confederate Army*. Richmond, VA: West and Johnson, 1861.
Hammond, William A. *Treatise on Hygiene with Special Reference to the Military Service*. Philadelphia: J. B. Lippincott & Co., 1863.
Letterman, Jonathan. *Medical Recollections of the Army of the Potomac*. New York: D. Appleton and Company, 1866.
Porcher, Francis Peyre. *Resources of the Southern Fields and Forests, Medical, Economical, and Agricultural, Being also a Medical Botany of the Confederate States; with Practical Information on the Useful Properties of the Trees, Plants, and Shrubs*. Charleston, SC: Steam-Power Press of Evans and Cogswell, 1863.
Sanitary Commission No. 31: Report of a Committee appointed by Resolution of the Sanitary Commission, to Prepare a Paper on the Use of Quinine as a Prophylactic against Malarious Diseases. New York: Wm. C. Bryant & Co, 1861.
Tripler, Charles S. *Manual of the Medical Officer of the Army of the United States, Part I: Recruiting and the Inspection of Recruits*. Cincinnati, OH: Wrightson & Co., 1858.
Warren, Edward. *An Epitome of Practical Surgery, for Field and Hospital*. Richmond, VA: West and Johnson, 1863.

National and State Government Documents

UNITED STATES OF AMERICA

The General Statutes of the Commonwealth of Massachusetts. Boston: William White, 1860.

Journal of the House of Representatives of the United States. Vols. 58–59. Washington, DC: Government Printing Office, 1861–1863.

Journal of the Senate of the United States of America. Vols. 53–54. Washington, DC: Government Printing Office, 1861–1862.

Public Acts of the Thirty-Seventh Congress of the United States. United States Statutes at Large Collection (Digitized), Library of Congress, Washington, DC.

Report of the Joint Committee on the Conduct of the War, at the Second Session Thirty-Eighth Congress: Army of the Potomac, Battle of Petersburg. Washington, DC: Government Printing Office, 1865.

Revision of 1860, containing all the Statutes of a General Nature of the State of Iowa. Des Moines: John Teesdale, State Printer, 1860.

United States. Naval War Records Office. Official Records of the Union and Confederate Navies in the War of the Rebellion. 27 vols. Washington, DC: Government Printing Office, 1894–1922.

United States. War Department. War of the Rebellion: A Compilation of the Official Records of the Union and Confederate Armies. 128 vols. Washington, DC: Government Printing Office, 1880–1901.

United States Statutes at Large. Vols. 12–13, 1861–1864.

United States Christian Commission. United States Christian Commission, for the Army and Navy. Work and Incidents. First Annual Report. Philadelphia, PA: February 1863.

United States War Department. Revised Regulations for the Army of the United States, 1861. Philadelphia, PA: J. B. Lippincott, 1861.

CONFEDERATE STATES OF AMERICA

An act to prohibit the importation of luxuries, or articles not necessary or of common use. Richmond, VA: s.n., 1864.

Circular... [concerning issue of alcoholic stimulants]. Charleston, SC: s.n., 1863.

Circular... [concerning the administration of alcoholic stimulants]. Charleston, SC: s.n., 1864.

Circular no. 10 ... [relating to abuse of administration of alcoholic stimulants]. Richmond, VA: s.n., 1864.

C. S. A. Surgeon-General's Office. Guide for Inspection of Hospitals and for Inspector's Report. Richmond?: s.n., between 1861 and 1865.

C. S. A. War Department. Message of the President: Richmond, Va., Jan. 6, 1865: to the House of Representatives, in response to your resolution of the 19th November last, I herewith transmit a communication from the Secretary of War, which conveys the information desired, relative to the impressment of brandy, so far as the records of his office enable him to furnish it.... Richmond, VA: s.n., 1865.

Matthews, James M., ed. Public Laws of the Confederate States of America, Passed at the Fourth Session of the First Congress, 1863–4. Richmond, VA: R. M. Smith, Printer to Congress, 1864.

———, ed. The Statutes at Large of the Confederate States of America. Richmond, VA: R. M. Smith, Printer to Congress, 1864.

Memminger, C. G. [Regulations "prescribed for the government and directions of all officers of the revenue, to carry into effect the provisions of the act to prohibit the importation of luxuries, or of articles not necessary or of common use, approved February 6th, 1864"]. Richmond, VA: s.n., 1864.
Regulations for the Medical Department of the C. S. Army. Richmond, VA: Ritchie and Dunnavant, 1862.
Regulations for the Subsistence Department of the Confederate States of America. Richmond, VA: n.p., 1861.
Regulations for the Subsistence Department of the Confederate States. Richmond, VA: Ritchie and Dunnavant, 1862.
Regulations prescribed for the government and directions of all officers of the revenue, to carry into effect the provisions of the act to prohibit the importation of luxuries, or of articles not necessary or of common use, approved February 6th, 1864. Richmond, VA: s.n., 1864.

Georgia
Acts of the General Assembly of the State of Georgia, Passed in Milledgeville, at the Annual Session in November and December, 1861. Milledgeville, GA: s.n., 1862.
Acts of the General Assembly of the State of Georgia, Passed in Milledgeville, at an Annual Session in November and December, 1862. Milledgeville, GA: s.n., 1863.
Candler, Allen D., ed. *The Confederate Records of the State of Georgia.* 6 vols. Atlanta, GA: Charles P. Byrd, 1909–11.
Journal of the Senate at an Extra Session of the General Assembly of the State of Georgia, Convened . . . March 10, 1864. Milledgeville, GA: s.n., 1864.

Mississippi
BlackPast, B. *(1866) Mississippi Black Codes.* Accessed March 10, 2021. https://www.blackpast.org/african-american-history/1866-mississippi-black-codes/.
Journal of the House of Representatives of the State of Mississippi, Called Session at Macon, August 1864. Meridian, MS: J. J. Shannon & Co., State Printers, 1864.
Journal of the House of Representatives of the State of Mississippi, Called Session at Columbus, February and March, 1865. Meridian, MS: J. J. Shannon and Co., State Printers, 1865.
Laws of the State of Mississippi, Passed at a Called a Regular Session of the Mississippi Legislature, Held in Jackson and Columbus, Dec. 1862 and Nov. 1863. Selma, AL: s.n., 1863.
Laws of the State of Mississippi, Passed at a Called Session of the Mississippi Legislature, held in Macon, March 1864. Meridian, MS: J. J. Shannon & Co. State Printers, 1864.

North Carolina
. . . *An ordinance for the suppression of distilleries, February 1862.* Raleigh, NC: s.n., 1862.
. . . *An ordinance to restrict the distillation of grain, and to raise revenue.* Raleigh, NC, John W. Syme, 1862.
. . . *Ordinance upon distilled spirits, November 1861.* Raleigh, NC: s.n., 1861.
Ordinances and Resolutions of the State Convention of North Carolina, Third Session in January and February, 1862. Raleigh, NC: s.n., 1862.
Public Laws of the State of North-Carolina, Passed by the General Assembly, at Its Session of 1862–'63. Raleigh, NC: s.n., 1863.

South Carolina

Acts of the General Assembly of the State of South Carolina, Passed in December, 1862, and February and April, 1863. Columbia, SC: s.n., 1863.

... *A bill to prohibit the undue distillation of spirituous liquors from the cereal grains in this state, first read on December 3, 1862.* Columbia, SC: s.n., 1862.

... *A bill to prohibit the sale of spirituous liquors in small quantities during the war, first read on December 15, 1862.* Columbia, SC: s.n., 1862.

Journal of the Senate of South Carolina: Being the Session of 1862. Columbia, SC: s.n., 1862.

Texas

Laws of the Eighth Legislature of the State of Texas: Extra Session. Austin, TX: s.n., 1861.

Virginia

Journal of the House of Delegates of Virginia, for the Session of 1861–62. Richmond, VA: s.n., 1861.

Published Personal Accounts

Andrews, Eliza Frances. *The War-Time Journal of a Georgia Girl, 1864–1865.* New York: Appleton-Century-Crofts, 1908.

Armstrong, Hallock. *Letters from a Pennsylvania Chaplain at the Siege of Petersburg, 1865.* Privately published by Mary M. Brown Armstrong, 1961.

Ayling, Augustus D. *A Yankee at Arms: The Diary of Lieutenant Augustus D. Ayling, 29th Massachusetts Volunteers.* Edited by Charles F. Herberger. Knoxville: University of Tennessee Press, 1999.

Beaudry, Louis N. *War Journal of Louis N. Beaudry, Fifth New York Cavalry: The Diary of a Union Chaplain, Commencing February 16, 1863.* Edited by Richard E. Beaudry. Jefferson, NC: McFarland, 1996.

Bellard, Alfred. *Gone for a Soldier: The Civil War Memoirs of Private Alfred Bellard.* Edited by David Herbert Donald. Boston, MA: Little, Brown, 1975.

Bereman, S. O. "Civil War Journal of S. O. Bereman," Garth Hagerman Photo/Graphics. Accessed August 31, 2012. http://garthagerman.com/fambly/bereman7.php.

Billings, John D. *Hardtack and Coffee: The Unwritten Story of Army Life.* Lincoln: University of Nebraska Press, 1993.

Bissell, Lewis. *The Civil War Letters of Lewis Bissell.* Edited by Mark Olcott. Washington, DC: Field School Educational Foundation Press, 1981.

Bircher, William. *A Drummer-Boy's Diary: Comprising Four Years of Service with the Second Regiment Minnesota Veteran Volunteers, 1861 to 1865.* St. Paul, MN: St. Paul Book and Stationery Co., 1889.

Blackford, Susan Leigh, comp. *Letters from Lee's Army, or Memoirs of Life In and Out of the Army of Virginia during the War between the States.* Edited by Charles Minor Blackford III. New York: Charles Scribner's Sons, 1947.

Boudrye, Louis N. *Historic Records of the Fifth New York Cavalry, First Ira Harris Guard.* Albany, NY: S. R. Gray, 1865.

Boyd, Belle. *Belle Boyd in Camp and in Prison, with an Introduction by a Friend of the South.* 2 vols. London: Saunders, Otley, and Co., 1865.

Bragg, Junius Newport. *Letters of a Confederate Surgeon, 1861–65.* Edited by Helen Bragg Gaughan. Camden, AR: The Urley Company, 1960.

Bratton, John. *Letters of John Bratton to his Wife.* Edited by Elizabeth Porcher Bratton. Privately published, 1942.

Brewster, Charles Harvey. *When This Cruel War Is Over: The Civil War Letters of Charles Harvey Brewster.* Edited by David W. Blight. Amherst: University of Massachusetts Press, 1992.

Brown, Augustus Cleveland. *The Diary of a Line Officer.* Privately published, 1906.

Butler, Benjamin Franklin. *Private and Official Correspondence of Gen. Benjamin F. Butler, During the Period of the Civil War.* 5 Vols. Springfield, MA: Plimpton, 1917.

Campbell, John Quincy Adams. *The Union Must Stand: The Civil War Diary of John Quincy Adams Campbell, Fifth Iowa Volunteer Infantry.* Knoxville: University of Tennessee Press, 2000.

Carter, John C., ed. *Welcome to the Hour of Conflict: William Cowan McClellan and the 9th Alabama.* Tuscaloosa: University of Alabama Press, 2007.

Carter, Robert Goldthwaite. *Four Brothers in Blue, or Sunshine and Shadows of the War of the Rebellion: A Story of the Great Civil War from Bull Run to Appomattox.* Austin: University of Texas Press, 1978.

Cavins, Elijah Henry Clay. *The Civil War Letters of Col. Elijah H. C. Cavins, 14th Indiana.* Compiled by Barbara A. Smith. Owensboro, KY: Cook-McDowell, 1981.

Chase, John W. *Yours for the Union: The Civil War Letters of John W. Chase, First Massachusetts Light Artillery.* Edited by John S. Collier and Bonnie B. Collier. New York: Fordham University Press, 2004.

Chesnut, Mary Boykin Miller. *Mary Chesnut's Civil War.* Edited by C. Vann Woodward. New Haven, CT: Yale University Press, 1981.

Child, Lydia Maria Francis. *Letters of Lydia Maria Child with a Biographical Introduction by John G. Whittier and Appendix by Wendell Phillips.* Boston, MA: Houghton, Mifflin and Co., 1883.

Conyngham, D. P. *The Irish brigade and its campaigns: With some account of the Corcoran Legion and sketches of the principal officers.* New York: William McSorley, 1869.

Cooke, Chauncey Herbert. *Soldier Boy's Letters to His Father and Mother, 1861–5.* Independence, WI: News-office, 1915.

Cooke, John Esten. *The Life of Stonewall Jackson from Official Papers, Contemporary Narratives, and Personal Acquaintance.* Richmond, VA: Ayres and Wade, 1863.

Corby, William. *Memoirs of Chaplain Life: Three Years with the Irish Brigade in the Army of the Potomac.* Edited by Lawrence Frederick Kohl. New York: Fordham University Press, 1992.

Corson, William Clark. *My Dear Jennie: A Collection of Love Letters from a Confederate Soldier to His Fiancee during the Period 1861–1865.* Edited by Blake W. Corson Jr. [S.I.]: B. W. Corson, 1982.

Cumming, Kate. *Kate: The Journal of a Confederate Nurse.* Edited by Richard Barksdale Harwell. Baton Rouge: Louisiana State University Press, 1998.

Cummins, Simon Burdick. *Give God the Glory: Memoirs of a Civil War Soldier.* Edited by Melvin Jones. Melvin Jones: 1979.

Dana, Charles A. *Recollections of the Civil War: With the Leaders at Washington and in the Field in the Sixties.* New York: D. Appleton, 1913.

Dana, Charles A., and James Harrison Wilson. *The Life of Ulysses S. Grant, General of the Armies of the United States*. Springfield, MA: Gurdon Bill and Company, 1868.

Daniel, John Warwick. *Character of Stonewall Jackson*. Lynchburg, VA: Schaffter and Bryant, Printers, 1868.

Daniels, Nathan W. *Thank God My Regiment an African One: The Civil War Diary of Colonel Nathan W. Daniels*. Baton Rouge: Louisiana State University Press, 1998.

Day, David L. *My Diary of Rambles with the 25th Massachusetts Volunteer Infantry*. Milford, MA: King and Billings Printers, 1884.

Dexter, Seymour. *Seymour Dexter, Union Army: Journal and Letters of Civil War Service in Company K, 23rd New York Volunteer Regiment of Elmira*. Edited by Carl A. Morrell. Jefferson, NC: McFarland, 1996.

Dixon, William Daniel. *The Blues in Gray: The Civil War Journal of William Daniel Dixon and the Republican Blues Daybook*. Edited by Roger S. Durbam. Knoxville: University of Tennessee Press, 2000.

Donaldson, Francis Adams. *Inside the Army of the Potomac: The Civil War Experience of Captain Francis Adams Donaldson*. Edited by J. Gregory Acken. Mechanicsburg, PA: Stackpole, 1998.

Dooley, John Edward. *John Dooley, Confederate Soldier: His War Journal*. Edited by Joseph T. Durkin. Notre Dame, IN: University of Notre Dame Press, 1983.

Downing, Alexander G. *Downing's Civil War Diary*. Edited by Olynthus B. Clark. Des Moines: Iowa State Department of History and Archives, 1916.

Duff, Levi Bird. *To Petersburg with the Army of the Potomac: The Civil War Letters of Levi Bird Duff, 105th Pennsylvania Volunteers*. Edited by Jonathan E. Helmreich. Jefferson, NC: McFarland, 2009.

Dwight, Wilder. *Life and Letters of Wilder Dwight: Lieut-Col. Second Mass. Inf. Vols*. Boston, MA: Ticknor and Co., 1891.

Ellis, Thomas T. *Leaves from the Diary of an Army Surgeon; or, Incidents of Field, Camp, and Hospital Life*. New York: John Bardburn, 1863.

Emerson, Sarah Hopper, ed. *Life of Abby Hopper Gibbons: Told Chiefly through Her Correspondence*. 2 vols. New York: G. P. Putnam's Sons, 1896.

Evans, Clement Anselm. *Intrepid Warrior: Clement Anselm Evans, Confederate General from Georgia, Life, Letters, and Diaries of the War Years*. Edited by Robert Frier Stephens Jr. Dayton, OH: Morningside, 1992.

Fleharty, Stephen F. *"Jottings from Dixie": The Civil War Dispatches of Sergeant Major Stephen F. Fleharty, U.S.A*. Edited by Philip J. Reyburn and Terry L. Wilson. Baton Rouge: Louisiana State University Press, 1999.

Fleming, George Thornton, ed. *Life and Letters of Alexander Hays, Brevet Colonel United States Army, Brigadier General and Brevet Major General United States Volunteers*. Compiled by Gilbert Adams Hays. Pittsburgh, PA: Privately published, 1919.

Fletcher, Elliot H. *The Civil War Letters of Captain Elliot H. Fletcher of Mill Bayou, Mississippi County, Arkansas, July to December 1861*. Little Rock, AR: Pulaski County Historical Society, 1963.

Ford, Worthington Chauncey, Charles Francis Adams Jr., and Henry Adams. *A Cycle of Adams Letters, 1861–1865*. 2 vols. Boston, MA: Houghton Mifflin, 1920.

Forbes, Eugene. *Diary of a Soldier; and Prisoner of War in the Rebel Prisons.* Trenton, NJ: Murphy and Bechtel Printers, 1865.

Forbes, John Murray. *Letters and Recollections of John Murray Forbes.* Edited by Sarah Forbes Hughes. 2 vols. Boston, MA: Houghton Mifflin, 1900.

Foroughi, Andrea R., ed. *Go If You Think It Your Duty: A Minnesota Couple's Civil War Letters.* St. Paul: Minnesota Historical Society Press, 2008.

Fremantle, Sir Arthur James Lyon, Coldstream Guards. *Three Months in the Southern States: April, June, 1863.* Mobile, AL: S. H. Goetzel, 1864.

Fullam, George Townley. *Our Cruise in the Confederate States' War Steamer Alabama: The Private Journal of an Officer.* Cape Town, Western Cape Province: South African Advertiser and Mail, 1863.

Fuller, Richard F. *Chaplain Fuller: Being a Life Sketch of a New England Clergyman and Army Chaplain.* Boston, MA: Walker, Wise, and Company, 1863.

Gillaspie, Ira. *The Diary of Ira Gillaspie of the Eleventh Michigan Infantry.* Edited by Daniel B. Weber. Mount Pleasant: Central Michigan University Press, 1965.

Gregg, J. Chandler. *Life in the Army in the Departments of Virginia, and the Gulf, including Observations in New Orleans, with an Account of the Author's Life and Experience in the Ministry.* Philadelphia, PA: Perkinpine and Higgins, 1866.

Haines, Zenas T. *In the Country of the Enemy: The Civil War Reports of a Massachusetts Corporal.* Edited by William C. Harris. Gainesville: University of Florida Press, 1999.

———. *Letters from the 44th Regiment M.V.M.: A Record of the Experience of a Nine Months' Regiment in the Department of North Carolina in 1862–63.* Boston: The Herald Job Office, 1863.

Hancock, Richard Ramsey. *Hancock's Diary: or, A History of the Second Tennessee Confederate Cavalry, with Sketches of First and Seventh Battalions.* Nashville, TN: Brandon Print Co., 1867.

Haupt, Herman. *Reminiscences of General Herman Haupt Giving Hitherto Unpublished Official Orders, Personal Narratives of Important Military Operations, and Interviews with President Lincoln, Secretary Stanton, General-in-Chief Halleck, and with Generals McDowell, McClellan, Meade, Hancock, Burnside, and Others in Command of the Armies in the Field, and His Impressions of These Men.* Milwaukee, WI: Wright and Joys Co., 1901.

Haydon, Charles B. *For Country, Cause, and Leader: The Civil War Journal of Charles B. Haydon.* Edited by Stephen W. Sears. New York: Ticknor and Fields, 1993.

Hess, Frederick. *Letters to Tobitha: A Personal History of the Civil War, Letters by Frederick Hess.* Edited by David Primrose. New York: iUniverse, 2006.

Higginson, Thomas Wentworth. *Army Life in a Black Regiment.* Boston, MA: Fields, Osgood and Co., 1870.

History of the 127th Regiment Pennsylvania Volunteers: Familiarly Known as the "Dauphin County Regiment." Authorized by the Regimental Association and Prepared by Its Committee. Lebanon, PA: Report Publishing Company, 189?.

Holmes, Emma. *Diary of Miss Emma Holmes, 1861–1866.* Edited by John F. Marszalek. Baton Rouge: Louisiana State University Press, 1979.

Holt, Daniel M. *A Surgeon's Civil War: The Letters and Diary of Daniel M. Holt.* Edited by James M. Greiner, Janet L. Coryell, and James R. Smither. Kent, OH: Kent State University Press, 1994.

Holt, David. *A Mississippi Rebel in the Army of Northern Virginia: The Civil War Memoirs of Private David Holt.* Edited by Thomas D. Cockrell and Michael B. Ballard. Baton Rouge: Louisiana State University Press, 1995.

Hosmer, James Kendall. *The Color-Guard: Being a Corporal's Notes of Military Service in the Nineteenth Army Corps.* Boston, MA: Walker Wise and Co., 1864.

Howe, Henry Warren. *Passages from the Life of Henry Warren Howe, Consisting of Diary and Letters Written During the Civil War, 1816–1865. A Condensed History of the Thirtieth Massachusetts Regiment and Its Flags, Together with the Genealogies of the Different Branches of the Family.* Lowell, MA: Courier-Citizen Co. Printers, 1899.

Hubbs, G. Ward, ed. *Voices from Company D: Diaries by the Greensboro Guards, Fifth Alabama Regiment, Army of Northern Virginia.* Athens: University of Georgia Press, 2003.

Hundley, Daniel Robinson. *Prison Echoes of the Great Rebellion.* New York: S. W. Green, 1874.

Jackson, Edgar Allan, James Fenton Bryant, and Irvin Cross Wills. *Three Rebels Write Home: Including the Letters of Edgar Allen Jackson (September 7, 1860–April 15, 1863), James Fenton Bryant (June 20, 1861–December 30, 1866), Irvin Cross Wills (April 9, 1862–July 29, 1863), and Miscellaneous Items.* Franklin, VA: New Pub. Co., 1955.

Jackson, Oscar Lawrence. *The Colonel's Diary: Journals Kept Before and During the Civil War by the Late Colonel Oscar L. Jackson, Sometime Commander of the 63rd Regiment O.V.I.* Edited by David P. Jackson. Privately published, 1922.

Johansson, M. Jane, ed. *Widows by the Thousand: The Civil War Letters of Theophilus and Harriet Perry, 1862–1864.* Fayetteville: University of Arkansas Press, 2000.

Johnson, Jonathan Huntington. *The Letters and Diary of Captain Jonathan Huntington Johnson: Written During His Service with Company D—15th Regiment New Hampshire Volunteers from October 1862 through August 1863 while Part of the Banks Expedition.* Privately published by Alden Chase Brett, 1961.

Johnston, Frontis W., and Joe A. Mobley, eds. *The Papers of Zebulon Baird Vance.* 3 vols. Raleigh, NC: State Department of Archives and History, 1963–2013.

Jones, Jenkin Lloyd. *An Artilleryman's Diary.* Wisconsin History Commission, 1914.

Kamphoefner, Walter D., and Wolfgang Helbich, eds. *Germans in the Civil War: The Letters They Wrote Home.* Translated by Susan Carter Vogel. Chapel Hill: University of North Carolina Press, 2006.

Kinsley, Rufus. *Diary of a Christian Soldier: Rufus Kinsley and the Civil War.* Edited by David C. Rankin. Cambridge: Cambridge University Press, 2003.

Larimer, Charles F., ed. *Love and Valor: The Intimate Civil War Letters between Captain Jacob and Emeline Ritner.* Western Springs, IL: Sigourney, 2000.

Lauderdale, John Vance. *The Wounded River: The Civil War Letters of John Vance Lauderdale, M.D.* Edited by Peter Josyph. East Lansing: Michigan State University Press, 1993.

Lewis, Richard. *Camp Life of a Confederate Boy, of Bratton's Brigade, Longstreet's Corps, C.S.A.: Letters written by Lieut. Richard Lewis, of Walker's Regiment, to His Mother, during the War, Facts and Inspirations of Camp Life, Marches, &c.* Charleston, SC: News and Courier Book Presses, 1883.

Lusk, William Thompson. *War Letters of William Thompson Lusk: Captain, Assistant Adjutant-general, United States Volunteers, 1861–1863, afterward M.D. Ll. D.* New York: W. C. Lusk, 1911.

McAllister, Robert. *The Civil War Letters of General Robert McAllister.* Edited by James I. Robertson Jr. New Brunswick, NJ: Rutgers University Press, 1965.

McDaniel, J. J. *Diary of Battles, Marches and Incidents of the Seventh S.C. Regiment.* Privately published, 1862.

McFall, William, and James McFall. *Civil War Correspondence: Letters of William and James McFall of the South Carolina Palmetto Sharpshooters.* Edited by F. Lawrence McFall Jr. Danville, VA: n.p., 2000.

McGuire, Judith White Brockenbrough. *Diary of a Southern Refugee during the War.* 3rd ed. Richmond, VA: J. W. Randolph and English, 1889.

McIntyre, Benjamin F. *Federals on the Frontier: The Diary of Benjamin F. McIntyre, 1862–1864.* Edited by Nannie M. Tilley. Austin: University of Texas Press, 1963.

Meade, George. *The Life and Letters of George Gordon Meade, Major-General, United States Army.* 2 vols. New York: Charles Scribner's Sons, 1913.

Miller, Alonzo. *Diaries and Letters, 1864–1865.* Prescott, WI: Privately published, 1958.

Molyneux, Joel. *Quill of the Wild Goose: Civil War Letters and Diaries of Private Joel Molyneux, 141st Pennsylvania Volunteers.* Edited by Kermit Molyneux Bird. Shippensburg, PA: Burd Street, 1996.

Moore, Frank, ed. *The Rebellion Record: A Diary of American Events.* 11 vols. New York: Putnam and Van Nostrand, 1861–68.

Moore, Nancy E. *The Journal of Eldress Nancy: Kept at the South Union, Kentucky, Shaker Colony, August 15, 1861–September 4, 1864.* Edited by Mary Julia Neal. Nashville, TN: Parthenon, 1963.

Moore, Robert A. *A Life for the Confederacy, as Recorded in the Pocket Diaries of Pvt. Robert A. Moore, Co. G. 17th Mississippi Regiment, Confederate Guards, Holly Springs, Mississippi.* Jackson, TN: McCowat-Mercer, 1959.

Morse, Charles Fessenden. *Letters Written during the Civil War, 1861–1865.* Privately published, 1898.

Myers, John C. *A Daily Journal of the 192d Reg't, Penn'a Volunteers, Commanded by Col. William B. Thomas; in the Service of the United States for One Hundred Days.* Philadelphia, PA: Crissy and Markley, 1864.

Myers, Robert Manson, ed. *The Children of Pride: A True Story of Georgia and the Civil War.* New Haven, CT: Yale University Press, 1972.

Nisbet, James Cooper. *Four Years on the Firing Line.* Edited by Bell Irvin Wiley. Jackson, TN: McCowat-Mercer, 1963.

Pate, James P., ed. *When This Evil War Is Over: The Correspondence of the Francis Family, 1860–1865.* Tuscaloosa: University of Alabama Press, 2006.

Patrick, Robert. *Reluctant Rebel: The Secret Diary of Robert Patrick, 1861–1865.* Edited by F. Jay Taylor. Baton Rouge: Louisiana State University Press, 1959.

Patterson, Edmund DeWitt. *Yankee Rebel: The Civil War Journal of Edmund DeWitt Patterson.* Edited by John G. Barrett. Chapel Hill: University of North Carolina Press, 1966.

Pember, Phoebe Yates. *Southern Woman's Story: Life in Confederate Richmond.* Jackson, TN: McCowat-Mercer, 1947.

Pender, William Dorsey. *The General to His Lady: The Civil War Letters of William Dorsey Pender to Fanny Pender.* Edited by William W. Hassler. Chapel Hill: University of North Carolina Press. 1988.

Perry, John Gardner. *Letters from a Surgeon of the Civil War*. Compiled by Martha Derby Perry. Boston, MA: Little, Brown, 1906.

Peter, Frances. *A Union Woman in Civil War Kentucky: The Diary of Frances Peter*. Edited by John David Smith and William Cooper Jr. Lexington: University Press of Kentucky, 2000.

Petty, Elijah P. *Journey to Pleasant Hill: The Civil War Letters of Elijah P. Petty, Walker's Texas Division, C.S.A.* Edited by Norman D. Brown. San Antonio: University of Texas Institute of Texan Cultures, 1982.

Powers, Elvira J. *Hospital Pencillings: Being a Diary while in Jefferson General Hospital, Jeffersonville, Indiana, and Others at Nashville, Tennessee, as Matron and Visitor*. Boston, MA: E. L. Mitchell, 1866.

Ravenel, Charlotte St. J. *Two Diaries from Middle St. John's, Berkeley, South Carolina, February–May 1865; Journals kept by Miss Susan R. Jervey and Miss Charlotte St. J. Ravenel, at Northampton and Pooshe Plantations, and Reminiscences of Mrs. (Waring) Henagan*. Pinopolis, SC: St. John's Hunting Club, 1921.

Reinhart, Joseph R., ed. *August Willich's Gallant Dutchmen: Civil War Letters from the 32nd Indiana Infantry*. Kent, OH: Kent State University Press, 2006.

———, ed. and trans. *A German Hurrah!: Civil War Letters of Friedrich Bertsch and Wilhelm Stangel, 9th Ohio Infantry*. Kent, OH: Kent State University Press, 2010.

———, ed. and trans. *Two Germans in the Civil War: The Diary of John Daeuble and the Letters of Gottfried Rentschler, 6th Kentucky Volunteers*. Knoxville: University of Tennessee Press, 2004.

Reminisco, Don Redro Quarendo. *Life in the Union Army: or Notings and Reminiscences of a Two Years' Volunteer*. New York: H. Dexter, 1863.

Richards, Lewis. *Eleven Days in the Militia during the War of the Rebellion: Being a Journal of the Emergency Campaign of 1862*. Philadelphia, PA: Collins Printer, 1883.

Riley, Frankin Lafayette. *Grandfather's Journal: Company B, Sixteenth Mississippi Infantry Volunteers, Harris' Brigade, Mahone's Division, Hill's Corps, A.N.V., May 27, 1861-July 15, 1865*. Edited by Austin C. Dobbins. Dayton, OH: Morningside House, 1988.

Robbins, Rufus. *Through Ordinary Eyes: The Civil War Correspondence of Rufus Robbins, Private, 7th Regiment, Massachusetts Volunteers*. Edited by Ella Jane Bruen and Brian M. Fitzgibbins. Westport, CT: Praeger, 2000.

Russell, William Howard. *My Diary North and South*. Boston, MA: T.O.H.P. Burnham, 1863.

Sangston, Lawrence. *The Bastiles of the North*. Baltimore, MD: Kelly, Hedian and Piet, 1863.

Schurz, Carl. *The Reminiscences of Carl Schurz*. 3 vols. London: John Murray, 1909.

Sheeran, James B. *Confederate Chaplain: A War Journal of Rev. James B. Sheeran, c.ss.r., 14th Louisiana, C.S.A.* Edited by Joseph T. Durkin. Milwaukee, WI: Bruce, 1960.

Smith, George Gilbert. *Leaves from a Soldier's Diary, the Personal Record of Lieutenant George G. Smith, Co. C, 1st Louisiana Regiment Infantry Volunteers (White) during the War of the Rebellion*. Putnam, CT: George G. Smith, 1906.

Stephens, George E. *A Voice of Thunder: The Civil War Letters of George E. Stephens*. Edited by Donald A. Yacovone. Urbana: University of Illinois Press, 1997.

Stevens, Thomas N. *"Dear Carrie...": The Civil War Letters of Thomas N. Stevens*. Edited by George M. Blackburn. Mount Pleasant, MI: Clark Historical Library, 1984.

Stott, William Taylor. *For Duty and Destiny: The Life and Civil War Diary of William Taylor Stott: Hoosier Soldier and Educator*. Edited by Lloyd A. Hunter. Indianapolis: Indiana Historical Society Press, 2010.

Strong, George Templeton. *Diary*. Edited by Allan Nevins and Milton Halsey Thomas. 4 vols. New York: Macmillan, 1952.

Taylor, Guy C. *Letters Home to Sarah: The Civil War Letters of Guy C. Taylor, Thirty-Sixth Wisconsin Volunteers*. Edited by Kevin Alderson and Patsy Alderson. Madison: University of Wisconsin Press, 2012.

Tenney, Luman Harris. *War Diary, 1861–1865*. Edited by Frances Andrews Tenney. Cleveland, OH: Evangelical Pub. House, 1914.

Thompson, Harriet Jane. "Civil War Wife: The Letters of Harriet Jane Thompson, Part I." Edited by Glenda Riley, *Annals of Iowa* 44, no. 1 (Winter 1978): 214–31.

Thompson, Robert Means, and Richard Wainwright, eds. *Confidential Correspondence of Gustavus Vasa Fox: Assistant Secretary of the Navy: 1861–1865*. 2 vols. New York: De Vinne, 1920.

Toalson, Jeff, ed. *Mama, I Am Yet Still Alive: A Composite Diary of 1863 in the Confederacy, As Seen by the Soldiers, Farmers, Clerks, Nurses, Sailors, Farm Girls, Merchants, Surgeons, Riverboatmen, Chaplains, and Wives*. Bloomington, IN: IUniverse, 2012.

Trobriand, Regis de. *Four Years with the Army of the Potomac*. Translated by George K. Dauchy. Boston, MA: Ticknor and Co., 1889.

Twichell, Joseph Hopkins. *The Civil War Letters of Joseph Hopkins Twichell: A Chaplain's Story*. Edited by Peter Messent and Steven Courtney. Athens: University of Georgia Press, 2006.

Tyler, Mason Whiting. *Recollections of the Civil War: With Many Original Diary Entries and Letters Written from the Seat of War, and with Annotated References*. Edited by William S. Tyler. New York: G. P. Putnam's Sons, 1912.

Von Olnhausen, Mary Phinney, Baroness. *Adventures of an Army Nurse in Two Wars*. Edited by James Phinney Munroe. Boston, MA: Little, Brown, 1903.

Wainwright, Charles S. *A Diary of Battle: The Personal Journals of Colonel Charles S. Wainwright, 1861–1866*. Edited by Allan Nevins. New York: Harcourt, Brace, and World, 1962.

Watson, Robert. *Southern Service on Land and Sea: The Wartime Journal of Robert Watson*. Edited by R. Thomas Campbell. Knoxville: University of Tennessee Press, 2002.

Welch, Spencer Glasgow. *A Confederate Surgeon's Letters to His Wife*. Washington: Neale Publishing Company, 1911.

Weld, Stephen Minot. *War Diary and Letters of Stephen Minot Weld, 1861–1865*. Boston: Massachusetts Historical Society, 1979.

Welles, Gideon. *The Diary of Gideon Welles, Secretary of the Navy under Lincoln and Johnson*. Edited by Howard K. Beale. 3 vols. New York: W. W. Norton, 1960.

Wells, Seth James. *The Siege of Vicksburg, from the Diary of Seth J. Wells, Including Weeks of Preparation and of Occupation after the Surrender*. Detroit, MI: William H. Rowe, 1915.

West, John Camden. *A Texan in Search of a Fight*. Waco, TX: Press of J. S. Hill and Co., 1901.

Wheeler, William. *Letters of William Wheeler of the Class of 1855, Y.C.* Privately published, 1875.

Wilder, Burt G. *Practicing Medicine in a Black Regiment: The Civil War Diary of Burt G. Wilder, 55th Massachusetts*. Edited by Richard M. Reid. Amherst: University of Massachusetts Press, 2010.

Wiley, William. *The Civil War Diary of a Common Soldier: William Wiley of the 77th Illinois Infantry*. Edited by Terrence J. Winschel. Baton Rouge: Louisiana State University Press, 2001.

Wills, Charles Wright. *Army Life of an Illinois Soldier: Including a Day by Day Record of Sherman's March to the Sea: Letters and Diary of the Late Charles W. Wills, Private and Sergeant 8th Illinois Infantry, Lieutenant and Battalion Adjutant 7th Illinois Cavalry, Captain, Major and Lieutenant Colonel 103rd Illinois Infantry*. Compiled by Mary E. Kellogg. Washington, DC: Globe Print Co., 1906.

Secondary Sources

Abzug, Robert H. *Cosmos Crumbling: American Reform and the Religious Imagination*. Oxford: Oxford University Press, 1994.

Adams, George Worthington. *Doctors in Blue: The Medical History of the Union Army in the Civil War*. Baton Rouge: Louisiana State University Press, 1996.

Ash, Stephen V. *When the Yankees Came: Conflict and Chaos in the Occupied South, 1861–1865*. Chapel Hill: University of North Carolina Press, 1995.

Beattie, Peter M. *The Tribute of Blood: Army, Honor, Race, and Nation in Brazil, 1864–1945*. Durham, NC: Duke University Press, 2001.

Bederman, Gail. *Manliness and Civilization: A Cultural History of Gender and Race in the United States, 1880–1917*. Chicago: University of Chicago Press, 1995.

Bensel, Richard Franklin. *Yankee Leviathan: The Origins of Central State Authority in America, 1859–1877*. Cambridge: Cambridge University Press, 1990.

Bernstein, Iver. *The New York City Draft Riots: Their Significance for American Society and Politics in the Age of the Civil War*. Oxford: Oxford University Press, 1990.

Beverly and Tom Lowry Database of Civil War Courts-Martial. *The Index Project, Inc.* http://www.theindexproject.com/.

Blair, William. *Virginia's Private War: Feeding Body and Soul in the Confederacy, 1861–1865*. Oxford: Oxford University Press, 1998.

———. *With Malice toward Some: Treason and Loyalty in the Civil War Era*. Chapel Hill: University of North Carolina Press, 2014.

Blakey, Arch Fredric. *General John H. Winder, C.S.A.* Gainesville: University of Florida Press, 1990.

Bledsoe, Andrew S. *Citizen-Officers: The Union and Confederate Junior Officers Corps in the American Civil War*. Baton Rouge: Louisiana State University Press, 2015.

Bleser, Carol K., and Lesley J. Gordon, eds. *Intimate Strategies of the Civil War: Military Commanders and Their Wives*. Oxford: Oxford University Press, 2001.

Blocker, Jack S., Jr., ed. *Alcohol, Reform and Society: The Liquor Issue in Social Context*. Westport, CT: Greenwood, 1979.

———. *American Temperance Movements: Cycles of Reform*. Boston, MA: Twayne, 1989.

Bordin, Ruth. *Woman and Temperance: The Quest for Power and Liberty, 1873–1900*. Philadelphia, PA: Temple University Press, 1981.

Boyer, Paul. *Urban Masses and Moral Order in America, 1820–1920*. Cambridge, MA: Harvard University Press, 1978.

Bray, Chris. *Court-Martial: How Military Justice Has Shaped America from the Revolution to 9/11 and Beyond*. New York: W. W. Norton, 2016.
Broomall, James J. *Private Confederacies: The Emotional Worlds of Southern Men as Citizens and Soldiers*. Chapel Hill: University of North Carolina Press, 2019.
Bynum, Victoria E. *Unruly Women: The Politics of Social & Sexual Control in the Old South*. Chapel Hill: University of North Carolina Press, 1992.
Carlson, Douglas W. "'Drinks He to His Own Undoing': Temperance Ideology in the Deep South." *Journal of the Early Republic* 18, no. 4 (Winter 1998): 659–91.
Carmichael, Peter S. *The War for the Common Soldier: How Men Thought, Fought, and Survived in Civil War Armies*. Chapel Hill: University of North Carolina Press, 2018.
Carpenter, John A. *Sword and Olive Branch: Oliver Otis Howard*. New York: Fordham University Press, 1999.
Cary, Samuel F. *Historical Sketch of the Order of the Sons of Temperance*. Halifax, Nova Scotia: W. Theakston, Printer, 1884.
Cashin, Joan E., ed. *The War Was You and Me: Civilians in the American Civil War*. Princeton, NJ: Princeton University Press, 2002.
Catton, Bruce. *Grant Moves South*. Boston, MA: Little, Brown, 1960.
———. *Grant Takes Command*. Boston, MA: Little, Brown, 1968.
Coker, Joe L. *Liquor in the Land of the Lost Cause: Southern White Evangelicals and the Prohibition Movement*. Lexington: University of Kentucky Press, 2007.
Conlin, Michael F. "The Dangerous *Isms* and Fanatical *Ists*: Antebellum Conservatives in the South and the North Confront the Modernity Conspiracy." *Journal of the Civil War Era* 4, no. 2 (June 2014): 205–33.
Connelly, Thomas L. *The Marble Man: Robert E. Lee and His Image in American Society*. Baton Rouge: Louisiana State University Press, 1978.
Conroy, David W. *In Public Houses: Drink and the Revolution of Authority in Colonial Massachusetts*. Chapel Hill: University of North Carolina Press, 1995.
Cunningham, H. H. *Doctors in Gray: The Confederate Medical Service*. Baton Rouge: Louisiana State University Press, 1958.
Cutter, Barbara. *Domestic Devils, Battlefield Angels: The Radicalism of American Womanhood, 1830–1865*. DeKalb: Northern Illinois Press, 2003.
Dannenbaum, Jed. *Drink and Disorder: Temperance Reform in Cincinnati from the Washingtonian Revival to the WCTU*. Urbana: University of Illinois Press, 1984.
Delo, David M. *Peddlers and Post Traders: The Army Sutler on the Frontier*. Salt Lake City, UT: Kingfisher Books, 1992.
Donald, David Herbert, ed. *Why the North Won the Civil War: Six Authoritative Views on the Economic, Military, Diplomatic, Social, and Political Reasons behind the Confederate Defeat*. Rev. ed. New York: Simon and Schuster, 1996.
Dorsey, Bruce. *Reforming Men and Women: Gender in the Antebellum City*. Ithaca, NY: Cornell University Press, 2002.
Dotson, Rand. "'The Grave and Scandalous Evil Infected to Your People': The Erosion of Confederate Loyalty in Floyd County, Virginia." *Virginia Magazine of History and Biography* 108, no. 4 (Autumn 2000): 393–434.
Escott, Paul. *Military Necessity: Civil-Military Relations in the Confederacy*. Westport, CT: Greenwood, 2006.

Eslinger, Ellen. "Antebellum Liquor Reform in Lexington, Virginia." *Virginia Magazine of History and Biography* 99, no. 2 (April 1991): 163–86.
Fahey, David M. *Temperance and Racism: John Bull, Johnny Reb, and the Good Templars.* Lexington: University Press of Kentucky, 2007.
Faust, Drew Gilpin. *Confederate Nationalism: Ideology and Identity in the Civil War South.* Baton Rouge: Louisiana State University Press, 1984.
———. *Mothers of Invention: Women of the Slaveholding South in the American Civil War.* Chapel Hill: University of North Carolina Press, 1996.
———. *This Republic of Suffering: Death and the American Civil War.* New York: Alfred A. Knopf, 2008.
Fellman, Michael. *Inside War: The Guerrilla Conflict in Missouri during the Civil War.* Oxford: Oxford University Press, 1989.
Fialka, Andrew. *Of Methods and Madness: A Spatial History Approach to the Civil War's Guerrilla Violence.* http://ehistory.org/projects/of-methods-and-madness.html, published April 2015, accessed August 14, 2019.
Flannery, Michael A. *Civil War Pharmacy: A History of Drugs, Drug Supply and Provision, and Therapeutics for the Union and the Confederacy.* New York: Pharmaceutical Products Press, 2004.
Fletcher, Holly Berkley. *Gender and the American Temperance Movement of the Nineteenth Century.* New York: Routledge, 2008.
Foote, Lorien S. *The Gentlemen and the Roughs: Manhood, Honor, and Violence in the Union Army.* New York: New York University Press, 2010.
Foster, Gaines M. *Moral Reconstruction: Christian Lobbyists and the Federal Legislation of Morality, 1865–1920.* Chapel Hill: University of North Carolina Press, 2002.
Gallagher, Gary W. *The Confederate War: How Popular Will, Nationalism, and Military Strategy Could not Stave Off Defeat.* Cambridge, MA: Harvard University Press, 1999.
Gallman, J. Matthew. *Defining Duty in the Civil War North.* Chapel Hill: University of North Carolina Press, 2015.
Gates, Paul W. *Agriculture and the Civil War.* New York: Knopf, 1965.
Genovese, Eugene D. *Roll, Jordan, Roll: The World the Slaves Made.* New York: Vintage, 1976, c1974.
Giesberg, Judith. *Army at Home: Women and the Civil War on the Northern Home Front.* Chapel Hill: University of North Carolina Press, 2009.
———. *Civil War Sisterhood: The U.S. Sanitary Commission and Women's Politics in Transition.* Boston, MA: Northeastern University Press, 2000.
Glatthaar, Joseph T. *General Lee's Army: From Victory to Collapse.* New York: Free Press, 2008.
Gleeson, David T. *The Green and the Gray: The Irish in the Confederate States of America.* Chapel Hill: University of North Carolina Press, 2013.
Goff, Richard D. *Confederate Supply.* Durham, NC: Duke University Press, 1969.
Griffin, Clifford S. *Their Brother's Keepers: Moral Stewardship in the United States, 1800–1865.* New Brunswick, NJ: Rutgers University Press, 1970.
Grimsley, Mark. *The Hard Hand of War: Union Military Policy toward Southern Civilians, 1861–1865.* Cambridge: Cambridge University Press, 1995.
Hale, Grace Elizabeth. *Making Whiteness: The Culture of Segregation in the South, 1890–1940.* New York: Vintage, 1998.

Handley-Cousins, Sarah. *Bodies in Blue: Disability in the Civil War North*. Athens: University of Georgia Press, 2019.

Headrick, Daniel R. *The Tools of Empire: Technology and European Imperialism in the Nineteenth Century*. New York: Oxford University Press, 1981.

Herbert, Walter. *Fighting Joe Hooker*. Indianapolis, IN: Bobbs-Merrill, 1944.

Hess, Earl J. *The Civil War in the West: Victory and Defeat from the Appalachians to the Mississippi*. Chapel Hill: University of North Carolina Press, 2012.

———. *Civil War Supply and Strategy: Feeding Men and Moving Armies*. Baton Rouge: Louisiana State University Press, 2020.

Hettle, Wallace. *Inventing Stonewall Jackson: A Civil War Hero in History and Memory*. Baton Rouge: Louisiana State University Press, 2011.

Hoganson, Kristin L. *Fighting for American Manhood: How Gender Politics Provoked the Spanish-American and Philippine-American Wars*. New Haven, CT: Yale University Press, 1998.

Hu, Tun Yuan. *The Liquor Tax in the United States, 1791–1947: A History of the Internal Revenue Taxes Imposed on Distilled Spirits by the Federal Government*. New York: Columbia University Graduate School of Business, 1950.

Huebner, Timothy S. "Joseph Henry Lumpkin and Evangelical Reform in Georgia: Temperance, Education, and Industrialization, 1830–1860." *Georgia Historical Quarterly* 75, no. 2 (Summer 1991): 254–74.

Humphreys, Margaret. *Marrow of Tragedy: The Health Crisis of the American Civil War*. Baltimore, MD: John Hopkins University Press, 2013.

Hurt, R. Douglas. *Agriculture and the Confederacy: Policy, Productivity, and Power in the Civil War South*. Chapel Hill: University of North Carolina Press, 2015.

Johnson, Mark A. *Rough Tactics: Black Performance in Political Spectacles, 1877–1932*. Jackson: University Press of Mississippi, 2021.

Jordan, Winthrop D. *White over Black: American Attitudes toward the Negro, 1550–1812*. Chapel Hill: University of North Carolina Press, 1968.

Keller, Christian B. *Chancellorsville and the Germans: Nativism, Ethnicity, and Civil War Memory*. New York: Fordham University Press, 2007.

Keller, Morton. *Affairs of State: Public Life in Late Nineteenth Century America*. Cambridge, MA: The Belknap Press of Harvard University Press, 1977.

Kleppner, Paul. *The Cross of Culture: A Social Analysis of Midwestern Politics, 1850–1900*. New York: Free Press, 1970.

———. *The Third Electoral System, 1853–1892: Parties, Voters, and Political Cultures*. Chapel Hill: University of North Carolina Press, 1979.

Krout, John Allen. *The Origins of Prohibition*. New York: Alfred A. Knopf, 1925.

Langley, Harold D. *Social Reform in the United States Navy, 1798–1862*. Urbana: University of Illinois Press, 1967.

Lawson, Melinda. *Patriotic Fires: Forging a New American Nationalism in the Civil War North*. Lawrence: University Press of Kansas, 2005.

Lebsock, Suzanne. *The Free Women of Petersburg: Status and Culture in a Southern Town, 1784–1860*. New York: W. W. Norton, 1984.

Lewis, Michael. *The Coming of Southern Prohibition: The Dispensary System and the Battle over Liquor in South Carolina, 1907–1915*. Baton Rouge: Louisiana State University Press, 2016.

Linderman, Gerald F. *Embattled Courage: The Experience of Combat in the American Civil War.* New York: Free Press, 1987.
Longacre, Edward G. "Fortune's Fool." *Civil War Times Illustrated* 18, no. 2 (May 1979): 22–31.
Lord, Francis A. *Civil War Sutlers and Their Wares.* New York: Thomas Yoseloff, 1969.
MacDonald, Robert H. *Sons of the Empire: The Frontier and the Boy Scout Movement, 1890–1918.* Toronto: University of Toronto Press, 1993.
Mammina, Laura. "The Home Front as Battlefront: Interactions between Union Soldiers and Southern Women during the American Civil War." PhD diss., University of Alabama, Tuscaloosa, 2017.
Marten, James. *Sing Not War: The Lives of Union and Confederate Veterans in Gilded Age America.* Chapel Hill: University of North Carolina Press, 2011.
Martin, Scott C. "'A Soldier Intoxicated Is Far Worse than No Soldier at All': Intoxication and the American Civil War." *Social History of Alcohol and Drugs* 25, no. 2 (Fall 2011): 66–87.
Matt, Susan J. *Homesickness: An American History.* Oxford: Oxford University Press, 2011.
Maxwell, William Quentin. *Lincoln's Fifth Wheel: The Political History of the United States Sanitary Commission.* New York: Longmans, Green, 1956.
McClurken, Jeffrey W. *Take Care of the Living: Reconstructing Confederate Veteran Families in Virginia.* Charlottesville: University of Virginia Press, 2009.
McCurry, Stephanie. *Confederate Reckoning: Power and Politics in the Civil War South.* Cambridge, MA: Harvard University Press, 2010.
McGirr, Lisa. *The War on Alcohol: Prohibition and the Rise of the American State.* New York: W. W. Norton, 2016.
Meyer, Sabine N. *We Are What We Drink: The Temperance Battle in Minnesota.* Urbana: University of Illinois Press, 2015.
Miller, Wilbur R. *Revenuers and Moonshiners: Enforcing Federal Liquor Law in the Mountain South, 1865–1900.* Chapel Hill: University of North Carolina Press, 1991.
Mitchell, Reid. *Civil War Soldiers.* New York: Viking, 1988.
———. *The Vacant Chair: The Northern Soldier Leaves Home.* Oxford: Oxford University Press, 1993.
Mittelman, Amy. *Brewing Battles: A History of American Beer.* New York: Algora, 2008.
Monaghan, Jay. *Civil War on the Western Border, 1854–1865.* Boston, MA: Little, Brown, 1955.
Morone, James A. *Hellfire Nation: The Politics of Sin in American History.* New Haven, CT: Yale University Press, 1994.
Mosse, George L. *The Image of Man: The Creation of Modern Masculinity.* New York: Oxford University Press, 1996.
Mott, Frank Luther. *A History of American Magazines, 1741–1930.* 5 vols. Cambridge, MA: The Belknap Press of Harvard University, 1958–1968.
Murphy, John Thomas. "Pistol's Legacy: Sutlers, Post Traders, and the American Army, 1820–1895." PhD diss., University of Illinois, Champaign-Urbana, 1993.
Myers, Barton A. *Rebels against the Confederacy: North Carolina's Unionists.* Cambridge: Cambridge University Press, 2014.

Neely, Mark E., Jr. *The Fate of Liberty: Abraham Lincoln and Civil Liberties*. Oxford: Oxford University Press, 1991.

———. *Southern Rights: Political Prisoners and the Myth of Confederate Constitutionalism*. Charlottesville: University Press of Virginia, 1999.

Neff, John R. *Honoring the Civil War Dead: Commemoration and the Problem of Reconciliation*. Lawrence: University Press of Kansas, 2005.

Nelson, Megan Kate. *Ruin Nation: Destruction and the American Civil War*. Athens: University of Georgia Press, 2012.

Nissenbaum, Stephen. *The Battle for Christmas*. New York: Vintage, 1996.

Ogle, Maureen. *Ambitious Brew: The Story of American Beer*. Orlando, FL: Harcourt, 2006.

Osborne, Charles C. *Jubal: The Life and Times of General Jubal A. Early, CSA, Defender of the Lost Cause*. Chapel Hill: Algonquin Books, 1992.

Ownby, Ted. *Subduing Satan: Religion, Recreation, and Manhood in the Rural South, 1865–1920*. Chapel Hill: University of North Carolina Press, 1990.

Paludan, Philip Shaw. *A People's Contest: The Union and Civil War, 1861–1865*. Lawrence: University Press of Kansas, 1996.

Parsons, Elaine Frantz. *Manhood Lost: Fallen Drunkards and Redeeming Women in the Nineteenth-Century United States*. Baltimore, MD: Johns Hopkins University Press, 2003.

———. "Slaves to the Bottle: Smith's Civil Damage Liquor Law." *Annals of Iowa* 59, no. 4 (Fall 2000): 347–73.

Pearson, C. C., and J. Edwin Hendricks. *Liquor and Anti-Liquor in Virginia, 1619–1919*. Durham, NC: Duke University Press, 1967.

Pease, Jane H., and William H. Pease. *They Who Would Be Free: Blacks' Search for Freedom, 1830–1861*. New York: Atheneum, 1974.

Pryor, Elizabeth Brown. *Reading the Man: A Portrait of Robert E. Lee through His Private Letters*. New York: Viking Penguin, 2007.

Rable, George C. *Civil Wars: Women and the Crisis of Southern Nationalism*. Urbana: University of Illinois Press, 1989.

———. *The Confederate Republic: A Revolution against Politics*. Chapel Hill: University of North Carolina Press, 1994.

———. *Fredericksburg! Fredericksburg!* Chapel Hill: University of North Carolina Press, 2002.

———. *God's Almost Chosen Peoples: A Religious History of the American Civil War*. Chapel Hill: University of North Carolina Press, 2010.

Raitz, Karl. *Bourbon's Backroads: A Journey through Kentucky's Distilling Landscape*. Lexington, KY: South Limestone Books, 2019.

Ramold, Steven J. *Baring the Iron Hand: Discipline in the Union Army*. DeKalb: Northern Illinois University Press, 2010.

Ringold, May Spencer. *The Role of the State Legislatures in the Confederacy*. Athens: University of Georgia Press, 1966.

Ritter, Luke. *Inventing America's First Immigration Crisis: Political Nativism in the Antebellum West*. New York: Fordham University Press, 2021.

Roberts, Rita. *Evangelicalism and the Politics of Reform in Northern Black Thought, 1776–1863*. Baton Rouge: Louisiana State University Press, 2010.

Robertson, James I., Jr. *Stonewall Jackson: The Man, The Soldier, The Legend*. New York: Macmillan, 1997.

Robinson, William M., Jr. "Prohibition in the Confederacy." *American Historical Review* 37, no. 1 (October 1931): 50–58.

Rorabaugh, W. J. *The Alcoholic Republic: An American Tradition*. Oxford: Oxford University Press, 1979.

Rosen, Hannah. *Terror in the Heart of Freedom: Citizenship, Sexual Violence, and the Meaning of Race in the Postemancipation South*. Chapel Hill: University of North Carolina Press, 2008.

Ruminski, Jarret. *The Limits of Loyalty: Ordinary People in Civil War Mississippi*. Jackson: University Press of Mississippi, 2017.

Salinger, Sharon V. *Taverns and Drinking in Early America*. Baltimore, MD: Johns Hopkins University Press, 2002.

Samito, Christian G. *Becoming American under Fire: Irish Americans, African Americans, and the Politics of Citizenship during the Civil War Era*. Ithaca, NY: Cornell University Press, 2009.

Sellers, James Benson. *The Prohibition Movement in Alabama, 1702–1943*. Chapel Hill: University of North Carolina Press, 1943.

Shively, Kathryn. *Nature's Civil War: Common Soldiers and the Environment in 1862 Virginia*. Chapel Hill: University of North Carolina Press, 2013.

Shprintzen, Adam D. *The Vegetarian Crusade: The Rise of an American Reform Movement, 1817–1921*. Chapel Hill: University of North Carolina Press, 2013.

Silber, Nina. *Daughters of the Union: Northern Women Fight the Civil War*. Cambridge, MA: Harvard University Press, 2005.

Simpson, Brooks D. *Ulysses S. Grant: Triumph over Adversity, 1822–1865*. Boston, MA: Houghton Mifflin, 2000.

Sinha, Manisha. *The Slave's Cause: A History of Abolition*. New Haven, CT: Yale University Press, 2017.

Smith, Andrew F. *Starving the South: How the North Won the Civil War*. New York: St. Martin's, 2011.

Smith, Michael Thomas. *The Enemy Within: Fears of Corruption in the Civil War North*. Charlottesville: University of Virginia Press, 2011.

Spar, Ira. *Civil War Hospital Newspapers: Histories and Excerpts of Nine Union Publications*. Jefferson, NC: McFarland, 2017.

Stewart, Bruce E. "'The Forces of Bacchus Are Fast Yielding': The Rise and Fall of Anti-Alcohol Reform in Antebellum Rowan County, North Carolina." *North Carolina Historical Review* 87, no. 3 (July 2010): 310–38.

———. *Moonshiners and Prohibitionists: The Battle over Alcohol in Southern Appalachia*. Lexington: University Press of Kentucky, 2011.

———. "Select Men of Sober and Industrious Habits." *Journal of Southern History* 73, no. 2 (May 2007): 289–322.

———. "'This County Improves in Cultivation, Wickedness, Mills, and Still': Distilling and Drinking in Antebellum Western North Carolina." *North Carolina Historical Review* 83, no. 4 (October 2006): 447–78.

Stotelmyer, Steven R. *The Bivouacs of the Dead: The Story of Those Who Died at Antietam and South Antietam*. Baltimore, MD: Toomey, 1992.

Stubbs, Brett J. "Captain Cook's Beer: The Antiscorbutic Use of Malt and Beer in Late 18th Century Sea Voyages." *Asia Pacific Journal of Clinical Nutrition* 12, no. 2 (June 2003): 129–37.
Szymanski, Ann-Marie E. *Pathways to Prohibition: Radicals, Moderates, and Social Movement Outcomes*. Durham, NC: Duke University Press, 2003.
Tapson, Alfred J. "The Sutler and the Soldier." *Military Affairs* 21, no. 4 (Winter 1957): 175–81.
Thomas, Emory M. *The Confederacy as a Revolutionary Experience*. Columbia: University of South Carolina Press, 1991.
———. *The Confederate Nation: 1861–1865*. New York: Harper and Row, 1979.
———. *The Confederate State of Richmond: A Biography of the Capital*. Austin: University of Texas Press, 1971.
———. *Robert E. Lee: A Biography*. New York: W. W. Norton, 1995.
Thompson, Charles D., Jr. *Spirits of Just Men: Mountaineers, Liquor Bosses, and Lawmen in the Moonshine Capital of the World*. Urbana: University of Illinois Press, 2011.
Thompson, H. Paul, Jr. *A Most Stirring and Significant Episode: Religion and the Rise and Fall of Prohibition in Black Atlanta, 1865–1887*. DeKalb: Northern Illinois University Press, 2013.
Thompson, Lauren K. *Friendly Enemies: Soldier Fraternization throughout the American Civil War*. Lincoln: University of Nebraska Press, 2020.
Tyrrell, Ian R. "Drink and Temperance in the Antebellum South: An Overview and Interpretation." *Journal of Southern History* 48, no. 4 (November 1982): 485–510.
———. *Sobering Up: From Temperance to Prohibition in Antebellum America, 1800–1860*. Westport, CT: Greenwood, 1979.
Ural, Susannah J., ed. *Civil War Citizens: Race, Ethnicity, and Identity in America's Bloodiest Conflict*. New York: New York University Press, 2010.
———. *The Harp and the Eagle: Irish-American Volunteers and the Union Army, 1861–1865*. New York: New York University Press, 2006.
Vargas, Mark A. "The Progressive Agent of Mischief: The Whiskey Ration and Temperance in the United States Army." *Historian* 67, no. 2 (Summer 2005): 199–216.
Veach, Michael R. *Kentucky Bourbon Whiskey: An American Heritage*. Lexington: University Press of Kentucky, 2013.
Veit, Helen Zoe. *Modern Food, Moral Food: Self-Control, Science, and the Rise of Modern American Eating in the Early Twentieth Century*. Chapel Hill: University of North Carolina Press, 2013.
Volk, Kyle G. *Moral Minorities and the Making of American Democracy*. Oxford: Oxford University Press, 2014.
Walters, Ronald G. *American Reformers, 1815–1860*. Rev. ed. New York: Hill and Wang, 1997.
Waugh, Joan. *U.S. Grant: American Hero, American Myth*. Chapel Hill: University of North Carolina Press, 2009.
Wells, Jonathan Daniel. *The Origins of the Southern Middle Class, 1800–1861*. Chapel Hill: University of North Carolina Press, 2004.
Wiley, Bell Irvin. *The Life of Billy Yank: the Common Soldier of the Union*. Indianapolis, IN: Bobbs-Merrill, 1951.
———. *The Life of Johnny Reb: the Common Soldier of the Confederacy*. Indianapolis, IN: Bobbs-Merrill, 1943.

Willis, Lee L. *Southern Prohibition: Race, Reform, and Public Life in Middle Florida, 1821–1920*. Athens: University of Georgia Press, 2011.
Winkle, Kenneth J. *Lincoln's Citadel: The Civil War in Washington, DC*. New York: W. W. Norton, 2013.
Woodworth, Steven E. *While God Is Marching On: The Religious World of Civil War Soldiers*. Lawrence: University Press of Kansas, 2001.
Wright, Ben, and Zachary W. Dresser, eds. *Apocalypse and the Millennium in the American Civil War Era*. Baton Rouge: Louisiana State University Press, 2013.

Index

abolitionists, 4, 168
abstinence: American Temperance Union on, 3, 4, 20, 23; as impractical in wartime, 14; and middle-class values, 35, 36, 37, 41; of teetotaling soldiers, 35, 147; and women's letters to soldiers, 72, 77
Adams, Charles Francis, Jr., 24, 50, 85
African American men: citizenship of, 10, 159, 160, 161, 166, 178n24; disloyalty accusations against, 158–59; drunkenness associated with, 9, 94, 133, 135, 137, 158, 159; self-restrained masculinity ideals of, 10, 158, 166; as soldiers, 9, 50, 55, 57, 135, 159, 160; troops plying with alcohol for entertainment, 67; white Southerners' characterization of, 135, 206n123
African Americans: and Black Codes, 168, 211n7; as civilian liquor sellers, 94, 161; fight for full inclusion in American society, 9; patriotism of, 9–10; on prohibition, 170; sobriety of, 160–61; temperance organizations of, 3, 9, 158, 159, 170; and vigilantism, 94, 206n123. *See also* enslaved people
African Methodist Episcopal church, 3
A. I. Simmons (distiller), 204n100
Albus, Junius, 160
alcoholic tonics, 18
Alleman, H. C., 38–39, 65
American Anti-Slavery Society, 176n10
American Revolution, 14, 115
American Temperance Society, 2, 3, 175n4
American Temperance Union (ATU): on abstinence, 3, 4, 20, 33; on African Americans, 160; on cold water as curative, 20, 32; on Abraham Lincoln and Hannibal Hamlin as temperance men, 1, 175n1; on liquor license laws, 114, 116, 119; on liquor traffic, 119–20, 121, 162; on medicinal liquor, 19, 32–33; membership of, 1, 3, 114, 175n4; on prohibition, 114, 120, 121, 169; on spirit rations, 120–21; on sutlers, 121, 122; tracts for soldiers published by, 74, 75, 76
amputations, 16, 76, 179n20
Andrews, Eliza Frances, 136, 165
Army of Central Kentucky, 105
Army of Mississippi, 105, 110
Army of Northern Virginia, 49, 51, 62, 91, 108
Army of Tennessee, 31
Army of the Cumberland, 47
Army of the James, 57
Army of the Potomac: Ambrose Burnside's Mud March, 61; Christmas celebrations of, 48; and civilian liquor sellers, 97–98; and Joseph Hooker, 142; and malaria, 17, 18; military discipline of, 66; nurses of, 29; officers of, 38, 65, 67, 91; St. Patrick's Day celebrations of, 47; spirit rations of, 17, 18, 25, 61–62, 180n24; sutlers of, 89, 122; trade prohibited in, 92
Army of the Tennessee, 23, 140, 144, 154
Atkinson, Thomas, 161–62
Augustin, Albert, 156–57
Ayling, Augustus D., 42–43, 99, 101

Baggs, John, 49
Bagley, David, 31
Baltimore and Ohio Railroad, 63
Banks, Nathaniel, 82
Barnwell, R. W., 33–34
Bauer, Georg, 52
Beaudry, Louis N., 78, 81
Beauregard, P. G. T., 110–11

Beecher, Henry Ward, 48, 143, 207n31
Bellard, Alfred, 44, 47
Berry, James H., 180n27
Bertsch, Friedrich, 27, 42
Beverly and Tom Lowry Database of Civil War Courts-Martial, 191n117, 191n119, 191n131, 195n68, 196n81
Bickerdyke, Mary, 30
Bissell, Lewis, 80, 156
Black, Samuel N., 80
Black Codes, 168, 211n7
Blackford, Charles Minor, 147
Blackford, Elizabeth, 30
Boston Herald, 46
Boteler, Alexander R., 148
Bowler, James Madison, 42, 73
Boyer, Paul, 176n6
Bragg, Braxton, 105–6, 110
Bragg, Junius Newport, 43, 98
Bratton, John, 124
brewing industry: and German Americans, 9, 108, 117–18, 170–71, 209n97; regulation of, 117, 128, 149; and temperance movement, 176n6
Brewner, Austin, 102
Brewster, Charles Harvey, 72
Bright, M. H., 25–26
Brinton, D. G., 17
Brown, Augustus Cleveland, 22–23, 64, 82, 90
Brown, John, 157
Brown, Joseph E., 125, 126–27, 128, 130, 131, 203n77
Brown, R. H., 63
Bryant, William Cullen, 144
Buchanan, James, 146
Buckner, Simon Bolivar, 146
Bullen, Joseph D., 69
Burke, Jim, 133
Burke (colonel), 182n93
Burns, Harry, 83
Burnside, Ambrose, Mud March of, 61
Butler, Benjamin, 22, 24, 44, 54–55, 100–101, 110, 120, 181n52
Butterfield, Daniel, 143

Cabell, S. G., 130
Cameron, Simon, 88
Campbell, John Quincy Adams, 23, 48, 99, 101
Camp Ledlie, New York, 85
Camp Washington, New York, 85
Canby, Edward R. S., 104
Carmichael, Peter S., 177n20
Carney, Kate, 135–36
Carr, Glenn, and Wright (distiller), 204n100
Carter, Robert Goldthwaite, 96
Carter brothers, 93, 154
Castle Thunder prison, Richmond, 31
Cavins, Ben, 73
Cavins, Elijah, 51, 73, 97
Chase, John, 91
Chase, Samuel, 91
Chesnut, Mary, 133–34
Chicago Daily Tribune, 122
Child, Lydia, 210n129
Chisolm, John Julian, 16–17
Cincinnati Volksfreund, 27
civilian liquor sellers: and Army of the Potomac, 97–98; contracts granted to, 109, 193n15; and disloyalty, 86, 92, 97, 103, 110; and Federal occupation, 99, 102–3, 104, 109, 110–11; and oaths of loyalty, 102; prices of, 89, 108; profits of, 97–98, 104, 108; soldiers' access to, 90–91, 93–95, 98, 107–8, 109; and Southern states' closure of, 7–8, 86, 92, 104–7, 108, 109–10, 111, 123; temperance reformers on, 119, 121; Union officials' regulation of, 86, 94–96, 97, 99–104, 109, 196n81
civilian reformers, 60, 61, 70, 71–72, 77, 84
civilians: and conciliatory policies, 86, 98, 102–3, 196n99; disloyal citizens, 9, 86, 92, 95, 96, 97, 102, 103, 105, 106–7, 110, 111; liquor shipped to soldier-relatives, 92; on liquor traffic, 123, 127; soldiers' interactions with, 91, 94, 95, 100, 104, 110, 111, 112, 113, 121, 135–36; and Union blockade, 124, 125
Civil War: dehumanizing carnage of, 12, 43–44, 55, 75, 177n20, 185n42; disruption

of death customs, 75; liquor problem in context of, 1, 8, 10; providential terms of, 176n17; and temperance movement, 1, 2, 5, 8, 9, 10, 11, 176n6; veterans of, 2, 89, 167, 169–70, 212n13. *See also* Confederate armies; Union armies

Clark, Charles, 132

class status, 177n20. *See also* middle class; middle-class evangelicals; middle-class values; working class

Coker, Joe L., 176n12

colleges, 185n56

Confederate armies: acceptability of liquor consumption in, 36; Christmas celebrations of, 48, 49–50, 51; and civilian liquor sellers, 86, 105–8; coffee shortages of, 26; confiscation of family-supplied liquor, 92; control of soldiers' access to liquor, 7, 85; on drunkenness of Union armies, 148–52; hospital inspectors of, 32; ideals of masculinity in, 6, 177n20; inconsistent alcohol policies of, 178n25; liquor-related problems of, 11, 61–62, 104–6; liquor shortages of, 49; and martial law, 8, 86, 105–6, 177n21; and medicinal liquor, 15, 16–17, 26–27, 31, 33, 41–42, 130, 131–32, 204n100; middle-class volunteer efforts for, 33–34; military discipline problems of, 61, 81–82; and officers' abuse of alcohol, 54, 56, 66; payday liquor consumption of, 52–53; rebellions in, 69; soldiers' liquor consumption in, 46; spirit rations in battle, 63; spirit rations in health regimens, 1, 7, 13, 14, 16, 18, 22, 25, 26, 28, 30–31, 34; subsistence department of, 179n23; supply shortages of, 14, 15, 26, 49, 108; and sutlers, 87–88, 90, 192n11; temperance meetings of, 78–79; temperance regiments of, 71–72; temperance tracts and papers distributed to, 74–75, 76; women nurses of, 182n97

Confederate Congress, on liquor traffic, 124, 129–30

Confederate States Prison, 105

Cook, Matthew, 79–80

Cooke, Chauncey Herbert, 67, 79, 151

Coolidge, Richard H., 179n23

Cooper Institute, 118

Copperheads, 9, 162–63

Corson, William Clark, 53

Couch, Darius N., 65, 96

Cowin, John Henry, 26, 91

Cowin, Samuel, 91

Cox, Jacob, 27

Craig, James, 103

Crimean War, 75, 178n3, 182n96

Cromwell, Oliver, 140

Cumming, Kate, 28, 31, 56

Cummings, J. F., 130, 204n100

Cummins, Simon, 31, 73

Curtis, Samuel R., 149

Daeuble, John, 67

Dana, Charles A., 63, 144–45, 207n37

Daniels, Nathan W., 58

Davis, George, 131

Davis, Jefferson: control of liquor traffic, 106, 124, 130, 162, 202n71; and Cyrus Franklin's complaint of drunken officers, 66, 153; and martial law, 107, 108; support for, 136, 158

Day, David, 24, 25, 26, 82

death customs, Civil War's disruption of, 75

Declaration of Independence, 126–27

Delevan, Edward C., 20

Democratic Party, 113–14, 121, 163, 164, 170, 171

Dent, Frederick, 109

de Trobriand, Regis, 38, 67

Dexter, Seymour, 46, 78

diets: for health benefits, 18–19, 169; and vegetarianism, 212n12

disloyalty: of African Americans, 158–59; and civilian liquor sellers, 86, 92, 97, 103, 110; of distillers, 112, 113, 137, 164–66, 211n136, 211n137; of draft dodgers, 9, 161, 163; and drunkenness, 161–62, 163, 164–65; of guerrilla bands, 9, 148, 152–53,

238 Index

disloyalty (cont.)
  162, 164; of immigrant communities, 153–58, 163, 164, 166, 171, 209n100; and liquor as national enemy, 9, 137, 161–62; of secessionists, 9, 10, 158, 161–62, 164. See also loyalty
distilling and distillers: and adulteration of liquor, 149, 208n57; and copper as war materiel, 125, 126; disloyalty accusations against, 112, 113, 137, 164–66, 211n136, 211n137; and food preservation in Southern agricultural life, 4, 5, 6, 8, 26, 128–29, 165, 204n92; of medicinal liquor, 6, 8–9, 16, 42, 128–32, 165, 204n100, 205n104; North's excise taxes on, 115–16; and personal use, 128–29; prices of, 124; profits of, 113, 127, 130, 132, 165, 166; Southern states' regulations on, 5, 8–9, 11, 26, 104, 106, 112, 113, 123–29, 130, 131–32, 168, 197n1, 201n59, 202n65, 204n92, 205n104
Dixon, William Daniel, 17, 27
Donaldson, Francis Adams, 26, 40, 83–84, 143
Donaldson, J. L., 25
Dooley, John Edward, 47, 91
Dotson, Rand, 211n140
Douglas, Hugh T., 23
Dow, Neal, 140–41
Downing, Alexander, 167
draft: immigrant communities' objections to, 9, 156–57, 163; New York Draft Riots, 160, 163–64, 176n6
draft dodgers, 9, 55, 161, 163
drunkenness: African American men associated with, 9, 94, 133, 135, 137, 158, 159; and alcohol dependence as disease, 32; and alcoholic tonic prescriptions, 18; and assumptions about enemies, 148–52; and Christmas celebrations, 49; chronic drunkenness, 53, 54, 59, 65, 84, 198n19; cowardice associated with, 151–52; and dangers to national success, 11, 137; and desertion, 83, 191n131; and disloyalty, 161–62, 163, 164–65; effect on soldiers'

performance, 13, 27, 28, 31, 32, 34, 61, 71, 81–82, 139, 149–51; of immigrant working men, 2; and insubordination, 60; liquor consumption distinguished from, 14, 61; of male nurses and stewards, 29–30, 32; of medical officers, 28–29, 30, 32, 59; medicinal liquor leading to, 42; and military discipline, 60, 61, 62, 66–67, 70, 81–82, 84, 95–96, 100, 191n117, 195n62; military officials on mishaps resulting from, 7, 8, 22, 23, 59, 60–61, 84; and mutinies, 69–70; and New Year's Eve celebrations, 50; of officers, 37, 40, 54, 55–58, 59, 60, 61, 65, 66–67, 140, 153, 187n129; and payday celebrations, 51, 52–53; perception shaping understanding of war, 11; punishments for, 81–84, 95–96, 98, 101, 191n117, 191n119, 191n123, 191n131, 191–92n133; rumors of drunken generals, 9, 11, 139, 141–45, 147, 148; of St. Patrick's Day celebrations, 47; selfish drunkenness, 59; and soldiers' interactions with civilians, 91, 94, 95, 100, 104, 110, 111, 112, 113, 121, 135–36; soldiers on reckless drunkenness, 7, 61; soldiers' solidarity with, 61; Southern states' protection of civilians from, 8, 86; temperance movement on, 1, 3; temperance reformers on, 3, 19, 74, 81, 139–41; temperance tracts on, 75
Duff, Levi Bird, 66–67, 69–70, 150, 210n130
Dupré, Alexander, 87
Dupré, Emile, 87, 156

Early, Jubal, 11, 107, 148
Eighteenth Amendment, 171, 172
Einstein, Max, 93
Ellsworth, Elmer, 138
emancipation, 47–48, 159
Emancipation Proclamation, 134, 160, 168
Emerson, Sally Gibbons, 28–29
enlisted men: confiscation of officers' liquor, 91; criticism of officers, 57, 64, 67; dependence on officers for supplies, 58, 187n129; election of company officers, 54;

families supplying liquor to, 92; frustrations with officers' abuse of alcohol, 54, 56, 57–58, 65–66; and military discipline, 61, 64, 67, 83, 84; obtaining liquor during marches, 62; on sobriety, 80; spirit rations of, 7, 56; sutlers prohibited from selling liquor to, 40, 44. *See also* soldiers; volunteer soldiers

enslaved people: drunkenness associated with, 9; escape to Union lines, 158–59; and medicinal liquor, 132; officers' illicit trading with, 57; prohibition of alcohol consumption, 4, 123, 133, 159, 160–61; as targets of white rage, 10; white Southern women's fear of enslaved men's access to liquor, 123, 133–36. *See also* African Americans

Erwin, Robert, 65
Escott, Paul D., 177n21
evangelical Christianity: on Christmas celebrations, 48, 49, 51; on masculinity, 6, 36, 38, 53, 58; on patriotic holidays, 48; perfectionism stressed by, 3, 6; on sobriety, 2–3, 35, 36, 46. *See also* middle-class evangelicals
Evans, Clement Anselm, 148
Ewell, Richard, 107

Farr, John B., 164
federal government: civilian behavior controlled by, 177n21; morality enforced by, 12; sutlers regulated by, 8, 86, 87, 88–90, 114
femininity, 38, 70
Fisher, James P., 77
Fisk, Clinton B., 152
Fleharty, Stephen F., 103
Fletcher, Elliott H., 54
Fletcher, Holly Berkley, 176n6
Floyd, John B., 146
Forbes, John Murray, 144
Foreign Missionary Society, 159
Forrest, Nathan Bedford, 135, 152
Franchsen, Wilhelm, 80, 156

Franklin, Cyrus, 66, 153
free people of color, 4, 10, 133, 159, 161
French Americans, 101
Friends of Temperance, 168, 211n6
Fuller, Richard, 78

George (colonel), 22
German Americans: and brewing industry, 9, 108, 117–18, 170–71, 209n97; citizenship of, 178n24; as civilian liquor sellers, 108; dual identities of, 153, 155; liquor consumption of, 6, 9, 46–47, 50, 101, 155–56, 158, 170, 209n93; nativist attacks on, 9, 153, 155, 156, 163, 171; as soldiers, 46–47, 50, 141, 153, 155, 156–57, 209n100; and Sunday Laws, 117–19, 153, 156, 157, 199n25; as targets of liquor regulation, 117
German Republican Committee, 118
Gerstein, Dietrich, 40
G. F. and H. E. Oliver (distiller), 204n100
Gibbs, George C., 105
Gillespie, Ira, 94
Gordon, John B., 62
Govette, William, 73
Graham, Albert G., 202n71
Grand Division of the Sons of Temperance of Virginia, 71
Grand Templars of Kentucky, 168–69
Granger, Robert S., 152
Grant, Julia, 144
Grant, Ulysses S.: Confederate capture of soldiers, 150–51; Charles Dana's biography of, 207n37; on liquor traffic, 99–100; migraine headaches of, 144; and patriotic holidays, 47; and payday celebrations, 51; prohibition of whiskey sales in camps, 90; rumors of liquor consumption and alcoholism of, 11, 144–45; wartime successes of, 23, 145
Gray, R. H., 32
Greeley, Horace, 158
Gregg, J. Chandler, 39, 93, 184n15
Griffin, Clifford S., 175n4, 183n115
Grimsley, Mark, 196n99
Grinnell, Josiah, 115

guerrilla bands: "drunkenness" and "disloyalty" labels applied to, 9, 148, 152–53, 162, 164; Irish Americans compared to, 154; irregular tactics of, 152; suppression of, 103–4; violence of, 101–2

Haines, Zenas T., 46
Halleck, Henry, 22, 63, 109, 120, 144, 181n52
Hamilton, A. S., 107
Hamlin, Hannibal, 1, 175n1
Hammond, William A., 15
Handley-Cousins, Sarah, 212n13
Haupt, Herman, 29–30
Haydon, Charles B., 43, 51–52, 68, 95
Herald of Health and Water-Cure Journal, 20
Herbert, Walter H., 207n31
Hermanns, Carl, 156
Herring, Charles, 84
Herring, Joseph, 69
Hess, Frederick, 57
Heyer, John, 108
Higginson, Thomas Wentworth, 50
Hoffman, W., 29
Hoge, Moses Drury, 150–51
Holden, C. N., 118
Holmes, Emma, 33–34
Holt, Daniel, 52
Holt, David, 42
Hooker, Joseph, 11, 48–49, 92, 141, 142–44, 145
Hooper, Edward, 161
Horstmann, August, 50
Hosmer, James Kendall, 58–59
Howard, Oliver Otis, 17, 140–41
Howe, Henry Warren, 25, 44, 52, 191–92n133
Hubbard, Bobby, 72
Hughes, D. H., 27
Hundley, Daniel Robinson, 164
Hussy and Williams (distiller), 204n100
Hutzler, Moses, 194n38

I. A. Taylor (distiller), 204n100
immigrant communities: and disloyalty accusations, 153–58, 163, 164, 166, 171;
209n100; liquor consumption in, 2, 6, 9, 10, 117–18, 153, 164, 166, 171; on sobriety, 36, 158; soldiers from, 9, 46; and Sunday Laws, 117–19, 119n25, 137, 153. *See also* German Americans; Irish Americans
Independent Order of Good Templars, 3, 71, 168, 169
Indiana Supreme Court, 103
industrialization, 70
Iowa, liquor licensing law in, 116–17, 198n19
Irish Americans: citizenship of, 178n24; dual identities of, 153, 154, 155; liquor consumption of, 6, 9, 46–47, 154, 158, 164, 170; nativist attacks on, 9, 153, 154, 155, 163, 164; as soldiers, 46–47, 48, 153, 154–55; and Sunday Laws, 118, 153

Jack (enslaved man), 158–59
Jackson, Oscar Lawrence, 99
Jackson, Thomas "Stonewall," 11, 41–42, 106–7, 141, 146–47
Jenifer, W. H., 63
Jennings, William W., 38–39
Jewish Americans, 178n24
Johnson, Bushrod R., 63
Johnson, Jonathan Huntington, 62
Johnston, Joseph, 106
Jones, Charles, 133–34
Jones, Jenkin Lloyd, 23, 37–38, 66–67, 99, 101
Jones family, 41–42, 133, 154
Journal of the American Temperance Union (JATU): on donations for tracts for soldiers, 74, 189n80; on Neal Dow, 140; on drunkenness, 139–40; on drunkenness of soldiers on trains, 62; on excise tax on liquor dealers, 116; on Ulysses S. Grant, 145; on postwar temperance, 167; readership of, 175n4; on soldiers' habits of drunkenness, 70; on spirit rations, 13, 181n52; on U.S. Navy, 120–21; on wartime opinions, 10

Kappner, I. G., 180n27
Kendrick, M. L., 92

Kennett, John, 102–3, 196n99
Kiddoo, Joseph B., 57
Kinsley, Rufus, 38, 47–48
Kite's stillhouse and apple orchard, 107–8

Lange, John Gottfried, 108–9, 157–58
Lansing, H. S., 63
Lauderdale, John Vance, 101, 143, 155, 163
Law, John, 115
Le Duc, William G., 22
Lee, Albert L., 98
Lee, Fitz, 147
Lee, Harry "Light Horse," 147
Lee, Robert E.: and Christmas celebrations, 49, 51; and Jubal Early, 148; liquor consumption of, 11, 147; on liquor for soldiers, 91, 108, 147; as moral hero, 146–47; on spirit rations, 18; surrender, 53; teetotalism of, 147
Lehmann, Ludwig, 56
Letterman, Jonathan, 18, 25, 180n24, 181n68
Lewis, Richard, 51
Liberator, 158
Likens, James B., 56
Lincoln, Abraham: on Bull Run, 141; Democratic Party's opposition to, 163; Emancipation Proclamation of, 134; federal government's control of civilian behavior, 177n21; and liquor traffic, 162–63; martial law authorized by, 103, 177n21; presidential election of 1860, 1, 5; suspension of writ of habeas corpus, 177n21; temperance habits espoused by, 175n1; and Union blockade, 125
Linderman, Gerald F., 177n20, 185n42
liquor consumption: of Civil War veterans, 170, 212n13; cultural opinions on, 13; dangers of adulterated liquor, 149, 208n57; debates on meaning of, 10–11, 54, 59, 64, 112; and drunken brawls, 47, 61, 63, 68–69, 85, 159, 188n46; as form of enslavement, 5, 176n6; gunpowder-and-whiskey cocktail myth, 151; health benefits of, 13, 14, 17, 31, 41, 55, 91; in

immigrant communities, 2, 6, 9, 10, 117–18, 153, 164, 166, 171; and masculinity, 2, 6–7, 12, 14, 35–36, 84, 133, 170, 172, 177n20; in military culture, 1, 6, 7, 10, 14, 35–36, 37, 46, 70, 73, 75; military regulations on, 37; moderation in, 2, 3, 4–5, 15, 19–20, 27, 41, 95, 147; and national duty, 9, 10, 12, 185n42; national well-being linked with, 2, 5–6, 9, 10; and patriotism, 2, 9, 55, 73, 116; ramification of excessive drinking, 9; social drinking, 6; as substitute for food and water shortages, 14, 25; and success on battlefield, 11, 178n25
Liquor Dealers' Association, 115
liquor license laws: American Temperance Union on, 114, 116, 119; in Iowa, 116–17, 198n19; in North, 4–5, 8, 10, 86, 113, 114, 117, 136, 198n22
liquor regulation: German Americans as targets of, 117; in military culture, 36, 44–45, 53, 81–82; in North, 1, 4, 8
liquor traffic: and civil damage laws, 117, 198n19, 198n21; and civilian liquor sellers, 86, 121, 123; and fermented liquors, 115–16, 117; German American brewers demonized as liquor-traffickers, 9; Ulysses S. Grant on, 99–100; national well-being linked with, 2, 5, 86, 114, 119–20, 122; North's regulation of, 113, 114, 116–17, 119, 121, 122–25, 136–37, 198n21, 202n63; as predatory, 117, 198n19; prices of, 89, 193n25, 193–94n26, 194n29; protection of women from, 124, 127, 132–33, 168; and smuggling operations, 86, 92–93, 100, 124–25, 129–30, 162, 196n81; Southern states on, 8, 112–13, 117n21, 123–25, 136–37, 200n54, 200n55; taxation of, 8, 113, 114, 115–16, 123–24, 136, 137, 200n54, 200n55; temperance reformers on, 114, 116, 119, 121–24, 172; U.S. Congress on, 114–16, 125, 202n63. *See also* sutlers
Lockard, Ed, 83
Lost Cause, 146

loyalty: as demonstrable through behavior, 178n24; and liquor consumption, 10; national conversations about, 2, 9; North's definition of, 177n23; Southern states' definition of, 177n23. *See also* disloyalty
Lusk, William Thompson, 69
Luther, Martin, 138
Lynchburg Republican, 22

McAllister, Robert, 38, 39, 80, 81, 193n22
Macbeth, Charles, 33
McClellan, George B., 22, 66–67, 92, 120, 159, 164, 181n52, 210n130
McClellan, William, 73
McClernand, John, 144
McCook, Alexander, 149
McCurry, Stephanie, 203n84
McDaniel, J. J., 154–55
McDowell, Irvin, 11, 141–42, 143, 144, 145
McGuire, Judith, 134, 136
Madison Lodge of the Independent Order of Good Templars, 71
Maine Laws, 4, 9, 11–12, 71, 112–13, 117, 121, 126, 140, 170
malaria, 13, 17–18, 20, 21, 31, 34
Mallard, Mary, 154
Mammina, Laura, 206n128
manhood: competing notions of, 46, 53, 54, 58, 61; culture of restrained manhood, 6, 11, 35, 36–37, 58, 71, 138–39, 140, 153, 158, 171; and liquor consumption, 32, 45, 70, 148, 176n6; of officers, 55, 57–58, 61; unselfishness as trait of, 58–59. *See also* masculinity
Mapping Alcohol in the Civil War project, Missouri Southern State University, 178n11
Marsh, John, 74
Martin, Scott C., 178n25
masculinity: appropriate definitions of, 2, 6–7, 169, 170, 206n5; aristocratic ideals of, 6, 37, 64; courage as cornerstone of, 177n20; democratic expressions of, 2, 84; and discipline, 36; evangelical Christianity on, 6, 36, 38, 53, 58; and family support, 51–52, 53; fluid definitions of, 53, 177n20; of immigrant soldiers, 153; and liquor consumption, 2, 6–7, 12, 14, 35–36, 84, 133, 170, 172, 177n20; and middle-class values, 38, 39, 53, 57; and morality, 74, 139, 140; and national duty, 11; officers' standards and privileges of, 6, 7, 37, 39, 41, 54, 56, 64, 66, 84, 138–39, 140; and patriotism, 64, 68, 73, 74, 137, 139, 166; and payday celebrations, 51; regular army's definitions of, 6; sectional definitions of, 6, 177n20; and self-control, 36, 37, 44, 58, 64, 73; self-restrained masculinity of African American men, 10, 158, 166; soldiers' definitions of, 43–44, 61, 64–65, 68, 84; teetotaling masculinity, 2, 6, 7, 11, 171; virility and athleticism associated with, 169, 212n12; wartime definitions of, 6, 7, 14, 58–59, 64, 68, 165, 166, 177n20. *See also* manhood
Masons, 3
Matt, Susan J., 184n37
Meade, George, 47, 122, 143–44
Meagher, Thomas, 154–55
medical officers: on alcohol as stimulant, 15–16, 17, 31, 34, 120; on amputations, 16, 179n20; chloroform as preferred anesthetic used by, 179n18; drunkenness of, 28–29, 30, 32, 59; evaluation for moral habits, 28; on health benefits of liquor consumption, 13, 14, 17, 31; homesickness of, 43; medicinal liquor used by, 15–17, 18, 31, 41
medicinal liquor: acquisition of alcohol from natural resources, 16; alcohol abuse creating tensions with use of, 14, 28, 32, 34; anesthesia used with, 16, 179n18; brandy as source of, 15, 16, 17, 28, 124, 179n13; cold water as substitute for, 13, 18, 19–21, 32, 34, 75–76, 178n3, 179n20; and Confederate armies, 15, 16–17, 26–27, 31, 33, 41–42, 130, 131–32, 204n100; debates on, 32, 34, 172; distilling of, 6, 8–9, 16, 42,

128–32, 165, 204n100, 205n104; false requisition of, 28; in field surgery, 16–17, 41; medical officers' use of, 15–17, 18, 31, 41; middle-class volunteers providing, 33–34; physicians on, 14, 15–16, 19, 20, 21, 132; private stores of, 14, 182n93; rations of, 7, 13, 14, 16, 18, 28, 31, 35, 68, 183n115; soldiers' use of, 41–43, 61; temperance reformers on, 14, 18–19, 20, 32–33, 34, 42, 75, 180n36; whiskey as preferred source of, 15, 16, 17, 28, 178n11, 179n13, 179n15, 180n27

Mehrländer, Andrea, 209n100

Meigs, Montgomery C., 25

Memminger, C. G., 202n63

middle class: African Americans of, 158, 159; and alcoholic tonic prescriptions, 18; on Christmas celebrations, 48; debates on meaning of liquor consumption, 10; and moderate liquor consumption, 20, 41; wartime volunteers of, 33, 183n115; working class distinguished from, 2, 36

middle-class evangelicals: on abstinence, 35; on perfectionism, 3; on self-control, 54; values of, 36, 61, 139

middle-class values: and abstinence, 35, 36, 37, 41; on acceptability of liquor consumption, 44; on balance of masculine work and feminine domestic sphere, 70; and definition of restrained manhood, 6, 36, 58; and Ulysses S. Grant, 145; lack of dominance of, 36; masculinity defined by, 38, 39, 53, 57; officers' mocking of, 37, 38, 40

Miles, Nelson A., 64

military chaplains, 60

military culture: aristocratic ideals of masculinity, 6, 37, 64; liquor consumption in, 1, 6, 7, 10, 14, 35–36, 37, 46, 70, 73, 75; liquor regulation in, 36, 44–45, 53, 81–82; martial masculine culture of, 14; military discipline associated with slavery, 177n20; sectional differences in, 177n20; temperance societies contrasted with, 81; tensions over abuse of alcohol, 54, 57–58, 61

military discipline: for control of drunkenness, 60, 61, 62, 66–67, 70, 81–82, 84, 95–96, 100, 191n117, 195n62; liquor consumption undercutting, 61, 69–70; for marches, 61–62, 63, 65, 82; and morality, 79; and mutinies, 69–70, 83, 192n134; officers' responsibility for, 62, 63, 64, 65, 81–84; and patriotism, 68; and punishments, 81–84, 95–96, 98, 191n117, 191n119, 191n123, 191n131, 191–92n133; and sobriety, 71, 73; soldiers' resistance to martial traditions, 61; standards of acceptable behavior, 66, 84; and sutlers, 88, 90–91; for troop movements, 61–63; in Washington, D.C., 95–96, 97, 104–5, 106, 195n62, 195n68

military officials: debates on meaning of liquor consumption, 10, 59; on health benefits of liquor consumption, 13, 41; medicinal liquor distributed by, 15; on mishaps resulting from drunkenness, 7, 8, 22, 23, 59, 60–61, 84; and policies on spirit rations, 22, 27

millennium, 3, 5

Miller, Alonzo, 26, 53, 186n108

Mississippi, dispensary system of, 131–32, 137

Missouri State Militia, 102

Mitchell, Reid, 177n20

Mitteldorfer, Marx, 91, 194n38

Moore, Robert A., 42, 91, 191n133

Moore, Samuel Preston, 31

Moore Hospital, Richmond, Virginia, 178n11

morality: and American nationalism, 119; conceptions of, 58; and heroism, 139, 140, 141–46; individualistic pursuit of personal morality, 6; and liquor traffic, 113; in long nineteenth century, 176n6; and masculinity, 74, 139, 140; and military victory, 113, 141–45; of Northern cause, 5; and pledges of sobriety, 3, 71, 73, 77, 78, 79–81, 144; and protection of

morality (cont.)
    civilians from dangers of alcohol, 11; restoration of moral balance, 70–72, 168; and soldiers' interpretation of violence, 84; and Southern states' closing of civilian liquor shops, 86; and Southern states' prohibition of distilling, 126–27; temperance reformers' use of moral suasion, 3, 4, 7, 71–72, 74, 75–76, 79, 81, 84, 138–39; of women, 30, 70, 72–73
Morgan, Edwin D., 121
Morse, Charles Fessenden, 40
Morton, S. W., 97
Moseley, John Baxter, 51, 147
Mott, Frank Luther, 175n4
Myers, Barton A., 211n136
Myers, Jon C., 191n133

National Archives and Records Administration (NARA), 10, 179n23, 191n117
national duty: and liquor consumption, 9, 10, 12, 185n42; wartime development of ideas of, 11, 177n23, 206n5
National Prohibition Party, 169
National Temperance League, 143
National Temperance Society, 169
Native Americans, citizenship of, 178n24
nativism: and immigrant communities' liquor consumption, 6, 9, 10, 117–18, 153; and Sunday Laws, 117–18, 153, 199n25; and temperance organizations, 3; and wartime service of immigrants, 9
Need, William, 88
Neely, Mark, Jr., 177n21, 202n71, 203n77
Newton, Isaac, 138
New York Draft Riots, 160, 163–64, 176n6
New York Herald, 80, 121, 150
New York Independent, 143
New York Times, 25, 114, 118, 155–56, 161, 181n72
New York Tribune, 121, 158
Nisbet, James Cooper, 90, 107
North: civilian liquor sellers regulated in, 86; debates on meaning of liquor consumption, 10; liquor license laws in, 4–5, 8, 10, 86, 113, 114, 117, 136, 198n22; liquor prices in, 193–94n26; liquor regulation in, 1, 4, 8; liquor traffic regulation in, 113, 114, 116–17, 119, 121, 122–25, 136–37, 198n21, 202n63; loyalty defined in, 177n23; and medicinal liquor, 14; middle-class ideals in, 6; on mishaps created by drunken armies, 8; patriotism defined in, 177n23; prohibition in, 4, 8, 11–12, 112, 113–14, 116–17, 136; Sunday Laws in, 8, 10, 115, 117–19, 137, 153, 199n25; temperance societies in, 3, 5, 9; urbanization of, 2
Northrop, Lucius, 26
Norton, E. R., 164–65
Nugent, Robert, 163

Odd Fellows, 3
officers: ability to purchase and obtain liquor, 40, 57; abstinence of, 38–39; abusive use of alcohol, 53, 54, 55, 56, 57, 60, 61, 65–67, 70; and camp-life doldrums, 39, 46; and Christmas celebrations, 48–49; on civilian liquor sellers, 86; company and regimental elections, 37, 54; debates on meaning of liquor consumption, 54, 61, 64; drunkenness of, 37, 40, 54, 55–58, 59, 60, 61, 65, 66–67, 140, 153, 187n129; folk remedies used by, 41; food and liquor obtained from families, 37, 40, 41; ideals of citizen-officers, 37; junior officers' reports on, 57–58; liquor access from civilian liquor sellers, 95, 107; liquor access from sutlers, 37, 40, 88, 89–90, 91; liquor consumption compromising ability to perform duties, 39, 40, 41, 54, 55–56, 57, 60, 61, 65, 66–67; liquor consumption for homesickness, 43; liquor consumption for self-care, 53, 61, 166; manhood of, 55, 57–58, 61; military discipline as responsibility of, 62, 63, 64, 65, 81–84; and payday celebrations, 51; and pledges of sobriety, 80; preference for liquor consumption, 36, 37–40;

private stores of liquor, 6, 7, 37, 38, 40, 91, 92; on republicanism, 37; response to drunken mishaps, 64–65; social pressures for liquor consumption, 38; on soldiers' excessive liquor consumption, 64–65, 92; soldiers influence by behavior of, 66–67; spirit rations dispensed by, 39, 44, 49, 61–62, 63, 66, 67, 120; standards of masculinity including privilege to drink, 6, 7, 37, 39, 41, 54, 56, 64, 66, 84, 138–39, 140; and sutlers' privileges, 87; tolerance of undisciplined soldiers, 43; vexation at undisciplined soldiers, 51. *See also* medical officers

Official Records of the War of the Rebellion, 10
Ogle, Maureen, 209n97
Osborn, E. D., 145
Overton, John, 68

Paine, Eleazer, 103
Palmer, R. B., 110
Parsons, Elaine Frantz, 176n6, 198n19
Patrick, Marsena, 122
Patrick, Robert, 57, 58, 68
patriotism: of civilian liquor sellers, 94, 95, 104; of distillers, 9, 112, 113, 127, 137; and liquor consumption, 2, 9, 55, 73, 116; and masculinity, 64, 68, 73, 74, 137, 139, 166; and military discipline, 68; sobriety associated with, 9–10, 55, 71, 73, 112, 171; wartime development of ideas of, 58, 177n23
Patterson, Edmund DeWitt, 42, 45–46, 49–50, 154
Pember, Phoebe Yates, 30, 182n96
Pender, William Dorsey, 32, 88
Perry, John Gardner, 68
Perry, Theophilus, 42
Peter, Frances, 151
Peters, De Witt C., 28
Petty, Elijah P., 42, 49
physicians: on alcohol as stimulant, 15, 16, 17, 18, 20, 21, 22, 41; on medicinal liquor, 14, 15–16, 19, 20, 21, 132; on mental and physical health, 181n62

Pillow, Gideon, 146
Pleasonton, Alfred, 143, 144
Porter, Andrew, 96–97, 106
Porter, David Dixon, 54
presidential election of 1860, 1, 5
presidential election of 1864, 164
Preston, Caroline, 134
Price, Billy, 53
prisoners of war, on stewards, 29
prohibition: debates on, 113–14, 116–17; hardline supporters of, 5; in North, 4, 8, 11–12, 112, 113–14, 116–17, 136; in postwar decades, 2, 11, 168–71; repeal of prohibition laws, 4–5; Southern states' support for, 1, 4, 5, 8, 9, 12, 112, 124, 125–27, 137, 168, 176n12, 177n21, 197n3; studies of, 176n6; and Sunday Laws, 8, 10, 115, 117–19, 199n25; temperance movement on, 1–2, 4; temperance reformers on, 5, 8, 11, 113, 127, 168–72; wartime experiments with, 8

Ramsey, James B., 162
Randolph, George, 107
Rappahannock Expedition, 208n60
Ravenel, Charlotte, 135
Rawlins, John, 63, 144
rebel spy networks, 97
Reconstruction, 12
Redpath, James, 48
Redwood (doctor), 28
Reminisco, Redro Quarendo, 39–40, 56
republican citizenship: ideals of, 6, 36, 37, 47, 48, 64, 66, 127, 139; and notions of "home," 70
Republican Party, 5, 114, 119, 164, 170, 171, 175n1
Resources of the Southern Fields, 16
respectability, 58
Richards, Louis, 94
Richardson, Israel, 87
Richmond, Virginia: Castle Thunder prison, 31; civilian liquor sellers in, 104–5, 196n107; Federal occupation of, 109; martial law in, 107, 108, 197n113; Moore Hospital, 178n11

Richmond *Daily Dispatch*, 123, 142, 146, 150, 162, 166
Richmond Enquirer, 46, 148, 153
Richmond Whig, 151
Ritner, Jacob, 54, 72, 80
Robbins, Rufus, 96
Robison, James D., 31
Rogers, Sion H., 131
Rorabaugh, W. J., 180n36
Rosser, Thomas L., 27
Ross General Hospital, Mobile, Alabama, 178n11
Rossi, Robert, 50
Ruminski, Jarret, 211n138
rural Americans, 36, 44, 61, 117n20, 170
Russell, William Howard, 39, 62, 95, 96, 133, 154

Sabbath Convention, 119
St. Patrick's Day, 47
Samito, Christian G., 178n24
Sangston, Lawrence, 182n93, 193n26
Schurz, Carl, 141, 143–44
Scott, Winfield, 13–14
secession and secessionists: conciliatory policy toward, 103; and control of enslaved people, 133; "drunkenness" and "disloyalty" labels applied to, 9, 10, 158, 161–62, 164; sympathizers of, 97; and temperance movement, 1
Second Great Awakening, 2–3
Seddon, James A., 131, 205n104
self-control: "home" as influence on, 70; and masculinity, 36, 37, 44, 58, 64, 73; middle-class evangelicals on, 54; of officers, 38, 64; value of, 2, 37
Semmes, Mary, 136
Semmes, Raphael, 81
Seward, William, 97, 150
Seymour, Horatio, 163
Sharwood, Dendy, 40
Sheeran, James, 79
Shelby, Joseph, 152–53
Sherman, Francis Cornwall, 118–19
Sherman, William T., 51, 154

Shields (private), 83–84
Shively, Kathryn, 181n62
Shprintzen, Adam D., 212n112
Sickles, Daniel, 62, 143
Sigel, Franz, 141
Silber, Nina, 189n64
slave codes, 4
slavery: military discipline associated with, 177n20; and presidential election of 1860, 1; and second party system, 5; slavery as national sin, 168; and temperance movement, 1, 5, 175n5
Smith, Andrew F., 193n25
Smith, Kirby, 86
Smith, Thomas Kilby, 65
Smith's Civil Damages Liquor Bill, 117, 198n19
sobriety: and definition of restrained manhood, 6, 11, 58, 71, 138–39, 171; evangelical Christianity on, 2–3, 35, 36, 46; immigrant communities on, 36, 158; and military discipline, 71, 73; national survival linked to, 1, 2, 5, 8, 9; patriotism associated with, 9–10, 55, 71, 73, 112, 171; pledges of, 3, 71, 73, 77, 78, 79–81, 119, 144, 167; and republican ideals, 64; sense of "home" as influence on, 70–71; soldiers' reevaluation of, 45, 58, 59; strength of, 138; temperance tracts on, 75, 138; and value of self-control, 2, 6, 37
soldiers: abusive use of alcohol, 53; alcohol-free recreation for, 77–78; capitalization of distributed spirit rations, 53–54; care packages of, 37, 41, 49, 50, 56, 91, 92, 94; Christmas celebrations of, 48, 49–51, 186n81; coffee used as currency by, 53, 186n108; debates on liquor consumption, 37, 47, 54, 61, 64, 65–66; definitions of masculinity, 43–44, 61, 64–65, 68, 84; dependence on officers for supplies, 58, 187n129; diet of, 25; drunken wandering of, 69, 98–99; expansion of definitions of acceptable liquor consumption, 44, 61; families supplying liquor to, 41, 42, 49–50, 91, 92,

194n38; family duties of, 73–74; folk remedies used by, 41–42; ideals of citizen-soldier, 37; immoral effects of liquor consumption on, 60; liquor access during troop movements, 49, 62, 63; liquor access from civilian liquor sellers, 90–91, 93–95, 98, 107–8, 109; liquor access from smuggling, 92–93, 94; liquor access from sutlers, 85–87, 88, 89–90, 91; liquor consumption for arduous tasks, 39, 44, 58, 61; liquor consumption for boredom of camp life, 41, 45; liquor consumption for homesickness, 41, 43, 45, 48, 50–51, 53, 184n37; liquor consumption for mental health, 43–44, 50, 53, 58, 61, 185n42; liquor consumption for self-care, 44–45, 53, 58, 166; liquor consumption in winter, 45–46, 53; liquor use of, 1, 7, 10, 13, 41; medicinal liquor used by, 41–43, 61; New Year's Eve celebrations of, 50; on officers' abuse of alcohol, 54, 55, 56, 57, 60, 65–67; officers' behavior as influence on, 66–67; patriotic holidays celebrated by, 47–48; payday celebrations of, 51–52, 53; and pledges of sobriety, 71, 73, 77, 78, 79–81, 119, 167; preference for liquor consumption, 36; railroad transport of, 62–63; recreational liquor consumption of, 44, 45, 67–68; reputations guarded by, 72–73; response to drunken mishaps, 64–65; sense of "home" for sobriety, 70–71; snowball fights of, 45; on soldiers' abuse of alcohol, 62, 67; steamer transport of, 63; sutlers prohibited from selling liquor to, 40, 49, 86, 88, 91; teetotalism of, 35, 46, 53–54, 72–73, 74, 78, 79–80; teetotalism rejected by, 52–53; temperance clubs for, 74, 78, 80, 81, 84; temperance societies in regiments for, 76–78; temperance tracts distributed to, 74–77, 189n80; temporary camp homes of, 44–45, 49–50; tributes of liquor demanded by pickets, 44. *See also* enlisted men; volunteer soldiers

solidarity, 58, 61
Sons of Temperance, 3, 4, 6, 32, 77–79
South Carolina Tract Society, 75, 76, 138
Southern states: aristocratic forms of masculinity and luxury in, 6; and boredom-induced debauchery, 21; civilian liquor sellers closed in, 7–8, 86, 92, 104–7, 108, 109–10, 111, 123; civilians on war profiteers, 88; conflicts over sovereignty in, 177n22; debates on meaning of liquor consumption, 10; and distilling regulations, 5, 8–9, 11, 26, 104, 106, 112, 113, 123–29, 130, 131–32, 168, 197n1, 201n59, 202n65, 204n92, 205n104; Federal occupation in, 99, 102–3, 104, 109, 110–11, 135–36, 157, 201n58; food shortages in, 8, 26, 110, 113, 124, 125, 127, 129, 132, 166, 168, 201n59; grain shortages in, 15, 26, 112, 113, 124, 125, 126, 201n58; liquor consumption as marker of privilege, 138; liquor shortages in, 98, 99, 100; on liquor traffic, 8, 112–13, 123–25, 136–37, 177n21, 200n54, 200n55; loyalty defined in, 177n23; martial law in, 8, 105–6, 107, 108, 109–10, 157, 196n107, 197n113, 203n77; and medicinal liquor, 14, 15, 16; middle-class ideals in, 6; moral military heroes of, 146; national independence of, 5; patriotism defined in, 177n23; prices in, 89, 108, 193n25, 194n29; prohibition support in, 1, 4, 5, 8, 9, 12, 112, 124, 125–27, 137, 168, 170, 176n12, 177n21, 197n3; racial social order of, 133; rural nature of, 4, 6; state and national authority debated in, 113, 127–28, 131, 132, 137, 203n84; support for temperance movement in, 4; temperance movement in, 9, 21, 74–75, 123–24, 126, 138–39, 152; temperance societies in, 3, 176n12; Union confiscation of liquor in, 124, 129–30, 200–201n58; Unionism in, 105, 110, 111, 165, 211n136, 211n140; urbanization in, 4; wealthy families' alcohol consumption, 4–5
Spirit of the Age, 10, 21, 124

spirit rations: amounts of, 16, 179n15; in battle, 61, 63–64, 66; for Christmas celebrations, 48–49; as compensation for poor diet, 25, 34, 64, 181n72; in Confederate armies, 1, 7, 13, 14, 16, 18, 22, 25, 26, 28, 30–31, 34; distribution of, 22, 31, 53–54; for exposure, 22–23, 24, 25, 35, 44, 61, 73, 152; for extreme fatigue, 23, 24, 25, 27, 35, 44, 61, 152; federal regulation of, 8, 21–22; for marches, 23, 25–26, 61–62, 63, 66; for mental exhaustion, 23–24, 27, 181n62; for morale, 23–24, 27, 44, 63; officers' dispensing of, 39, 44, 49, 61–62, 63, 66, 67, 120; overuse of, 32; for picket duty, 23, 24–25, 42; quality of, 26; soldiers' capitalization of distribution of, 53–54; statistics on, 179n23; temperance reformers on, 5, 8, 13, 14, 18, 20–21, 75–76, 113, 119, 120, 199n34; as trade for additional wages, 24, 53; in Union armies, 1, 7, 13–14, 16, 17, 20–26, 34, 114, 179–80n23, 180n24. *See also* medicinal liquor
Stanton, Edwin, 55, 144
Starr, Samuel, 88
state authority, 2, 177n21
states' rights, 107
Stephens, George E., 92–93, 159–60
Stevens, Isaac Ingalls, 69
Stott, William Taylor, 35, 54, 186n81
Strong, George Templeton, 145
Strong, William A., 132
Stuart, J. E. B., 92
Sturgis, Samuel, 135
Sunday Laws: and German Americans, 117–19, 153, 156, 157, 199n25; in North, 8, 10, 115, 117–19, 137, 153, 199n25; in Southern states, 133
sutlers: and Confederate armies, 87–88, 90, 192n11; federal government's regulation of, 8, 86, 87, 88–90, 114; fines levied against, 90; goods peddled by, 87; licensing of, 87, 88, 90, 109, 192n11, 193n15, 193n18; and military discipline, 88, 90–91; officers' ability to purchase liquor from, 37, 40, 88, 89–90, 91; prices of, 89, 90, 93, 193–94n26, 194n29; profits of, 89–90, 193n22; soldiers' access to, 85–87, 88, 89–90, 91; temperance reformers on, 5, 8, 20, 113, 119, 121–22; and Union armies, 87, 89–90, 122, 192n11; unscrupulous behavior of, 87, 89, 90, 91

Taylor, Guy C., 76, 164
Taylor, John, 107
Taylor, Thomas H., 106
temperance movement: on abstinence, 20; in antebellum period, 2, 3, 8, 176n6; and Civil War, 1, 2, 5, 8, 9, 10, 11, 176n6; on home as prevention against liquor consumption, 45, 70; on mobilization of armies of volunteer soldiers, 5–6; on prohibition, 1–2, 4; and slavery controversy, 1, 5, 175n5; in Southern states, 9, 21, 74–75, 123–24, 126, 138–39, 152; on spirit rations, 14; studies of, 176n6; and values of sobriety, 6
temperance reformers: and abolitionists, 4; on adulterated liquor, 149, 208n57; and African Americans, 160; on alcohol as medical stimulant, 18–19, 20, 120; approaches to drunkenness, 3, 19, 74; on civilian liquor sellers, 119, 121; on Civil War, 11; on cold water as curative, 18, 19, 20–21, 32, 34, 75–76, 79, 146; crusades of, 10; debates on meaning of liquor consumption, 10–11; on drunkenness, 3, 19, 75, 81, 139–41; on Elmer Ellsworth, 138; on Ulysses S. Grant, 145; on Oliver Otis Howard, 140–41; on influence of home, 70–71; on "King Alcohol" as enemy, 149–50; legal suasion as strategy of, 4, 81; on liquor excise taxes, 115; on liquor traffic, 114, 116, 119, 121–24, 172; on masculine duty to support families, 51; on masculinity, 2, 6, 51, 138; on medicinal liquor, 14, 18–19, 20, 32–33, 34, 42, 75, 180n36; on moderate liquor consump-

tion, 19–20; moral suasion as strategy of, 3, 4, 7, 71–72, 74, 75–76, 79, 81, 84, 138–39; on officers' responsibilities, 57–58, 187n129; postwar temperance crusade, 167–71; and presidential election of 1860, 1; on prohibition, 5, 8, 11, 113, 127, 168–72; on soldiers in warm climates, 20–21; on soldiers' liquor consumption, 46, 62, 70; on spirit rations, 5, 8, 13, 14, 18, 20–21, 75–76, 113, 119, 120, 199n34; on sutlers, 5, 8, 20, 113, 119, 121–22; on taxation and regulation of liquor, 8
temperance regiments, 71–72
Templars Magazine, 1
Ten Islands Baptist Association, Calhoun County, Alabama, 123
Tenney, Luman, 47
Terry, Alfred, 109
Thirteenth Amendment, 168
Thompson, Harriet Jane, 72
Thompson, Lauren K., 177n20
Thompson, M. Jeff, 47
Trall, R. T., 20
Tripler, Charles S., 13, 17–18, 24
Tripp, Porter D., 80
Twichell, Joseph, 93, 94, 95
Tyler, Mason Whiting, 31, 33, 55
typhoid, 13, 17, 20, 41, 43, 76
typhus, 13, 17, 32
Tyrrell, Ian R., 113, 175n5

Union, preservation of, 5, 113
Union armies: acceptability of liquor consumption in, 36; blockade of, 124–25, 129, 150, 162; Christmas celebrations of, 48–49; and civilian liquor sellers, 86, 94–96, 97, 99–104, 109, 196n81; Commissary of Subsistence, 17, 25–26, 179–80n23; confiscation of family-supplied liquor, 92; confiscation of liquor in Southern states, 124, 129–30, 200–201n58; control of soldiers' access to liquor, 7, 8, 85–86; destruction of whiskey, 27, 149; on drunkenness of Confederate armies, 148–52; election of company officers, 54; hospital inspectors of, 32; ideals of masculinity in, 6, 177n20; inconsistent alcohol policies of, 178n25; liquor-related problems of, 11, 61; and martial law, 103, 110; on masculine responsibility to family, 51; medicinal liquor in hospital stores of, 15, 17, 27, 33; middle-class volunteer efforts for, 33; military discipline problems of, 61, 81–82; officers of, 40, 54; payday celebrations of, 51, 52; rebellions in, 69; in Southern states, 134; spirit rations in battle, 63; spirit rations in health regimens, 1, 7, 13–14, 16, 17, 20–26, 28, 34, 114, 179–80n23, 180n24; supply shortages of, 14, 26; and sutlers, 87, 89–90, 122, 192n11; temperance regiments of, 71–72; temperance societies of, 76–78, 119; temperance tracts and papers distributed to, 74–77, 189n80; in warm climates, 20–21
U.S. Christian Commission (USCC), 33, 74, 76–78, 91
U.S. Colored Troops, 50, 55, 57, 160
U.S. Congress: on Joseph Hooker, 143; on income taxes, 115; on liquor traffic, 114–16, 125, 202n63; and spirit rations, 8, 13; on sutlers' goods and prices, 88, 193n18; on U.S. Navy, 120–21
U.S. Navy, 53, 54, 120–21, 122, 199n39
U.S. Sanitary Commission (USCC), 17–18, 33, 88, 145, 183n115
U.S. War Department, 29
universal manhood suffrage, 2
urbanization, 2, 4, 177n20
Uterhard, Carl, 29

Valley Campaign (1862), 107
Vance, Zebulon, 129, 131, 165, 204n92, 205n104, 211n137
Van Cleve, Horatio, 89
Vandevender, Hiram T., 35
vegetarianism, 18

Vicars, Hedley, 75–76, 178n3
volunteer soldiers: families supplying liquor to, 91; and military culture, 36; and military discipline, 85; mobilization of armies of, 5–6, 85; on morality of drinking, 6, 58; personal observations of, 10; and republican citizenship, 66; and sectional definitions of masculinity, 177n20; temperance societies of, 7; in Washington, D.C., 95–96
von Olnhausen, Mary Phinney, 30

Wadley, Sarah Lois, 133
Wainwright, Charles S., 40, 142–43, 154
Wallace, S. W., 129
War of 1812, 115
Warren, Edward, 15–16
Washington, D.C., military discipline in, 95–96, 97, 104–5, 106, 195n62, 195n68
Washington, George, 48
Washingtonians, 3, 4, 6
Watson, Robert, 50, 56, 65, 66
Weer, William, 56
Weld, Stephen Minot, 69, 144
Welles, Gideon, 143, 207n31
Wells, Seth James, 73
West, John Camden, 154
Wheeler, William, 52, 164
Whig Party, on prohibition, 113–14
white Southerners, 8, 9, 11, 12, 21, 123, 133–36
white supremacy, 170
Whittle, James M., 112, 128
Wilder, Burt, 28, 31
Wiley, William, 53, 65
Williams, Seth, 65
Wills, Charles Wright, 151–52, 188n46
Wills, Irvin Cross, 50
Wilson, Henry, 121
Wilson's Bill (March 19, 1862), 91, 122, 193n18

Winder, John H., 105, 106, 197n113
Winn, Martha, 80
Winn, Robert, 76, 79–80
Wittenmyer, Annie, 33
women: and alcoholic tonic prescriptions, 18; as civilian liquor sellers, 93–94; as dependent on officers, 58; as distillers, 129; Federal occupation troops' protection of, 135–36, 206n128; and guerrilla bands, 153; and influence of domestic realm, 70–71, 72, 74, 77, 189n64; letters to soldiers on abstinence, 72, 77; and medicinal liquor, 132; morality of, 30, 70, 72–73; as nurses, 29–30, 182n96, 182n97; protection from liquor traffic, 124, 127, 132–33, 168; and soldiers' drunkenness, 62, 70, 107, 110; Southern white women's fear of enslaved men's access to liquor, 123, 133–34; support for soldiers, 52; as temperance reformers, 51; temperance tracts on soldiers' relationships with, 75
Women's Christian Temperance Union, 33, 169
Wood, S. A. M., 105
Woodruff, Christian, 118
Woolfork, T. J., 57, 58
working class: on acceptability of liquor consumption, 44, 170; definitions of masculine recreation, 61; draft resistance of, 163; middle class distinguished from, 2, 36; and Sunday Laws, 137; temperance organizations of, 3, 6; urban work of, 71
World War I, 171

Yates, D. P., 180n27
yellow fever, 20

Zouaves, 39, 95, 138

www.ingramcontent.com/pod-product-compliance
Lightning Source LLC
Chambersburg PA
CBHW021853230426
43671CB00006B/378